GUILTY ~

"More g   story, an

"Compe intervent (includir new tria reviews the criminal justice system.   —Booklist

"Searing and shocking . . . Many readers will have to fight not to finish *Guilty Until Proven Innocent* in a single sitting."   —*Publishers Weekly*

"A nonfiction whodunit in which the villain is our criminal justice system and the hero is an innocent youth who is jailed, tried, and convicted—while the real killer escapes unknown."   —*School Library Journal*

GUILTY UNTIL
PROVEN INNOCENT

DONALD S. CONNERY

BERKLEY BOOKS, NEW YORK

THE BERKLEY PUBLISHING GROUP
Published by the Penguin Group
Penguin Group (USA) Inc.
375 Hudson Street, New York, New York 10014, USA
Penguin Group (Canada), 90 Eglinton Avenue East, Suite 700, Toronto, Ontario M4P 2Y3, Canada
(a division of Pearson Penguin Canada Inc.)
Penguin Books Ltd., 80 Strand, London WC2R 0RL, England
Penguin Group Ireland, 25 St. Stephen's Green, Dublin 2, Ireland (a division of Penguin Books Ltd.)
Penguin Group (Australia), 250 Camberwell Road, Camberwell, Victoria 3124, Australia
(a division of Pearson Australia Group Pty. Ltd.)
Penguin Books India Pvt. Ltd., 11 Community Centre, Panchsheel Park, New Delhi—110 017, India
Penguin Group (NZ), 67 Apollo Drive, Rosedale, North Shore 0632, New Zealand
(a division of Pearson New Zealand Ltd.)
Penguin Books (South Africa) (Pty.) Ltd., 24 Sturdee Avenue, Rosebank, Johannesburg 2196,
South Africa

Penguin Books Ltd., Registered Offices: 80 Strand, London WC2R 0RL, England

The publisher does not have any control over and does not assume any responsibility for author or
third-party websites or their content.

GUILTY UNTIL PROVEN INNOCENT

A Berkley Book / published by arrangement with the author

PRINTING HISTORY
G. P. Putnam's Sons hardcover edition / October 1977
Berkley mass market edition / January 2010

ISBN: 978-0-425-23323-8

BERKLEY®
Berkley Books are published by The Berkley Publishing Group,
a division of Penguin Group (USA) Inc.,
375 Hudson Street, New York, New York 10014.
BERKLEY® is a registered trademark of Penguin Group (USA) Inc.
The "B" design is a trademark of Penguin Group (USA) Inc.

PRINTED IN THE UNITED STATES OF AMERICA

10 9 8 7 6 5 4 3 2 1

to all who saw that
justice was done

Acknowledgments

This book, in part, is a distillation of documents: transcripts of court proceedings, police reports, witness statements, lawyers' briefs and the private papers of Barbara Gibbons and Peter Reilly. They make a pile four feet high. But documents give only the bare bones of the Reilly case. The flesh is provided by those who were caught up in the story and who were good enough to talk at length about what they know. Most police officers and court officials would speak frankly only on the assurance that they would not be quoted by name. A few were dismayed, or at least puzzled, by what was being done in the name of the State and volunteered information at some risk. I am particularly grateful for the opportunity to have heard the infamous confession tapes.

Those who came to Peter's defense were generous with their time and endured hours of interviewing. I thank them all just as I thank Peter himself for submitting so graciously to so much exploration of his personal history and feelings. Special appreciation must go to Marion and Mickey Madow and members of their family. Their home became a storm center from the moment they opened their arms to Peter Reilly and made him a third son. They were unfailingly kind and selfless to journalists and other callers who too frequently interrupted their lives to learn the latest news of the Reilly case and to gather information. I became the worst offender. Like Peter himself, the Madows weathered the storm with great dignity.

I was helped enormously by the newspaper reporters whose work on the Reilly case was exceptionally fine—and a far cry from the sensational journalism of other celebrated murders. Some are named in this book. Joseph O'Brien's detailed coverage of the case in its entirety for the *Hartford Courant* is a gold mine for any researcher. Judith Boucher's fine reporting appeared first in the *Lakeville Journal* and then in the *Waterbury Republican*. Roger Cohn, before moving on to the *Philadelphia Inquirer*, followed his investigative reporting for the *Torrington Register* by doing more digging for me in the summer of 1976. He was able to interview sources who would not talk to me. His contribution to this book is invaluable. The end product, of course, is my responsibility and I alone am accountable for what follows.

My wife, Leslie, inspired me to undertake this work, and my daughter Carol served as my secretary. Perry Knowlton was more than a literary agent: his personal interest in the Reilly case counted greatly in the shaping of the manuscript. And then I had the good fortune to turn it over to the ministrations of a skilled and sensitive editor, Hugh Howard.

—D. S. C.

INTRODUCTION

In the 1970s, that woeful time of Watergate, the Vietnam War and the Patty Hearst kidnapping, the Peter Reilly story was sensational.

A friendly, mild-mannered, law-abiding high school senior in a quintessential New England town, Peter had confessed to killing his mother, the only parent he had ever known. The bloody assault in their tiny home was conducted in such an orgy of stabbing, stomping and sexual cruelty that she was nearly beheaded.

The State Police had his words on tape: "I definitely did do what happened to my mother last night. But the thing that I don't realize is the exact steps that I took doing it."

Did he really do it?

Peter's manslaughter conviction half a year later triggered a wave of protests by the normally reticent folk of Connecticut's rural northwest corner. The spectacle soon ballooned into a national cause célèbre.

Playwright Arthur Miller, a Litchfield County resident, enlisted the free services of an outraged former prosecutor and a crack private investigator to lead a rescue party. Both the nation's most famous pathologist and a world authority on psychological coercion signed on. William Styron, Elizabeth Taylor, Mike Nichols and other celebrities rallied to the cause.

Mike Wallace brought his *60 Minutes* crew to Falls Village to film the bake sales and other money-raising efforts by residents anxious to help Peter prove his innocence. Front-page investigative reports in the *New York Times* exposed the police's blind focus on the wrong suspect. A valiant judge—who had initially chastised Peter for his "lack of remorse" but later allowed his defenders to present evidence about other suspects—stretched the limits of the law to correct the miscarriage of justice that had occurred in his own courtroom.

The lead headline in the *New York Times* of March 15, 1976, proclaimed, "Reilly Wins Retrial in Mother's Slaying," though Peter's full exoneration was achieved without a second trial. After the state's attorney dropped dead on a golf course, his successor's inspection of the files led to the discovery that the prosecutor and the lead detective had concealed evidence that made the youth's innocence obvious.

That bombshell set off a firestorm which was further fueled by a one-man grand jury probe of law enforcement's misconduct and by the State Police's insistence that they had evidence of Reilly's guilt under a new theory of the crime. At one point, the newly appointed state's attorney, refusing to bend to pressure from the cops, threatened to arrest the State Police commissioner. It took the intervention of the nation's first elected female governor, Ella Grasso, to put things right.

Almost forgotten in the uproar was the victim, Barbara Gibbons, the brilliant eccentric who once said she had pulled her son's Irish name "out of a hat." Though compelling facts and disclosures always pointed to the likeliest killer or killers, her murder remained unsolved.

As an author, independent journalist and former foreign correspondent for *Time* and *Life* magazines, and as a father whose four children attended the regional high school with Peter, I was so caught up in the great moments of the Reilly drama that writing this book became inevitable.

I had been a wire service reporter covering Senator Joe

McCarthy's rampage of false accusations of treason during the Red Scare in the 1950s. In the Soviet Union and other "police states," I had first-hand exposure to places where the law is a sham and innocence is irrelevant. Yet here, in my own country, I encountered evil at the heart of our criminal justice system.

The shock of it all altered my life—changing my career path from foreign affairs to criminal justice—even as Peter's trauma and deliverance turned an unpolished boy into a passionate advocate for justice.

With the passage of a third of a century, you would think that the Reilly case belongs to a distant dark age of primitive crime solving. Surely in this new time of DNA exonerations and CSI depictions of wondrous forensic technology we no longer tolerate convictions based on "admissions" wrung from suspects by interrogation-room tactics that amount to psychological torture.

The terrible truth is that Peter's ordeal is as fresh today as it was in the 1970s. The case is considered a false-confession classic, often mentioned in courtrooms and regularly cited in books and studies of police interrogations.

The human rights abuse of a false accusation and a corrupt prosecution, as related in this book (with the original text virtually unchanged), is echoed in present-day "wrong man" cases. The innocent accused—numbering in the tens of thousands each year and largely drawn from society's least advantaged and most vulnerable—are at risk of imprisonment and even execution for crimes they did not commit.

The big difference in the Reilly story is that the small-town teenager did not become one of America's "disappeared." Most of the wrongly incarcerated simply vanish, their cries unheard. Peter, in contrast, was saved in just four years by the passion of his neighbors and the kindness of strangers.

1 ▪ MURDER

SGT. KELLY: Well, I think we got a little problem here, Pete.
PETER REILLY: What do you mean?
SGT. KELLY: About hurting your mother last night.
PETER REILLY: I didn't do it.

Barbara Gibbons was still alive at 9:30 on the night of September 28, 1973. She was alone, probably, in her Falls Village cottage in northwest Connecticut. She was drunk; that was not unusual. Often her eighteen-year-old son, Peter Reilly, would telephone home to let her know that he was all right and receive no answer. Because she was partly deaf, he would explain to his friends that "my mom must be sleeping on her good ear and can't hear the phone." Maybe so, they would think, but it was just as likely that she had passed out.

That night, however, Barbara Gibbons was still functioning and she was worried. She had been operated on for cancer of the uterus three years earlier, and she had recently undergone tests to see whether there had been a recurrence. She had told friends that she thought she was dying of cancer.

Anxious to know the results of the tests, she telephoned her surgeon, Dr. Frank Lovallo, at his Sharon residence. He was not home, but she finally reached him at a dinner party in Salisbury. "Her manner of speaking was aggressive," he told the police, "and she sounded upset. I advised her to contact me Monday and I would check to see if the results were in. . . . The call from Mrs. Gibbons came in after we started dinner and I would place it between 9:20 and 9:40 P.M." She never did learn that the tests revealed that she was not dying of cancer.

At the same time, on West Main Street in North Canaan, a town just above Falls Village, Peter Reilly was standing outside the Canaan United Methodist Church, saying good night to friends. He and two dozen other people had been meeting in the church basement since eight o'clock to discuss the future of the Canaan Youth Center. Although Falls Village is officially the town of Canaan as distinct from the town of North Canaan, it is customary to think of "Canaan" as the two towns combined—which is exactly the way it was until they were split apart in 1858.

Many of the townspeople at the meeting were older than Peter, but he was comfortable in the company of adults. He seemed able to get along with everyone. Better spoken and better mannered than most of his contemporaries, he was a slight, almost frail youth who looked younger than his eighteen years. He was easygoing, more lethargic than energetic, but he was bright and well informed despite his average grades. In retrospect, he had a kind of Billy Budd innocence and amiability that his seniors found appealing.

Peter, his schoolmates insisted, was no "goody-goody." He could get into mischief, smoke pot, race his car, and carry on like any other teenager. But he also had a sense of restraint and kept out of serious trouble. Except for a minor automobile accident, he was, as one officer described him, "clean as a whistle" as far as the police were concerned. And that surprised them because they thought his mother was a "screwball." In school his deportment was exemplary; everyone from the principal on down had a good word for him.

If he was too impressionable and too eager to please and be liked, that seemed only natural. Here was a young man who had never known his father, who was not really sure that Barbara Gibbons was his mother, and who did not even know why his last name was "Reilly." He knew only that his mother had a fertile imagination, and that she had given various explanations for his name and origins. Besides, his neighbors said, just look at his home life.

Barbara Gibbons was much discussed because of her drinking and her promiscuous and belligerent behavior. Some thought her a lesbian; others spoke of the men she entertained; some said she was bisexual. Yet Peter seemed to have a way of floating above it all. He saw nothing special about her sex life; he did not consider her an alcoholic. She was "my mother" or "my mom" and never "the old lady." Though they sometimes argued and swore at each other, he seemed more proud than ashamed of her eccentric ways, perhaps because she had persuaded him that she was more sophisticated and liberated than their small-town neighbors.

Even so, he clearly enjoyed being in other places with other people. He spent most of his evenings away from home, especially since he had started playing the guitar in a rock band. When he finished this, his last year in high school, he would have a decision to make: whether to strike out on his own, or to stay home and take care of his mother.

The fall night was cool and crisp, and few cars or pedestrians were to be seen. Except for the clusters of houses in the several hamlets of the Canaan area, most homes are scattered about the hills and valleys. Most of their occupants were watching television, catching up on their reading, doing homework or hobbies, or preparing for bed.

Two horror films were being shown at the Canaan Drive-In Theater: *Slaughter Hotel* and *Don't Look in the Basement*. Frank Finney, a young painting contractor and auxiliary state trooper, and his wife, Wanda, decided to leave the second feature during a particularly gruesome scene. A woman's tongue was being cut out.

The leaves of the Litchfield Hills were just beginning to turn. Soon there would be people driving up from the city to see the spectacular views. At night, however, an overwhelming darkness and silence settle over the small towns and make their isolation even more pronounced. Like a remnant of old New England or a relic of Norman Rockwell's America, the communities in Connecticut's northwest corner go to sleep early.

Directly across the street from the entrance to the Methodist church is the parish house that was once the home of J. Clinton Roraback, a most influential man in Canaan in his day. The law offices of his niece, Catherine Roraback, a well-known civil-rights attorney, are nearby. Immediately across the street from where Peter stood is the Bianchi house, as it is known locally, both for John A. Bianchi, an Italian immigrant who became a successful merchant in Canaan, and his son, John F. Bianchi, who was, in 1973, the chief prosecutor of Litchfield County.

State's Attorney John Bianchi was in Boston that night, attending a Holy Cross College reunion. If he had been at home and had stepped out on his front porch when the Youth Center meeting was breaking up he would have been delighted to exchange a few words with Peter Reilly and the others. Everyone knew "Smiling John" and he made it a point to know everyone. Bianchi was a popular man in Canaan; a born politician.

A friend of Peter's, sixteen-year-old John Sochocki, asked if he could have a ride home. Peter agreed even though he would have to go out of his way. They climbed into the "royal blue" Corvette, complete with a white convertible top and all the trimmings, that his wealthy godmother in New York had bought for him the year before. He was a fortunate young man, people thought, to be able to drive around in a car like that while he and his mother lived on welfare. Still, they didn't resent him for it. He was too nice a boy for anyone to dislike. His mother, of course, was something else.

The Reverend Paul Halovatch, an energetic young priest who was well liked in Canaan, cautioned Peter to drive slowly in the powerful car. Peter smiled and drove off, but at first he crept along by inches to tease Father Paul. Then he speeded up, moving east on Main Street.

The territory was familiar to the boys of Canaan. They bought their blue jeans in Bob's Clothing Store and took their girls to movies at the Colonial Theatre. John Bianchi worked above the shops in the State's Attorney's office.

Peter pulled up to John Sochocki's house, the home of his aunt, Judy MacNeil. "There were six of us sitting in the kitchen," Mrs. MacNeil recalled later. "We said, 'John, you're home early,' and he said, 'Yeah, Peter drove me back.'" She looked at the electric clock hanging on the wall. The clock read 9:45, but it was a few minutes fast.

If Barbara Gibbons was alone in her cottage when she telephoned Dr. Lovallo, she surely was not alone by 9:45. After putting down the telephone she might have poured herself another drink. The alcoholic content in her body at that time was high enough to put most people on the floor. Barbara, however, "had two hollow legs," according to a former neighbor, and she was somehow able to read day and night even while drinking heavily.

She was known locally as a character, partly for the things she said and the pranks she pulled and partly because she seemed to spend almost all of her time sitting under an outside light in front of the cottage reading books. She had even been seen reading under an umbrella in the pouring rain and while wrapped in a raccoon coat in a snowstorm, her book protected by a transparent plastic sheet.

Barbara Gibbons probably had been reading that Friday night, before and perhaps after calling the doctor, as she lay on a sleeping bag on the top bunk of the double-decked beds that she shared with her son. If she was reading, it was probably a murder mystery. She had become addicted to figuring out fictional murders.

After delivering John Sochocki at the MacNeil house, Peter was seen in his Corvette by Frank and Wanda Finney as they made their way home from the drive-in theater near the police barracks. Peter passed through the heart of Canaan, heading for Falls Village and home. The five-and-a-half-mile journey from the MacNeil home took Peter about eight minutes. He recalls that he cruised along at 40 MPH because the car ahead of him had the look of a police cruiser. But even if he had had the straightaway all to himself he says that he would not have pushed the Corvette faster than 45. Since he had put superwide tires on the front wheels, the car could hardly be controlled at high speed. It lunged from side to side.

"I didn't have any reason to hurry anyway," Peter says. "I was going to hit the sack as soon as I got home. I was really exhausted."

He was driving on Route 7, a two-lane road that follows the scenic undulations of the Housatonic River most of the way south from the Massachusetts border to Danbury. It passes the only two covered bridges still used in Connecticut.

The final stretch that Peter drove is a black corridor at night. At first there are some signs of civilization—the volunteer firehouse, the VFW building with a World War II tank in front, the factory that used to make Wash'n Dri packets, the old chinchilla ranch—but soon there are only woods and swamps and the looming hills. A driver has to watch out for the raccoons, porcupines, skunks and rabbits that wander across the road—and for the deer that suddenly leap through the beams of headlights.

After this spooky passage, the security lights of the Texaco station loom dead ahead, where 7 meets Route 63. Just across 63 from the gas station a little white cottage sits between a small red barn and an old two-story house. The cottage has a kerosene-stove chimney and a little picket fence close by to protect the flower beds. From March 1967 until September 28, 1973, this was the home of Barbara Gibbons and Peter Reilly.

When Peter reached home that night, he pulled the Corvette up to the front of the house, fussed a bit with a faulty headlight, locked the car and then opened the front door. Both the wall light and the ceiling light were on. There was no sign of the cat. A book was open on the living room card table but facedown in a way that might hurt the binding. Peter was surprised to see that. "She was a library sort of person, with a respect for books," Peter says of his mother. He figured that she must have been reading in bed earlier and had gotten up to see who was at the door, putting her book down for a moment.

He called out, "Hey, Mom, I'm home," as he usually did, when he entered the house. Hearing no answer, he glanced into the bedroom at his right. First he noticed that the reading lamp was on, the one attached to the top bunk. She often read there, though it was his bed. Both bunks were empty.

When he looked down, Peter Reilly saw his mother sprawled on her back on the floor, five feet from the door. Her feet were nearest to him, her head close to the three-speed English bicycle that they kept in the bedroom against the far wall. Her legs were spread and her arms were outstretched. She was naked except for a white T-shirt and an unbuttoned shirt that had been pulled above her breasts. The clothing covered a great gaping neck wound and severed vocal cords. Barbara Gibbons had almost been beheaded. Her battered face was turned to the left and her dark hair was matted with blood. Her body had been slashed, smashed and stomped upon. She lay motionless on a dirty rug crimson with her blood. More blood was spattered about the room—on a green chair, on the bunk beds, on freshly laundered shirts hanging from a curtain rod.

People react in different ways to horrifying sights. Barbara Gibbons was the only parent Peter Reilly had ever known. He loved her and he had enjoyed a unique kind of comradeship with her. Peter might have rushed into that bedroom to touch or shake or embrace his mutilated parent. He might have tried to determine whether she was dead or alive, especially since he heard something that sounded like breathing. He might have rushed out of the house screaming for help. He could have run next door to his elderly landlord, Fred Kruse, or up the street to the Dickinson family.

What Peter Reilly did do, with such self-possession that it would later count against him in the minds of the police and the State's Attorney, was most sensible. He went straight to the telephone to call for an ambulance. Then he tried to call his doctor. Then he called the nearest hospital. The hospital, in turn, called the State Police. Help arrived within minutes: friends, ambulance, police. They swarmed into the cottage while Peter stood shaking in a corner. Finally he was told: Your mother is dead.

Twenty-four hours later, after a prolonged interrogation that led to the signing of a confession, Peter Reilly was arrested for the murder of his mother, Barbara Gibbons.

2 ▪ SEPTEMBER 28, 1973

SGT. KELLY: She could have went at you. And, this is strictly a self-defense thing where you had to protect yourself against her.

PETER REILLY: Right.

SGT. KELLY: You follow me?

PETER REILLY: Yes. But still, I'd still have to have a problem. I mean, self-defense goes just so far.

SGT. KELLY: All right. But this is where you went off the handle. You lost complete control of your mind and your body.

PETER REILLY: Mm-hm. I almost wish I hadn't gone home last night. I wish I stayed at the Teen Center later.

During the next four years, the events of the night of the murder—and especially the time between Peter Reilly's departure from the church and the arrival of the State Police at the cottage at 10:02—were to be repeatedly recalled, reviewed, disputed and dissected by Peter, the prosecutor, the lawyers, the witnesses and everyone else whose life was touched by the tragedy.

Suddenly an orphan, and still in his teens, with no close ties to relatives, Peter was subjected to four great shocks in a day's time: the murder of his mother, the realization that he was suspected of being the murderer, his own amazed agreement that he might be his mother's killer and his arrest. He was put behind bars and there he remained for 143 days before going on trial.

In and out of the courtroom, he would be asked over and over again—as if he were a loop of recording tape going round and round in a machine—to tell the story of his ride home and exactly what he did when he arrived. He was asked about his life and his mother's life and their relationship with each other. He was asked to remember in exact detail all the events of a day that was not all that exceptional—until the commission of one of the most ghastly murders in Connecticut history.

From the evidence of the old photographs in the living room, Peter's schoolmates could see that his mother had been both strikingly beautiful and athletic in her youth. They knew that she used to ride motorcycles and take part in many activities that seemed more masculine than feminine, like shooting, fishing, driving fast cars and working like a grease monkey underneath an automobile. But now she was middle-aged and very much the worse for wear. At 5 feet 2 inches and 115 pounds she was a chunky little woman whose poor health in the last few years had sapped her strength.

Peter was just 5 feet 7 inches and only six pounds heavier than his mother. He seemed undernourished. He was a nice-looking boy: hazel eyes, prominent nose, broad smile, cleft chin and a long mop of sandy hair. He was something of a waif, the kind of youngster who would be the last one to be picked if sides were being chosen for a rough game. He brought out the mothering instincts of the Canaan women who knew him. They worried about him.

Caroline Wakefield, then the head of the Housatonic Valley Regional High School Guidance Department, would one day write to the judge at the Reilly trial to say, "I have been aware of the boy and his mother for about 15 years. This is a small town and people care about one another. Whenever I found myself in a group which was expressing concern for Peter, I joined them. But we did nothing about it. More recently, during his high school years, I stood by and 'wrung my hands in despair' about Peter's deplorable home life. Again, I did not act. Why not? I wanted to avoid any encounter with Barbara Gibbons. I reasoned that Peter seemed to be coping and making the best of his situation. Soon he would be self-sufficient and could get away. Now this tragedy."

The presence of Barbara Gibbons' name on the welfare rolls did not mean that she and Peter lived in dire poverty. Peter's godmother took care of many of their bills and helped out with major expenses. Indeed, Barbara and Peter ate out every so often in one or another of the local restaurants. But Peter's diet was poor. He never ate breakfast and he sometimes skipped supper if he was doing something else at that time of night. He existed on school lunches and soft drinks.

On September 28, fifty-one-year-old Barbara Gibbons was up and about before the sun, as usual, while Peter slept until the last possible minute before rushing off to school, as usual. Her sleeping habits were unorthodox. Often she would rest during the day and then prowl about the cottage at night. Peter's friends enjoyed staying overnight with Barbara and Peter because they were, for a mother and son, a fun couple, but they admit that she could be difficult between midnight and dawn. Paul Beligni, a frequent overnight guest, says that "You could be sleeping on the cot in the living room at three in the morning, and Barbara might get up if the whim hit her, plug in the vacuum cleaner and vacuum you in your sleeping bag. Or else she'd start singing opera. You had to laugh. But she was also the kind of person who'd put an extra blanket over you if she thought you were cold."

Barbara probably poured herself a glass of S. S. Pierce sherry (she prided herself on drinking "only the best"). She might have puttered about the cottage before turning on the radio at six to catch the Bob Steele show on a Hartford station.

Steele's raffish sense of humor appealed to Barbara. She was an intelligent woman whose education had begun at a private school in England. She had been the editor of a magazine for a major insurance company and, though she was down and out, she still took an interest in things. She viewed the world pessimistically and found amusement in the stupidities of people in authority. She had a sharp, sarcastic tongue. She was, or at least she tried to be, a rebel, a maverick, a one-in-a-million individualist. She got her kicks out of beating the system, fooling the law and showing up fools.

At seven she probably turned on the *Today* show. She preferred books to television, but she watched the news and documentary programs closely, as well as some of the more challenging quiz shows, especially *Jeopardy*. She devoured everything about Watergate and the troubles of her pet hate, Richard Nixon.

Peter could have driven himself to school in the Corvette, but his mother needed the car for shopping. He would have taken the school bus except that his two closest friends, Paul Beligni and Geoff Madow, arrived in a car with several other youngsters. They pried Peter out of bed and hurried him into his clothes: "blue Landlubber jeans, brown knit shirt, gold sneakers," as he would testify. They got to the high school in a few minutes because it lies within the Falls Village township.

Peter recalls that it was a "beautiful, sunny, gorgeous day." The hours in school passed as usual, save for a special outdoor assembly in the early afternoon to honor a janitor who was retiring after working at the school since its founding in 1939. "We split about five minutes before the bell rang," Peter remembers. Geoff, Paul and another friend, Conrad King, drove him to his house before going on to their homes in East Canaan.

Peter saw his mother across the road at the Texaco station, chatting with its operator, Kenneth Carter, a bright young businessman with a West Point education. Peter also wanted to talk to Carter. He walked over and made an arrangement to go to Carter's house in Litchfield the next day to pick up an old motorcycle. Peter, of course, never had a chance to keep that Saturday appointment. ("Do you know who finally got that motorcycle?" Carter asked Peter when they met in New Hampshire two and a half years later. "A state trooper.")

After talking to Carter, Barbara and Peter walked back to the house. In his statement to the police two days later, Carter emphasized that "they both seemed normal" and said he thought highly of both mother and son. He said Barbara had told him earlier that day that a certain local character was a "flasher." She explained that this man had come over to her house a few days before, leaned against his car and exposed himself. But Carter also told the police that "Barbara told me a lot of things. After telling me she then would say she was just 'pulling my leg.' She had quite an imagination but was very intelligent, and I enjoyed talking with her. She never mentioned having any problems with Peter. I always thought that they got along very well."

Although Ken Carter had been, for more than a year before the murder, a constant observer of Peter Reilly's relationship with his mother and was one of the last persons to see them together, the State Police did not go to him for a statement. Perhaps they would have eventually, but after waiting two days he persuaded a trooper, Dean Hammond, to hear him out and take his statement. Although he recalls that he mentioned a number of persons in the area who seemed to him capable of carrying out a brutal murder, the one-page statement that the trooper wrote out for his signature was confined to his observations about the warm relationship between Barbara and Peter and to Barbara's story about the local flasher.

Carter was never again questioned by the State Police about his knowledge of the Gibbons-Reilly relationship. His statement to the police was never turned over to Peter's attorneys.

Although Carter would have made an excellent character witness for Peter Reilly, no one ever approached him about testifying. He did not come forward because he was sure, until the conclusion of the trial in Litchfield, that both the prosecution and the defense knew what they were doing. Finally, in his frustration "about what was being done to Peter," he wrote a letter to Judge John A. Speziale. But by then, in May 1974, it was too late.

As the owner of Falls Village Texaco from August 1972 to October 1973, I came to know Peter Reilly and his mother, Barbara Gibbons, quite well. The station is located directly across the street from their house, and they frequently came over every day.

The impression I formed of Peter was one of a happy, popular boy who took things in stride with little fuss or anxiety. While other children in the neighborhood took delight in giving me much trouble, Peter and his friends frequently helped me out without asking for anything in return.

I came to like Barbara also, with all of her moods and

eccentricities. Here was an extremely complex personality which I could not begin to fathom. Nothing that Barbara did came as a surprise, and her actions were entirely unpredictable.

I last saw the two of them together on the afternoon of the terrible tragedy. When I left them they were in jovial spirits, kidding each other about some kind of game. The next day I was informed by my employee of Barbara's tragic death. This news was shocking in itself, but when he told me that Peter was a suspect and was being held by the State Police, I became absolutely incredulous. My first thought was that the police must be using Peter as a trap to get the real killer.

I cannot for the life of me for one minute entertain the idea that Peter was capable of such an act, either physically or emotionally. Only a week before her death Barbara had told me during a conversation that Peter was not capable of hurting a fly inasmuch as his nature was non-violent and nonaggressive.

Unless there is some physical evidence linking Peter to this crime of which he has been convicted, I will go to my grave believing that a grave injustice has been done to an innocent person. Peter will always remain a friend, and I will continue to enjoy the presence of his company.

When Barbara went into the house with Peter in the early afternoon, as he recalls, she asked him to turn the mattress on his bed and then she made up the bed. They decided to play cards—a game of rummy. They talked, and she told him that she had bought a wallet in North Canaan that morning and had cashed a check in Falls Village. Both the check and the wallet would be much discussed in the Reilly case.

The $100 check was from Peter's godmother, Miss Barbara Sincerbeaux of Forest Hills, New York, and it had arrived that very morning in a letter that said:

"Whatever happened to those dishwashing jobs? You'll never feel well until you get out and pull your weight in society. Why don't you do something??? Who wants to be a parasite? Think about it and get moving! You've got to come to grips with reality. Further—my resources have had it!"

The wallet, which Barbara showed Peter, was a replacement for a wallet that had been stolen from the house less than two weeks earlier. The police had been notified because $120 as well as Barbara's driver's license and other identification cards were gone. The wallet was missing when Peter went to get his lunch money early one morning, and he assumed that someone had sneaked into the cottage during the night.

Neither the new wallet nor any of the $100 from Sincerbeaux was found in the Gibbons cottage after the murder. Nonetheless, the State, in mounting its case against Peter, discounted the strong possibility that robbery might have been either the motive or an afterthought for the murderer.

Barbara had driven to Canaan village in the late morning to buy both the wallet (for $7.50) and a lightweight nylon jacket ($12.95) at Bob's Clothing Store. As usual, she charged both items, which meant that the proprietor, Bob Drucker, would send the month's bill to Barbara Sincerbeaux.

At two minutes to twelve she appeared without an appointment at the West Main Street office of her optometrist, Dr. Arthur S. Boylen, Jr., to pick up a pair of glasses that she had ordered several weeks earlier. He fitted them for her. The glasses were to be paid for by the Welfare Department.

When Barbara got back into her car she could not start the engine. Fred Wohlfert, who lived in the nearest house, was just returning home for lunch in his truck and helped her start the Corvette. Barbara drove away. More than a half years later, the State Police, still trying to show that mother and son were in some state of hostility that day, questioned both Boylen and Wohlfert about an argument that was said to have taken place between Barbara and Peter at noon because her car wouldn't start. There was no argument, Wohlfert told them: Barbara Gibbons was alone. Dr. Boylen said he had heard no argument and had not seen Peter, who was in school.

Probably Barbara was home before one o'clock and ate before Peter arrived at around two. That was one thing you had to say for Barbara Gibbons, her neighbors stated later: She made it a point to be there whenever Peter came home.

*　*　*

The rummy game between Barbara and Peter was interrupted at three by a phone call from Geoff Madow. He was driving to Great Barrington, Massachusetts, fifteen miles north of Falls Village, and asked Peter to go with him. Peter agreed. Geoff arrived a few minutes later in his car. Barbara was on her own for the next three and a half hours. A well driller named Aldo Beligni passed by the house soon after Peter and Geoff left. As he told the police, "I saw Miss Gibbons seated outside near the barn in a lawn chair and she appeared to be asleep."

In the late afternoon she drove to the center of Falls Village to do some shopping. Because of conflicting accounts of her movements, it is conjectured that she made two shopping journeys. Eleanor Schindler, then the proprietor of the package store, remembers Barbara coming in to buy a half gallon of S. S. Pierce sherry, something Barbara did regularly, often two or three times a week. She is sure that there was no conversation because she had learned that Barbara was more inclined to argue than talk.

Barbara apparently visited the Falls Village Market to buy some groceries after leaving the package store. Duke Moore, a private contractor who sometimes works as a reporter, remembers seeing Barbara drive up to the market. Because all the parking spaces were filled she simply parked in the street, blocking three cars parked by the sidewalk. An elderly lady came out of the store and tried to maneuver her car around the Corvette. She hit the Corvette just enough to cause it to rock, Moore recalls, waited a moment, then drove off.

Barbara finished her shopping and went to the checkout counter. Dana Shores, the owner of the market, was able to tell the police that he remembered seeing her new wallet that day because he was accustomed to her exhibiting her money. "She seemed to be farsighted and would make a production of holding the wallet out toward me and thumb through the money. She usually seemed to have a large amount of cash."

By 6:30 Barbara was back home again. She was seen crossing the road by a farmer named Joseph Downey and his wife as they drove by.

Peter, in the meantime, was on the road with Geoffrey Madow: first to Great Barrington, where Geoff picked up a paycheck and inquired about his job at a supermarket, then to Geoff's house in East Canaan. Peter ate cookies and watched television while Geoff had his supper in the kitchen. Geoff's parents, Meyer (Mickey) and Marion Madow, asked Peter if he wanted to eat, but he said he would have supper when he got home.

Geoff finally drove Peter home but only after they spent some time finding out who was in an ambulance that they passed on the road. Peter reached his house at about 6:45 and went in with Geoff.

"My mother was a little irritated with me for being late for dinner," he testified at his trial, "and I apologized for being late. She was eating a TV dinner and I sat down and watched the national news with her." Geoff went outdoors and sat in Barbara's chair for a while, petting the cat and watching the sunset. Peter had had only lunch and cookies during the last twelve hours, but he skipped dinner entirely. "I went in," he testified, "washed up, shaved, if you want to call it shaving, and then, around 7:20 to 7:30, we went to Canaan." He was still wearing the same clothes that he had worn all day. He didn't bother to put on a jacket because the sun was still up and he felt no chill.

When Peter's attorney interviewed him in jail four days after the murder, he mentioned, according to her notes, that his mother "asked again if he was going out—she couldn't seem to remember things." He said he didn't know whether his mother was drunk: "She just always drank wine steadily."

Soon after arriving home, Peter had telephoned Joanne Mulhern, the wife of State Trooper James Mulhern, to ask whether a Youth Center meeting was scheduled for that evening. She told him that there would be a gathering in the Methodist Church at 8 P.M. Peter and Geoff drove to the church in separate cars and waited outdoors until Mrs. Mulhern arrived and opened the basement door with a key.

The meeting concentrated on the problem of finding a new location for the Center. Everyone present, without exception, recalls that Peter was his usual self. There was no agitation, no sign of problems at home, no reason to think that he was angry or overwrought. If Peter Reilly went into a towering rage that night and slaughtered his mother, as the State of

Connecticut would insist, then there was no forewarning. There was no suggestion beforehand that mild-mannered Peter Reilly would, within the hour, prove capable—according to the police and the prosecutor—of a vicious murder.

The contention of the State would be that Peter not only attacked his mother immediately after reaching his house, as the result of a sudden argument, but that he telephoned for help while she was still alive. Then, knowing that the ambulance and the police were on their way, he went back to the body and finished the job. Various wounds were said to have been inflicted after death, and they must have been inflicted by Peter Reilly, the State insisted, because he himself had said on the telephone that his mother was still breathing when he called for help.

Peter actually made five telephone calls that night, including two to Directory Assistance. Even by the State's version of events, the calls could only have been made very shortly after his arrival home. By his own account he had seen his mother's body on the floor and rushed to the kitchen to call for help instead of going into the bedroom.

His first thought, as he told his attorney a few days later, was "Oh, my God . . . suicide." Barbara had told him six months earlier that she had considered suicide because she was so depressed but did not have the nerve to go through with it. There was blood all over the place, Peter said. His mother's eyes were closed. She seemed to be having trouble breathing, as sounds were coming from the body that he took to be breathing.

Peter was never asked in court to describe the sounds, even though his belief that his mother was breathing was, along with his "confession," the bedrock of the State's case against him. "It was like gurgling," he says today. "A little bit. Not a lot. A little bit of gurgling. I just looked and I heard something and maybe thought I saw something and I went straight to the phone. I went back and looked one more time when they asked me to. And I said I thought it was getting shallower. It was gurgling, not breath going in and out."

When asked why he didn't shake her or do something to

make sure if she was dead or alive, he replies, "Because I *thought* she was alive so I didn't have to shake her to see if she was alive. But I knew she had to have help, so I went to the phone. Besides, I was scared. I couldn't stand the sight of blood. I can deal with it now. I couldn't deal with it then. I was horrified, absolutely horrified. I didn't want to go in the bedroom. I was scared to go in."

Something else went through Peter's mind. Not only his mother but the Madows—Mickey, Marion and their sons, Art and Geoff, all volunteer workers for the VFW ambulance squad—had told him what to do in a medical emergency. Don't touch anything unless you are qualified, they said. Get help.

The first of his five calls was to the Madows who were ten minutes away by car. Marion Madow was watching television when the phone rang. She told the police the next day that "Peter told me 'There is something wrong with Ma' or 'Something happened to Ma. There's blood all over the place and I think she's unconscious.'" Mrs. Madow said that they would get the ambulance right away and instructed Peter to call the family doctor. Then she and her husband and a visitor from Salisbury, Frances Kaplan, rushed out to Marion's car and drove to Geer Memorial Hospital, an institution for the elderly on Route 7, where the VFW ambulance was garaged. At the same time, Geoff asked Miss Kaplan if he could take her Toyota and go directly to Peter.

Peter's second call was to Directory Assistance for the home number of Dr. Carl Bornemann in Falls Village. Then he telephoned the doctor. When a woman answered, Peter assumed that she was Mrs. Bornemann, but she was actually the physician's daughter-in-law, Jessica Bornemann, who lives in Nova Scotia.

"He sounded very upset," she stated afterward, "and he said either, 'My mother, Barbara Gibbons, is injured, lying on the floor, with blood all over the place,' or 'My mother is injured and there's blood all over the floor.'" Because Dr. and Mrs. Bornemann were away on vacation, she gave Peter the names of other physicians to call, but he said they would take too long to reach the house. "I realized that he had an emergency and I stopped to think, and finally I told him to call the hospital." She estimated that the conversation lasted nearly three minutes. "After I hung up, I felt badly because I realized I hadn't given him the number of the hospital."

Peter dialed Directory Assistance again, and on his fifth call reached the hospital. Elizabeth Swart, the switchboard operator, told police that "The person calling stated he was Peter Reilly. He had just gotten home and had found his mother on the floor and breathing hard and blood all over the place. He also stated he had called the Canaan ambulance and Mickey Madow, who was a friend, and what should he do next. At this time I paged Mrs. Barbara Fenn, evening supervisor, and told her to stay with me on this call. Both of us listened to the conversation and the boy repeated everything again. He also asked Mrs. Fenn if she wanted his name. . . . When the boy was speaking with me he sounded panicky, but he had calmed down some when he was speaking with Mrs. Fenn."

In her statement to the police two days after the murder, Barbara Fenn said that she "heard a young male, soft-spoken voice, extremely upset, breathless, say, 'I am at the home of Barbara Gibbons. She is lying on the floor and having trouble breathing, and there is a lot of blood over the place.' I asked him if the patient is conscious, to which he responded, 'I don't know.' I requested that he check and there was a pause and he responded, 'No, she isn't.' I then stated I was dispatching an ambulance from Falls Village after getting directions, but he stated he had already called the Canaan ambulance. I asked why he had called Canaan, and he stated that he knew Mickey Madow was at home. I then asked him if he knew artificial respiration and he said, 'No.' I then concluded by saying I would dispatch the Falls Village ambulance and would call the State Police. I called the Falls Village ambulance and the State Police. At no time during the conversation did he reveal his name or relationship to the patient."

After making his calls, Peter hurried outside to clear the way for the ambulance. He hurled aside the outdoor grill near the front door. He moved the Corvette to the side of the house and turned on the flashers. Then he stood before the house, looking into the dark distance, alone in the terrible silence.

The roads were empty. The filling station had been closed since seven o'clock. In the house next door, Fred and Helen Kruse were asleep. They had last seen Barbara Gibbons outside reading at about 8:30. A little later they observed a light on in the house. Except for the murderer—or murderers— they were probably the last persons to see her alive.

Mrs. Marie Ovitt is the sister of two boyhood friends of Peter Reilly's, Timothy and Michael Parmalee, whose names would ultimately make headlines in the Reilly case. She told the State Police that she had seen a car parked in front of Barbara's house a half hour or so before the murder. She had been working at her evening job at the Bicron Electric plant in Canaan. "I left for home at exactly 9:00 P.M. and arrived at about 9:10 P.M. When I passed Barbara Gibbons' home, which is only several hundred yards north of mine, I noticed a normal-sized car parked right in front. I don't remember the color, make or anything about it. I'm quite sure it was a regular size, however. The house was dark. This I remember because it is usually well lit."

This was almost exactly fifty minutes before Peter Reilly found himself standing alone in front of the house, his mother's savaged body inside. As Peter related to his attorney, in a taped interview, "I jumped up and down. I was waiting for something, you know. . . . I saw this little car coming like a bat out of heck. He must have been doing 70, 75, 80 miles an hour down the road. It was Geoff. He pulled in the yard and said, 'Where is she?' I said, 'In the house,' so he went straight in the house. And, well, I went in right behind him and looked, and his first impression is, it looked like somebody raped her. I said, 'Well, come on, let's go back outside and wait for the police.' We got out and then we saw the lights and everything flashing and I was jumping up and down—must have jumped two, three feet in the air—waving them into the yard, you know."

Geoff Madow was then a tall, gangling seventeen-year-old. His shoulder-length dark hair was even longer than Peter's, He had followed his parents' car until they turned into Geer Hospital, then raced on alone to the cottage, arriving at just about the time that his parents were starting the ambulance and State Trooper Bruce McCafferty, cruising on Route 44 in East Canaan, received his orders to go to the Gibbons cottage.

The two teenaged boys on the murder scene didn't know what to do next, or even what to say to each other. Everything had been so normal just two and a half hours earlier when they had been with Barbara before driving to the church. Now Barbara was sprawled on the floor and Peter looked "glazed," according to Geoff.

Long after that night, Geoffrey Madow described what happened. "I drove in and parked the car. I was out of the door in one smooth motion and I was in the house. I was moving pretty quickly. I went into the bedroom and stopped in the door jamb. And that was it. I took one look at her and I noticed there was a cut on her abdomen, but there was no blood on it. It was clean. I didn't understand that. I could see the cuts everywhere. The neck was covered up. I could see the blood around it. There was blood on the face and the face looked battered. Definitely. I took maybe two steps in to about a foot in front of her feet. I put one hand on the bed and leaned way over to see if her chest was moving. It wasn't. I turned around and walked back out into the living room and Peter was over by the kitchen door and I just looked at him and we didn't say nothing. Then I looked at the clock, but I can't remember what time it was. And I just looked around the wall and then I turned to Pete and said, 'I think she's been raped.'

"We just sat there and talked for a minute, then we heard this car barreling into the driveway, and the front end of McCafferty's cruiser comes up next to the door, four feet away. The flashers going. No siren. He must have really flown. There was another cop with him. McCafferty walked in and went into the bedroom. He checked her pulse. Pete and I were just standing there, scared out of our heads. I didn't know what to do and Pete looked the same way. Peter said, 'We'd better move things out of the way for the stretcher.' We started moving things, but McCafferty came out and said, 'Don't move a thing. Don't touch a thing.' We put everything down and stopped. Then my father came in, followed by Fran and then my mother. And Fran walked over and she knew there was nothing we could do. My mother walked over and stood there by Pete. I never said anything. I never said, 'Pete, she's dead.' I didn't know how to turn around and say it. But Peter knew it. It looked like he knew it. I think it was Lieutenant Shay who finally told him she was dead. Then a whole bunch of other cops came running in. Not even three minutes after. They came in and told me to get out of the house. They told everybody to get out. Except Pete."

As the Madows and Fran Kaplan hurried to the cottage in the VFW ambulance, they radioed the State Police barracks. They were told that a trooper was on his way. McCafferty came up quickly behind them on Route 7 and Mickey, who was driving, pulled over to let him go by.

When they arrived at the Gibbons house, the auxiliary trooper, who had been riding with McCafferty, approached Mickey Madow and said, "Better hurry up; it's messy in there." Mickey got the stretcher out of the ambulance. Fran Kaplan grabbed a resuscitator and asked, "Where the hell is she?" They ran into the house. Miss Kaplan, then employed as an X-ray technician at Sharon Hospital, went into the bedroom and tried to see if she could discover any signs of life. She pushed aside a tool box near the body, stepped over the left arm and reached for the right wrist. She could find no pulse or chest movements. She noticed the abdominal wound and a large amount of blood that had come from the ears, nose and mouth.

"Forget it," she said to Mickey. "She's dead. Get me a goddamn blanket." After checking again for a pulse, they covered the body with a white blanket from the ambulance. Peter told Marion later that "I realized she was dead when you and Mr. Madow didn't put her on the stretcher and take her out."

As Fran Kaplan told the police, "Mrs. Madow then walked over to Peter Reilly, who was still sitting on the chair, and asked him, 'Are you okay?' and they hugged each other. While I was standing there I heard Peter ask Mrs. Madow if he could go home with her and she replied, 'Yes.' Peter then asked, 'Are you sure it's all right?' And Mrs. Madow replied, 'Of course,' and Peter again hugged Mrs. Madow. Peter was visibly shaking so Mrs. Madow asked her son Geoffrey for his jacket for Peter. Geoffrey gave his jacket to Peter, who then put it on."

In the meantime, Fran Kaplan unthinkingly picked up a set of keys on a silver ring that were on the bedroom floor near the right foot of the corpse. She placed them on the living room table. Peter recognized them as his mother's house and cabinet keys and later asked a policeman for permission to use them to get cigarettes from a cabinet. He never carried a house key of his own because, as he explained afterward, "We didn't lock the doors. Either she was home or she'd leave the door unlocked if she went out and knew I was coming. I got locked out of the house only once, in my freshman year in high school." Nonetheless, the police speculated that the keys belonged to Peter and that he had dropped them in the bedroom while attacking his mother.

Bruce McCafferty was a rookie cop who had been stationed in Canaan for less than a year. After his first view of the corpse he went to the cruiser and radioed for a supervisor to come to the scene. He returned to the bedroom, took another look and called the barracks again. "It looks like I have a 125." The response was, "Are you kidding? You'd better seal off the area then."

The number of people at the scene grew and grew. The Falls Village ambulance arrived. Lieutenant James Shay, the commander of State Police Troop B at the Canaan Barracks, having driven at top speed from his Granby home, took charge soon after 10:30. He was not in uniform. He began by berating Mickey Madow for covering the body with a blanket. He asked Mickey why he did it. "Because her son was standing there and she was nude. I did it only out of decency." Shay said, "Well, don't ever do it again."

The Madows remained on the scene as the police began their investigation. They had to give statements about what had happened. They also expected to take Peter home with them. In her statement, Marion Madow recalled that when she went to Peter because he was shaking, he said to her, "I called you and Mr. Madow because I didn't know what else to do. Did I do the right thing?" She replied, "Yes." He asked whether he could stay at her house. At this point, Sergeant Percy Salley, the shift supervisor who responded to

McCafferty's first call, approached Peter to look for signs of blood or bruises or anything suspicious. Peter remarked later that as he removed his shirt and watched the officer inspect his body and peer at his fingernails he realized for the first time that he might be a suspect in the slaying of his mother.

Geoff Madow was also an early suspect because when the police arrived at the murder scene two persons were present: Peter and Geoff. The boys were placed in separate police cruisers, about twenty-five feet apart, on the other side of the road from the house. They sat and sat while all the commotion went on around them.

Shortly before eleven o'clock, McCafferty sat behind the wheel of the car in which Peter was waiting and said that he needed to take a statement about Peter's activities that day. He asked Peter to read and sign his constitutional rights as they were printed on the statement forms. Peter learned that he had these rights:

1) You have a right to remain silent. If you talk, anything you say can and will be used against you in court. 2) You have the right to consult with a lawyer before you are questioned, and may have him with you during questioning. 3) If you cannot afford a lawyer, one will be appointed for you, if you wish, before any questioning. 4) If you wish to answer questions, you have the right to stop answering at any time. 5) You may stop answering questions at any time if you wish to talk to a lawyer, and may have him with you during any further questioning.

Peter could have said that he preferred to say nothing until he had the assistance of a lawyer. Today, he believes that this is what he should have said. At that time he could think of no reason to remain silent if he had nothing to hide. Quite willingly, as Trooper McCafferty would testify, Peter Reilly told the story of his day, slowly enough for the officer to write it all down in capital letters:

I, Peter A. Reilly, age 18 (DOB 03-02-55) of Route 63, Falls Village, Conn., make the following voluntary statement.
    I went to Great Barrington, Mass., with Geoffrey

Madow this afternoon. Geoffrey had to check to see if be was working this weekend. He works at Shop Well in Great Barrington. We left for there between 3:00 and 3:30 P.M. When we left there we went to Geoffrey's house and watched TV. Geoffrey ate dinner and we started to my house. We passed an ambulance by Deeley Road in Canaan. We figured it was going to pick up Geoffrey's uncle who had been having chest pains. After passing the ambulance we went to the Arco Station located at the intersection of Rt. 7 and Rt. 44. Geoffrey bought $1.00 worth of gas and we went back to see where the ambulance was going. When we found it, it was by Locust Hill Road in East Canaan. We followed the ambulance back to Norfolk. Then turned around and went back to Geoffrey's house to see if it was his uncle. I waited in the car when Geoffrey went into the house. We left Geoffrey's house and went directly to my house. We arrived at my house at 6:45 P.M. I was late for dinner and apologized to my mother for being late.

We both stayed (Geoffrey and myself) at my house until 7:20 P.M. At this time we both left for the Teen Center in North Canaan. Geoffrey drove his car and I drove my mother's car. We got there around 7:30–7:35 P.M. and waited until about 7:50 P.M. for Father Paul to get there. We stayed there until about 9:30 P.M. I dropped John Sochocki off at his house located on the road to the dump. After dropping John off I came directly home. I arrived home between 9:50–9:55. I parked the car in front of the house and got out to fix a headlight. I got back in the car and shut it off. I got out and locked the car. I went inside and said, 'Mom, I'm home.'

My mother didn't answer. I looked through the doorway and didn't see her in bed. I then saw her lying on the floor. She was having problems breathing and she was gasping. I saw the blood at this time. I didn't touch my mother but went straight to the telephone and called Mickey Madow and told her [Marion Madow] that my mother was lying on the floor and having trouble breathing and said that there was blood all over the place. Mrs. Madow told me to call my family doctor and that they would be right down. I then called Information and asked for Doctor Bornemann in Canaan. I got the number and called him. I got Mrs. Bornemann and told her the situation. She told me Dr. Bornemann was out of town and that I should call the Sharon Hospital Emergency Room. I went outside and threw the charcoal grill out of the way. I then moved my car to the north side of the house. I then went to the driveway and waited for the police or ambulance. While I was waiting, Geoffrey Madow came and we both went in and looked at my mother. Then we went back outside to wait.

The statement took more than half an hour to write down. At 11:35 P.M. Peter signed it. He hoped that he could go home with the Madows. He had been up for more than sixteen hours.

As Peter later told his attorney in a taped interview, "Lieutenant Shay came over and they asked me to go to the Kruses' house. They closed all the doors and everything, and they had me take off all my clothes and everything, and they looked them over. They checked through my hair, checked everything. Then he let me put my clothes on."

His lawyer asked if there was any blood on his body at all. "Not a spot. Not a spot." What about your shoes? "Not a spot. Not one single drop of blood. I never went through that bedroom. I do not ever remember going through that bedroom. I *know* I never went through that bedroom. All the transactions I made—the telephone, the moving part—everything, were between the front door and the kitchen. I never went through that bedroom.

"They went through all the searching stuff and I went back out, said good-bye to Mr. and Mrs. Kruse before I went out. I'm sure I did. It wouldn't be like me not to. And I went back out and sat in the cruiser and, oh, Bill Dickinson, Mr. Dickinson, came over by the cruiser, and he told me that if I needed anything, don't hesitate to get in touch. And Bob Belcher was there. Came up and he asked what was going on."

Geoff Madow, still sitting in a police cruiser, remembers seeing Peter get back into McCafferty's car. "He just sat there looking off into space. All of a sudden he looked up and saw me and he waved. Then he looked off into space again."

Feeling the midnight cold, Geoff slipped out of the cruiser for a moment to ask Peter if he could have his pea jacket back. After a while, Sergeant Salley told Geoff to come with him to the front of the cottage. The sergeant talked to Lieutenant Shay who told him to take both Peter Reilly and Geoff Madow to the police barracks. Salley mentioned to Shay that Geoff's father was on the scene. Well, in that case, Shay said, just take Reilly to the barracks and come back with the van. Geoff watched as the sergeant drove away with Peter. "That was the last time I saw Pete until December."

Salley returned quickly with the big police van. While a trooper took Mickey Madow's statement, another trooper led Geoff into the van. "Pretty soon Shay comes in," Geoff remembers, "and says, 'I want to strip you, make sure there's nothing on you.' I said, 'Are you out of your minds, it's cold here tonight.' He took my boots that weren't in such great shape anyway and ripped them apart. I don't know what he was looking for. He stripped me all the way down to my shorts and socks. And he says, 'Okay, drop your shorts.' I told him to 'Fuck off.' That's exactly what I said to him. He said, 'Do it; it's not my week for boys.' So I did it. He let me keep my socks on. After I got dressed and left the van he went through my pea coat, pulling out all the pockets. All my clothes were a mess. I was put back in the cruiser for a few minutes and then they let me go home. My father was pretty sore when he found out about it."

Mickey Madow protested to Shay about the strip search of his seventeen-year-old son. Madow recalls that the lieutenant told him that he didn't know that the boy's father was present; he just wanted to search the boy to eliminate any doubts.

Marion Madow had already gone home. It was now past midnight. Mickey and Geoff, assured that Peter would be questioned only briefly at the barracks, drove home to wait for Peter. But the State police did not deliver Peter Reilly to them that night. Or the next day. As the hours went by, Geoff became more and more agitated. He said over and over again to anyone who would listen, "They're doing something to Pete."

3 ■ INVESTIGATION

LIEUT. SHAY: Don't be afraid to say, "I did it."

PETER REILLY: Ya, but I'm incriminating myself by saying I did.

LIEUT. SHAY: We have, right now, without any word out of your mouth, proof positive—

PETER REILLY: That I did it?

LIEUT. SHAY: That you did it.

PETER REILLY: So, okay, then I may as well say I did it.

Peter Reilly was taken to the State Police Barracks shortly before two o'clock Saturday morning, four hours after the murder. He had sat in a police cruiser for most of the previous three and a half hours, alone with his thoughts, while the drama of a police homicide investigation went on just across the road. He could see the police going in and out of the cottage, special investigators going about their work, spectators gossiping behind a rope barrier, and cars rushing up and down a highway that is normally deserted after midnight.

Peter was driven to the barracks, a grim, two-story, redbrick building with a green neon "State Police" sign out front, by Sergeant Percy Salley. On the way, in an attempt to make conversation, Peter said that "this is an interesting case." The sergeant would relate this to a jury: It fit nicely into the State's picture of an unemotional young killer who had remained cool and untearful after his terrible deed.

To Peter, his words seemed natural. He was glad to have someone to talk to at last, and he did not feel uneasy because he was with a policeman. The state cops might be known as "the blue meanies" because they prowled the roads in their blue cruisers but, like most of his companions, Peter looked upon the State Police more as friends—or at least as friendly adversaries—than enemies. They were authority figures, of course, and The Law was somehow awesome, but because the barracks for the northwest corner of the state was in Canaan, the kids of Canaan knew many of the troopers, especially those who lived in town.

The teenagers of the Litchfield Hills have a relationship with the police that is peculiarly old-fashioned for America of the 1970s. The troopers are almost "neighborhood" cops, since towns like Falls Village and North Canaan, which together have but four thousand residents, do not have town police. The townspeople can no more afford to hire full-time policemen than they can afford professional firemen. They put out their fires with volunteers and they depend on the State Police for law enforcement.

Although they are kept busy with occasional major crimes and a great variety of minor matters—from hunting for deer-jackers to breaking up family fights—the men of Troop B spend most of their time on the road as highway patrolmen. At any one time scarcely half a dozen Canaan troopers are cruising about the Litchfield Hills.

The typical state trooper may have just managed to get through high school, then one day he suddenly appears on Main Street as a uniformed guardian of the law, his eyes alert for wrongdoers. He cuts an impressive figure, but he is still a small-town kid who became a rural cop. One state trooper says of New York City, a two-and-a-half-hour drive south of Falls Village, "You wouldn't ever catch me in that place without my gun."

Before the murder of his mother, Peter Reilly thought about applying to the State Police after graduation. On the very night of the murder, he said to Trooper McCafferty that he would like to become a state trooper. According to McCafferty, "He questioned me as to what kind of marks you needed in high school to be eligible for the job." Possibly this was Peter's way of ingratiating himself; perhaps he was wondering about his future now that his mother was dead. A trooper, after all, earns at least $10,000 a year and spends most of his day behind the wheel of a car, a job bound to appeal to Peter.

Besides, he liked the troopers. He thought Jim Mulhern a friend as well as a fellow member of the Youth Center Steering Committee. He and other teenagers had recently helped Mulhern when he began work on a new sidewalk for his house. Jim had been to Peter's house when his mother complained to the police about harassing telephone calls; Jim had written down the details. The Madows liked Jim Mulhern, too. Jim and Mickey played golf together. Art Madow once stayed with the Mulherns after a row with his parents.

On the night of the murder, Joanne Mulhern was so disturbed by the news that she telephoned Father Paul to see what could be done to help Peter.

Then there was Trooper John Calkins. Peter had "tapped the teenage underground," to use Peter's phrase, to help him on a case. As Calkins stated in an official report:

> During the past month or so Peter Reilly has been supplying information to the writer. This information concerned a missing teen-age girl who had at one time been a steady girlfriend of Reilly's. I was requested by another police agency to see if Peter Reilly could shed any light on the girl's whereabouts. Reilly apparently got the word that I wanted to speak to him as he called on the phone at this troop. I explained what I wanted and he agreed to try and obtain the information and call me back. His attitude was quite friendly. Subsequently I received several phone calls from Peter while on duty at which time he did supply information on the missing person. He even took the trouble on at least one occasion to call me early in the morning while the writer was working the midnight shift. The missing person was also subsequently located during this period. Reilly and the writer became friendly, though we never met face to face.

Trooper Calkins was on desk duty at the barracks when the first calls came in about the Gibbons murder; Trooper Mulhern drove Peter to the interrogation in Hartford and wrote out his so-called confession; and Trooper Calkins escorted him to jail. Both troopers testified for the State in the Reilly trial.

When Peter was taken to the barracks for questioning, he was not like an inner-city teenager confronted by cops he didn't trust. He felt an affinity for the troopers because he was a "gearhead." Peter explains that "gearheads are crazy about automobiles: The cars draw the girls and the girls decorate the cars."

Peter became a supergearhead once he started driving around in a Corvette. He and his friends had a Tom-and-Jerry relationship with the highway patrolmen. The troopers had to put a stop to any high-speed driving that endangered life and limb, but they were inclined to go easy about minor infractions of the law.

Art Madow remembers the times he sat in cruisers with police, "just talking to pass the time," and the times he and his friends would go to the barracks to wheedle the desk sergeant out of a couple of gallons of gasoline.

A long time after the murder, Art, a husky young man who had become almost an older brother to Peter, said that "I blame myself for Peter's arrest. You see, I got to know the cops pretty well, but I didn't trust them. Pete got to know them well too, but his trouble was, he trusted them. If only I had wised him up."

When Sergeant Salley reached the Canaan Barracks, ten miles north of the Gibbons cottage, he took Peter into a 12-by-18-foot room that was used as a coffee lounge by the troopers. The furniture consisted of counters lining two walls, a table and chairs, a sink and a refrigerator and vending machines. Salley gave Peter a soft drink. Later, Peter bought himself a candy bar, his first food since the cookies at the Madows in the late afternoon. "I couldn't eat the darn thing," he said later. "I had no appetite at all after everything started happening."

From two to six in the morning, Peter remained in the room waiting to be questioned. No one suggested that he rest in one of the bedrooms on the second floor. Although Sergeant Salley testified that Peter did not ask him about sleeping, Peter insists that he said several times that he wanted to sleep somewhere and was told to wait until Lieutenant Shay returned to the barracks. "The Madows are waiting for me," Peter said. "The lieutenant wants to talk to you first," Salley said. The two of them just sat there.

A detective had said to Lieutenant Shay at the murder scene, "I wouldn't let Reilly out of my sight until you find out what the story is." Long after that night, the same detective, not wanting to be quoted by name, conceded that if Peter had not agreed to go to the barracks the evidence against him would have been insufficient for an arrest. "He was very cooperative. He'd do anything they said." Still insisting on Reilly's guilt, he added that "This didn't surprise me. In my experience, it's the guilty people who are usually the most cooperative. It's the innocent ones who often put up the most resistance."

Resistance was not in Peter's nature. Though he was not under arrest, and had a right to counsel and a right not to answer questions, he raised no objection to being isolated for hours in a police cruiser and in a police building. "Somebody murdered my mother," he explained later. "I wanted to help the police find out who did it. It never occurred to me that I should not cooperate." When Mike Wallace on the CBS program *60 Minutes* in January 1976 asked him why he thought he didn't need a lawyer, Peter said, "Because I hadn't done anything wrong and this is America and that's the way I thought it was."

The police force of a major American city, with hundreds of homicides to investigate every year, would probably not find the murder of a middle-aged woman of poor reputation who lived on wine and welfare unusual. But a savage murder in Litchfield County is rare enough to make it the prime topic of everyone's conversation. It could be the major event of the year for the local State Police force and could make or break careers, or at least burnish or tarnish reputations.

Lieutenant James Shay faced those risks. A tall, dark-haired, broad-shouldered officer, he was a married man with six daughters. He had been a member of the State Police for twelve years, a detective for the last eight, and commander of Troop B for little more than four months. The *Lakeville Journal*, the principal weekly newspaper in the area, had described him as "one of the department's top detectives."

Although some officers who had known Shay for years had misgivings about his competence as an investigator ("He's a bull in a china shop," one said) and spoke of his heavy-handed way of dealing with the public, they had to admit that he had moved quickly up the State Police hierarchy, and was very much a "hard-nosed, take-charge kind of guy." The trouble is, said a colleague from Shay's days as a recruit, "there's such a thing as being too hard-nosed. You can get to be too stubborn for your own good."

A homicide investigation begins by accumulating every scrap of information that might conceivably pertain to the circumstances of the killing, the character, behavior and associations of the victim, and to the identity of the killer. Or killers. Some murders tell their own story: The victim lies dead on the floor, clearly punctured with bullets, while the murderer conveniently lets himself be caught, gun in hand. He blurts out a confession. Then the police are engaged in a mopping-up operation. Every care must be taken that the evidence proves the defendant's guilt in court, but the pressure is off. The experts go about their business.

The solution to the Gibbons killing was not so apparent. The victim had been repeatedly assaulted and mutilated. The crime was an exceptionally vicious and bloody all-out attack. Moreover, it appeared to be a sexual assault as well as a killing. No one stood about with blood on his hands, body or clothes. Neither murder weapon nor motive was obvious. And not a single witness to the murder or the flight of the murderer came forward. The next-door neighbors, eighty-four-year-old Fred Kruse and his wife, had slept through it all. They awakened only when the State Police rapped on their windows.

The police had plenty of manpower on the scene, including the veteran County Detective, Sam Holden, and specialists from the State Police crime laboratory in Bethany. Jim Mulhern was assigned to knock on doors in the immediate neighborhood and take statements from the inhabitants. Pictures were taken and sketches were made, but the task was not easy in the tiny cluttered bedroom. The floor space between the bunk beds and the wall was only seven feet wide and was dominated by the corpse.

The grounds, the house, the bedroom, the body—all were measured and photographed. An inventory of key household items was prepared. One little item not listed was a platinum ring with three diamond chips. "My mom wore it all the time," Peter says. "My aunt Steffie gave it to her. It disappeared after the murder just like the wallet and the money." Since the authorities ruled out robbery as motive for the murder, and because Peter's defense made only a weak effort to deal with the robbery, the missing ring played no part in the Reilly trial.

One officer, after making a rough sketch of the four rooms, gave this description:

> Interior of house very dirty. Large amount of dust and dirt visible on floor and furnishings. Many books in living room. Rooms very small. Kitchen very dirty as well as cooking utensils and dishes and silver. Many knives around the house. A leather pouch in kitchen contained three fish cleaning knives. Long thin sheathed blades. Sharp. Point broken off one of them. Large machete hanging by front door and pouch with ice pick. Several rifles hanging on wall in living room. Pistol in case in drawer in kitchen.

Trooper Marius Venclauskas examined the various sharp instruments and took such interest in a wooden-handled knife with a broken point—it appeared to have some blood on its six-inch blade—that he scratched his initials on a brass fitting. Another trooper rummaged through drawers and came up with an empty worn-out wallet (the third wallet of the Reilly case) that Barbara had not used for years. The search went on in the early morning hours, but not until the following afternoon did Trooper Donald Moran come upon an old-fashioned, barbershop-style straight razor inscribed "7000 Made in Germany." It was on a living-room bookshelf, in plain sight. The razor was closed. There was no blood on the blade.

The investigators took notice of the blood-spattered furniture, the unusual amount of dirty laundry strewn about the bedroom, the penny and the dime next to the body, the nickel on the living-room floor, and the bloody footprint near the body—a footprint that would never be identified. Sink traps were examined. Preparations were made for flushing out the septic tank.

The panties and dungarees next to the victim's left foot were of special interest. Peter remembers being led to the doorway of the bedroom by a police officer. "My mom's pants were on the floor near her and they were soaking wet. He asked me to feel them. He said, 'Are these your pants or your mother's?' I said, 'Can I look at them?' He said, 'Sure.' So I pulled at them—you know, apart. They were all crumpled up in a ball. I looked at them and I noticed the cuffs were rolled up and they were straight pants. I told him they were hers because mine—I always wear bell-bottom jeans and I never roll the cuffs up on them."

During the on-the-scene medical examination the bottom parts of the shirts the victim was wearing were discovered to be wet. The rug was damp, but only underneath the body. No one found out what fluid had caused all this wetness. Lieutenant Shay said later that he knew it was not urine because it didn't smell like urine. But what accounted for the damp clothes, the damp body? Did Peter Reilly try to cleanse his mother after killing her, as the State would suggest? Had Barbara Gibbons been knocked into a nearby swamp by a car while wandering on the road and then brought into the house and killed, as some of Peter's defenders speculated?

Sergeant Gerald Pennington, a fingerprint specialist from the State Police crime laboratory, found only one fingerprint of consequence, as well as a front-door palmprint that would defy identification. Located on the exterior of the side screen door, the fingerprint was clear enough to be identified, but the State Police, for all the resources at their command, seemed unable to determine who the owner might be. Consequently, it played no part in the Reilly trial. The mystery would remain unsolved for more than two years, and then the solution would have a dramatic impact on Peter's fortunes.

Geoffrey Madow remembers walking by the side of the

house with Lieutenant Shay and Sergeant Salley. "I noticed that the back door was open and it was hanging off and the cop was brushing it for prints. I said, 'The back door is open.' Shay goes, 'Huh,' like that. I said, 'The back door is open. That door is never open. The outside latch is left on.'" When Shay asked Peter, Peter said that the door was kept locked except when his mother occasionally used it.

Several weeks after the murder, when the police took down their barriers and warning signs and Fred Kruse, the landlord, was able to approach the cottage closely for the first time, he noticed that the bottom hinge of the side screen door had been pushed out of the door frame. He set to work plugging the screw holes and making the necessary repairs. The fact of the broken hinge was not revealed until long after the Reilly trial. Kruse says that he knew for sure, as a conscientious handyman, that the door had been in good order before the murder. His opinion is that "someone was in there, heard Peter come home, and kicked out the back door so that he could get away."

When a reporter asked him, "Did you testify at the trial about the door being damaged?" Kruse said, "No. Nobody ever asked me."

"The Corvette," Peter says, "was a very loud car. Whoever it was must have heard me coming before I reached the house. Then because I took so long fixing the headlight and locking the car door, he had time to get away through the side door. You could open the two bolts on the inside door with your hand, but if the screen door was latched on the outside, as usual, you'd have to force it open."

The primary object of attention at the murder scene, of course, was the body of the victim. Dr. Ernest M. Izumi, a pathologist from Sharon Hospital, arrived at 11:30 after driving from his Colebrook home. A bespectacled Japanese-American with a round face and closely-cropped hair, Dr. Izumi functioned as the local assistant to the State Medical Examiner, Dr. Elliot Gross. While waiting for Dr. Gross to arrive, he decided that he had better declare the patient dead. As he later reported:

I accompanied Lt. Shay to the bedroom, being careful not to touch or move anything. A white cotton blanket was removed from the body. The victim was pulseless, left arm was cold (rigor mortis absent), but abdomen was warm (11:45 P.M.). The victim was supine with white "T" undershirt pushed up over breasts around neck covering in part multiple neck cuts surrounded by clotted and dried blood. Over the undershirt was a blue shirt, part of which covered the abdomen. No further clothing. Victim laying beside a double deck bed, on floor with blood around head and neck. Upper bunk bed reading lamp was on, bloody shirt hanging off bedpost. Sleeping blankets and pillows were orderly except upper bunk where blanket was open.

Blood was confined chiefly to area surrounding body. One or two small spots of blood on shirts (ironed) hanging from adjacent curtain rods. Adjacent to body on left side was laundry basket with clothes, pile of laundered socks, shoes and metal tool box (no blood on any item). Above the head was bicycle approximately three feet away standing against wall. On right side was the bunk bed approximately two feet away. At the feet on left side was denim jeans and underpants (separated) which were wet from the waist to cuffs of leg. The body was not closely examined until Chief Elliot Gross arrived and pictures were taken.

Dr. Gross looked over the situation and asked Dr. Izumi to carry on with the examination. The report continues:

At approximately 4:40 A.M. again examined because of delay in obtaining photos. Examination of clothes shows they are wet. The back of shirts wet and warm (fluid not blood). The lower back reveals multiple cuts, no blood oozing. Shirts were removed. Buttons (2) torn off—one on floor, other on victim. The shirt shows no tears nor any cuts.

Before removing the clothing, Dr. Izumi held the hands while Lieutenant Shay put transparent plastic bags over them and tied them on. Izumi's work was done by 5:15.

The cause of Barbara Gibbons' death was clear:

"exsanguination of blood due to multiple wounds in the neck and body caused by sharp object and aspiration of blood." Dr. Izumi wrote this account of his examination:

> Supine position of white female, hair matted with wet and dried blood. Blood on face, both eyes discolored blue extending across bridge of nose. Blood oozing from mouth, head and face leaning on left side. Blood around cut areas of neck and on surrounding carpet. Upper lip shows an abrasive laceration on margin. No teeth were broken.
>
> T-shirt and blue shirt described. Small wounds on abdomen (six or more); midline healed scar; gaping open wound (4″) horizontal with no blood in left lower quadrant.
>
> Legs widely separated exposing external genitalia. Blood on both thighs. Left upper thigh had a small round wound (1″) in diameter, brownish in color. On right upper thigh an oval crescent-shaped abrasion ½″ in diameter.
>
> Right hand shows a defense wound on palmar surface across crease, approximately ¾″. Also ragged wound on dorsal surface of right hand, 1″ above second and third fingers. Right inner elbow shows a contusion about 1½″ in diameter. Left hand shows a crescent-shaped abrasion on dorsal surface.
>
> On the lower back and to the left of the midline there are approximately five stab wounds in regions above the posterior ileum (each measures ¼″).
>
> Blood oozing from vaginal orifice and on carpet between legs. Blood present on right and left anterior thighs. The body was carefully lifted and rolled so that white sheet could be placed under body for removal.
>
> Body removed to Sharon Hospital morgue at approximately 4:40 A.M. Sept. 29, where an autopsy is to be performed.

Lieutenant Shay remained at the murder scene for an hour after the removal of the corpse. He telephoned the barracks to tell Sergeant Salley to read Peter his constitutional rights again. Salley did so after first telling Peter, in response to a question, that he was not being charged with anything.

When Lieutenant Shay arrived at about six o'clock he took Peter to an interview room on the second floor and again read him his rights. He asked Peter to sign two Constitutional Warning and Waiver of Rights forms to show that he had heard and understood his rights. As Shay would later testify, Peter asked him, "Am I actually a suspect?" Shay said, "Yes, you are a suspect." When the lieutenant said that the State would supply him with an attorney if he could not afford one, Peter said there was an attorney in his family. He was confident his godmother would help him if there was any legal or financial problem: Her brother was a prominent Manhattan attorney. Peter did not ask to speak to a lawyer before being questioned. He still took the view that you only need a lawyer if you have something to hide. Lieutenant Shay was "struck by the fact that he was very calm, very poised and showed no emotion."

The questioning began at about 6:30. It was being taped in Shay's office on the first floor. He had activated the machine himself before going upstairs. The lieutenant began by asking Peter, "What time did you leave school today?" Peter related his movements that afternoon and evening, just as he described them in his original statement to Trooper McCafferty, and then spoke of returning home and looking into the bedroom.

"The bed was turned down and I took a double take. . . . She wasn't on the top bunk. I looked down and I saw her on the floor." A transcript of a portion of the taped interview, as heard by Peter's attorney, states that "Reilly's voice breaks down at this point." Peter is heard to say to Shay that he either said or thought, "Oh, my God," when he saw the body. Peter explains about going to the telephone and making his calls. He insists that "I didn't touch her. If you touch someone you can get into trouble."

The interrogation continued:

Q: How long was the first call?
A: Thirty seconds, a minute.
Q: How long were you on the phone?
A: Four or five minutes, maybe less. I looked and saw blood all over the place. I never went into the room. I never went through the bedroom door.
Q: Was your mother alive?

A: She was breathing but having trouble. She was unconscious. She didn't answer when I called to her.

Q: Were her eyes open?

A: No, I think they were closed. I'm almost sure, but I can't definitely say.

Q: How long did you observe her breathing?

A: Just a couple of seconds. Then she stopped.

Q: How was she dressed?

A: She had on a T-shirt and nothing else, maybe a coat. I'm not sure.

Q: Did you see any blood?

A: Yes, the T-shirt was pulled up and there was blood on the chest. And on the floor. Possibly on her face and throat, I'm not sure. (Reilly seemed to be choking up at this point.)

Q: It's normal.

A: I was really shaken. We were very close. She did as much as she could. She did a very good job. She always tried to do things. If I wanted something, if there were any problems, we'd always work them out.

Q: Could someone think otherwise?

A: I haven't been at home that much in the evenings for the last several months. We swore at each other when we got mad.

Q: Which was quite often.

A: Not really. She changed a little after the hysterectomy. I wouldn't want to discuss things with her. She'd fly right off the handle.

Q: Did she have a drinking problem?

A: She drank wine quite consistently.

Q: People who drink a lot get irritable.

A: Yeah. (Mumbles something, then says) I have long hair. I would cut it if she asked me to.

Q: Did you ever see your mother having sex?

A: No, but I heard it once, I heard heavy breathing and the bedsprings.

Q: Did it bother you?

A: No. I argued that if I can do it she can.

Q: Do you have any brothers or sisters?

A: No, an only child.

Q: What names did you call your mother?

A: Fuck you, dumb bitch. She called me the same, you sonofabitch and things like that. Otherwise we got along fairly well.

Q: Why didn't you touch her?

A: I knew I didn't know what I was doing. The first thing I'd do was to get someone who knew what they were doing. First person I could think of was Mrs. Madow. I wanted to get someone there. You don't expect to see your mom in a pool of blood. It's been drilled into me not to touch her. I'd be more than willing to take a lie detector test.

Q: We'll arrange it. What entrance did you use?

A: Front door.

Q: Ever use the back door?

A: No.

Q: When was the last time you used it?

A: Week or two ago, at least.

Q: Did your mother use the door?

A: Yes. She hung out laundry there.

The rest of the tape of this conversation, which lasted for an hour and a half, was garbled beyond transcription. Questions were asked, Peter believes, about his godmother and his relatives and where they might be found. He was questioned about his mother's sex life and whether he had ever had relations with her. Peter was upset about this, and he even became "a little mad" when Sergeant Salley came in and began asking him the same questions when Shay stepped out of the room. When Shay returned Peter asked him if he had studied psychology. Shay said he had. "I figured so," Peter told him; there had to be some reason for all the questions.

Shay finally suggested to Peter that he might need some sleep. He was taken down the hall to one of the bedrooms. It was now 8:30 in the morning. Peter had been awake for twenty-five hours. Lieutenant Shay took his sneakers: "I guess they wanted to analyze them or something," Peter said later. He lay down on the bed fully clothed, and was left alone for the next four hours. But the door was kept open so that an auxiliary trooper, sitting on a chair in the hallway, could watch him.

As Lieutenant Shay continued to direct the investigation, Dr. Izumi drove to Sharon Hospital to do the autopsy on Barbara Gibbons. Five witnesses were present. The autopsy took more than six hours, starting at 9:50 Saturday morning when Peter was sleeping—or trying to sleep—in Canaan and ending at 3:45 in the afternoon when Peter was in Hartford taking a lie detector test.

The twelve-page autopsy report begins with a "clinical resume" about "this 51-year-old white female" that misstates the approximate times of two occurrences. It gives 9:30 instead of 9:50 as the time Peter Reilly discovered the body and 10:35 instead of 10:05 as the time that Frances Kaplan arrived on the murder scene and found that there was no pulse.

Dr., Izumi described the major mutilation as "a gaping horizontal incised wound" of the neck. This great wound, ellipsoid in shape, was six inches long, two and a half inches wide at the center and a full four inches deep. Two and perhaps three other neck wounds, when combined with the primary wound, meant that the slashing of Barbara Gibbons' neck was so severe that the head was practically severed from the body. None of this was seen by Peter, the Madows or any of the first arrivals at the cottage because the neck was covered by the bunched-up shirt and undershirt.

Other wounds and injuries were examined and described in excruciating detail, including interior tears of the vagina, leg fractures and cuts on both the stomach and back. The extent of the assault on Barbara Gibbons is evident from a ten-point summation of the wounds and injuries:

1. Stab wound through her hand.

2. Blow to elbow.

3. Blow to face, breaking nose.

4. Minor brain contusion.

5. Several slashes of the throat.

6. Multiple stab wounds in the lower back.

7. Gash wound in abdomen.

8. Three broken ribs.

9. Deep penetration of the vagina with an unknown object.

10. Two broken femurs (thighbones).

Trooper Venclauskas collected in specimen containers items worthy of analysis by the crime lab experts. He gathered a blood sample, scrapings from the soles of both feet (which were very dirty), fingernail and toenail scrapings, samples of hair from several parts of the body, and five or six hairs that were found with the dried blood in the palm of the right hand. Barbara Gibbons had tried to protect herself: Some of the cuts were judged to be defense wounds. Still more interesting was Dr. Izumi's opinion that some of the blows and cuts had been inflicted after death—after the victim had stopped breathing.

As the autopsy continued, key findings and conclusions were passed on to Lieutenant Shay. They proved useful in the interrogation of Peter Reilly.

Where *was* Peter? The police knew, but his friends weren't sure. Mickey Madow had remained at the murder scene until about 2:30 Saturday morning, after the rest of his family had left, and then he drove home in Fran Kaplan's Toyota. His conversations with several troopers had led him to believe that Peter would shortly be brought to his house.

Half an hour after Madow reached his home, a Corporal Logan called and asked if Mickey and his wife and Miss Kaplan would come to the barracks later in the morning to give the police some additional information.

"Look," said Mickey, "as long as we are up right now, why don't we come down right away?"

"No," the trooper replied. "Get a little rest."

"How about Peter Reilly? Will he be able to come home?"

"No, we are going to be with him for about another half to three quarters of an hour."

"Do you want me to come down and get him then?"

"No, we'll run him up to your house."

A bed was made up for Peter in the den and a light was left on outdoors. He never appeared.

4 ▪ INTERROGATION

PETER REILLY: Does that actually read my brain?

SGT. KELLY: Oh, definitely, definitely. And if you've told me the truth this is what your brain is going to tell me.

PETER REILLY: Mm-hm.

SGT. KELLY: If you—

PETER REILLY: Will this stand up to protect me?

SGT. KELLY: Right, right.

PETER REILLY: Good. That's the reason I came up to take it, you know, for the protection of having—

SGT. KELLY: Let me put it this way, Pete. If you didn't hurt your mother last night, I'll be only too happy to say so. All right? If you did, I'll have to say that. All right?

PETER REILLY: Right.

Peter dreamed about his mother. He dreamed she was alive and that he had decided not to go to the Youth Center meeting after all. He dreamed that he was with her when someone came to the cottage door Friday night.

He had closed his eyes after lying down on the bed in the barracks. "But I was restless," he told his lawyer afterward. "I couldn't go to sleep. Every time I'd start to go to sleep, you know, I'd wake up again. I must have been there for an hour and a half, two hours, before I finally fell asleep. It only seemed like I could sleep for a minute or two. I didn't get that much sleep that it did any good."

On the first floor of the police building there was great commotion, as if the place were under siege. While some troopers handled routine police business, other officers, working full time on the Gibbons murder, rushed in and out. People were being questioned about their movements the night before and what they knew about Barbara Gibbons and Peter Reilly.

All leads had to be followed, and all possible suspects checked out. Solving the case quickly would be a great feather in the cap of the commanding officer, but to let the killer slip away by mischance would be a personal disaster. By mid-day Saturday, however, no suspect had been found, except Peter Reilly, and no physical evidence pointed to his guilt. His own account of his movements, however, suggested that his mother was killed either while he was approaching the cottage or inside the cottage. His claim of innocence seemed to rest on an extraordinary coincidence: that he had appeared on the scene just minutes or seconds after a murderer finished the job and vanished.

The one great advantage to the police in their investigation was Peter's willingness to be kept in custody and to answer questions without a lawyer present. If he was the killer, then getting a confession out of him was vital before anyone could interfere. Keeping information about their work from leaking out was important.

"Not one word of this is to get out to anybody," Lieutenant Shay ordered his men at the Canaan Barracks. "I'm telling you now: being forewarned is forearmed. If anything gets back to me, there will be hell to pay." Shay was practically shouting at the troopers, according to Marion Madow, who heard his raised voice while dictating a statement to Trooper Mulhern in an adjoining room.

At noon, Peter awoke to Mulhern's voice. Shay had sent him to ask Peter if he wanted anything to eat. Though twenty-four hours had passed since his last meal, the high school lunch, Peter said he didn't feel hungry. Mulhern left and Peter rested for another forty minutes. Then Mulhern returned and announced that they were going to Hartford for the lie detector test. Peter was taken into another room and told to wait. At the same time, the trooper's wife, Joanne Mulhern, in the adjoining room, was asked to scrutinize Peter through a one-way glass.

One of the oddities of the Reilly case was that a police officer and his wife, both of whom were acquainted with the accused, should find themselves on opposite sides, with one testifying for the prosecution and the other for the defense. Trooper Mulhern did as he was told in the investigation and interrogation, playing his part in the prosecution's effort to demonstrate Peter's guilt. By simply describing what she had seen and heard, Joanne Mulhern helped make the case for his innocence.

Mrs. Mulhern had seen Peter at the Youth Center meeting. She had a good idea of what clothes he was wearing, what car he was driving and when he left the church. When she returned home from the meeting, she had called the Sharon Hospital on a personal matter.

"Hold on a minute," the switchboard operator said to her, "I cannot connect you at this time. It is very busy here."

"Oh," said Mrs. Mulhern, "I won't bother you now. Why is it so busy?"

"I have called an ambulance to Canaan."

"All right, I won't bother you."

Mrs. Mulhern had telephoned at the exact time that Peter was asking the hospital to send help for his mother. Because her husband was called out to work on the murder, she was one of the first of Peter's friends to learn what had happened. At the Canaan Barracks, she looked closely at Peter and his clothes. She said that they were the same clothes he had worn at the church. She signed a statement to that effect.

Peter's clothing mattered because the prosecutor in the Reilly trial would suggest, despite the testimony of Mrs. Mulhern and others, that Peter had taken off his bloody clothes after killing his mother and had somehow disposed of them. One witness would claim that Peter had told him about driving away from the house with a bundle of bloody clothes to hurl them away before returning home to await the ambulance and the police. No bloody clothes were ever found. No bloodstains were discovered in the Corvette.

After being secretly observed by Joanne Mulhern, Peter was driven to Hartford by Jim Mulhern. "Mulhern was driving so fast that I was kind of scared. I trusted his driving but I had my foot on the brake, if there had been a brake on the passenger's side, all the way." They talked about motorcycles and television commercials but not the murder; Mulhern had been ordered not to discuss the case.

They arrived in Hartford at two o'clock and drove to the State Police Headquarters at 100 Washington Street, a few minutes' walk from the golden-domed state capitol building. The State Police Commissioner and his assistants work in the imposing but outdated stone building facing the street, while Troop H operates out of another structure directly behind. Peter remembers being taken into a waiting room in the main building and sitting on a bench for twenty minutes. He could see secretaries typing. He smoked a cigarette. He looked the way he felt: a thin, weary, unwashed teenager in scruffy clothes and sneakers. "I went into a bathroom, washed my face and hands, combed my hair. I tried to wake myself up, but it didn't do any good."

Mulhern returned and took him upstairs to meet Sergeant Jack Schneider, a pleasant, soft-spoken man who had been with the State Police for ten and a half years. Schneider explained to Peter that his partner, Sergeant Tim Kelly, the head of the Polygraph Unit, was going to conduct the lie detector test. But first they needed Peter's signature on a form stating that he was taking the test voluntarily. Peter signed his name. The time was 2:40 P.M.

Schneider asked Peter for some basic data about himself, saying that "This is confidential information. It stays here. Everything that we do today or any forms we make out remain here." His whole approach was friendly and relaxing, as if Peter had nothing to worry about and would soon be free to go. The emphasis was on the future. He asked what Peter was going to do when he got out of school. Peter said he was thinking of trying a blue-collar job for a while, but "if I don't like it then my godmother is going to pay my way to go to college if I want to."

The sergeant asked Peter if he had had any kind of intoxicating liquor during the past twenty-four hours. No, Peter said, nor had he used any drugs. He admitted to having smoked marijuana in the past. "Who don't smoke grass at eighteen years of age, right?" Schneider said cheerfully.

Schneider's job, of course, was to soften up the subject for the lie detector test. When he commented to Peter that "You're very calm," Peter said, "Well, I figure I would save my tears for later. This is more important than that." Peter was so grateful for the kindly treatment that he commented, "You're the only person who has been straightforward with me in the last twenty-four hours. I've been drilled and drilled and drilled and gone over and gone over."

Schneider told Peter that there would be no trick questions in the polygraph test: "You and Tim are going to talk it over. He's going to make up some questions. You're going to go along with him in making up these questions. He'll only ask you what you want and you answer yes or no. Okay?"

The time had come to take Peter to the polygraph room. Schneider explained that "The reason we have the double doors and everything, and the reason we can't smoke in here is because we try to make the room as soundproof as possible."

The room was a former bedroom fitted with yellow acoustical tiles and green carpeting. The polygraph machine was built into a regular desk. Peter was asked to sit next to the desk in a straight chair with a leather back, a leather seat and adjustable arms. Schneider called it "the seat of honor." Peter was asked to roll up his sleeve and flex his muscle. The sergeant placed a Childs Cardio-cuff on his left arm and explained that "we're measuring your blood pressure, your heartbeat, your pulse, you see, because that's very important because that's the only muscle in your body you can't control." A rubber device was fastened to Peter's chest to measure his respiration and electrodes were attached to two fingers of his left hand to measure his body electricity.

Schneider had a final word for Peter. "There are three things we can say here today. You told us the truth, you didn't tell us the truth, or there's some mental or physical problem, we can't test you. For some reason we can't test you, we'll test you again some other day. Okay? As long as you want to."

Peter sat alone in the polygraph room after Schneider left. He was nervous but also eager to start the test because he was confident that the lie detector would come to his rescue. He had been unable to convince Lieutenant Shay that he was telling the truth, but the polygraph would do it for him. Then, at last, he could get back to Canaan, go to bed and start a new life on his own.

He had volunteered for the test, Peter told his attorney later, "because I was so sure of my innocence. I just wanted to get all the police garbage out of the way so I could get some rest and be with my friends. I was, of course, quite unhappy, as you can well understand. I was so sure of myself, you know. I had no worries."

Daniel Defoe, best known as the creator of *Robinson Crusoe*, anticipated by two centuries the present-day use of the polygraph as an instrument for separating the guilty from the innocent. In a pamphlet published in 1730, grandly entitled *An Effectual Scheme for the Immediate Preventing of Street Robberies and Suppressing all Other Disorders of the Night*, he wrote:

> Guilt carries Fear always about with it; there is a Tremor in the Blood of a Thief, that, if attended to, would effectually discover him; and if charged as a suspicious Fellow, on that Suspicion only I would always feel his Pulse, and I would recommend it to Practice. . . .
>
> It is true some are so hardened in Crime that they will boldly hold their Faces to it, carry it off with an Air of Contempt, and outface even a Pursuer; but take hold of his Wrist and feel his Pulse, there you shall find his Guilt; . . . a fluttering Heart, an unequal Pulse, a sudden Palpitation shall evidently confess he is the Man, in spite of a bold Countenance or a false Tongue.

Today's sophisticated "lie box" records a variety of physiological reactions on moving graph paper as a suspect is asked a series of questions—some innocuous, some likely to be emotionally upsetting to a guilty person. By sensing blood pressure, pulse, respiration, muscular activity and even skin reactions, a polygraph enables a trained operator to determine, in most cases, whether a suspect is lying or telling the truth.

The polygraph machine, like its operator, is not infallible, and thus the very term "lie detector" is a misnomer. Some people cannot be effectively recorded on the instrument, whether guilty or innocent, and ever present is the risk of an erroneous interpretation by even the most conscientious expert. So much depends on the skill of the operator, in fact, that leading law-enforcement figures, including J. Edgar Hoover, have always been wary of the machine. American courts of law routinely reject polygraph tests as direct evidence.

Which does not mean, of course, that the polygraph is not a valuable tool for unearthing evidence and persuading the guilty to tell all. It is certainly a more humane means of extracting information from reluctant subjects than the old "third degree." Often the mere existence of the lie detector does the job, quite apart from the test results. A standard textbook in police academies states that "the instrument, the tests, and the accompanying procedures have a decided psychological effect in inducing admissions and confessions from guilty individuals."

The lie detector is also useful as an introduction to a full-scale interrogation. A person who volunteers for a polygraph test, thinking the machine is all that he has to face, may suddenly find himself on the defensive as several police officers fire a barrage of questions. He is no longer being tested according to an agreed-upon procedure; he is being accused directly and told that he might as well confess because his guilt is obvious. In his confusion he is likely to forget that he has a right not to answer questions at all. He stumbles ahead and incriminates himself. If he is truly guilty, then his confession, especially if he furnishes verifiable information about how the crime was done, will greatly simplify the police investigation. If he is innocent, and if the police are too eager or too careless, his "confession" may be accepted by them as proof of his guilt even in the absence of verifying evidence.

The interrogation of Peter Reilly, including the polygraph test, lasted eight hours. Virtually every word was recorded on five reels of RCA magnetic tape. Microphones were in every room of the Polygraph Unit that Peter was taken to. The taping was supervised by Sergeant Schneider. The tapes provide a dramatic record of a confrontation between the eighteen-year-old and four experienced police officers, taking turns or working in pairs. To Peter's defenders, the tapes reveal a classic case of brainwashing: an instance of psychological coercion so effective that the accused actually joined his interrogators in a desperate search for his reasons and actions in an outburst of violence that he could not remember. To others, of course, the tapes simply portray the police doing their job and finally winning a confession despite Reilly's clever evasions.

State's Attorney John Bianchi did not listen to the interrogation tapes before seeking a grand-jury indictment for murder. He did not hear the tapes in full until the Reilly trial when they were played for the jury. No transcript of the tapes was made until *after* the trial when it was too late to read what was actually said on tapes that were difficult to hear in the courtroom and which were almost inaudible in many passages.

A senior State Police officer has stated, not for attribution, that he would have destroyed the Reilly tapes if he had had the chance because they raised too many questions. "Look at what happened to Nixon," he said. In his view the confession counts, not the dialogue that leads up to it. In the Reilly case, however, there can be no real understanding of what happened to Peter Reilly without an awareness of what was said and done at the Polygraph Unit of the Connecticut State Police on the afternoon and night of September 29, 1973.

Peter was told to relax by Sergeant Schneider when he was left alone in the polygraph room. He was unaware that his voice was being recorded or that Lieutenant Shay and the other officers were watching him through a one-way glass. Shay had arrived in Hartford soon after Peter and Trooper Mulhern. He gave Sergeant Kelly a thorough briefing on the Gibbons murder and the reasons for suspecting Peter. Kelly, like Shay, was in civilian clothes—a uniformed interrogator has more difficulty earning the confidence of a suspect. He had spent nearly twenty-one years with the State Police, all of them in Hartford, and he would soon retire to Florida.

On the tape, Peter can be heard clearing his throat, but otherwise sits quietly, waiting for Kelly to appear and the polygraph test to begin. The door squeaks open and closes with a bang. "Peter, how are ya?" says Kelly. He speaks slowly. His deep voice is warm and friendly. He does not want Peter to feel threatened. "This is a new day," he explains. "I'm a new person." He talks about Peter's constitutional rights, saying, "You can leave here any time you want. You just say, hey, Tim, I want to go home, let me take the equipment off, and you can go home, Fair enough?"

Peter agrees that it is fair. Kelly explains the questions for the test will be reviewed beforehand because "I'm not here trying to trick you or anything like that." Peter comments that "Even if you are, it's for the better" because it will help get out the truth. "Well," says Kelly, "I'm not, in no way, trying to trick you."

Tricks, however, are the stock-in-trade of a police interrogator. A widely used textbook, *Criminal Interrogation and Confessions* by Fred E. Inbau and John E. Reid, says flatly that "We do approve of such psychological tactics and techniques as trickery and deceit that are not only helpful but frequently necessary in order to secure incriminating information from the guilty."

Before beginning the test, Kelly and Peter talk about the events of the previous day. Kelly reveals that Peter's mother, according to the autopsy, had two broken legs. Peter expresses surprise and he is encouraged to speculate about how they could have been broken. He is asked how his mother's clothes got wet, but he doesn't know. Kelly asks whether he has told the truth in his earlier statements to the police. Peter says he has. Now they will all know for sure, Kelly says, because the polygraph "reads your brain for me."

"Does it actually read my brain?" Peter asks.

"Oh, definitely, definitely. And if you've told me the truth this is what your brain is going to tell me."

"Will this stand up and protect me?"

"Right, right."

"Good. That's the reason I came up to take it, you know."

Peter is so eager that he says, "Let's go!" when he thinks the test is about to begin. Kelly says they don't want to rush things: "We take our time, all right?"

When Kelly, still asking preliminary questions, asks Peter if he has ever done anything that he is really ashamed of in his life, Peter doesn't want to answer unless he is promised his words will not leave the room. Kelly assures him that the answer will stay "right here," just between the two of them. Peter reveals that he is ashamed because a homosexual once made an advance on him. Although "nothing really happened," the incident has stuck in his mind. He mentions, too, that he lied to his mother about smoking marijuana, but that seems to be the extent of his shameful memories. He agrees with Kelly that murdering his mother would be "a damned shameful thing," but he says, "It would be ridiculous for me to come down and volunteer for this test" if he wasn't confident that he was innocent.

This may seem logical to Peter, but, Kelly observes, "I've had people actually come in here and take this test because they knew they were guilty but they didn't know how to tell somebody." He says to Peter: "Maybe you're looking for somebody to help you, I don't know. . . . A lot of time people come here and take this test, then let the test say they need help."

The test questions are discussed and Kelly leaves the room for a minute "to write these up on a form so I can read them intelligently." He says that "the truth will be on that tape [the polygraph chart] very shortly."

When he returns, Kelly tightens the arm cuff, like a doctor taking blood pressure. He tells Peter that "your arm may get slightly red, but I guarantee it won't fall off."

Then come the questions. There are twelve, a mixture of relevant, irrelevant and "control" questions, according to standard practice in the profession. Kelly pauses for about twelve seconds after each answer before asking the next question.

1. "Were you born in the United States?" (Peter answers, "Yes.")

2. "Do you live in Connecticut?" ("Yes.")

3. "Last night do you know for sure how your mother got hurt?" ("No.")

4. "Are you wearing a brown shirt?" ("Yes.")

5. "Last night did you hurt your mother?" ("No.")

6. "Did you ever deliberately hurt someone in your life?" ("No.")

7. "Is your first name Peter?" ("Yes.")

8. "Do you know how your mother's legs were broken?" ("No.")

9. "Last night did you talk to your mother when you came home?" ("No.")

10. "Do you know how your mother's clothes got wet?" ("No.")

11. "Besides what we've talked about, have you done anything else you're ashamed of?" ("No.")

12. "Is the statement you made to the police the truth?" ("Yes.")

Peter has a question of his own when the test is over: "How'd I do?" Kelly gives a cautious answer: "You're very cooperative, let me put it that way." The reaction is not what Peter expected. Disappointment and confusion cloud his voice when he asks, "What do you mean?"

Kelly explains that the first test was just a warm-up and that to give the results from the polygraph chart wouldn't be fair because "You're nervous. . . . Definitely nervous this first time." Kelly reassures Peter that he is not lying to him about how the test is conducted: "We run it once to show you there's no electric shock or tricks. I'm not going to lie to you one iota. . . . I don't make it a habit to lie to people."

Kelly asks whether any of the questions bothered Peter. If so, he might have to change the wording.

"Well, one thing I noticed is that, like, the question whether I harmed my mother or not."

"Why?" Kelly asks.

"Well, that question—like they told me up at the barracks yesterday that—how some people don't realize—all of a sudden fly off the handle for a split second and it leaves a blank spot in their memory."

This is an important observation by Peter, even though it

would not be given any emphasis at the trial. It reveals that someone at the barracks had already put into Peter's mind the thought that he might have killed his mother in a sudden rage and then blanked it from his mind, "Well, I thought about that last night," Peter says, "and I thought and I thought and I thought, and I said no, I couldn't have done it. . . . And now, when you ask me the question, that's what I think of."

Kelly comments, "If you did it, this is probably how it could have happened."

"What do you mean?"

"Bango, just like this . . . if you did it, it was a split-second thing that you did. You lost your head." Kelly goes on to suggest that Peter might have been high on narcotics when he did the killing or maybe there was an argument or maybe his mother attacked him. "If anything like that happened, I'll know it over here on these charts."

Peter is told that in the next exercise he will be asked to deliberately lie so that they can be sure that they are getting proper recordings from him. Kelly says that 8 percent of the people tested cannot be usefully recorded on the machine because "they're just blah."

Sergeant Schneider is brought back in to run a test with a deck of playing cards. "This is the person's opportunity to beat the polygraph," he tells Peter, because if the instrument cannot detect a person lying about the number of the card in his hand then it will be of no use on the serious questions.

When the test is over, Schneider compliments Peter on being a "textbook reactor. You give me such responses in here that you must be so honest that I don't think the sun would come up. . . . Pete, you're about the best reactor I've had in here for a long time. . . . You know the difference between right and wrong . . . when you tell a lie you go right to the top of the chart. . . . In other words, this is great for us because we'll have no trouble here today."

Peter thinks it is good news too. "I'm perfect," he says.

"You're perfect," Schneider repeats. "You're no pathological liar."

"Right," Peter says. When Schneider leaves and Kelly returns to the room, Peter proudly announces, "I'm a textbook reactor."

Kelly tightens the arm cuff and runs through the twelve questions again. Peter gives the same answers. He denies hurting his mother or knowing who hurt her. Kelly looks at the chart and says he wants to do the test one more time: "I think I have the answer, but I want to make absolutely sure."

Again the questions are asked, but this time in different order. And instead of asking "Are you wearing a brown shirt?" as the twelfth and last question, Kelly injects two completely new questions despite having assured Peter that there would be no tricks, no surprises. The questions set the stage for the more than six hours of interrogation by Kelly, Shay and Mulhern that are still to come.

"Do you have a clear recollection of what happened last night?" Kelly asks.

"Yes," Peter answers.

"Is there any doubt in your mind, Pete?"

"Can you stop the test?"

"Okay."

"I didn't understand that last question. I didn't understand—"

"I think we've got a little problem here, Peter."

"—that last question."

"I was just trying to probe your subconscious there a little bit, okay?"

"But, the thing was, I wasn't sure whether you meant what happened to her or whether I knew who did it to her and everything."

"Well, I think we got a little problem here, Pete."

"What do you mean?"

"About hurting your mother last night."

"I didn't do it."

Expecting the machine to confirm his truthfulness, Peter is stunned when he is told that the machine indicates that he is lying. From then on, he is no longer the confident volunteer, but an accused person struggling to demonstrate his innocence. The polygraph examination is blended so skillfully with an all-out interrogation that he seems unaware of what is happening.

Kelly tells Peter that "You're giving me a reaction, that's why I put in these questions towards the end there. I'm just wondering, do you have any doubt in your mind?" Peter explains his confusion by referring back to the dialogue in the barracks: "About hurting my mother. Because the thing is, like, when we went over, and over, and over it. . . . When he told me I could have flown off the handle I gave it a lot of consideration."

"All right," Kelly says.

"But, I don't think I did."

"But, you're not sure, are you?"

"That's right. Well, I could have."

"Okay," says Kelly. "Now I think you possibly did from what I'm seeing here, okay?"

Peter explains that "I'm sure what I did," but says he is not sure what happened in the house. Kelly speculates that he might have hit his mother with the car outside the house and then "set it up to look like something really violent happened in the house."

Peter protests that "it wouldn't have been, like me . . . honestly, if I had hit my mom the first thing I would have done was call the ambulance." Kelly says that "I think you got doubts as to what happened there last night. Don't you?"

"I've got doubts because I don't understand what happened and—"

"What do you mean you don't understand?"

"—well, I mean, I'm afraid to uh—"

"Are you afraid that you did this thing?"

"Well, yeah, of course I am. That's natural."

A little later, when Peter says that not being sure "scares me a little bit," Kelly says, "I don't think you're *crazy* or anything like this, but I think you need a little help."

"With a psychiatrist?" Peter asks.

"Yes," says Kelly.

The exchange is the beginning of a constant refrain: that Peter has a mental problem and that is why he cannot remember murdering his mother. Peter feels, however, that the bad reaction on the polygraph must be due to nervousness—"I mean my mother did die"—and says that "I'd like to come in and take another test. I mean rather than go by this one."

Kelly puts him off, saying that "what I'm interested in here, Pete, is that you said you're not sure if you hurt your mother or not last night."

Peter's response is that "What I say I did, I'm absolutely sure of. But if I had a lapse of memory, that's what I'm not sure of." Kelly asks whether he thinks he had a lapse of memory and Peter says flatly, "No." He is just as firm in denying that he is covering up for somebody else.

No longer able to rely on the lie detector to get him out of this fix, Peter turns to another hope. He says, "If I did it and I didn't realize it, there's got to be some clue there in the house anyway that's gonna connect with it . . . there *has* to be something in that house, someplace. If I did it. Or whoever did it. There's got to be something, somehow, somewhere."

The dialogue goes on. Peter is asked whether he has any doubt about hurting his mother and says that "this test is giving me doubt right now." He speaks of having been "drilled and drilled" and then he tries to recall what he had been told back in the Canaan Barracks. He remembers the proposition that he might have killed his mother and "the fact that I could have forgotten . . . that really shook me because I never heard of anything like that before."

The sergeant steps out of the room briefly and comes back with the news that Peter's mother had talked on the telephone to Dr. Lovallo shortly before she was murdered. Kelly's interpretation is that this "puts you home almost at the exact same time." When Peter says that that was the time he left the Youth Center, Kelly says that he is speaking of the approximate time and adds, "Pete, I think you got a problem. I really do. . . . And Jack feels the same way when he looked at these charts. . . . These charts say you hurt your mother last night."

When Peter says that he cannot remember, Kelly suggests that "what happened here was a mercy thing"—perhaps Peter's mother had a fatal disease and he was doing her a favor by ending her life. On the other hand, Kelly says, Peter might have hit her with his car and then panicked. If so, "this is only an accident." But Peter insists that he did not even hit her with the car.

"Then if you didn't," Kelly says, "then you killed your mother deliberately."

"I didn't though," Peter responds. "I don't remember it."

"Then why does the lie chart say you did?"

"I don't know. I can't give you a definite answer."

"You see? But you don't know for sure if you did this thing, do you?"

"No, I don't."

"Why?"

"I just don't. I mean, like your chart and everything says I did."

"Okay."

"But *I* still say I didn't."

The interrogation is a contest of wills: Peter versus the polygraph as interpreted by Kelly. Peter is still attached to the machine, two hours after the session began. Kelly removes the last of the connections, but the interrogation continues in the polygraph room. Kelly speculates that "something happened between you and your mother last night and one thing led to another and some way you accidentally hurt her seriously."

Peter says, "But how? It's not like me." He adds: "I wouldn't mind so much if they could *prove* I did it. . . . I'm positive to myself that I didn't. Consciously. But subconsciously, you know, who knows?"

By this time his confidence is gone, "Now I'm afraid," he says, "because I was so sure, you know, that I didn't do something. . . . And I still want to stay in school. I don't have any place to go. . . . I don't want to go into—like Newtown or something."

By "Newtown" Peter means Fairfield Hills Hospital in Newtown, Connecticut, a mental-health institution. Peter seems persuaded that he has a mental problem. Kelly encourages this belief, saying that "This isn't the end of the world. I've talked to a lot of people who have been involved in a lot of serious things and they're normal individuals today. Once they got it straightened out upstairs."

When Kelly insists that Peter "did it" even though Peter cannot remember doing it, Peter asks if there is any way "they can kind of pound it out of me, if I did it?" Kelly seems to be shocked. He exclaims, "Peter!"

Soon Peter admits that "now there's doubt in my mind. Maybe I did do it." He says, "We got to keep drilling at it" to get the answer.

The search begins in earnest, with Peter as an active participant, to figure out how he could have carried out the terrible deed. Once again, Peter relates the story of his homecoming. But now he says that when he entered the house and looked up at the top bunk in the bedroom "I thought I saw her" lying in the bed. "See?" Sergeant Kelly says. "I think this is probably where you flipped over a little bit. You probably *did* see your mother standing there." But Peter says, "No, laying in bed." He explains about his mother's habit of lying in bed reading with all her clothes on when it is too cold to read outdoors.

Kelly seems to feel that he is getting closer to a confession. When Peter says that "I wish I could go out and have that cigarette now," Kelly leaves the room briefly to get an ashtray and cigarettes. As they light up, Peter muses that "the thing that's messing me up" is not whether or not he killed his mother, but "the fact that *if* I did it, why don't I remember it?"

Kelly says that Peter is so ashamed of what he did that he is afraid to admit it and says that he thinks Peter is deliberately lying to him. Denying that he is lying, Peter once again asks about clues: "Are my footprints going into the bedroom there?" Kelly says that such things take time to check out. He continues with the line that Peter is too ashamed to admit his guilt. "Once we get this out in the open and we get you the proper help it will be over with. . . . No one's going to lock you up and throw the keys away."

Peter says that "I *want* to tell you I did it now, but I'm still not sure I did do it." Kelly is virtually telling him that the only penalty will be a short spell of psychiatric treatment: "As I said, Peter, three months out of your life—that's not a very long time." Peter accepts that he has a serious mental problem. "I think I've been sliding for a long time, to something. . . . I've *always* had a question in my mind if I was mentally right." He had worried about his family's history of mental problems and alcoholism.

The dialogue between Peter and the sergeant becomes increasingly unreal. They are face to face in a little room in Hartford because a horrible murder has been committed. The victim is Peter's mother. Peter is the prime suspect. But Kelly talks of Barbara Gibbons as having been "hurt" by Peter, and a penalty of no more than a little psychiatric counseling, and Peter talks about band practices. He tells Kelly that "If I had to give up the band, I'd have no outlook on life anymore." He wouldn't want to go away for mental treatment because "it would stop the band." He says, "I got to go to the dance this week. We got contracts and can't break contracts." Kelly tells him that Peter can continue in the band only if he faces up to what he has done.

Kelly and Peter speculate together about why Peter "went off the handle." Or what he did when his mother "flew off the handle and went at you or something and you had to protect yourself." Peter is being offered an opportunity to claim that he acted only in self-defense, but he does not accept it because "self-defense goes just so far."

After they both agree that Peter is not a cold-blooded killer but just "a guy sitting here with a problem," Kelly asks again what happened and Peter says, "I'm still in a fog. I don't know."

They seem to be getting nowhere. Long pauses occur on the tape as Peter thinks and thinks, but cannot come up with any reason for having a battle with his mother. "I'm so damned exhausted," he says. "I'm just going to fall asleep. I know I am." Kelly says that "I bet you won't fall asleep" and leaves the room. Peter lets out a long sigh.

Like police interrogators elsewhere in the country, the experts at Hartford had been taught that an isolated room without distracting noises is vital to good questioning. Within such a room, the deprivation of cigarettes, food and sleep will keep emotional tension high. They can be offered as rewards for cooperation. The interrogator should be friendly but persistent. He should seem to be on the side of the suspect by sympathizing with him and condemning the victim of his crime.

In *Criminal Interrogation and Confessions*, Inbau and Reid urge interrogators to maintain a "trusting" atmosphere and "display an air of confidence in the subject's guilt." They should "call attention to the subject's physiological and psychological 'symptoms' of guilt," and minimize the seriousness of the crime by suggesting that "anyone else would have done the same, under the circumstances." A sudden direct accusation might surprise the subject into confessing guilt, but a danger exists that if the subject is innocent "he may become so disturbed and confused that it will be more difficult for the interrogator to ascertain the fact of the subject's innocence."

If the subject clings to his story and refuses to confess, then an alternate method of interrogation, is to try to unnerve the suspect with a "bad cop" and offer him relief with a "good cop." Finally, a written confession should be obtained as soon as possible after an oral confession so that the subject will not have time to think things over and change his mind.

The U.S. Supreme Court, in *Rogers vs. Richmond* in 1961, said that "ours is an accusatorial and not an inquisitorial system—a system in which the State must establish guilt by evidence independently and freely secured and may not by coercion prove its charge against an accused out of his own mouth." The words from his own mouth, extracted in the intimidating atmosphere of a police interrogation, would point the finger of guilt more strongly at Peter Reilly than any evidence. His own words set off a chain reaction: They were compressed in a written confession that convinced the State Police who convinced the State's Attorney who convinced a grand jury to indict Peter for murder.

Policemen understandably see intense questioning of the likeliest suspect as the shortest and fastest route to the solution of a crime. The abuse of police interrogations and the risk of false confessions have been so great, however, that the police are obliged to work under tight restraints. As a result of the U.S. Supreme Court's 1966 *Miranda* decision on the admissibility of confessions, the prosecution in a trial may not use, as evidence, statements made by a defendant "stemming from custodial interrogation of the defendant" unless the prosecution can demonstrate that a confession is truly voluntary and not coerced. Procedural "safeguards" must be carefully followed. The defendant must be assured of his Fifth Amendment protection against being compelled to incriminate himself.

Although *Miranda* and other decisions have induced police officers to be meticulous about reading the defendant his rights, as in the Reilly case, whether this is enough of a safeguard is debatable. Many authorities maintain that a police interrogation cannot be truly voluntary or noncoercive, even if the defendant is aware of his rights and has waived them, so long as he is on his own, without counsel.

"For most, if not all of us," says Henry H. Foster, Jr., professor of law at New York University, "the policeman and prosecutor are authority figures, and the situation of being subjected to their questioning triggers off emotions varying from apprehension to panic. The physical setup of a station house in itself is intimidating. In the absence of counsel or some friend or relative to lend a supportive role, most suspects will talk, although the experienced or professional criminal may preserve his silence. If the interrogation is protracted, done in relays, and fatigue sets in, suspects may confess to almost anything."

Professor Foster believes that confessions made outside of a courtroom are inherently unreliable and should not be admitted at trial. Proof of guilt should be established by more cogent evidence. Skillful police interrogators, without necessarily realizing it, can have a hypnotic effect, especially with easily influenced personalities.

"Police, or anyone else, including the subject himself," Foster says, "can learn to induce hypnoticlike trances. And under police station conditions, whether we call it a hypnotic trance or submission to suggestion, suspects may be manipulated by authority figures. In order to maintain conditions which allow an individual to exercise critical control and his best judgment, there must be alertness, time for reflection, and the support of counsel or friend. Otherwise, the hostile atmosphere of police station interrogation will overwhelm most suspects unfamiliar with police methods, and there can be no assurance that a confession is genuine."

* * *

When Sergeant Kelly returns to the polygraph room he tells
Peter that he has been on the telephone with the investigators
in Canaan. "I think I have a reason why it happened." He
says that the police have learned from Peter's friends that
"your mother was always on your back. Constantly," She was
always telephoning around for him. "She'd been bugging you
so fucking long that last night you came in the house and
started bugging you again and you snapped. Am I right?"

"I would say you're right," Peter replies, "but I don't
remember doing the things that happened. That's just it.
I believe I did it now."

His words are the beginning of the confession. Peter has
snapped at the bait. He is hooked. Now it is just a matter of
reeling him in and getting his signature on a formal confession. But the process will take many more hours of "drilling,
drilling, drilling." As he told his attorney later, "They started
brainwashing, making me think I really had a mental problem. So you know, I started really believing that maybe I'm a
little nutty. So I started dreaming things up."

Kelly tells Peter that he "lost self-control" and that he was
"like a prisoner being tortured." His mother had treated him
so badly that naturally he finally blew up.

"Am I right, Pete?"

"You're right," Peter agrees. Straining to be helpful, he
adds, "Somewhere in my head a straight razor sticks in."
He remembers that there is a straight razor in the house. He
speculates that his mother might have been mad at him for
using the car in case she needed it. All the while, Peter yawns
repeatedly and finally asks if he can have something to drink,
maybe even something to eat. "I haven't had anything to eat
in about twenty-four hours except a candy bar—part of one."
Kelly sends Schneider for a couple of soft drinks, but he tells
Peter that "you're not going to be able to eat because this is
going to be preying on your mind." First talk, then eat. "Once
you get this out," Kelly says, "you're going to eat like you've
never eaten before." When Peter mentions how tired he is,
Kelly adds, "Well, once you get this out, Pete, you'll be able
to sleep for a week."

"When I get this out," Peter asks, "I'd possibly be totally cured too?"

"Could be," Kelly answers.

For a moment, Peter seems almost exultant about a situation that seems to be purging him of his troubles. He speaks of feeling so free now, "like all the things that have had a hold of me all around are letting go." Suddenly, some other part of him remembers what his mother was like, at her best, and how, just a few hours ago, he had awakened and thought of going to his mother for help "because, if I ever got in trouble—like something like this—she'd be right there."

Peter vacillates. He says, "I believe I did it," but then, after further questioning, he doubts that he did because he doesn't think he had any right to take his mother's life. He still cannot remember any details about the murder so he takes incidents from earlier days—his mother complaining about cigarettes or the old Ford that he tried to repair in the backyard—and wonders whether they could have cropped up on the murder night. Kelly, like Shay, asks if he ever had relations with his mother. Once again, Peter says no, but he recalls an affair that his mother had with a man: "Once she started having relations with this other guy it all started going downhill." Peter seems persuaded of his guilt and asks whether he might murder again if he should get married and find his wife having relations with another man.

Peter is encouraged to feel sorry for himself. He speaks of the nice homes of his friends in contrast to his own and how annoying sharing an automobile with his mother was. "I hated being home," Peter says. On the other hand, when he was away from home, "I'd miss my mom." But once home again he would want to get away because of her nagging. Kelly wants to know specifically what she was nagging him about that caused him to "go off the deep end."

Peter says he doesn't know, but as he rummages through his mind he finds that "violence is coming into it now. With the straight razor, slashing and stuff. But, not much. I—one thing toward her throat. I think. I may be imagining it. And shaking her up a lot."

"How about her legs?" Kelly asks. "What kind of vision do we get there?"

Peter says that "I don't want to remember that because I think I'm going to get sick if I do."

"Why?"

"Because something like that makes me sick anyway—and to think I did it!"

"Peter, you're not going to get sick. Did you step on her legs or something? When she was on the floor, and jumped up and down or something, and break them like that or what?"

"I could have."

"Or did you hit her?"

"That sounds possible."

"Or did you hit her with something?"

"No, 'cause if I hit her with something it probably would have been my guitar and no matter what I did, I'd have never used my guitar."

"I don't blame you."

"'Cause that thing, that's my piece of life over a car, over anything in lifetime."

"Can you remember stomping her legs?"

"I think. But, I'm not sure because you say it then I imagine I'm doing it."

"No, no, no. You're not imagining anything. I think the truth is starting to come from you now. Because you want it out. You want that second chance."

When Peter speaks of his worry that people will look at him and say, "Hey, he murdered his mother," Kelly says that it was not murder because "I don't think you planned it. I don't think it was premeditated. I think something happened between you and her there last night and you just went off the fucking deep end and you just kept slashing and kicking and hitting, and it was too late. You had lost all your composure because of all the build-up over the past year or two years and all this came out at one time. And it came out violently."

Kelly asks about the straight razor. Peter thinks he "probably" found it on the kitchen table and then after using it "maybe I gave it a heave or something."

Kelly obviously wants to know where Peter disposed of the razor because this might be the murder weapon. (Back in Canaan, Trooper Moran has already come upon the straight

razor, closed and without bloodstains, on a living room shelf.)
Peter speculates that he might have heaved the razor behind
the gas station or over the barn. "They're the most natural
places I'd think of throwing it," he explains. "Because, I
whenever I wanted to get rid of something, that's where I'd
throw it."

When Kelly asks where he cut his mother with this razor,
Peter says "the throat is the only thing I can think of" and
he makes a motion with his hand to show how he could have
done it. He says he made only one slash. He can't think of any
other place where he might have cut her. As for cleaning up
his mother with water afterward, Peter is puzzled and asks,
"Wouldn't I have been out of breath if I'd carried her in and
back and done all that? . . . If I'd taken her into the bathroom
and cleaned her up or something?"

He asks Kelly, "Do you think we could quit now—where
we are—so I could get some sleep? I'm so dead, nothing's
happening."

"I think it's happening now, Pete. I think it's coming out
now. I think it's coming right out now."

"I think I'm saying things that I don't mean to say
though."

When Kelly insists that Peter is now finally telling the
truth and that "you know it was you," Peter says, "What
would you do if something came up where it turned out that
it absolutely wasn't me? If it happened?"

"I'd apologize to you," Kelly replies, "but this isn't going
to happen, Peter."

The speculation continues. Peter wonders whether he
could have put himself into a state of hypnosis the night
before. "Wish I weren't so tired because things come into
my head and they go right out again." Peter supposes that
either his mother or he picked up the razor. He is not sure,
but "I remember slashing like that. . . . I remember doing
the damage." And he thinks he "could have jumped up and
down on her. . . . Maybe I could have kicked her." He thinks
so because, even though he has never been in a real fight, he
thinks you have to fight dirty to win.

*   *   *

The interrogation has been underway for four hours. Kelly seems to feel that he has done all he can do for the moment. He wants Lieutenant Shay to take over for a while. He suggests to Peter that they go across the hall to another room where they can be more comfortable. He leads him to the interrogation room of the Polygraph Unit, complete with a leather lounge chair and a leather couch. Peter sits on the couch by himself while Kelly confers outside with Shay, A window is open and children can be heard playing on the street.

When the two men enter the room together, Peter announces to the lieutenant that "the polygraph thing didn't come out right. It looked like I've done it."

Kelly asks, "Well, what's it look like now?"

"It really looks like I did it."

"You did it?"

"Yes."

Peter thinks he used the straight razor. When Shay suggests that he used a knife as well, Peter says, "Maybe. I think. I'm not absolutely *sure* of it, though."

Kelly leaves the room and Shay carries on. He learned how to question suspects at the State Police academy, and he once attended lectures by Fred Inbau at the University of Maryland. He explains to Peter that "we on the State Police are not your enemies." They want to help him. Peter says that before he goes any further, "I've got to have someone to talk to." Shay tells him that "you got us to turn to in this case."

Peter seems to feel more alone and vulnerable than before. He speaks of needing "one particular person who's going to be on my side and help me. I don't mean a lawyer or something like that. I mean someone like an adult. A father, a mother or something." He is afraid of being taken out of school. He feels "so guilty" about what has happened. He wouldn't mind seeing a psychiatrist once or twice a week, "but I *cannot* be taken away from the band. That's my life." He wants to find the answer to the puzzle. "I've got to get this out in the open so I can see what happened. And say, it's done. I've done it. I've got to live with it."

He tries again to describe how he might have killed his mother. As he does, sirens scream in the background. He offers "three possible things that we could have been arguing about." He is now so convinced of his guilt that he apologizes for causing his interrogators so much trouble: "I didn't realize I was lying on that lie detector. . . . You're really busting your ass trying to help me right now and I really appreciate it."

Shay asks Peter to trust him and to begin trusting people, and then lies to him. "We have, right now," he says, "without any word out of your mouth, proof positive that you did it."

"So okay," Peter responds, "then I may as well say I did it."

As Peter worries about what is going to happen to him—his name in the papers, having a record, missing school—he becomes a little less convinced of his guilt. When Sergeant Kelly returns to the room, Peter asks, "Should I really come out and say something that I'm not sure?"

"Peter, I think you're sure," Kelly says.

"Pete, you're sure," Shay adds.

"No, I'm not," Peter says. "I mean, I'm sure of what *you've* shown me that I did it, but what I'm not sure of is how I did it. It's still not all coming to me."

He tries to describe the murder to them, but nothing is clear except his coming home and seeing his mother on the floor. He can't seem to fill in the space between looking at the top bunk and the sight of the body on the floor. Shay becomes exasperated and accuses Peter of "not being honest." He says Peter is trying to trick him.

Peter offers to go back on the polygraph, but Shay says that "You've been playing head games with us here for two days. You know it and I know it."

Peter protests, "I don't know it!" And after further argument he pleads, "I'm trying hard as I can. Just—I mean it's bad enough realizing and finding that my mom's dead, but to find that I did it and not realizing that I did it makes it even worse."

Shay continues the questioning. Again, Peter is encouraged to feel sorry for himself. He had earlier protested when Shay spoke of his need for decent parents by saying, "I don't think my mom was that indecent." Now he agrees that he's been treated like an animal. "I've been given my food and I've been given my place where I slept, but I've never been shown affection." Now that his mother is off his back, he says, he has to find someone to help him. When Shay says that "If you trust me, I'll see that you get the help you need," Peter asks, "You personally?" When Shay says, "Yes," Peter speaks of his dream of finding someone like Shay to help him. He begins to cry. Between tears, he explains that "I haven't cried 'til I found someone to turn to." He asks where Shay lives and whether there is any chance that he would take him in.

"Sure there's a chance," Shay answers.

"God, I'll do anything," Peter says. "Work around the house, chores, anything. I'd love to do it."

He tells Shay that he now realizes, "I definitely did do what happened to my mother last night. But the thing that I don't realize is the exact steps that I took doing it."

Shay is now indulgent, allowing Peter to ramble on about life and death and God and the wonder of good, close families like the Belignis and the Madows. Peter speaks of "getting more and more trusting" and he asks for a chance to get at the truth gradually. Shay decides that a little food might help the situation. He leaves the room. Peter sits alone.

Jim Mulhern appears with a ham-and-cheese sandwich, two chocolate cupcakes and a can of Coca-Cola. Peter has not seen his Canaan friend for six hours but Mulhern has been watching him through one-way mirrors. Peter volunteers to Mulhern the news that "it turned out I did it."

"Did what?" Mulhern asks.

"What happened to my mother."

"You killed your mother? How did you do that?"

Peter does not really know and he still cannot figure out why there is no blood on him. "There's nothing on me. I'm still wearing the same clothes. I can't understand that."

It is now past eight o'clock. Lieutenant Shay returns to the room and orders Mulhern to reduce Peter's admissions to writing, a difficult assignment because Peter is saying he can "imagine" himself cutting his mother's throat "and the chances are that I did do it . . . but I'm not positive." Shay accuses him of playing "head games" and leaves the room. Peter appeals to Mulhern: "I don't know what to do, Jim. I'm still not positive any of that happened. . . . It seems like I'm being pushed into saying things. . . . Why should I say something that I'm not sure of if it can be used against me?"

Mulhern does not respond. He is conscious, as Peter is not, that every word being said can be overheard by his superiors and is being recorded. The time has passed, anyway, to give advice to his young friend. He simply says that he will write down whatever Peter tells him. Peter asks him three times to be sure to put in the statement that he is not really sure of what he is saying. Mulhern promises but he does not, in fact, include that qualification in the confession.

Shay returns in time to hear Peter tell Mulhern that it is "almost like I'm making it up." He gets angry and charges Peter with "playing head games with us now for too long a period. . . . We have definitely established that you were in that house when your mother was killed. Okay, now look. There are many things that we can do to make this thing a very difficult process for you."

He asks, "You realize that?" Peter meekly answers, "Yes."

Shay then launches into a five-minute tirade as he tells Peter that "I've been fooling around here now for a lot of hours with you and I'm getting tired. I don't want you to treat me like some kind of jerk." As Peter says, "I'm not," Shay's voice becomes louder. He is yelling as he says that "we have proved conclusively with a tape where you lied repeatedly. . . . Now you know, I tried to treat you like a human being. I tried to be understanding but it seems you've had a rough upbringing and that you reject every offer that we've made to be kind to you. . . . Now you're trying to treat us like muck. . . . If you want to play this way we'll take you and we'll lock you up and treat you like an animal."

Shay bellows that "it's about time you sat up in that chair and you faced us like a man and you realize that trying to talk to two State Policemen like they're two goddamn idiots, it's not gonna work." He continues:

Now, you are here because you are responsible for the death of your mother. I am not sitting in judgment of you.

I am not saying it was right or wrong. It is a death that we must investigate. . . . Let's stop the nonsense and let's get going here. . . . [At] some point in your life you've got to realize that you've got to trust somebody. And we're telling you that this is it. That you've got to trust us. And put your faith in us and deal with us as human beings as we will deal with you. . . .

We know what your life has been like. We know what your mother's reputation is. We know a lot more than you give us credit for knowing. I'm not even saying that you were wrong doing what you did. But you've got to get yourself some help. Now, if you will not get yourself some help then we will—you will force us to force this treatment on you. We have no choice. Now, you know you're not gonna get away with a situation like this. You can't—there's no way in hell that you can continue without getting your psychological and your emotional problems resolved. . . .

I don't want to see you in prison. That's not what I get paid for. I don't get paid by the number of people I put in jail. . . . If we can help you or any other citizen or any kid, that's what we're paid for and that's what we're trying to do. Now somebody is dead. You are responsible; we know. We can prove it with extrinsic evidence. Now, we're telling you that we are offering you our hand. Take it.

By this time, Lieutenant Shay has calmed down and is no longer yelling, but when Peter asks, "You say you can prove it?" Shay erupts again and says that "I'm not going to play head games." He tells Peter that "your mother called the doctor at nine thirty. You called the hospital at ten minutes of ten."

"I called there at ten of ten?" Peter asks.

"That's correct," Shay says. "We can place your mother's death in that fifteen-minute period. . . . Now, if you think you can beat that, you're crazy. And if you're going to act like a hardened criminal, John Dillinger, try to beat the police, you're nuts."

Peter says softly, "I'm not." Shay tells him to "sit there like a man" and understand that he is going to go to a mental hospital, not the gas chamber or prison. "You are in no condition to think or to make judgment as to what your problem is."

When Peter tries once again to describe what happened in the cottage, he speaks of a "double take": thinking he saw his mother in his bunk and then seeing her on the floor. Shay tells him "there's no such thing as a double take. You're not a camera. You're a human being."

The questioning goes on, but Peter insists that all he can remember is cutting his mother's throat and jumping on her stomach. The only blood he can remember seeing is "when I was back in reality again" after having "flown off the handle."

Peter, at this moment, is not exactly in "reality." When Shay steps out of the room Peter asks, "After having this on my record, is there any chance I can still get on the State Police?"

Mulhern, of course, can say only that it depends on what happens. Long pauses occur as Mulhern laboriously writes out the confession for Peter to sign. Peter asks if "you could put little quotes in between the part where I was slashing my mother's throat to where I jumped on her legs? You know, so you can tell that section is the stuff I—that I'm digging up."

Peter looks over the confession and signs it. Then when Mulhern leaves with the document and Shay returns to the room, Peter has a question for the man who only minutes before threatened to treat him like an animal. "I was wondering," Peter asks Shay, "if some way . . . I could possibly live with your family if you had the room? . . . I wouldn't want to impose and I know my godmother would pay my way."

Shay responds that "It would be a rather unusual turn of events," but Peter explains that "I've taken a liking to you—you know, kind of father image and I trust you. . . . I would like to live with a family, like a complete family, for a while anyway."

Peter rambles on about the pleasures of real families, apparently thinking his ordeal is over. But Sergeant Kelly reappears and tells him that "Something's still wrong here,

Pete." Shay and Kelly have learned the details of Dr. Izumi's autopsy and they know that Barbara Gibbons was sexually mutilated. A large object was thrust into her vagina with sufficient force to cause internal injuries.

"What's really burning inside of you that you don't want to tell us about," Kelly asks, "that you did to your mother?"

Peter says, "I don't know," and starts to ask whether he raped her. Then quickly—as if to forestall any further charges of playing head games—he says, "I think I raped her." He explains by saying that "It seems like I did. That's what everything looks like I did."

But the answer is not the right one. Kelly knows that Barbara Gibbons was not raped by Peter or anyone else. Kelly persists. He keeps asking for the worst thing that Peter did, but all Peter can think of is rape. Nothing worse comes to mind and rape is not the right answer. Kelly tries another tack by reminding Peter that he had said something about kicking his mother as well as jumping on her. When Peter speculates that "I may have kicked her in the side," Kelly announces that Peter's mother had three broken ribs. Now, he says, "There's one other detail that we need," and he is back to the question of what Peter did when his mother was "flat on the floor."

Peter keeps trying. Rape? No. Sexual assault? "In a way," says Kelly. Could he have put his penis in her mouth? Kelly doubts it. Peter explains that rape sticks in his mind because of Geoff Madow's comment that he thought someone had raped his mother. Finally Peter comes close to the answer by asking, "Someone wouldn't try to cut out her sex organs would they?" But when Kelly wants to know if this is what Peter did, he is told, "I wouldn't know how. I wouldn't know, you know, exactly what to do." Straining to be cooperative, he adds, "If I was that mad I would have tried anything, right?" Like "mutilate or damage her." Kelly says, "Right, right" But Peter is not much help on details. He can only think of the straight razor. When Kelly asks what made him think that he had cut out her sexual organs, Peter says, "That's all I could think of left."

* * *

Again, the officers switch places. Kelly goes out, Mulhern comes in. Mulhern wants more details about the throat slashing. Peter figures that he must have made a slash using his right hand and going from left to right. He is "pretty sure" that he saw the razor cut through, but "it's almost like in a dream."

As Mulhern adds these details to the confession, Peter asks him, "Do you feel bad about knowing me now that you know what I've done?" Mulhern replies that what Peter did is not all that bad: "Five years from now I may do the same thing."

Peter persuades himself that his situation is not too serious. "It's not a case where I need punishment. Correct? Whereas going to jail will punish me. Getting the help is something that I need." He believes that he is in for a few months of psychiatric treatment.

Mulhern, having combined Peter's statements into a single confession, asks for his signature again. And now, at long last, Peter wonders whether he will need a lawyer. Mulhern tells him that "You can have an attorney at any time that you want." Peter indicates that he knows this, but he still clings to the idea that you don't need a lawyer so long as you don't lie. "Everything I said I mean," he tells Mulhern. "I mean, it *is* the truth." Even so, Peter says, he would like to have "one particular person" to advise him and he specifies Lieutenant Shay. Mulhern points out the impracticality of that idea. Peter seems distressed, but then his mind turns to practical matters. He wonders what will happen about the house and the car, and who will take care of the cat and the parakeet. And when he goes to the mental hospital, can he take his guitar? He realizes he is going to be booked for murder, "but it's not like premeditated because I didn't plan."

Mulhern asks why Peter has not finished his sandwich, but Peter still has no appetite, a day and a half after his last meal. Peter sits alone as Mulhern leaves to give the signed confession to Shay.

At nearly eleven o'clock at night, the tape recorder is at last turned off. Five boxes of tapes, each numbered and marked "MURDER, FALLS VILLAGE, 9/29/73," are placed on top of a filing cabinet. A confession, said to be "the queen of evidence," is in hand. The murder of Barbara Gibbons has been solved. Peter has declared himself the killer.

I, Peter A. Reilly, age 18, DOB 3/2/55 of Rte. 63, Falls Village, Conn., make the following voluntary state-ment without fear, threat or promise, knowing it may be used in Court against me.

On the evening of Friday, September 28th, 1973, I attended a meeting of the Canaan Youth Center at the Methodist Church in North Canaan, Conn. I left the church at about 9:30–9:35 P.M. and took John Sochocki of West Main Street, North Canaan, home. After leav-ing him at his house I proceeded to my home arriving at about 9:50–9:55 P.M. I parked directly in front of the house, got out of the car and pushed down the front left headlight unit, and turned off the car. I entered the front door of the house and yelled, "Hey Ma, I'm home."

There was no answer so I looked to the right into the bedroom. At first, I thought I saw my mother, Bar-bara Gibbons, in the top bunk and then I saw her on the floor. I remember "slashing once at my mother's throat with a straight razor I used for model airplanes. This was on the living room table. I also remember jumping on my mother's legs." I am not sure about washing her off. Next I saw blood on her face and throat, and, I think, I'm pretty sure on her T-shirt which was rolled up to the bottom of her breasts.

Then I went to the telephone and called the Mad-ows to get an ambulance. Next I called information for the family doctor's number, Dr. Borneman [sic], I spoke with Dr. Borneman's wife, I assume or a woman answered, and she gave me two other doctor's names who were covering for Dr. Borneman who was on vacation. I again called information for the Sha-ron Hospital's telephone number as Mrs. Borneman instructed me. I was connected with the hospital emer-gency room and was asked if I knew artificial respira-tion to which I replied, "No." I was told they would notify the State Police and dispatch an ambulance. I told the woman I already called the ambulance.

I hung up the phone and went outside and unlocked the car and moved it to the side of the house, the north side, facing the road and left on the flashers. I also threw a hibachi grill out of the way as it was near the front steps on the cement. I stood in the driveway until Geoffrey Madow arrived and we both went inside to look at my mother. Geoffrey stated she looked as though she had been raped. We both went back outside and waited for the police cruiser to arrive.

I would like to clarify one point in this statement. When I slashed at my mother's throat with the straight razor I cut her throat. This is all I wanted to clarify. I have read the above statement and it is the truth.

(signed) PETER REILLY

5 ■ IN JAIL

PETER REILLY: You know, Jim, after what I said, I honestly don't think I did this.
TROOPER MULHERN: This is something you're going to have to make up your mind about.
PETER REILLY: I really don't think I did it.

The time had come to arrest Peter for murder. "Jim Mulhern took me downstairs," he told his lawyer soon afterward, "and put me through the processing. He fingerprinted me and he was teasing me when he took my pictures. He was really good about it because we are on very good terms. Then he took me to Canaan."

Peter was now officially dangerous. He had been lightly guarded in Canaan and enroute to Hartford but, as a confessed killer, handcuffs became necessary. Mulhern sat next to him in the rear of the police cruiser while a rookie cop drove. They reached the Canaan Barracks at 12:30 Sunday morning. Mulhern took the handcuffs off and turned Peter over to Trooper John Calkins—who promptly handcuffed him behind his back—for the drive to the Litchfield Correctional Center, the old redbrick county jail facing the village green in one of New England's most beautiful and best-preserved historic towns.

To make sure that Peter would not get away from Trooper Calkins, Sergeant Norman Soucie followed Calkins' cruiser in another vehicle. The beginning of the half-hour drive to Litchfield was a rerun of Peter's Friday-night journey home. All was quiet in North Canaan. They saw few cars on Route 7 as they speeded south toward Falls Village. The familiar lights of the Texaco station appeared at the junction with Route 63, but something was different about his house. Peter could see ropes and warning signs. It was being guarded. He was concerned because his Corvette was nowhere in sight, but Calkins told him that the police had taken it in for safekeeping because of the expensive accessories.

Although Peter would remember both the drive to Canaan and the drive to Litchfield as "mostly a blur," Calkins would one day testify that he was "relaxed, in good spirits, friendly, alert" and talkative. They had discovered, soon after leaving the barracks, that they had spoken on the telephone several times when Peter helped Calkins in the case of the missing teenager. After passing the cottage, Peter commented that Lieutenant Shay was a nice man, and he inquired whether "this thing" would interfere with his becoming a policeman.

When Calkins asked about "this thing," Peter gave him a thumbnail version of what he had confessed to just a couple of hours earlier. Calkins thought this was interesting enough for him to make notes about soon afterward and to write up as a report, though not until a month and a half later. (When asked about his notes during the Reilly trial he said he had lost or destroyed them.)

The key passages in his report describe Peter as stating to him that he had returned home, looked in the bedroom, thought he saw his mother in bed and then "there was a blank in his memory and the next thing he remembers he was standing over his mother who was lying on the floor. . . . He also remarked that he was not sorry for what he had done in a way, even though he realized it was wrong. At this particular time I asked him why it happened and he remarked that 'she' had been on his back for four months."

The prosecutor would emphasize these comments. Peter's words, as related by Calkins at the trial, were portrayed as an admission of guilt volunteered by Peter to a friendly cop who was not conducting a formal interrogation. Others would argue that Peter at this point was practically a sleepwalker who was so thoroughly befogged and brainwashed that he really did believe that he was responsible for his mother's death.

Litchfield looked as empty as a ghost town. The jail was the only place open for business. Calkins and Soucie escorted Peter inside and turned him over to two officers. "A receipt for him was obtained," Calkins reported.

"They took me in and we stood at the desk," Peter relates. "And I remember someone saying something about a $100,000 bond. They took me down to where, I found out later, was the conference room which was between the cell block and the boundover section. They had me take off all my clothes, asked me what my weight was and my height and so on. Then they gave me jail clothes, and then they took me in a jail cell, which I found out later was number 32 cell."

At half past one on Sunday morning, September 30, the jail was quiet except for the snores of other prisoners and the clanging of the iron door that closed behind Peter. He put his blanket on the bed and lay down.

Peter's final thought before sleeping was this: "I thought I was going to be there for the rest of my life. That was all I could figure." For the last day and a half, he had felt a terrible sense of abandonment. He was completely on his own as he struggled to make sense out of his predicament, and as he tried and failed to persuade the police and then himself that he was not his mother's slayer. No friend or relative had appeared to speak up for him. For all he knew, not one person in the whole world knew about his plight or cared what happened to him.

Since the morning after the murder, however, telephones had been ringing all over Canaan, and the people who knew him best were asking each other, "Where's Peter?" and "What's happened to Peter?"

They knew that he was in police custody. They had been told that he was helping the police with their inquiries. Young Eddie Dickinson, whose father had offered Peter help the night before while he sat in the police cruiser, went to the barracks Saturday to see Peter, but was told that he could not.

Like the Madows, the Dickinsons were willing to have Peter stay with them. At the Madow house, Geoff kept on insisting that "They're doing something to Peter." His mother said, "You watch too many TV shows, Geoffrey. Nowadays they don't do those kind of things. They don't use rubber hoses. They're just asking Peter questions. They have to find out who his mother knew or who knew his mother."

Mickey and Marion Madow made repeated efforts Saturday, both on the phone and in person at the barracks, to find out if Peter was all right. They were not told that he was a suspect or that he had been taken to Hartford. Peter was halfway through the interrogation when Mickey drove to the barracks at six o'clock Saturday evening and spoke to Sergeant Salley. "I asked how Peter was doing and he said, 'Fine.' He said that Peter wanted to cooperate as fully as he could, and he had eaten, and that he was cooperating and he wanted to stay at the barracks because he felt safer there. And at that point I said, 'Would he need an attorney?' He said, 'No, not at this point.'"

Lieutenant Shay, however, had telephoned the Canaan Barracks from Hartford soon after 5:30 P.M. with instructions to try to locate Stanley Herman, the public defender. The police called his home, his office and even a couple of restaurants, but to no avail.

The State Police contacted Peter's out-of-state relatives while keeping his Canaan friends at arm's length. Barbara Gibbons had so alienated members of her family that she had not been in regular contact with any of them for years. Her married cousins June and Victoria, once they were drawn into the murder case, feared the notoriety and begged reporters not to use their names.

June was reached on the telephone by a trooper in her New Jersey home between 3:00 and 3:30 Saturday afternoon. "He told me that Barbara had been murdered, or was dead, one or the other. I was very stunned, and I said, 'You'll have to give me a minute, now, just a minute. I know there are some things I want to ask you and I just need a minute to think about it.' And I said, 'There's a boy, Peter. I want to know where he is. Is he there with you? Is he there?' And he said, 'He's not here right now.'" June asked the police to locate him; she was especially worried that he would return to the house where his mother had just been killed. "I didn't think it was right."

June called Victoria's house in upstate New York. The sisters and their husbands agreed that they should do what they could for Peter as quickly as possible. Victoria and her husband made plans to go to Canaan to get him and bring him home if he wished to come. The two families telephoned the Canaan Barracks a number of times to get more information.

During one talk with a trooper, June asked whether there were any friends of Peter's in Canaan who were with him. "They said, 'Well, we don't know anything about that.' And I said, 'He has no one? No friends? There's no one with him?' They said he had no one, no friends. I said, 'My God, you've got to find him for me. Where is he? Out wandering?' Well, they said they didn't know where he was. But he was with them all the time!"

June recalls speaking to an officer at about 8:30 Saturday night. When he would not specify where Peter was, she asked if Peter needed a lawyer. "It wouldn't be a bad idea," she was told. Then, at two o'clock Sunday morning, the police called to tell her that Peter had been arrested for the murder and would appear in court Monday morning.

For June, who had seen Peter only twice in the past thirteen years, and for Victoria, who had never seen him, the news that Barbara's son was believed to be her murderer was shocking, but their astonishment and disbelief could not match that of the Canaan families who knew Peter intimately. They were so stunned when they learned of Peter's arrest that they scarcely knew what they could do except call each other and exchange information. The telephone at the Belignis rang all day. Jean Beligni recalls speaking to Marion Madow and assuring her that "Everything will be all right as soon as Jim Mulhern gets down there. He knows that Peter couldn't possibly have done a thing like this."

One of the first questions that occurred to many of Peter's Canaan friends was whether Peter's godmother, "Auntie B," who had been giving Barbara and Peter financial help for many years, had heard about the killing and Peter's arrest. If anyone could help, she could. Only a few knew that her name was Barbara Sincerbeaux and that she lived in Forest Hills in the borough of Queens, New York City.

The State Police had been trying to contact her by phone since early morning Saturday. Peter had given them her name and they had found the letter that Barbara Gibbons apparently had received from Sincerbeaux on the day of the murder. The letter sounded like a warning that the money supply might be cut off at any moment. The Connecticut police finally asked the New York City police to call at Barbara Sincerbeaux's apartment. They learned that she had gone to Toronto, Canada, to visit her sister.

For many people, the first news of the tragedy reached them in their Sunday newspapers. The *Hartford Courant* story, under the headline "WOMAN, 51, DEAD WITH THROAT CUT," told of the discovery of the body of Barbara Gibbons by her son "Peter Riley. [sic]" The information about the murder was sparse and nothing was said about Peter's whereabouts. The investigating troopers were said to be searching for the murder weapon. "One chased away a news photographer who snapped a photo of troopers digging up the septic tank behind the house in the search for clues," the article stated. A grocery clerk was quoted as saying that the victim "was a well-educated lady with an elaborate sense of humor."

The press had not had time enough to determine that the son of the victim was under arrest and in a cell at the Litchfield Correctional Center. Peter himself scarcely knew where he was or what was going on when he was awakened soon after seven o'clock by a guard who brought his breakfast on a tray. The plate and the cup were paper because the jailers had discovered that he had a mouth infection which they did not want spread to other prisoners.

As Peter related in court, "I remember they spilled the milk that was in the cup. And then they closed the door and I sat there and I ate. Then I just rolled over and went back to bed. Sometime later on, that morning, they came down and they told me to pack up my things. They gave me a pack of cigarettes and a pen and a letter, and I packed that up and packed up a book that they had handed me when I came in, and my blanket and pillow. They took me over to the bound-over section."

He was placed in cell E at the end of a row. He would remain locked up for the usual observation period of forty-eight hours before he was allowed to move freely about the area like the other prisoners.

A middle-aged inmate named Robert Erhardt was drinking coffee when Peter was brought in by a guard. "He looked like a drowned rat," Erhardt recalls. The tan jail uniform that he had been given was several sizes too large. Erhardt remembers Peter's pale, bewildered face—and the tears. "The kid, if he wasn't in shock, was damned close to it. He was a physical wreck. His whole coordination was out of whack. He couldn't make his bed. He just lay on the bundle of sheets and blankets with all his clothes on."

Erhardt says that "The guard came over to me after locking him in, and he told me not to talk to the kid because he was in for some horrible crime and besides that he had a disease. I thought this was pretty funny. I asked him, 'What's he got, leprosy?' It turned out to be only trench mouth. So when the guard left I walked over to his cell, pulled up a bench and started to talk to him."

Robert Erhardt, who was then forty-five years old, is a husky, soulful-looking man with a sympathetic nature and a good mind. He has artistic skills and a thirst for knowledge, but no knack for successful armed robberies. He has tried and failed many times and, as a result, has spent more than half of his adult life in prison. He once spent half a year in a federal prison cell with former Teamster boss Jimmy Hoffa. "I've got a record as long as your arm and it's nothing I'm at all proud of," he says, "but at least I've never hurt anyone." He was in the Litchfield jail for robbing a local cinema, after having been out of prison for thirteen months.

Erhardt's analysis of his life is that his stormy relationship with his parents and his lifelong feeling of rejection led to his criminal activities. When he saw eighteen-year-old Peter Reilly appear in the Litchfield jail he saw himself, at the same age in the same place a quarter century earlier. In 1946 he was newly married and had just enlisted in the Navy when he "borrowed" somebody's car for a joyride. "I was arrested for auto theft and put in jail. There was a $1,000 bond, but my father wouldn't put up the money. He wanted to teach me a lesson. I spent a year in the Litchfield jail. Nobody helped me. That's where it all began."

He tried to make conversation with Peter, but it was difficult at first because, as Erhardt would relate in court, "he was really talking in circles" and "none of his statements were coherent."

He began by asking Peter what he was in for, but Peter just said it was something "unbelievable" that he was "too ashamed" to talk about. Erhardt could see that "the kid was all torn up," so he made him a cup of coffee and then sat for an hour or so while Peter rambled on about his schoolwork, his friends, his guitar and everything else that came to mind. Finally, saying that "I'm not a violent person," Peter edged closer to revealing the cause of his arrest. "You won't stop talking to me?" Peter asked.

Erhardt reassured him. "I said that I had known guys who had done everything you could imagine. I had even known mass murderers. That really made him sit up. Finally he told me that he was charged with killing his mother. I thought, oh boy, that's really serious, and I walked away to get some coffee. He called after me, practically crying, 'You're not going to walk away from me, are you?' So I went right back to him."

Erhardt would one day sit at his typewriter and put down his recollection of his dialogue with Peter because the police were trying to establish that Peter had admitted his guilt to his fellow prisoners in the Litchfield jail. He noted that Peter said that "I'm really a very shy person. I wouldn't fight with anyone. I'm not very strong. I don't bother anybody. But they are trying to charge me with . . . Will you understand?"

"Go ahead," Erhardt told him. "Get whatever it is off your chest."

"They are trying to say that I killed my mother," Peter said.

"Come on now, you got to be kidding. Do you know what you're saying?"

"I'm so confused. When I got home . . . I think I blacked out.

I couldn't have killed my mom . . . But I signed a statement . . .
I know I didn't kill her. . . . They kept asking questions and all I
can remember is I got very run down, and they kept asking and
asking questions. I was sleepy. . . . And yet I gave them a signed
statement."

"Did you admit to it?" Erhardt asked.

"I think I did," Peter said. "But I really don't know what
I said. . . . All I can remember is that I came home and Mom
was laying on the floor and I know she was bleeding. I called
for an ambulance and they came. And then I was brought to
the police barracks and questioned."

"Did you make a phone call to anyone?"

"No."

"Have you called a lawyer?"

"No, I haven't made any calls. I've seen no one but the
police."

"Well, I'll give you some good advice: Get a lawyer.
Because you are going to need one as soon as possible."

Because Peter was locked in his cell, Erhardt asked a
guard to bring them a Torrington telephone book so that
they could look up attorneys in the Yellow Pages. When they
came to the name Charles W. Roraback, Peter remembered
that there was a lawyer in Canaan, Catherine Roraback, who
was a famous civil-rights lawyer. "I said I would like Catherine Roraback," Peter later said in court. "They told me I
probably couldn't afford her, but that's who I said I wanted."
He was sure that his Auntie B would take care of the costs.

Peter requested permission to make a telephone call. He
decided to ask the Belignis to contact Miss Roraback for him.
He dialed the Beligni number, but it was busy and continued
to be every time he called. In the meantime, a public defender
named Henry Campbell arrived in the early afternoon to offer
his services to Peter. County Detective Sam Holden had suggested that he do so. Peter told him that he was going to have
private counsel. Peter kept getting busy signals from the Beligni
house all Sunday afternoon, but he finally got through.

"When Peter called me from prison," Mrs. Beligni says,
"he was still very confused." She recalls that their dialogue
went like this:

"They told me I need a lawyer."

"You certainly do, Peter, but I know you didn't do anything wrong."

"Well, they told me I did."

"But you didn't; I know you didn't do it."

"*They* know I did."

"But you didn't."

"I know *now* I didn't, so I need a lawyer."

Mrs. Beligni adds that "I asked him where he was and he wasn't too sure. He had to ask the other prisoners to be sure he was in the county jail. I said, 'Who do you want, Peter?' He said, 'I want Catherine Roraback.' I said, 'Okay, since we've been talking I've been thinking about it and I think she's a good choice.' I think he picked her because she did all these civil-rights things; she seemed to go for the underdog every time."

Peter spoke to other members of the Beligni family and to Art and Geoff Madow, who had stopped by at the Beligni home to find out whether anyone had any news about Peter. When they returned home and told their parents the latest developments, Marion Madow sat down and wrote Peter the first of the dozens of letters that she sent him during the next few months. She had already told him, while comforting him at the murder scene Friday night, that he could be part of her family and "I'll yell at you just like I yell at my kids." Now she said:

Dearest Pete: Just a note to let you know we all love you and are thinking about you every second. Peter, just remember that you have a place with us for as long as you need it. Come here and make this place your home. You are just like one of my boys to me. Keep the faith, Pete, ole boy, and just remember we are here when you need us. We know *you have not done anything wrong! We will see you as soon as they let us. Take care, Peter. Love from us all.*

MARION MADOW.

Jean Beligni tried repeatedly to reach Catherine Roraback by telephone. By nine o'clock, Sunday night, she was still unsuccessful.

As she related long afterward, "I said to Aldo, let's call John Bianchi. He can find Catherine Roraback for us. When he came to the phone I told him, 'John, this boy didn't do this thing,' and he said that he didn't know too much about the case because he'd been away all weekend, but he assured me that everything was fine with Peter. He said Peter didn't really need an attorney because they'll appoint him a defender and that when he appears in court the next morning it was just a formality to have the case bound over to Superior Court.

"Well, I said, 'Look, John, after all that's happened he must think we've all deserted him because we tried to see him and they wouldn't let us see him. They even told him that we hadn't been trying! And if Catherine Roraback isn't there with him in the morning, that kid's going to fall apart.' And he said to me, 'Oh, they wouldn't do that, Jeannie,' and I suddenly thought, here I am talking to the *opposition*. John's on the same side as the police. It was so stupid, that I didn't realize it. I've been brought up in a police atmosphere. My aunt works at the Canaan Barracks. My father was a deputy sheriff in town and he and John used to play golf together. My father was one of the pallbearers for John's mother. My cousin, Judge John Speziale, appointed John State's Attorney. I thought of John Bianchi as our friend and that if anything happened you called a policeman. I never dreamed they would do what they did to Peter."

John Bianchi's advice to Jean Beligni was to locate Catherine Roraback's secretary: She would have Miss Roraback's private home number. Mrs. Beligni remembered that her husband had only recently drilled a well for the secretary. The contact was made and early the next morning Catherine Roraback called to ask, "Where do they want me?"

6 ▪ THE LAWYERS

SGT. KELLY: Did you step on her legs or something? When she was on the floor, and jumped up and down or something, and break them like that or what?

PETER REILLY: I could have.

SGT. KELLY: Can you remember stomping her legs?

PETER REILLY: I think. But, I'm not sure because you say it then I imagine that I'm doing it.

SGT. KELLY: No, no, no. You're not imagining anything. I think the truth is starting to come from you now. Because you want it out. You want that second chance.

PETER REILLY: I know—

SGT. KELLY: But, you can't have that second chance until—

During his first day in the Litchfield jail Peter Reilly received a crash course in the workings of the criminal justice system from his fellow inmates. Robert Erhardt, older and more experienced than most of the others, had passed the word that Peter had been given a bum rap and should be treated with consideration. Walter Woods, a prisoner closer to Peter's age, explained to him how a man can get off scot-free for crimes he *did* commit and then have the bad luck to be punished for something he did not do. Other advisers simply told him to keep his mouth shut. Their counsel was reinforced by the public defender who told Peter, during their brief meeting, "Don't say anything to anyone except your lawyer."

Sunday night Lieutenant Shay came to the jail with a search-and-seizure warrant permitting him to take possession, for scientific examination, of the blue jeans, brown shirt, sneakers and other items that Peter had worn Friday and Saturday. The document stated that "the clothing worn by Peter Reilly was an instrument used in the crime of murder." In the warden's office, Shay, accompanied by a couple of troopers, asked Peter a few more questions.

"I was polite," Peter recalls. "I just said, 'I'm sorry, I would rather not answer any questions without my attorney being present.' That stopped him in his tracks. And then when I told him that I was getting my own lawyer instead of using the public defender—well, you should have seen the look on his face."

The meeting in the warden's office was Peter's first real show of defiance and it felt good. He would not know until late the next morning, however, whether Catherine Roraback could or would take his case. A busy woman, with offices in both Canaan and New Haven, she was attending an American Civil Liberties Union board meeting in New York that very weekend. Her secretary said that she could not be reached until early Monday morning when she would be back in Canaan.

Since his mother had followed the news so carefully, Peter knew of Catherine Roraback's reputation as an outspoken feminist and as a defender of unpopular causes and unpopular people. He was aware of her role in the heavily publicized Black Panther case in New Haven in 1970–71. She had defended Ericka Huggins, a Black Panther leader and a codefendant of Bobby Seale, against murder charges in the slaying of fellow Panther Alex Rackley. Seale and Huggins had been freed when a mistrial was declared in a trial that was said to have been the longest and costliest in Connecticut history. Jury selection alone had taken nearly four months, with 1,042 prospective jurors questioned.

A newspaper profile of "Katie" Roraback noted that she had been called everything from "Communist" to "champion of the underdog," but concluded that "She is simply a lawyer who many moons ago fell in love with the Constitution and the Bill of Rights."

Like Barbara Gibbons in her better days, Roraback was a chunky, quick-witted woman. She wore her hair cropped short and mannish suits. Her aggressive manner made her a formidable opponent in a courtroom. Some people in conservative Canaan scarcely knew what to make of her: Her ideas were unorthodox, her politics radical. Yet in the community, the Roraback name was long distinguished and well known in politics and public service. Catherine Roraback's letterhead listed three predecessors in the family law firm: Alberto T. Roraback, J. Henry Roraback and J. Clinton Roraback.

Her grandfather, Alberto T., born in 1849, was a noted jurist. Her granduncle, J. Henry, a turn-of-the-century lawyer who became Connecticut's "Mr. Republican," had been the political boss of the state for many years when he committed suicide in 1937. J. Clinton, her uncle, was an outstanding trial lawyer whose half century as a Canaan attorney made him one of the most influential figures in the area. She inherited his Canaan practice in 1955.

Catherine Roraback's father, Albert E., like many others in the family, went to Yale, but chose to enter the ministry instead of studying law. One of Albert Roraback's friends in the Class of 1902 was Frank Sincerbeaux, a brilliant attorney, whose daughter Barbara became Peter Reilly's godmother.

Born and raised in Brooklyn, Catherine Roraback attended Mount Holyoke College where she was one class behind Ella Grasso, a future governor of Connecticut. After several years of wartime work in Washington she went on to Yale Law School. Out of the 180 members in the Class of 1948 (including John Lindsay, a future mayor of New York), she was one of four women. She soon became famous, or infamous, for defending Communists in the Smith Act trials, pacifists who demonstrated at the New London submarine base, and assorted revolutionaries, reformers and demonstrators, many of whom were too poor to pay a lawyer. She defended birth-control advocates in the early 1960s, a litigation that concluded when the Connecticut Supreme Court struck down the state's anticontraceptive law. She was active in Mississippi during the civil-rights struggle. Not long before she accepted the Peter Reilly case, she was in the newspapers again as the attorney for the son of Peter's family physician, Dr. Carl Bornemann, who was fighting for classification as a conscientious objector during the Vietnam War.

*   *   *

As soon as she heard the sketchy details of Peter's arrest, Catherine Roraback knew that the case was one she could not refuse. State's Attorney Bianchi had told Jean Beligni that she would be too expensive for Peter, but money was not Roraback's first consideration and Peter's supporters were confident that enough funds could be raised. According to Mickey Madow's brother, Murray Madow, who would play an important role in the defense effort, "The attitude was that there would be plenty of money once Peter's godmother was reached. We were sure she was going to come through. We didn't worry about it." Jean Beligni bought $72.50 worth of clothing for Peter at Bob's Clothing Store so that he could be decently dressed for his court appearances. She knew Barbara and Peter had a charge account there and that the bills were routinely sent to his godmother.

Roraback had never met Peter Reilly. With her young associate, Peter Herbst, she hurried to Torrington, where Peter was waiting for her in the law library at the City Hall before his Circuit Court appearance. The morning was an emotional one for him because he had just met his mother's cousin Victoria and her husband, John, for the first time. He went quickly into Victoria's arms. All three wept. They told Peter that he could come and live with them if he wished as soon as his legal problems were solved.

Attorney Roraback's first important questions for Peter were, of course, about the murder. Did he do it? "No," he said, and he explained the peculiar events of the past two days. When they emerged from their private meeting place, Peter's face, according to a press account, was "pale and expressionless. He looked at no one. He held tight to a pack of cigarettes in hands cuffed behind his back."

They stood together before the Circuit Court judge for the arraignment. The charge was murder. The case was continued until the following week. In arguing for reduction of Peter's $100,000 bond, Roraback stressed that Peter had lived all his life in Canaan and that "a number of neighbors are extremely concerned about him." The bond was chopped to $35,000.

* * *

The State quickly moved the case from the Circuit Court to the Superior Court. The bond went up to $100,000 again. It had to be reduced if there was any hope of getting Peter out of jail.

Just six days after the murder, forty persons from the Canaan area went to the courthouse in Litchfield to speak in Peter's favor. Edward Kirby, his school principal, said to Superior Court Judge Anthony J. Armentano that "We've never had any difficulty with him whatever." The Reverend Paul Halovatch of St. Joseph's Church said that Peter "is respectful and has integrity." Catherine Roraback revealed that Peter had a choice of homes to go to and that both friends and relatives wanted him. Cousin Victoria was in the courtroom. Marion Madow stated that "He's like one of my boys. I'd take him anytime."

"Do you feel the same way, knowing he's been charged with murder?" Judge Armentano asked.

"Yes, sir, I do," Mrs. Madow replied.

Peter's backers argued for a greatly reduced bond, saying that he would not become a fugitive if released from jail. John Bianchi called $100,000 "a modest figure" inasmuch as Reilly was charged with a serious crime. Judge Armentano decided to reduce the bond to $50,000 in view of Peter's "strong community backing."

State's Attorney Bianchi was an imposing figure in the courtroom. He exuded self-confidence. He was a dark-haired, round-faced, broad-shouldered man of average height who fought to keep trim on the golf course. He was a natty dresser in finely tailored suits. He had been about to play golf on Saturday, during his college reunion in Boston, when County Detective Sam Holden telephoned him with the news of Barbara Gibbons' murder. Holden called him again the next day to report the arrest of Peter Reilly. Then the State Police briefed him on the case as soon as he returned to Canaan.

He had also spoken to a number of his Canaan friends who were upset about the police confinement of Peter and astonished by his arrest. He knew most of the forty persons who came to the Litchfield courthouse on Peter's behalf. Father Paul, for example, was the curate at his church, and

the Madows were old acquaintances. He and Mickey were
members of the same VFW post. Everyone was friendly at
that court appearance, but, nonetheless, John Bianchi, for
the State, and Peter Reilly's supporters were squaring off.
Neither he nor they could know that in this, the most important case of his career, he would come to be seen, at least by
some, as more of a persecutor than a prosecutor.

"Smiling John" Bianchi was the chief prosecutor for all
twenty-six towns of Litchfield County, population 150,000.
He was active in town affairs as a lawyer, as a businessman
who owned real estate in the area, as Canaan's town counsel
from 1950 until his appointment as State's Attorney in 1972
and as a member of everything from the American Legion to
the Knights of Columbus.

   He was on the Board of Directors of the Canaan National
Bank. He was active in scholarship programs for deserv-
ing youths and he was an umpire for the local Little League
(whose most celebrated product was Steve Blass, recently
a pitching hero for the Pittsburgh Pirates). He occasionally
chaperoned at the Youth Center and appeared regularly at the
high school to talk to students about crime and justice in the
Contemporary Problems class.

   While no one could say that John Bianchi did not give his
all for the best interests of Canaan, some said that he went too
far. He seemed to see himself as the protector of the town's
moral well-being. "Johnny is a friend of mine," one man said,
"but it seems to me that he comes down too hard on kids with
long hair and anybody who sounds like a bleeding-heart liberal. He feels very protective about Canaan. You remember
he fought the idea of Salisbury sharing our town dump. He
said he didn't want Salisbury people dumping their garbage
in his town. He's a very conservative man, like a lot of people around here. The superpatriots. During the Vietnam War
there was a peace vigil going on in Sharon every Saturday,
but you'd never see a thing like that in Canaan."

   Canaan is something of an exception in the Litchfield
Hills. The twin towns of North Canaan and Falls Village,

unlike Salisbury and Sharon, have few old moneyed families and wealthy retirees. They have a blue-collar style undiluted by too many gentlemen farmers or the presence of private schools like Hotchkiss or Kent, as in other nearby towns. Canaan's several small factories and quarries give the community a touch of industry that is absent in most of the Litchfield Hills.

During the past century, Canaan has become less of an old Yankee place and more of a hometown for Italian Catholics. The Italian influence is strong in Connecticut cities while the rural areas remain, for the most part, Anglo-Saxon Protestant. Canaan, however, is a bucolic Little Italy. Although most Canaanites are not Italian, the Belignis, Cecchinatos, Gandolfos, Minaccis, Perottis and Segallas give the town a flavor of its own. In 1973, no name was more prominent than John Bianchi's.

John A. Bianchi arrived in Canaan from Italy and started Bianchi's clothing store in 1910. John F. Bianchi was born a dozen years later, and it was not long before he was known as "the best-dressed boy in town." He was also an only child who, according to a lifelong friend, "was so overprotected by his mother, an Irish Catholic, that I really do think he was unhappy a lot of the time. Johnny grew up to be a big man, but he was a puny, sickly kid who would be kept out of school by his mother on the slightest excuse. If his nose ran, he didn't go to school. I used to have to deliver his homework to him. I don't think he was that sick, but she worried herself into an early grave. His mother became a very strange, very difficult person in her last years. Even when he was grown up and working as a lawyer she would tell people that she was worried that her boy was lost and would not be able to find his way home. She desperately wanted him to become a priest, but he went into the law instead. It was a very, very difficult relationship for him. She had always been so well groomed, but at the end she was unkempt and constantly crying all day so that you would have to avoid her. Johnny came home one day and found her dead. She apparently had taken a bath and had a heart attack. I've always wondered if he thought much about that when he heard about Peter Reilly going home to his mother on the night of the murder."

If John Bianchi was a mama's boy in his childhood, too precious for rough-and-tumble sports, his life changed when he was enrolled in a private Catholic boy's school—Cranwell in Lenox, Massachusetts—instead of the regional high school. He became active in sports and played baseball for his college team when he attended Holy Cross under the auspices of the Navy training program during World War II. He aspired to be a Navy flier, but he was not yet twenty-one and needed his parents' consent. His father gave it; his mother would not. But he did serve with the fleet in the South and Central Pacific before taking his degree. "After the war," he said in an interview, "I wasn't sure what I wanted to do. My father suggested law school, saying it was good background for various fields including business." He studied law at Fordham University and was admitted to the Connecticut bar in 1949.

Bianchi once told another attorney that he had few clients during his first years of practice because J. Clinton Roraback handled virtually all of the legal business in town. Clint Roraback was a jovial, back-slapping civic leader, and Bianchi might well have modeled himself on that style. He had asked for Roraback's help when he tried—unsuccessfully—to get into Yale Law School. When Clint died of a heart attack in a courtroom in 1955, his niece became Bianchi's rival for Canaan's legal business.

He had known Catherine Roraback since his childhood because she and her brother Albert had spent their summers in Canaan. Although they argued cases against each other in courtrooms and competed for clients, Bianchi told people that Catherine was a good friend. Nonetheless, his deeper feelings about the Rorabacks were obvious to other members of the bar and they could see the makings of a fascinating confrontation between "John and Catherine" in the Peter Reilly case.

They were opposites in personality, social background, religious affiliation (although he had married a Protestant), political orientation and social connections. Catherine Roraback had the Yankee background and the Ivy League degrees while John Bianchi had had to struggle for status—yet she was the social revolutionary and he the guardian of the status quo. During the Reilly case, he could be seen as a man who enjoyed the company of policemen, quite apart from the need to work intimately with them as State's Attorney, while she had seen enough police excesses over the years to view their work most skeptically.

7 ▪ PEOPLE FOR PETER

PETER REILLY: (to Sgt. Jack Schneider) You're the only person who has been straightforward with me the last twenty-four hours. I've been drilled and drilled and drilled and gone over and gone over, you know, and—

Grassy Hill Cemetery on Sand Road in Falls Village is located on a hillside, where the weather-beaten old gravestones are surrounded by tall evergreens. A dank stone storehouse, where bodies used to be kept through the winter until the spring thaw, still stands at the rear.

One day in late October, 1973, nearly a month after her murder, the body of Barbara Gibbons was brought to the side of the storehouse. A grave was dug by a tractor using a back scoop and she was soon buried. No relatives or friends of the deceased were present. Her only child was in jail, unaware of the event. No gravestone had been ordered. The burial was routine: just the next step after the delayed filing of a death certificate which said, among other causes of death, that Barbara Gibbons had choked on her own blood.

According to Father Paul, "There was a little item in the paper about the death certificate being issued that said the burial was scheduled that day. No one knew it was going to happen and it was all over with by the time we read about it. People were very upset by that. The family had not been notified. It was very poorly handled. The funeral parlor was probably told what to do."

Jean Beligni, Father Paul, the Madows and others decided to hold a graveside memorial service for Barbara Gibbons and to try to get permission for Peter to attend. Warden Charles Brownell in Litchfield said that Peter would be there. The service took place, with thirty people present, in the early afternoon of November 2. It was a simple, moving ceremony on a sunny day. Though no eulogy was read, everyone said the words to the Lord's Prayer.

Solemn as the occasion was, it gave Peter some of his warmest moments since his imprisonment five weeks earlier. He was surrounded by the boys and girls who were his best friends in school and by adults who were concerned about his arrest. His first time out of jail, except for his court appearances, he had his first look at his hometown since his arrest. A jail officer, in civilian clothes, stood at his side throughout, but gave him plenty of time to chat with his friends. The officer thoughtfully draped his coat over the handcuffs that held them together.

Peter's spirits had been buoyed up soon after his arrest by the realization that he was not alone and that all was not lost. Far from being forgotten, he had attracted an extraordinary amount of press attention and community support, as the headlines made clear:

SLAYING ARREST STUNS VILLAGERS

SLAYING SUSPECT, 18, GETS TOP LAWYER

RESIDENTS RALLY TO SUPPORT OF PETER REILLY

NEIGHBORS BACK YOUTH CHARGED WITH MURDER

The slaying itself quickly became secondary to the fact that the victim's son was accused of the murder and that so many people were convinced that the State Police had seized the wrong man. What happened to Barbara Gibbons seemed to be a question of far less importance than the fate of Peter Reilly. She became the forgotten woman. In all of the newspaper stories, magazine articles and television accounts that would appear in the next four years, little information about Barbara Gibbons' origins, her personal history, her relationships and the true nature of her comradeship with her son would be reported.

The emphasis was on Peter, for at least three good reasons:

1) He simply did not look the part of a murderer and virtually everyone interviewed by reporters spoke of his quiet, unaggressive nature and his warm feelings about his mother.

2) The Canaan people who knew Peter reacted to his arrest with utter disbelief, then anger and then action. Ordinary citizens who had seldom if ever questioned the work of the police were suddenly up in arms. In a remarkably short time they took a public stand, something many of them had never done before.

3) Because the State Police kept as much as possible of their investigation secret, no evidence was made known to the public that linked Peter Reilly to the murder. His confession would not be reported in the press until December 1973, and then it seemed to many to be tainted. What was known about the case was deeply disturbing to Peter's supporters because they felt his movements on the murder night left him with no time to kill his mother and dispose of incriminating evidence.

The public reaction was so swift that the State Police and then the State's Attorney were immediately put on the defensive. Most people, of course, in Canaan and in the surrounding area, remained uninvolved although interested. Some automatically assumed Peter was guilty. They became even more sure of his guilt as soon as they learned that "a bunch of do-gooders," as one man called them, was protesting his innocence. That many people were protesting was news, and the story gained momentum as more facts about Peter, the murder and the arrest became known.

The tone of the Reilly case was established in the first reports of the tragedy in the *Lakeville Journal*. This venerable and award-winning newspaper is one of the outstanding weeklies in the nation and the principal organ for the people in the northwest corner of Connecticut. Its owner-editor is Robert H. Estabrook, a veteran foreign correspondent and former editorial page editor for the *Washington Post*. Estabrook is an authority on freedom-of-the-press issues and a journalist whose championship of the public's right to know has frequently brought him into conflict with public officials who prefer closed meetings and the least possible disclosure about controversial matters.

The *Lakeville Journal*'s coverage of the case was so thorough that the police and the prosecutor felt that the paper was crusading unfairly against them. The editorial columns made clear that the *Journal* believed the case was grossly mishandled. One 1974 editorial, "The Issues in the Reilly Case," received a first-place achievement award from the Connecticut Civil Liberties Union Foundation. "Whatever else comes out of the Reilly case," the *Journal* said, "it ought to occasion a hard look at police procedures. . . . Surely the present misinformation and lack of information from police have contributed to the alienation of townspeople. If police officials want to know how to improve public relations, let them go over the record in this unfortunate episode."

The headline on the *Journal*'s report of October 4, 1973, was indicative: "SECRECY SHROUDS MURDER CASE IN FALLS VILLAGE." The Gibbons murder was the biggest crime story in the area in years and the paper gave it major front-page play—but few details were available about the how and why of the slaying. The story spoke of the "tight curtain of secrecy" drawn by the police. It said that persons interviewed by the police were ordered not to talk to anyone. "So extensive were police restrictions," the article stated, "that G. Roger Newkirk, Canaan and Lakeville funeral director, was not allowed to talk to Reilly as the next of kin to make funeral arrangements earlier in the week. Mr. Newkirk told the *Lakeville Journal* this was the first time he had ever experienced such restrictions."

Lieutenant James Shay was quoted as saying that there were very important reasons for restricting information. "First, I have to be sure that we release nothing that would prevent this boy from getting a fair trial. Second, as commanding officer here, I have to be conscious that we have a very major crime to be solved."

Many readers learned for the first time that the murder had been exceptionally brutal and that "Miss Gibbons sustained massive fractures as well as multiple stab wounds." The story spoke of the discrepancies in the time sequence of the killing and Peter's movements, insofar as information was known. And it reported the public reaction:

> As the grisly happening became known, a number of persons acquainted with young Reilly expressed astonishment at the murder charge against the youth. He reportedly had been at the Canaan Youth Center Friday evening until only a few minutes before the murder was discovered.
>
> A group of friends met Tuesday evening to organize a show of support for Reilly, and fellow students collected money at the high school to purchase a transistor radio for him. A Canaan family also had taken clothing and cigarettes to him at the Litchfield Correctional Center. . . .
>
> Friends found it difficult to believe that Reilly could be charged with murder. An associate in a rock band commented that "He was really good to his mom."
>
> Edward Kirby, principal of the Housatonic Valley Regional High School, said he had known Reilly as a student and that there never had been any problems with him.

The theme was the same in other newspapers. No one had a bad word for Peter Reilly and a remarkable number of people were willing to speak up for his good character. The *Torrington Register* reported that "His arrest shocked neighbors and friends at Housatonic Valley Regional High School where he was described as 'a nice kid.' Friends of Reilly told reporters 'they've got the wrong guy' . . . 'he couldn't have done it' . . . 'he liked his mother an awful lot.'"

The citizens' movement to help Peter had many beginnings because so many people were simultaneously concerned and eager to act. Some, like the Belignis, Madows and Dickinsons, had seen a lot of Peter in recent years. John and Priscilla Belcher and a few others had known him most of his life. Others knew nothing about him, but they sensed a terrible injustice and came forward, one by one, to help.

Beverly King was the mother of one of Peter's friends, Conrad King, but she had not met Peter. She had a special understanding of his plight, however. Some months before the murder, she and a few others in Canaan, including Beatrice Keith, Norma Hawver and the Methodist Church minister, had formed a committee to raise money for a young man who had been arrested for setting fire to several buildings. His guilt or innocence was not the issue; he was just someone who needed help. He was duly convicted, jailed, paroled and given psychiatric treatment. He was able to continue living and working in the community.

The committee found that a few dollars remained. "At our last meeting," Beatrice Keith recalls, "we were wondering what to do with this money when Bev King said, 'Did you hear about this Peter Reilly?' Well, I hadn't. She gave us some details about the situation and she said her son had come home and asked whether the legal defense money could be used to help Peter. Beverly said she heard about a small group in Falls Village that was going to have a meeting to help Peter, so we decided to call them and offer the money. They said, 'Great!,' and that's how it started."

Mrs. King was one of those "Canaan mothers" who would make the Reilly case a major part of her life while caring for her four children and holding a regular job. "When we started out," she recalls, "none of us had any idea that this was going to go on and on for so long. Any of us would have taken Peter into our home. We all treated him as though he were our own son. We've cried with him and laughed with him and we've gone through a lot of ups and downs. There were meetings, tag sales, bake sales, many hours on the telephone, going to the trial, raising money and then more money and more meetings. Peter certainly went through a lot—too much for someone his age—but we went through a lot too."

In Jean Beligni's words, "We ate, breathed and slept this thing. It went on not just months but years. People gave up an incredible amount of their time going to meetings every week and just doing anything to save Peter. It became a living, breathing cause. It was phone calls morning to night. Sometimes Bev King and I would talk on the phone until we were so tired we couldn't talk any more. Originally, when Peter was in jail, the big thing was raising money, but later on we felt that we had to solve this thing. We tracked down every lead. We were all being Perry Mason. We had to find out who did it. Somebody killed Barbara Gibbons and we knew it wasn't Peter."

Beatrice Keith was there at the beginning as was her invalid mother, Mrs. Florence Tompkins. Both mother and daughter had worked in show business and that, along with their political liberalism, set them apart from most people in Canaan, including other supporters of Peter Reilly. Mrs. Tompkins had been an actress and singer while Bea Keith had been an outstanding ballerina with the New York City Ballet and the Joffrey Ballet. Her late husband, Hal Keith, had worked with Sid Caesar, Wally Cox and other stars as a television director.

When the original fund-raising effort for Peter began, Bea was the treasurer while her mother wrote thank-you letters by the dozens. Later on, when her mother's eyesight weakened, Bea assumed the correspondence duties. They were drawn to this cause (as they were to the case of the young arsonist) because of their concern for justice and the rights of the individual. But Bea Keith, who had regularly stood in the Sharon Peace Vigil during the Vietnam War, soon found it politic to avoid the civil-rights issues of the Reilly case. Most of Peter's supporters did not consider themselves "liberal do-gooders." They were for "law and order," not protesting and demonstrating, and they were not accustomed to doubting the word of the police. Mrs. Tompkins would observe one day that "The Reilly case has changed a lot of people in this community. Before, if they read about an arrest, they'd believe the person was guilty. They trusted the authorities. It's not that way anymore."

Although one woman who joined the Reilly defense effort did so because, "knowing cops, I figured Peter was getting the shaft," most people became involved simply because

Peter's arrest seemed wrong on the face of it. One man stated that "Even if the cops had the right man, they went about it the wrong way. They really made it look as if they were trying to railroad him."

Murray Madow, the brother of Mickey Madow, is a manufacturer of horseshoes who calls himself an old-time horse dealer. "At the beginning," he says, "there were people like myself who didn't even know Peter Reilly." His wife, Dorothy, adds that "I only met Peter the day before his mother was killed. I was at Marion's house and she was on the telephone saying, 'Yes, Barbara, yes, Barbara,' because Peter was there and his mother was calling. I didn't think much about it. He just struck me as a nice, quiet, little boy. Then a few days later we find out that he's supposed to be a murderer."

"What got me right away," says Murray, "was that he hadn't been given a fair deal. I wasn't sure that he was guilty or not guilty, but I knew his rights had been violated. When I took a personal interest, trying to prove things to myself, I couldn't figure any way that he could be guilty. Then when I talked to Peter and found out how naive and gullible he was, well, I could see what had happened. At that point you get mad. You figure you have to do something."

At the beginning there were impromptu meetings in both Falls Village and North Canaan, in private homes and public halls. Within a few weeks after Peter's arrest a formal group came into being that everyone referred to as "the Committee." Meetings were held once a week and often in the Methodist Church parish house that had been Clint Roraback's home. Attendance fluctuated between ten and twenty-five people and more when Peter's high school friends took part. Although husbands like Mickey and Murray Madow, Aldo Beligni and Bill Dickinson were devoted to the cause, along with Father Paul, the women outnumbered the men. "Peter was the same age as our own kids," one woman said. "If this could happen to him then it could happen to them."

Many of the meetings were discouraging rather than inspiriting: No one was sure how to proceed. Money was needed for Peter's legal expenses and pledges of money were required for the $50,000 bond to get him out of jail. The bondsman's fee of $3,600 seemed attainable, but finding the

$50,000 security in property, stocks, bonds and bank books was not so easy.

None of the participants was wealthy. They were not people with particular influence or important connections. They could only hope that enough people like themselves would see things their way. If they could not get fifty people to pledge $1,000 each, then perhaps a thousand people willing to pledge $50 each could be found. They learned that most people prefer not to get involved in matters as controversial as a murder case.

Peter was grateful for the support he received. "All people that have written to me make me very happy," he wrote in a letter that was read aloud at an early committee meeting. "I must have been the happiest person in the world when I found my home town and people from the surrounding towns were behind me."

Peter was happy at times, but he was more often depressed or "just numb." He was to spend 143 days in the Litchfield jail, including the Christmas holidays, before enough money was raised to post the required bond in late February of 1974. Many of those days behind bars he came close to sinking into despair.

Bob Erhardt, who had befriended and protected Peter in his first weeks in Litchfield, was moved to a state prison in mid-October. In a letter some time later, Erhardt said:

I recall coming back to my cell after lunch one day. I was sitting on my bunk and I was getting ready to write some letters. When I looked up Peter was standing there. I told him to come in and sit on the bunk. He did and when I looked at him he was all flushed. I asked what was wrong but he didn't say a word. The tears were running down his cheeks. Being the emotional slob that I am I reached out and put my arm on his shoulder. I told him that it would all work itself out for him. After a couple of minutes he fought to get control of himself and he managed to do so. His eyes were puffy and red, like this had been going on longer

*than just the couple of minutes in my cell. I suggested
that we go play some cards or ping pong. Pete's face
lit up and he gave me a halfhearted smile.*

*One other time I saw Pete in his cell reading let-
ters and again crying. For the life of me I cannot see
how anyone would think that Peter showed no feelings
about any of this. There were many times that he tried
like hell to remain calm about things but you can bet
he was fighting hard to give this appearance. He was
in with men that didn't care if they were in jail or not
and I'm sure he fought hard to make it look like he
could handle it. If he had let his guard down and had
a breakdown, most of these guys would laugh him off
the block. Convicts are very cold in most cases.*

Litchfield, however, was too small and old-fashioned to
be as oppressive as a giant penitentiary. The warden was
reputed to be a decent man and the guards encouraged to
live up to the front-door sign that said THROUGH THESE
PORTALS PASS THE MOST <u>PROFESSIONAL</u> CORREC-
TIONAL OFFICERS IN THE WORLD. Peter found that he
had supporters on the inside as well as outside. Several of
them, signing themselves "Concerned Inmates," wrote to the
Waterbury Republican a few days after his arrival to express
their "deep concern and sympathy" and to charge that Peter
was being "cruelly treated." They said that he was "kept
locked in a cell approximately 6-by-4 feet, with no light and
a white bucket for a toilet," and that he was allowed to leave
his "dungeon" only an hour a day and given food unfit for
children.

The newspaper sent a reporter to the scene. The headline
on the resultant article read "PRISON LIFE OF REILLY NOT SO BAD."
The reporter noted that Peter had fish sticks, clam chowder,
parsley potatoes, lima beans and ice cream for his Friday
lunch and that he was seen "sitting on a bench in a fair-sized
common room watching television with a half-dozen other
men. One man was reading the *Waterbury Republican*, which
we don't like to think is cruel and unusual punishment."

True, the story said, Peter had been confined to his cell
for the first few days to determine whether or not he had any

special medical or psychological problems, but after that he had "the run of the common room, with its TV set, game boards and gymnastics equipment from 6:00 A.M. to 11:00 P.M." The section of the jail for persons awaiting trial had no lights or individual toilet facilities, unlike the cells for men serving sentences, but this only mattered for seven hours a night when the men were supposed to be sleeping.

The building, dating back to 1811 and facing the courthouse across the Litchfield Green, is an almost charming antique. Surely the jail is one of the few in the world that share a wall with a bank.

Peter found that everything in jail is done according to rules. Mealtimes were seven, noon and five, and he had to go to the mess hall whether he was hungry or not. Two blasts of the buzzer and a command on the loudspeaker meant that the inmates had to stand in their cells for a head count.

Except for attorneys and clergymen, visitors were limited to members of the "immediate family" who were eighteen years of age or over, and they could only enter the jail on Saturdays between 1:00 and 4:00 P.M. Warden Brownell was overwhelmed with visiting requests from Peter's well-wishers, especially his high school friends. He had to turn down almost all of them; although, since Peter had no immediate family, he permitted three sets of surrogate parents to visit on Saturdays: the Belignis, Dickinsons and Madows. Father Paul was a frequent caller.

Peter's only complaint, apart from being confined in the first place, was that he was prevented from having his guitar. He wanted to practice now, as never before, because music— and the experience of being a member of a rock band—had been his greatest pleasure in the last two years. Without music he felt punished as well as detained.

One reward of imprisonment was the chance to hear real-life cops-and-robbers stories. This was better than television and more authentic than James Bond. Peter's convict friends taught him about prison life as well as card tricks and new forms of gambling. He learned how contrabands like marijuana came into the jail, and he was told to keep his mouth shut around an inmate named McAloon. The man was a recognized "squealer," and had been known to give false testimony to help himself. Peter was advised by one jailhouse lawyer to "do your time; don't let your time do you."

Placed in the main cell block after two weeks in the ancient boundover section, he did a lot of reading, in and out of his cell. He became fond of paperbacks about crime and the law, and discovered a new hero, trial lawyer F. Lee Bailey, after reading his book *The Defense Never Rests*. He read about Bailey's encounters with New York's famed medical examiner, Dr. Milton Helpern, not knowing that Dr. Helpern would one day come to his defense.

Some of Bailey's observations were disheartening. About a man named Edgerly, Bailey said he "had been arrested and indicted simply because no other suspect could be found, and because it was politically expedient to come up with *some* solution to a frightening crime. . . . To the public, mere arrest implies solution—the general feeling being that the law enforcement agencies have done their job, and the trial is just a game. And the American people do not equate jury acquittal with innocence."

Bailey said of another client that "he had the wrong attitude from the beginning; he suffered from the delusion that because he was innocent he would be acquitted. . . . Ideally, police should have a continuing interest in determining a man's innocence. But expediency dictates otherwise."

And of the celebrated Dr. Sam Sheppard, Bailey wrote, "When I started speaking on Sam's behalf, a police officer in Cleveland had told me: 'If Sam Sheppard is innocent, I don't want to know it.' I was coming to realize how many members of Ohio's power structure felt the same way."

Peter had always enjoyed playing games with his mother. In prison he had many hours each day to play chess, poker, gin rummy, cribbage and other games. "I played a lot of Ping-Pong as well," he says, "but the funny thing is that I always lost to Bob Erhardt. I think I only beat him once. He showed me no mercy." What he did not realize was that Erhardt, at least initially, was deliberately trying to make him angry.

"I'd give Pete twelve points," Erhardt relates, "and then I'd beat his ass off. I got on him pretty heavy. I did everything I could to get a rise out of him. You want to know why? I was looking for a streak of temper because he was supposed to have gotten mad at his mother and killed her. I had to be sure he wasn't conning me. I've seen thousands of convicts and I know all the games. But I couldn't get him mad. There wasn't any temper. Anybody can browbeat that kid; he just takes it. He's a country bumpkin and he's the purest S.O.B. I've met. He's got nothing to hide. And every time he'd talk about his mother, he'd say, 'It's too bad you never met her.' "

Just to break the monotony of prison routine Peter attended a few Alcoholics Anonymous sessions in the jail. "I know it's hard to believe," he says, "but that was the first time that I really understood that my mom was an alcoholic. I knew she drank a lot but I just never thought of her that way."

At Housatonic Valley Regional High School in Falls Village, Peter was much on the minds of Principal Edward Kirby and Assistant Principal Richard Alto. Barbara Gibbons had telephoned them dozens of times during Peter's three years at the school. "Some of the calls were not as rational as they might have been," Kirby says, "but she was truly interested in his welfare."

Dick Alto remembers the time she insisted on a meeting, with Peter present, "so that she could motivate him about his reading. She really put him down in front of me, saying he doesn't try, he doesn't read. When I finally persuaded her to leave I said to Peter not to worry about it because she had been pretty rough with him. I expected him to say something against her, but he never did. Never at any time did he speak ill of her to me. He just said, 'Hey, Mr. Alto, she's right! I don't read as much as I should.' I thought it was marvelous the way he defended her."

Kirby, Alto and Peter's teachers made arrangements to provide books, school materials and homework assignments so Peter could carry on his senior-year studies. Permission had been granted by Warden Brownell. Peter tried to apply himself to his schoolwork, but his worries and the distractions were too great. "It just didn't work," he says. "It wasn't the same thing as being in class."

In the meantime, students at the high school had voted to stage a benefit rock concert starring Rick Beligni's band to raise money for Peter's defense. Many students wrote to him and the messages from some of the girls must have given him new confidence in his prowess with the opposite sex. Susie Gleason in Kent said that "I bet as soon as you come back to school you'll probably be kissed to death by all the girls. That's something to think about, isn't it?" Eddie Dickinson said that "I want you to know that the WHOLE SCHOOL IS ON YOUR SIDE." Another close friend wrote, "Boy, I bet you're horny as a castrated rabbit, with no women. But around here times are getting so bad that you're doing better than me."

The mail Peter received could not help but give him a sure feeling that people really did care about him. Eleven days after the murder, Elizabeth Tyburski sent two petitionlike documents that expressed "our deep concern in your time of trouble." They were signed by no less than seventy-four Falls Villagers.

Cousin June wrote from New Jersey to say that "it is fantastic to see the people who came to your side. Nothing but raves about you from everyone. . . . Your friends are fantastic, Peter, simply and completely beautiful loving people. . . . I know this nightmare will be over for you soon. Know that you give *us* inspiration by being the swell guy you are even through these bad times."

And Marion Madow: "You know, Doll, you have our family and the Belignis too. You're loaded with loving parents. . . . We are all with you every minute of the day. You are my last thought at night and my first in the morning. What you are going through is unfair but because we are human beings life deals us some awfully bad times. Perhaps it is to make us strong for the good times. I must admit, though, this is something unbelievable, like something in a book or movie, but it is happening."

East Canaan is a part of the township of North Canaan. The Madows of Locust Hill Road and the Belignis of Furnace Hill Road were among the few hundred families living in East Canaan, but until the Peter Reilly case the parents scarcely knew each other, even though their sons were good friends.

The Madows were among the very few Jewish families

in the area while the Belignis were part of the large Italian community. Aldo Beligni was a familiar figure in Canaan and surroundings. Mickey Madow was a salesman of industrial equipment who spent considerable time traveling. Both wives were clever and energetic. In addition to raising her three children, Jean Beligni kept the books for the well-drilling business and Marion Madow was the office manager and bookkeeper for her husband's business while raising her two sons.

Both families reacted in the same forceful way when Peter's troubles began, but the Belignis were Canaan insiders while the Madows were outsiders, though they had moved into the area nearly a quarter century before. "You can live here for fifty years," Marion says, "and it's still not the same as being born and bred in Canaan. We're accepted all right, but we've never been in the inner circle." She grew up in Queens, New York, while Mickey was raised in a part of Harlem that was then a Jewish and Italian neighborhood. His father, an Orthodox Jew, was in the horse-and-stable business. Mickey's brother Murray, the horse dealer, led the way to East Canaan during World War II. Their parents followed, then Mickey and Marion, who had married in 1947, moved to Lakeville and later built their house in East Canaan. With so few Jews in the area, says Marion, the family lost a good deal of its cultural heritage: "Our boys grew up Gentile."

In contrast, Aldo Beligni and his wife, Jean, the daughter of Sam Speziale, a popular barber, were hometown folks who were intimately involved in the church and social life of the Italian community. Jean Beligni was a lively, spunky woman who came out fighting for Peter instantly because she knew him well. During the Hartford interrogation Peter described Aldo Beligni as "the only person I've ever met who's totally honest." Jean Beligni, who says of her husband that "It's a privilege to be married to that man," was impressed by Peter's respect for Aldo's practice of old-fashioned virtues. And she delighted in the way he cared for Gina, her seven-year-old daughter.

"I knew that Peter was one of the gentlest human beings there is," she says, "and I had seen how he reacts when he gets mad. There was one incident when he hooked up his amplifier and it wouldn't work, and when he called the company it had changed names, and so on. I could tell he was furious. My son would have put his fist through the wall but Peter, he says, 'Is it okay if I go up to Ohler's and get a can of beer?' He was gone for longer than I expected so I asked him what happened. He said, 'Well, I drank my can of beer instead of bringing it home because I know Mr. Beligni doesn't drink and maybe if Gina saw me with a can of beer she'd think less of me.' And this from a terribly angry boy!"

In his letters from the jail, Peter addressed both the Belignis and the Madows as "Mom and Dad." Both families were ready to give him a home, but Jean Beligni was concerned that all the excitement about the case might be bad for little Gina. All agreed that Peter would go to the Madows but, of course, he would see a lot of the Belignis.

"Mrs. Madow and I were talking today," Jean Beligni wrote to Peter, "and I finally figured out why you picked the Madows and the Belignis. How many kids can have Yom Kippur, Hannukah, Christmas and Easter?"

The fund-raising activities for Peter were impressive for their fervor but discouraging in the results. There were high hopes at the beginning that required dollars could be raised, but the money came in slowly in tens and hundreds. The security pledges for Peter's bond amounted to only a tenth of the $50,000 required.

"Our whole trouble, Peter," Mrs. Beligni reported, "is that everyone is working very hard, but none of us has a great deal of money so we have to raise it the best way we can. The two Strattman girls from up the street stood in the lunch line this week and collected money, raising $58 from the kids at the high school. They brought it to Miss Roraback today. So please, dear Pietro, don't get discouraged. . . .

"It is a very slow process but this week we are sending appeal letters to every name in the phone book, including Winsted, Canaan, Lakeville, Salisbury, Sharon and Kent. We have some people lined up who are going to type envelopes for us and the stationery and stamps are being donated. Pretty terrific, huh?"

The mailing asked for contributions "in the name of justice and on behalf of young people all over." The response was disappointing, however. Bea Keith wrote Peter that she had placed a jar in Kauttu's Drug Store on Main Street, with the sign "HELP PETER REILLY TO GRADUATE." She said $22.32 had been collected so far.

Mrs. Beligni told Peter that "We had another dance last night and we made about $125 after expenses. Mr. Madow and Aldo went up to the stage halfway through the dance. Mr. Madow thanked everyone for coming for you and told everyone you said hello. It was a very nice little speech. All the 'Mother Hens' got teary eyed and all the kids cheered. So you see, Peter, everyone is still behind you even though things seem to move slowly now and then."

Jean Beligni also told of her efforts, like those of others, to persuade Peter's godmother to help him: "I have written to Auntie B and have talked to her on the phone. I really can't figure out why, but she certainly isn't being cooperative. I know the police have talked with her a couple of times and I really think she is worried about any problems that could arise because she was sending you and your mom money while your mother was collecting welfare. I think she figures that if she just sort of backs off into the background people will forget about her, which is exactly the opposite of what is happening."

Two detectives drove to Toronto soon after the murder to talk to Barbara Sincerbeaux about her relationship with Barbara Gibbons and Peter Reilly. Upon her return to her New York apartment, she went to the Canaan Barracks with an attorney for an interview that lasted at least four hours. According to John Bianchi, she told the police that she had been helping Barbara Gibbons in order to get her back on her feet, encourage her to work and be a better mother to Peter.

Bianchi said of her meeting with police, "She was cooperative, of course, but she played no part in this case. Her reasons for not assisting are her own, but I would assume that if you'd been helping somebody for twenty years and the help hasn't been, perhaps, appreciated, or anything like that, that finally I suppose she might have seen that something like this might have happened and she was just finished with it. What she wished to do with the survivor of this mother and son was her own personal business, but I am certain that she was just finished with them."

Bianchi added that "I, myself, never spoke to her, but I'm told she's very attractive, very much of a lady." He said he doubted the police had taken a statement from her—despite the length of her "visit." Bianchi was aware that she was a woman with good connections. He said that Senator Abraham Ribicoff's Hartford law office had telephoned him before the Reilly trial, on Sincerbeaux's behalf, to ask whether she would be called as a State's witness. He told them that he doubted it. She did not, in fact, testify for either the State or the defense in the trial.

Barbara Gibbons' cousin June had known of Barbara Sincerbeaux's close relationship to Barbara and Peter for many years. "I telephoned her several times after this thing happened," she says, "and I asked her to help Peter but she wouldn't. I felt that she was scared to death. She said her brother was a lawyer and that she had been advised to keep out of it." Other persons who contacted her felt that she wanted to help Peter, but her anxiety about the Sincerbeaux name being publicized in a sordid murder case kept her from doing so.

Auntie B did write four brief letters and a Christmas card to Peter while he was in jail. In her first note, on October 9, she said that "I am thinking of you, every minute," and in December she spoke of her ill health and recent surgery. "I am sure you are disappointed not to hear from me but please understand circumstances beyond my control prevented it."

On November 7, 1973, Peter was escorted from the jail and across the Litchfield Green to the Superior Court building to appear before a grand jury. Thanks to his supporters, he was better dressed than he had been at the time of his arrest. He wore a tan sport jacket, red turtleneck sweater, dungarees and tan-and-black shoes. In the courthouse he learned that he would sit through the grand jury deliberations without his attorney present. Judge Armentano denied motions by Catherine Roraback that she be allowed to be present and to have a stenographic record of the session. The eighteen-member grand jury began its work at 10:30 A.M. State's Attorney Bianchi had seven witnesses at hand for questioning by the grand jurors, but only four testified. Three were policemen. Dr. Ernest Izumi revealed what the murderer had done to Barbara Gibbons. Lieutenant James Shay, Sergeant Timothy Kelly and Trooper Bruce McCafferty described the events of the murder night, the questioning of Peter and his confession. In the late afternoon the grand jurors returned a "true bill."

> The Grand Jury of the County of Litchfield by this indictment accuses Peter A. Reilly of Canaan, Connecticut, of the crime of Murder and charges that at the Town of Canaan, on the 28th day of September, 1973, the said Peter A. Reilly, with intent to cause the death of Barbara Gibbons of Canaan, did cause the death of Barbara Gibbons, by slashing her throat, breaking bones in her body, and inflicting stab wounds all in violation of Section 53a-54 of the General Statutes of Connecticut.

Peter stood before the judge and voiced his plea of "not guilty," and asked to be tried by jury. Then he was taken back to jail.

The county sheriff, William Menser, commented that "This is the longest session we've had and the fewest witnesses." The headlines announced "JURY INDICTS REILLY FOR MOTHER'S MURDER," but Peter was prepared. He had learned that grand jurors usually respond like a rubber stamp when the prosecutor lays a case before them. They hear only witnesses for the State, none for the defense. The story will be different, his attorney assured him, when the case goes to trial—if it goes to trial. Because of the involuntary quality of the confession, the case seemed as if it might be thrown out of court altogether. That, at least, was what Catherine Roraback was aiming at. Her first action was taken immediately after the indictment when she filed a Motion for Discovery and Inspection that sought, among other things, copies of any admissions or confessions made by the defendant, copies of evidence obtained by the police and "any and all exculpatory information." The first of many efforts to obtain from the authorities information that might assist in establishing his innocence, Catherine Roraback's motion signaled the beginning of what would prove to be a struggle every inch of the way.

The grand jury indictment had the effect of affirming the contention of the police that Peter was the murderer. The main business at hand became the construction of the case against him. Thinking that Peter might have had an accomplice, the police briefly considered other Falls Village youths. One teenager, who would be linked two years later to the fingerprint on the back door of the cottage, was questioned at length by the police after they found that he had left town the day after the murder and remained away for a week. He was given a lie detector test in Hartford and denied any involvement in the Gibbons murder. The police decided that he was telling the truth and released him.

The State Police reacted vigorously six weeks after the killing when Elizabeth Mansfield, a Falls Village real estate agent, discovered a black wallet in the tall grass surrounding a vacant house that she owned on Route 63, about four hundred yards south of the scene of the murder. Mrs. Mansfield, one of the very first citizens to help Peter, was amazed to find that the wallet contained a driver's license and other papers belonging to Barbara Gibbons. There was no money, however.

Ultimately, the police determined that this was the wallet that had been stolen from the Gibbons' cottage two weeks before the murder, but, initially, they considered the possibility that it could have been the wallet that had disappeared after the killing. If so, the murderer—either Peter Reilly or someone else—might have thrown it away after extracting the money. And he might have thrown away other things too: perhaps the murder weapon or bloody clothing. Lieutenant Shay called out the troops. More than a dozen officers scoured the area for clues but without success. The discovery of the wallet was kept secret from the press and the public for nearly half a year, and went unmentioned in the Reilly trial.

* * *

A sign in the entrance hall of the Connecticut State Police headquarters reads "A judicial system exists not only to exonerate the unjustly accused but to convict the guilty. The latter no less than the former is an important means of protecting the innocent members of society."

In the early days of the Reilly case, Peter's supporters believed the police would recognize and admit their error in deciding so swiftly that Peter was his mother's killer as soon as they acquired more information about the murder. Only gradually did they realize that a commitment to Peter's guilt had been made. Jean Beligni remembers how it was: "Everybody was telling me that they were trying to find out that he was innocent, but they weren't. And we began to hear through the grapevine—you know, what different policemen and different people say—that we were stupid people and that Peter was conning us and taking us for a ride. He was supposed to be a mental case and he was so clever that he could play these head games with us and fool us into believing that he was innocent."

What disturbed Peter's supporters more than anything else was the determination of the police to prove Peter's guilt by portraying his life with his mother as one characterized by incessant argument that led inevitably to violence and death. Citizens who had willingly described the Barbara-Peter relationship in interviews with the police found that the troopers were not satisfied. They were asked the same questions again and again. Rosalind Ryan, for example, who had known Barbara and her son since Peter was a baby, said, "I was interrogated by detectives on three different occasions. There were three different men. They put me through all these questions and I finally told the third one, 'Look, I'm not changing my story. Don't come around again.'"

Some people were disturbed about the way their statements were written up by the troopers who questioned them. "When I read my statement," Marie Dickinson recalls, "I said to the trooper that this isn't what I said. He said, 'Well, it's more understandable that way.' I told him I would sign it only if he wrote it the way I said it."

According to her son, Eddie, "The police were really ripping at me, trying to get me to say that Peter and his mother used to fight like cats and dogs. The cop would slip it right in when you least expected it, getting me to say a yes or no."

The police succeeded in accumulating a number of statements that portrayed mother and son as having argued often and in profane language. Yet even the most vivid statements failed to picture Peter and his mother in violent combat. Geoff Madow, when questioned by Trooper Mulhern, said that Peter and his mother argued "quite often" and used strong language, but "During these arguments I never saw either Barbara or Peter strike one another or throw anything at each other."

A man who had once lived in the cottage with Barbara and Peter was questioned by the police four different times. "They kept on asking about Peter's fights with his mother and stuff like that. They wanted to know everything about how Peter hated his mother except that I *know* he didn't hate her. The whole idea is ridiculous. They told me they knew he was guilty. I said I couldn't believe he had killed Barbara because he's such a skinny little kid and he's squeamish about blood. 'Oh no,' they said, 'he's become a big rough boy.'"

One consequence of the State Police methods and careful secrecy was an eruption of "suspicions and fears in the region," as a *Lakeville Journal* article expressed it. Under the headline "POLICE WORRIED BY PUBLIC ATTITUDE IN MURDER CASE," Lieutenant Shay was quoted as saying that the public suspicions were regrettable. "I would like to assure them that we have acted only out of a sense of duty and in a professional way." He said that he thought the rural setting of the Gibbons murder had something to do with the public reaction. "Most people here aren't used to this type of major investigation. They are unaccustomed to its proportions."

In the next issue of the *Journal*, a Falls Village resident, Mildred Monahan, replied to Lieutenant Shay:

The groups that have formed to come to the aid of Peter Reilly have been formed from a desire to ascertain that this "rural-town boy" does get all the justice that our Constitution assures each individual.

It was due to the knowledge that (1) this young man is alone and until a year ago would have been considered a minor, (2) companions, students, former teachers and Cub Scout den-mothers, all think of this young man as one who is in a very bad and most regrettable position and needs possible financial and definitely moral aid, (3) and most of all, it is true that a feeling of the "unknown" has caused concern.

Never a wish to obscure justice or hinder the proper progress of fact-finding. But what are the facts? No one has an inkling as to the findings in the case. It is the ever-present air of mystery that causes the speculation.

One day Mickey Madow, who would no longer allow Geoffrey to go alone to the police barracks, when asked to make further statements, said to Lieutenant Shay, "I'm going to give you a suggestion, Lieutenant. Take it as you wish. You know you really ought to invest in a little public relations work. Let the people know what you're doing."

"This is police work," Shay told him. "We don't have to explain to the people what we're doing."

8 ▪ BEFORE THE TRIAL

PETER REILLY: I wish I could start all over from being born, you know.

SGT. KELLY: Well, Peter, once you get this out you're going to be reborn. All right? Except you're going to be reborn at eighteen. All this hassling and bullshit and it's all going to be in the past. You know. The nagging bits and all this.

PETER REILLY: Ya. Well, that's something I lived with all my life. Not with her, but my grandmother—

SGT. KELLY: All right. But that's what I say—

PETER REILLY: —nagging.

SGT. KELLY: —you're being reborn.

PETER REILLY: What time is it?

SGT. KELLY: Six thirty. No. Ya, Six thirty.

PETER REILLY: I keep thinking I got to be home so my mom doesn't miss me.

In a turn-of-the-century book, *The Bench and Bar of Litchfield County*, the story is told of a judge who could scarcely contain his temper as he listened to the case being tried before him. When he charged the jury, he said, "Now, gentlemen, if you believe this incredible story you will convict the prisoner, but if you do not believe it you must acquit him." The prisoner went free.

The special pride of Litchfield County, Connecticut, and of the town of Litchfield in particular, is its history of concern for justice and the emancipation of the oppressed. A person falsely accused of murder might consider himself lucky to have as the setting for his legal struggle an enlightened New England village that is famed as a fountainhead of the law in America.

Litchfield is the county seat, a place, more than two and a half centuries old, that has been called "New England's finest surviving example of a typical late-eighteenth-century New

England town." It has an abundance of handsome, lived-in, pre-Revolutionary homes. The center of Litchfield, including the courthouse and the jail building, has been designated a National Historic Landmark. It is the site of the first law school in America and the first institution in the United States for the higher education of women. Ethan Allen, Harriet Beecher Stowe and Henry Ward Beecher were born here.

Tapping Reeve established the law school in 1774. For the next fifty-nine years the little Litchfield institution prepared 1,100 young men for the bar, including two Vice Presidents—Aaron Burr (Tapping Reeve's brother-in-law and his first student) and John C. Calhoun—and a host of Supreme Court justices, U.S. senators, governors and other notables.

Like most of his neighbors in Canaan, half an hour's drive north, Peter Reilly had spent little time in Litchfield—he knew it as a place one passes through on the way to somewhere else. Peter's town was earthier, more ethnic, more working class; Litchfield was mannered, moneyed and conscious of its Christmas-card beauty. The two towns were indifferent about each other—until the Reilly case came along. Then a number of Canaan people virtually commuted to Litchfield. They could be seen swarming like starlings on the courthouse steps early each morning, waiting to be admitted to the courtroom.

Peter and his most loyal supporters became familiar figures around the Litchfield Green, especially after he was out on bail and able to join his friends during court recesses. The Canaan crowd could often be found at lunchtime in the friendly Village Restaurant just down the street.

The original Litchfield courthouse was built in 1751. The present courthouse went up in 1890, after two others had burned to the ground, and was made as fireproof as possible. In a town of wooden homes and brick buildings, it is a small fortress with thick walls of gray granite trimmed with white blocks. A tall clock tower surveys the Litchfield Green.

The courthouse has none of the impersonal grandeur of its big-city counterparts. Only a few cases each year attract much public notice. Spectators at proceedings as controversial as Peter Reilly's are able to become acquainted with the court functionaries and to feel at home in the place.

On December 12, 1973, soon after ten in the morning,

Judge Anthony Armentano, a former lieutenant governor of Connecticut, arrived in Superior Court to conduct a pretrial hearing. "The next matter to come before Your Honor," said State's Attorney John Bianchi, "is docket number 5285, State versus Peter Reilly."

Three newspapermen and a magazine writer were present in the courtroom as well as a small contingent of Peter Reilly's supporters, including Cousin June and one of her sons. Peter had been brought over from the jail and his handcuffs removed. To those who had not seen him before he looked more like a victim than a villain. His friends said that he must have gained a few pounds after eating regularly in the jail, but he still looked scrawny in his knit shirt and slacks. His hair was long and scraggly; the prison system had not insisted on a crew cut. He was able to flash shy smiles when he caught the eyes of friends, but he knew that these were crucial days. At best, he would soon be free to go home and pick up the pieces of his life. At worst, he would spend many more months in jail and then go to trial—and maybe to prison.

Everything hinged on the confession. His attorney believed that his incriminating statements had emerged because of indefensible police tactics. In a series of motions Catherine Roraback asked for the suppression, as evidence in a trial, of a number of things including:

> Any and all statements, confessions or admissions, oral, written or recorded, taken from him, on the grounds that the same were involuntary, coerced, taken during and after the defendant had been in custody and isolated for a substantial period of time, and without having counsel present during his interrogation, and in violation of his rights to privacy, to be secure in his person, to due process of law, not to be compelled to be a witness against himself, and to counsel, all as guaranteed him by the First, Fourth, Fifth, Sixth, Ninth and Fourteenth Amendments to the Constitution of the United States

If Peter's "admissions" about slashing his mother's throat and jumping on her body could be kept from a jury, then the

State might have to drop the charges. Without the confession only bits and pieces of circumstantial evidence remained. Or so Peter's supporters surmised because they believed Peter's story. Others, less emotionally involved, thought that the authorities were unlikely to have singled out Peter so swiftly as the murderer without hard evidence.

Roraback also challenged the makeup of the eighteen-member grand jury that had indicted Peter.

"It is not a jury of his peers," she insisted, "nor does it represent a cross-section of the community of Litchfield County." She argued that there were not enough single jurors, or females, or persons under age twenty-nine. The average age of the grand jury was forty-four. Not one was under twenty-seven; six were over fifty. All were married. Only six were female. Peter Reilly, she argued, is a student, but no grand juror was a student at a high school, college or other institution of learning.

With considerable passion she contended that a distinct "youth" class of individuals exists in American society and that youth and the older generations are engaged in what Erik Erikson has described as an "ethical dialogue." She spoke of a national crisis that "is particularly aggravated in the experience of youth—who feel most acutely the need, and inability, to 'participate meaningfully' in the life of the society. The *policy implications* of this situation for the judicial process and institutions of the country are clear. If a substantial number of youth are systematically denied the opportunity to serve on juries, as is their constitutional right, this will only exacerbate their feelings of disillusionment and distance from the dominant 'established' classes of society."

When the Superior Court resumed on the morning of the twelfth, after a brief recess, Roraback appealed for a further reduction of Peter's bond. She told the judge of the "extensive campaign" in the Canaan community and said $5,000 had been raised. She asked that the bond be set at that amount. John Bianchi, saying that "I don't think that there has probably been any prosecutor in the past fifteen years who has been more lenient on bond than I have," said that the normal bond for murder is $100,000. "I feel that a $50,000 bond is most lenient . . . where the offense is a very, very serious one."

Judge Armentano agreed with Bianchi: "The crime is a serious one, carries life imprisonment, and a man in this situation may be tempted by flight." The bond remained at $50,000.

The main business of the day was the presentation of four witnesses by John Bianchi to establish the validity of Peter's admissions to the police. All four were policemen: Trooper Bruce McCafferty, Sergeant Percy Salley, Lieutenant James Shay and Sergeant Timothy Kelly.

McCafferty, when asked to identify Peter in the courtroom, said, "It's the gentleman sitting with the red sweater." He told of sitting with Peter in his cruiser outside of the Gibbons cottage. He said that Peter had read his constitutional rights on a form before giving his initial statement. Both Bianchi and Roraback asked questions about the procedure and then the judge asked: "Was there anything about any conduct on his part that was unusual such as drinking or being under the influence of drugs or being emotionally disturbed, anything like that?"

McCafferty answered, "Didn't appear to be."

The judge: "No drugs, no alcohol, no emotional disturbance that you knew?"

"No."

"Anything about his physical appearance that didn't appear normal to you?"

"No."

Then John Bianchi had a question: "Was he crying, Trooper McCafferty?"

"No, he was not," the officer answered.

When Sergeant Salley took the stand and told of driving Peter from the house to the barracks some four hours after the discovery of the murder, Bianchi again wanted to know, "Was he in tears, Sergeant Salley?" Answer: "No, sir." Throughout the Reilly case the State's Attorney would put extraordinary emphasis on the fact that Peter did not weep and wail in the aftermath of his mother's death. He would bring out at every opportunity Peter's outward composure.

Bianchi asked Salley what else he could recall about the

ride to the barracks. Salley replied, "He told me he thought this was an interesting case."

Salley described how he presented Peter with his constitutional rights in the barracks. Then Lieutenant Shay, next on the stand, said that the first thing he did after returning to the barracks from the cottage "was explain to Peter that he had certain constitutional rights" and have him sign a waiver of rights.

The court recessed for lunch while Shay was on the stand. When it resumed, John Bianchi told the judge that reporters were present from three newspapers: the *Hartford Courant*, the *Lakeville Journal* and the *Berkshire Eagle* of Pittsfield, Massachusetts. He said he was concerned about the reporting in the press of evidence that may or may not be admissible in a trial, which could do irreparable harm to the accused. "It could create an inflammatory situation throughout the county where we have to select a jury against the accused." (A slip of the tongue, perhaps, but "a jury against the accused" is what he said.)

While the *Courant* and the *Eagle* had given the Reilly story "ordinary coverage," Bianchi went on, the *Lakeville Journal* had printed "practically a headline every week." He did not say in court what he was angrily saying in private: that the *Journal*, his local weekly, was handling the story almost as an exposé of police tactics. One four-column front-page headline read "FRIENDS SAY POLICE KEPT THEM FROM PETER REILLY." The article began, "Friends of accused murderer Peter Reilly contended this week that police kept them in the dark and obstructed their efforts to communicate with the 18-year-old Falls Village youth in the two days following discovery of the body of his mother, Barbara Gibbons."

The State's Attorney asked that "the balance of the hearing on the motion to suppress in this case be held in chambers." Catherine Roraback said that she would never join in or make a motion to exclude the press or the public in a trial or a pretrial hearing: "I think that it goes to the whole question of the manner in which our judicial proceedings are conducted and part of the whole history of our Constitution."

The judge spoke to the members of the press in chambers. Perhaps they would be willing to give assurances, he said, that they would not print anything that was highly prejudicial. He asked if they would be willing to censor themselves. Greg Erbstoesser, a young reporter for the *Journal*, and Joseph O'Brien, a veteran crime reporter for the *Hartford Courant*, said they preferred to leave any deletions to their editors. Stanley Moulton of the *Berkshire Eagle* and Joan Barthel, a writer for *New Times* magazine, seemed more willing to decide the contents of their writings themselves.

Back in the courtroom, Judge Armentano spoke of the constitutional right to a fair trial by an impartial jury and said, "It's been my experience that the press has been extremely cautious in this regard and has used good judgment in reporting news coverage from the court, and they always have a desire to not only maintain a free press but also to maintain a fair trial. I am going to deny the motion to have the matter heard in chambers. I don't think it is necessary, at this time. I can rely on the judgment of the press."

Judge Armentano's decision came as a great relief to Peter's supporters. They had been counting on the pretrial hearing to unleash some of the mysteries of the case. They knew from Peter that he had been interrogated under such conditions that he had confessed to a crime he had not committed. By rejecting the State's Attorney's move to exclude the press and public, the judge, they felt, was upholding their right to know. The *Lakeville Journal* reported that "Mr. Bianchi's bid to ban the press and public from court was said by courtroom veterans to be unique in this region. Joe O'Brien of the *Courant* said that in 15 years of covering trials in the area he could not recall such an occurrence."

During the pretrial hearing, John Bianchi was probably unaware of the true nature of the interrogation that had produced the confession. As he would say himself, at the close of the first day, "I have only heard a small portion of the tapes. I don't know what's on the tapes." He had accepted the confession at face value. He did not know how susceptible Peter was to suggestion. He may not have understood that the police had convinced Peter that he must have had a memory lapse. Presumably Bianchi did not realize how consistently Peter had qualified his statements with phrases like "I could have" and "I'm still not sure."

The situation was peculiar and paradoxical. The defense wanted the confession and other statements by Peter suppressed so that a jury could not hear them while at the same time it was willing to let the public know the facts. The State wanted a jury to hear what Peter told the police while seeking, at least at this stage, to conceal the facts from the public.

The fair trial–free press issue would surface again when the trial judge placed restrictions on reporting. A number of instances in other U.S. courtrooms of judges gagging the press in criminal cases would occur in the next three years. In a New Jersey murder trial the judge ruled that "Nothing which takes place outside the presence of the jury is to be printed." Press organizations said the ruling made a mockery of the Constitution. After a Nebraska judge imposed heavy restrictions on pretrial publication of various items in a sensational murder case, including matters of public record, the U.S. Supreme Court, on June 30, 1976, ruled that a judge may not, except in the most extraordinary circumstances, forbid publication of information about criminal cases even if the judge thinks such an order will help assure the defendant a fair trial by preventing prejudicial publicity.

Mr. Justice Brennan, in his opinion, said this:

Commentary and reporting on the criminal justice system is at the core of First Amendment values, for the operation and integrity of that system is of crucial import to citizens concerned with the administration of government. Secrecy of judicial action can only breed ignorance and distrust of courts and suspicion concerning the competence and impartiality of judges; free and robust reporting, criticism, and debate can contribute to public understanding of the rule of law and to comprehension of the functioning of the entire criminal justice system, as well as improve the quality of that system by subjecting it to the cleansing effects of exposure and public accountability.

When the pretrial hearing continued in midafternoon, after the judge spoke to the reporters in his chambers, Lieutenant Shay and Sergeant Kelly described Peter's interrogation. Roraback asked Sergeant Kelly if he remembered Peter asking him, "Do you think we could quit now? I am so tired, I think I am saying things I really don't mean." And if he recalled Peter saying, "I wish I wasn't tired, because things come into my head and go right out again." Kelly did. The tapes themselves were not heard until the following day.

Three of the five tapes were played, beginning at 10:37 and, with a break for lunch, ending at 4:36 in the afternoon. Like figures in a stone frieze, everyone sat silently, almost motionlessly—the judge, lawyers, sheriffs, reporters, spectators and Peter. Cousin June remembers her impression: "You could hear Peter falling and falling into the trap and you wanted to reach out and catch him."

The tapes played were confined to the interrogation in the polygraph room. The dialogue ended at the point where Sergeant Kelly suggested to Peter that they move across the hall into a more comfortable room. Although everyone in the courtroom would have preferred to continue the hearing the next day, Judge Armentano said he would be too busy. His explanation gave a little insight into the life of a Superior Court judge: "We're getting into a heavy domestic relations schedule. I have twenty-four pages on short calendar tomorrow, thirty divorces on Tuesday, thirty divorces on Wednesday, short calendar on Thursday. So this case will have to come to Hartford . . . but I do know I have nineteen sentences the first day so that would be out." The hearing, in fact, would not resume until a full month later.

One immediate effect of the playing of the tapes was to strengthen Peter's backers in their conviction that he was utterly innocent of his mother's killing. They heard on the tapes what they wanted to hear—his frequent assertions that he was not sure of what he was saying—just as the police heard what they wanted to hear. The journalists present were not about to conclude that Peter was guilty or innocent, but their stories emphasized the confusion of his admissions. The *Hartford Courant*, for example, highlighted Peter's belief that he might have raped his mother and Sergeant Kelly's response that there was no indication of rape. Joan Barthel, who had taken down the taped dialogue in shorthand, was so astonished and appalled at the interrogation that she began a magazine article that would have a major impact in the case.

No journalist had been allowed to interview Peter. His only public statement until then had been a "Thanks from Peter Reilly" letter in the *Lakeville Journal* expressing his appreciation for the support he was receiving and giving his Christmas greetings "to everyone who believes in truth and justice for all."

As luck would have it, however, a reporter for the daily *Torrington Register* interviewed Peter by accident. Roger Cohn, a Long Islander fresh out of Yale and just starting his newspaper career, had sat in on some of the pretrial hearing, though his paper had not, as yet, assigned him to the Reilly story. He went to the Litchfield jail to do a feature article about what spending the Christmas season behind bars was like. He was given permission to talk to several prisoners, one by one, in a small room in the maximum security section. "I was quite surprised," he told me later, "when a guard brought in Peter. He was wearing a white T-shirt, tan chinos and white sneakers. He seemed to me pathetically thin."

The guard had made a mistake. The warden asked Cohn afterward to omit from his article any matters that might prejudice the trial. Peter told Cohn that this was the first Christmas he had ever spent without his mother. "It's really a bummer to be in here," he said, "especially when it's a holiday and I know somewhere out there my mom's murderer is running around." When asked why he had signed a confession, he replied, "You'd be surprised what they can make you do."

In a recollection of that interview, Cohn writes:

Peter told me he'd received a lot of Christmas cards from friends but that he wasn't expecting many visitors for Christmas weekend because jail regulations prohibit visitors under 18. The Madows had already given Peter a Christian medallion as a Christmas gift. Peter said the medallion was "the only thing I really wanted this year." He talked quite a bit about how he'd been reading the New Testament and reassessing his values since coming to jail. He said the whole experience had made him reconsider what the truly important things in life are. He said he planned to be baptized a Catholic.

"When I lost everyone close to me, I started looking

for a friend," he said (obviously referring to his mother as "everyone close to me"), "Now the only ones I can trust are my closest friends and Jesus Christ." Peter's religious kick is another example of how impressionable he is. It seemed to me that Peter was doing what was expected of him, acting out the role of the innocent martyr who turned to religion, playing the part of the good youth left alone in the world who finds companionship in Christ. I'm not saying that Peter didn't mean what he was saying. I just think his religious convictions were shallow and were based on his confusion at that time. I didn't hear Peter talk much about Christ or religion after he was released from jail and during the trial.

Before the murder Peter had not been baptized and had rarely been to church. His mother was scornful of organized religion. Her next-door neighbors, the Kruses, belonged to an evangelical faith and held regular prayer meetings in their home. Barbara would occasionally sit in "just for laughs," sometimes with Peter in tow. Peter had never really thought much about religion—until going to jail. Then he began receiving many letters exhorting him to put his faith in God. Father Paul came to see him frequently and his influence was strong. Peter's gratitude to the Belignis flowed over into an appreciation of their Roman Catholic faith. In her letters to him, Marion Madow, to show that her family was behind him all the way, spoke of the strength of those who had suffered persecution: "The more people put you down, the harder you fight to get up." In another letter she said, "Keep your face happy and remember how many prayers are being said for you every minute of every day. Catholic ones, Protestant ones and Jewish ones. Now, how can you miss?"

Sometimes Peter felt sorry for himself because the worst possible things had happened to him, but wonderful things were happening as well.

His Christmas, for example, was happier than he expected. Jean Beligni convinced Warden Brownell to let her son Rick bring his Frosty Morning band to the jail to play for the prisoners just before Christmas. The warden not only agreed but said, "You might as well bring Peter's guitar and let him play." The rock concert was such a success that the inmates sent a petition to the warden asking for a return engagement in January.

"I went along to help set up the equipment," Paul Beligni recalls. "The warden was at the front desk and he sent out some of the prisoners without supervision to carry the stuff. I guess he knew they wouldn't take off. Pete was out of practice, but he went up on the stage with the rest of them and they let him take as many solos as possible. It was a pretty informal jail, it seemed to me. A nice place to visit, but I wouldn't want to live there."

On Christmas Day, the Madows, Belignis and Dickinsons all came to visit, and their boys were permitted to come along for the first time. Spirits were high. The pretrial hearing would be concluded in mid-January. If the judge ruled in his favor and if the prosecutor, unable to use the confession, decided to drop the case, Peter could be free in a matter of weeks.

The January 16 hearing before Judge Armentano was held in a Hartford courthouse. Four state troopers and County Detective Sam Holden testified. So did Mickey and Marion Madow and Cousin June, who told what the police had done and not done about communicating with Peter's relatives and friends in the aftermath of the murder. John Bianchi tried to show that the police had conducted the interrogation properly and that Peter's admissions of guilt were voluntary. Catherine Roraback, seeking to suppress all the incriminating statements, wanted to establish that the atmosphere of the interrogation was coercive.

After asking many questions about the recording of the interrogation and the custody of the tapes, Roraback appeared to be satisfied that they had not been tampered with. She was anxious to have the judge hear them in their entirety to get "the flavor, the background and the atmosphere" of the questioning. The judge decided that he would hear the remaining tapes in a few days, but outside of the courtroom, with Peter and his attorneys present. The reporters and spectators were disappointed. They had looked forward to hearing the remaining tapes.

John Bianchi maintained that "The best evidence, Your

Honor, is the testimony of the people who were there, and not reliance on the electronic gadget." Some of the police testimony, however, showed how faulty the version given by officers could be. Trooper Jim Mulhern, for example, could not recall that Lieutenant Shay had threatened Peter by saying, "We'll take you and we'll lock you up and treat you like an animal," even though he was in the same room when an angry Shay shouted these words.

Although she would have been more successful with a transcript of the tapes, Roraback found her notes of key interrogation passages were useful to show the difference between what Peter had tried to say to the police and what the police put into the confession that he finally signed. When questioning Lieutenant Shay, she asked about the confession and learned from him that "I took Trooper Mulhern aside and I told him what points should be in the statement." Roraback then asked, "And were you aware at any time, Lieutenant Shay, of statements of Peter Reilly to the effect that he wasn't sure of what he was saying?"

An objection by Bianchi saved Shay from answering. In her questioning of Trooper Mulhern, however, Roraback had more satisfaction.

Q: Do you remember Peter Reilly saying to you, "I don't know what to do, Jim. I'm still not sure of what happened. The only things I'm positive about, she was on the floor. And what I had in my original statement."

A: I believe so, yes.

Q: And do you remember Peter Reilly saying to you, "It seems I'm being pushed into things. He won't allow me to say what I think."

A: He may have said that. I don't recall it.

Q: And do you remember him saying to you, "I'm not sure. Can you say in the statement, the entire statement I make, I'm not sure of?"

A: Yes.

Q: Did that get put in the statement?

A: I believe it is in the statement.

Q: I'm referring now to State's Exhibit E, the four
pages [the confession]. Could you just tell me where
it appears in there?

A: It isn't in the statement, ma'am.

As a Canaan resident and as a friend of Peter and the
Madows, Jim Mulhern's testimony was expected to be as
scrupulous as possible, but his words were puzzling and disturbing to those who followed the case closely.

Mulhern had been on the force just six years. The Reilly
case was already a problem for him, and one day it would even
get him into a shouting match with Mike Wallace of CBS television when the *60 Minutes* team turned up in Canaan. (Yet
months later, when a writer spoke to him on the telephone,
he growled that "I couldn't care less" about the Reilly case or
what people wrote about it. "It doesn't interest me.")

In the early months after the murder he was known to be
concerned about what people thought of his performance in
the first days of the case. According to Joan Barthel in *New
Times* magazine, Jean Beligni said to him:

Ten years from now, Jim, will you let what happened to
Peter happen to your Michael? What you did to Peter is
morally wrong. You did your job, but your job could have
been tempered with a little bit of humanity. You should
have said to Peter: "You're in serious trouble, you ought
to get a lawyer." Jim Mulhern, you have a face that would
charm the angels, you have a blue jacket on, and I wouldn't
trust you as far as I could throw my stove. In one weekend you tore down things I have spent thirty-nine years
believing and seventeen years teaching my children. Now
I'd rather have my child say, "I want to be a hippie bum,"
rather than, "I want to be a policeman."

The outspoken Mrs. Beligni remembers that Trooper
Mulhern replied, "You've got to believe that we're trying as
hard to prove Peter innocent as we are to prove him guilty."
Her comment many months later: "Well, I don't believe him.
And after what I saw at that trial, I'll never believe him."

In the Hartford courtroom, when questioned by Bianchi, Mulhern said that during Peter's interrogation he was assigned to get some food for Peter. After purchasing a ham-and-cheese sandwich, cupcakes and a can of Coke from vending machines, he related, he entered the room where Peter was sitting alone and said, "Hi ya, Pete" or "Hello, Pete." Then he claimed that this dialogue took place:

REILLY: Hello. Are you ashamed to know me now?
MULHERN: What?
R: Are you ashamed to know me now?
M: Why should I be ashamed to know you?
R: Because, well, because I did it. I killed her.

Mulhern said that this took him by surprise and he did not immediately respond. But when he asked, "Why?," Peter said he was confused and didn't know. Then he quoted Peter as saying, "It seems that we are going into it now. We are going into it now, and it seems to be coming back to me." (Mulhern also testified that he only asked Peter one or two questions at this time. The tape transcript shows that he asked at least thirty questions. A reasonable supposition is that he was sent in by Shay, at just this point in the interrogation, in the hope that Peter would finally give details about the murder to his Canaan friend.)

Catherine Roraback had heard the interrogation tapes and she could not recall this dialogue at all. And for good reason: It was not on the tapes. Yet when she questioned Mulhern, he said that the tape recording had resumed "as I came through the door, I think it started after the door had been shut, or swinging shut." And he said that Peter asked the question about being ashamed "as I was putting the food on the table."

What the tapes reveal is that the following was the actual conversation:

MULHERN: Ham and cheese. Can you eat that?
REILLY: Yup.
M: Cupcakes.
R: Thank you very much.
M: What's happening?

R: Oh, I'm messed up.

M: You're messed up?

R: But it's getting all together and I really understand why.

M: Why what?

R: Why everything happened.

M: What do you mean, why everything happened?

R: Well, I mean, the way I was brought up. Things like that.

M: Oh, ya.

R: Background and—

M: Why, what happened?

R: Well, it turned out I did it.

M: Did what?

R: What happened to my mother.

M: You killed your mother? How did you do that?

R: Well, we haven't really gotten into it. I mean, like I've been digging and getting little things. And, I don't know. We've been digging and digging and digging. . . .

The tapes also reveal that as they continued to talk, Peter spoke about feeling terrible about it and said, "You knew me and you wouldn't expect me to do something like that." When Mulhern asked if he cut his mother's throat, Peter said, "That's right, I can remember it, yes." Also, much later, after further questioning by Lieutenant Shay, Peter remarked to Mulhern, "Do you feel bad about knowing me now that, now that you know what I've done?"

The difference between what Peter actually said to Mulhern, as revealed by the tapes, and what Mulhern claimed Peter stated is slight: It is almost a toss-up between Mulhern's version ("I did it. I killed her") and what actually was said ("It turned out I did it"), although nowhere in the entire interrogation did Peter use so strong a word as "killed" or "murdered." Mulhern could easily have admitted that his version was just his "best memory" of the actual dialogue, but he did not. He insisted under oath both at the pretrial hearing and at the trial that the unrecorded "I killed her" statement had taken place immediately before the conversation was recorded. State's

Attorney Bianchi not only accepted Mulhern's version, but he made it one of the pillars of his case against Peter. He would impress upon the jury repeatedly, and especially in his closing argument, that Peter Reilly and Jim Mulhern were the best of friends (an exaggeration) and that "Mulhern was taken aback" when Peter "blurted out" his admission about killing his mother. Said Bianchi to the jury: "If there was ever a confession, that, ladies and gentlemen, was it, right then and there. 'Because I killed her' to his good friend, Jim Mulhern."

John Bianchi, in short, made plain that he was willing to make use of the most dubious kind of testimony to have his way. If Mulhern and Bianchi are to be believed, then this is the sequence of statements during that portion of the interrogation:

1) Mulhern enters the room with the food. Immediately, Peter asks, "Are you ashamed to know me now?" and he confesses, "I did it. I killed her." Mulhern asks Peter why and Peter gives a rambling explanation.

2) Then Mulhern (as the tape starts recording) offers Peter the ham-and-cheese sandwich and the cupcakes. "Thank you very much," Peter says.

3) Mulhern asks, "What's happening?" Peter speaks of being messed up and after a while says, "Well, it turned out I did it."

4) Mulhern is surprised. "Did what?" he asks. Peter says, "What happened to my mother." Mulhern, apparently forgetting that Peter had confessed the killing just moments ago when he walked in the door, says, "You killed your mother? How did you do that?"

After the pretrial hearing, Bianchi and Roraback set to work on briefs for Judge Armentano as he considered the defendant's Motion to Suppress. Bianchi emphasized the reading of Peter's constitutional rights on four occasions and portrayed both the written confession and his verbal admissions as entirely voluntary. Trooper Mulhern, he said, had not even been questioning Peter when the defendant "blurted out" his admission that "I killed her."

In her brief, Roraback cited the U.S. Supreme Court's standard, from *Rogers v. Richmond:* "whether the behavior of the State's law enforcement officials was such as to overbear petitioner's will to resist and bring about confessions not freely self-determined." Quoting from another case that "coercion can be mental as well as physical," she emphasized that "The repeated promises of sleep, food, psychiatric help (after persuading him he needed it), and friendship and trust (Lieutenant Shay especially on this), all added to the totality of circumstances which clearly lead to the conclusion that any statements or confessions made were involuntary."

Judge Armentano decided for the State. In his ruling of February 13, 1974, he said, among other things, that "There may have been some repetitive, suggestive questioning, or the planting of ideas, by members of the State Police" but not enough to deprive the defendant of due process. He found that "The statements, confessions, or admissions of the defendant to members of the State Police were voluntary and were not the product of any improper threats, inducements, promises or coercive conditions." The Motion to Suppress was "denied in its entirety."

Although some who heard the tapes were overwhelmed by the image of an immature and hopelessly confused adolescent struggling to keep awake and to keep from breaking down in the face of constant questioning by four policemen, Judge Armentano had a different reaction. "The tape recordings," he said, "provide ample evidence that the defendant is a very intelligent, articulate, calm, alert individual who displayed no emotional anxiety, distress or despondency during his interrogation."

The judge's decision was a blow to Catherine Roraback as well as to Peter. She had clearly emphasized the constitutional issues involved, and, according to expert sources, had argued them well. Judge Armentano's ruling was announced on February 19, in Litchfield's Superior Court, and Roger Cohn remembers that Roraback was "visibly upset, brushing off reporters' questions. I felt that Roraback had been expecting to win that motion and thus the case. Without the confession, there probably would have been no trial." Jury selection began the very next day.

* * *

Despite all of their efforts, Peter's supporters had not been able to raise the money for his bail. Then a magazine that almost no one in Canaan had ever heard of appeared nation-wide with a picture of Peter Reilly and Barbara Gibbons on the cover above the words, "DID PETER REILLY MURDER HIS MOTHER?" Although *New Times*, as a newcomer to the news-stands, had only a modest circulation, the article by Joan Barthel had an extraordinary impact because of its liberal use of dialogue from the interrogation tapes. It was a stun-ning piece of journalism.

To many readers, the interrogation sounded like a brain-washing episode from a spy novel. They were touched by the way Peter's Canaan neighbors had gone to his aid and moved by the writer's remark that "I thought of all the eighteen-year-olds who must be lying around the Tombs and other city jails, unnoticed." The magazine published the address of the Peter Reilly Bond Fund and letters with checks began to pour in from all over the United States. They included $15 from a Pennsylvania couple on Social Security and $5 from a Louisiana prison officer, who wondered how many of his own prisoners might be innocent. A Connecticut resident, who sent $100, wrote: "I was very moved and hor-rified by the story of Peter and all the events surrounding his mother's death, not the least of which is the behavior of the Connecticut State Police in this matter."

But nothing could match the drama of the telephone call received by Jean Beligni. The caller was a woman in New York who had known nothing about Peter until she read the *New Times* account of the murder, the arrest and the fund-raising campaign. "How much do you need?" she asked. Jean Beligni said that they were still $44,000 short of the $50,000 required for Peter's bond. The lady said that she would send the money. All of it. Forty-four thousand dollars. As soon as she could.

She was Jacqueline Bernard of Riverside Drive, Manhat-tan. Although she asked that she remain anonymous, her name was eventually published. She had posted bond before: for her own eighteen-year-old son when he was a civil-rights worker in Mississippi. She said that the money for Peter was in memory of her mother, Louise H. de Sieyes, who had spent the last twenty-five years of her life in Washington, Connecticut, a beautiful town south of Litchfield. "My mother would never have done such a thing," she remarked to Barthel. "She was very New England, very reserved; everything about her was muffled. There was great fear, in women of her generation, of stepping out of the structure. But she had many vibrations of conscience and a deep concern for fairness, which she expressed so little."

The offer was widely described in Canaan as a miracle, but some said that it was too good to be true. Two weeks went by without any sign of the check. People did not realize that Peter's unknown benefactor needed time to make arrangements at her bank for a $44,000 loan, using stocks as collateral. The check arrived just as jury selection for the Reilly trial began in Litchfield.

Peter's supporters went into action. The $50,000 bond was posted during the morning session of the Superior Court on February 21, four months and three weeks after Peter's arrest. Marion Madow, who had agreed to act as surety for Peter, signed the bond papers. State's Attorney Bianchi said that he knew the Madows personally as "good, solid citizens" so he did not object to the granting of the bond. Judge John A. Speziale asked Marion Madow if she had any doubts about what she was doing. "None whatsoever," she said.

As he left the courtroom, Peter was asked by reporters what his plans were. He said he wanted to go back to school and graduate with his class, but he doubted that he could if there was going to be a trial. He spoke of the mail he had received from all over the country as a result of the *New Times* article. He said that many letter writers told him that they "couldn't believe the police worked as they did" and that they thought "the kind of tactics used by the police were left way back in World War II or with the Communists." Peter was more outspoken than the journalists expected, especially in light of restrictions that Judge Speziale was placing on comment about the case. But Peter, for all of his outward joy, was angry about what had happened to him—and the fact that his mother's murderer had gone scot-free. "I won't be happy until they catch the right person."

Peter went to lunch at the Village Restaurant with his lawyer, the Madows and several classmates. The Correctional Center's food, he announced, was tolerable but nothing like the hamburger, french fries, coleslaw and Coke that he had before him. He returned to the jail for half an hour to pick up his belongings and to say good-bye to his inmate friends. His new celebrity status was confirmed by the crowd on the sidewalk by the entrance. A young man on a bicycle stopped and asked a reporter, "Who the hell's in there anyway, Al Capone?"

As Peter joined Geoff Madow in the backseat of a car to be driven away from Litchfield he could hear the farewell yells and whistles of the men who remained in jail. When they passed through Falls Village he saw the little house where he had lived—the place was dark and empty, without life. His arrival at the Madow house in East Canaan is remembered by "Nan" Lavigne, the grandmother in the family: "When he got out of the car he came up to the door with his box of things. He didn't even have the courage to come in. I said, 'Peter, what are you standing out there for, honey? This is your home now.'"

The house filled with people, including Reilly Committee members who had never met him before. The telephone rang constantly and Peter placed a few calls of his own, including one to Jacqueline Bernard. When the boys went down to the basement where the band equipment was kept, the parents sat in the living room and talked about the coming trial. They were sure that Peter would be found not guilty. They worried about the money that they were going to have to raise for legal costs and to pay the interest on the $44,000 loan: over $400 every month.

If Peter had his own worries, he did not show them that first weekend. He played his guitar, called on friends, repaired a car and attended an early Sunday mass at St. Joseph's. He was enjoying his freedom but he was not truly free. He could not plan his life. He could not stray far from the Canaan area. He was an accused murderer, and John Bianchi had said that he would ask for a sentence of twenty-five years to life.

The State of Connecticut seemed to be trying to destroy

him. His mother's life had been taken, by someone, and now the State was taking from him what worldly assets she had left behind: the $704.29 she had squirreled away in a Massachusetts savings bank, the 16 cents found on the floor of the cottage after her murder, the Corvette (said to be worth $1,900) and the furniture ($1,105). Barbara's books were appraised at $50 and her jewelry at $43.

Altogether, the Gibbons' estate was reckoned at exactly $3,899.80, but Peter got only the 16 cents, which he kept as a remembrance in a plastic container, and a few personal belongings of his mother. After various creditors were paid off, the probate judge ruled that the balance of the estate, $461.13, be paid to the State of Connecticut as a reimbursement for the welfare money that Barbara Gibbons had collected.

Peter Reilly was, in short, broke, jobless and out of school as well as under arrest and facing a murder charge, but at least he had help from friends and even strangers, and plenty of it. Even with his closest supporters, however, he sometimes wondered whether they had doubts about his innocence and misgivings about going to his aid. One day, when the trial was underway, a Committee member drove him to the courthouse and was startled to hear Peter ask, "Are you sure you feel okay being alone in a car with me? I'm supposed to be a murderer." She hired him to babysit her children that very night to prove her faith in him.

Peter had no doubts about the Madows' faith in him. Peter addressed Marion and Mickey as "Mom" and "Dad." Art and Geoff were "my brothers." Hannah Lavigne, Marion's mother, was "Nan," his grandmother. An ordinary, seemingly unremarkable middle-class family living in a comfortable but not opulent single-story-with-basement house in a small town had made a place for Peter.

The Madows assumed a responsibility that would take a heavy toll of their energies and financial resources for four years. Mickey and Marion would give up many days of work and hundreds of hours of their spare time. They drove Peter to innumerable legal appointments. Their telephone bills were astronomical. By being Peter's surrogate parents they placed themselves at the center of the controversy. An exhausting and often alarming experience, it would cost them the friendship of some even as they won the admiration of others.

But for all that, the Madows felt that Peter was a gift to them, an adornment to their family. They were outgoing people; he was shy and quiet. While they brought him out of his shell, he had a way of introducing a note of harmony to their boisterous family life. According to Hannah Lavigne, "Peter was a little boy when he came here. Now he's a man. He's one of us now. This whole thing that happened to him, it's good coming out of bad. He lost his mother, he went to jail, but he came into our family and grew up as a good human being."

They all liked the way Peter so obviously enjoyed being part of a whole family. "This is nice," he would say to Marion, "coming home and smelling chocolate cake in the oven." But there was something else they liked and marveled about. Never, ever, did he speak of his good life now in contrast to his not-so-good life before. "Peter loved his mother," Mickey says, "and his memories are happy memories. As far as he's concerned, he lived in a palace."

9 ■ "A STRANGE LITTLE WOMAN"

SGT. KELLY: Jesus, Peter, I think you had a real problem with your home life.
PETER REILLY: I did, definitely. I hated being home.
SGT. KELLY: That's too bad.
PETER REILLY: That's why I'd go to my friend's house for a week or two weeks and then I'd miss home. I'd go home and I'd be there for an hour and I'd hate it all over again.
SGT. KELLY: Mm.
PETER REILLY: I'd miss my mom. And, once I was back there I'd have to get out again.

Barbara Gibbons was a character. Depending on who is speaking, she was a nut, a kook, a screwball, a bitch, a brain, a troublemaker, a practical joker, a bad mother, a good mother. She was a showoff, a loner, a lesbian, a gutsy female, a voracious reader, an expert on trivia, an amusing drinking companion, a drunk. She was a person of great independence, a welfare cheat, a lost soul, a tomboy turned she-devil. She was someone "who wanted to get her name in history."

In Falls Village and the other hamlets in the Canaan area, Barbara Gibbons had a certain value as a conversation piece. She was much discussed, both before and after that bloody Friday night in September 1973. She was impossible to ignore, as one old friend has put it, "because she was always up to something—some kind of mischief." She delighted in concocting hoaxes, creating a commotion or doing something to discomfit her more straitlaced neighbors, "She would do anything for a laugh," Peter says. She would also do anything to avenge what she deemed a slight. She once drove five hours from Falls Village to Manhattan and back to Falls Village to let the air out of the tires of a car owned by a woman who had annoyed her.

State's Attorney John Bianchi called her "a strange little woman." Aldo Beligni describes her as "one of the most intelligent women I have ever met, interesting as could be, but there was some quirk in her mind that made her do things she shouldn't have done." Neighbor Timothy Parmalee remembers her as "unpredictable. Like one minute she'd be nice to you, then you'd see her an hour later and she'd be in a terrible mood." Michael Parmalee says that "she always seemed like a good mother, but as the years got on, the older Peter got, the more possessive she became."

Many people in Canaan thought the worst about Barbara Gibbons and wondered "how it was possible for a woman like that to bring up a boy as nice as Peter." They remember her today as a "dreadful person," "a real wino," and as a woman who "went around with her usual pissed-off expression, looking as mean as any hard-nosed dyke." Yet her former employers at the Cole Insurance Agency in nearby Cornwall knew her as one of the most delightful and capable persons they ever hired. Or fired.

Without question, the once beautiful and vigorous Barbara Gibbons went into a sharp decline in the last decade of her life. She became a person to avoid. "You never really wanted to have a conversation with her," comments a Falls Village shopkeeper, "because she would start an argument with you." A Lakeville artist, who once lived in Falls Village and who had seen the changes in Barbara Gibbons, says, "Men were embarrassed around Barbara. She talked to you in such a way that you didn't know how to handle her. She was one of those people who tried to put you on the spot. She said what she thought. But I had the feeling that she was very lonely and that she was sorry when I wouldn't respond when she challenged me in a conversation. She was really a tragic, tragic figure, and she was bright enough to understand her own tragedy. She was a candidate for suicide except that she had to take care of Peter. In a way though, because she was self-destructive, she really was committing suicide in those last years."

Jean Beligni, knowing that this book would be written,

said that "I hope you will be kind to her because she had many good points. She was a compassionate person. There was the time my son was lost on the mountain all one night and Barbara came over and spent the entire night consoling my little daughter and telling her stories. That part of Barbara nobody knows."

Kenneth Carter says of her, "Barbara might have offended some people, but I knew her as someone you could really talk to. She was one of the few people in that area who had a decent education.

"When I first took over the Texaco station she was hesitant about coming over because of some trouble she had had with the previous operator, but eventually she came over to buy cigarettes, and then she'd stop by a lot just to talk. If she'd been drinking too much you could tell because she'd get a little sloppy in her speech and mannerisms, but she was still very pleasant. We'd talk about what was going on in that area, which in some ways was a real Gothic nightmare, full of the weirdest characters, and she would tell me about the latest murder mystery that she was reading. We had discussions about photography, for example, because she was a good photographer. She used to take pictures for her insurance company magazine. When things got too busy she would run the pumps for me or take care of the station if I had to take off for an hour or two. Now here was this woman that some people in the village thought was absolutely horrible, but I could trust her to go to the bank for me with an eight- or nine-hundred-dollar deposit when I wasn't able to get away from the station.

"I really liked her even though she once told me that she didn't like men. She was expressing a sexual preference. The idea some people have that she was sitting outside of the cottage under the light soliciting men is preposterous. I never saw anything like it.

"There was another side to her, though. She bragged about blackmailing someone in connection with her welfare payments. Apparently this was one of her lesbian friends and she had it all down on tape. I don't know whether the tapes actually existed or whether she was just trying to impress me with her control over people, but she bragged about those tapes. The thing is, she was extremely bitter about life in general. I remember saying, 'Barbara, why are you so bitter?' She wouldn't say, but one of the things that passed through my mind after the murder was that Barbara's getting a big kick out of this situation except for Peter's being involved. She would have appreciated the mystery. Peter didn't do it, so who really did it? She would have laughed her head off at the way the State Police screwed up the whole case."

Ken Carter's observation about how a ghostly Barbara Gibbons might have reacted to her own murder coincides exactly with something Peter once said: "My mom would have enjoyed this case if it weren't for the fact that the police decided right off that I was guilty instead of really investigating what happened. She would have enjoyed seeing the cops running around trying to figure out who killed her."

An investigator for the Connecticut Department of Adult Probation, assigned to write a presentence report in 1974 on Peter Reilly and his personal and family history, remarked on the contrast between Peter's standing in his hometown and his mother's. "The defendant himself enjoys a very good reputation within his community. He is generally described as a polite, respectful and sincere individual. Due to this fact, this case has become quite controversial in his community as many of the people feel that he was not capable of committing this crime. Regarding Barbara Gibbons herself, it appears that she was never capable of establishing a meaningful relationship with anyone. She was considered by her family to be a black sheep and was, for the most part, ostracized."

Her reputation, he wrote, "certainly leaves a lot to be desired. She was reported to be an alcoholic and quite promiscuous. Also, her relatives have stated that in her early years she was known to have had lesbian relationships. She was a person of above-average intelligence who had a large fund of general knowledge. While she was an attractive woman, she was not at all feminine. She enjoyed activities which are generally thought of being masculine in nature."

Her cousin Victoria, who had gone to school with her in

England and knew her as a lively teenager in New Jersey, says that "Barbara was a terrific person, but there were times when she was so exasperating that you could have wrung her neck." When, at last, someone repeatedly slashed that neck instead of merely wringing it, Victoria would react to the news as one who knew her cousin only too well. "Oh, Barbara," she thought, "what have you done now?"

In the weeks, months and years after the murder, Peter Reilly would be asked over and over again to explain his mother. "She was just a different person," he would say. "Maybe people in the country weren't ready for a person like my mother." She looked down on her neighbors; they looked down on her. She thought of herself as intellectually superior, with good reason; they saw her as morally inferior, with good reason.

The attitude of at least a few members of the Connecticut State Police was one of "good riddance to bad rubbish." The suggestion was that the killer did the community a service. Concluding that Peter Reilly was the murderer was easy because, as one trooper put it, "How could anyone live in the same house with that woman and *not* blow up one day?" John Bianchi told a number of people that he was "not surprised" that Peter had finally lashed out at his mother.

She died without dignity and was disposed of like surplus state property. The murder was bestial; her tortured body was further dehumanized by the necessary autopsy. Photographs and color slides of the bloodless corpse and its multiple wounds, external and internal, would be displayed in a courtroom.

When she died, Barbara Gibbons had few friends to mourn her. She had antagonized so many people that her best friends were Peter's friends. People of her own generation were put off by her unorthodox behavior; those of Peter's generation thought she was "a cool person" or "a really dynamite lady." One young man remembers how Peter was proud of her for "being a little different from everybody else."

Arthur Madow knew her in her last years as well as any of Peter's friends. "I really liked Barbara. She was great. It's hard to find the right words. She was weird in a way but she was cool. She was far-out. To understand her you'd have to listen to someone who is under thirty describe her as well as someone over thirty. She liked having me and Geoff and the rest of the kids over at the house. The conversations we used to have! They were unreal. She knew everything. You could bring up some subject, like eighteen-inch guns for the *Bismarck*, and she'd know all about it. You couldn't hold a candle to her in any argument. She was sharp! Superintelligent! Her ideas were different from most people. She made fun of all the poor slobs who weren't doing the things she was doing. But she wasn't happy and she was drinking a lot, though the funny thing is that in all the time I was in their house I never saw her drink. She could be pretty well tanked up, but she didn't drink in front of us.

"Sometimes I'd call up there to talk to Pete and when she'd answer the phone she'd say something like, 'Dr. Goldfarb's, obstetrics' or 'Los Angeles city morgue: you kill 'em, we chill 'em.' Stuff like that. She wasn't your conventional mother, but she was a lot of fun. But toward the end she must have been lonely a lot of the time.

"It's ridiculous, all this talk about her sex life, how she was supposed to be entertaining a whole line of men. I was down there a lot for at least a year and a half before she died and I never saw anybody around there. Pete and I could be driving around late at night, raising hell, and we'd stop by to grab a can of iced tea or something and she'd still be sitting there under the light, reading a book. We never got hassled. We'd just take off again and she'd still be reading. She was probably reading some mystery book when she was murdered. That's why we never grieved about her so much, because, you know, I think she really wanted to die that way. I know it sounds strange, but I think she wanted to die and become a murder mystery, I really do."

Barbara Gibbons, in Peter's phrase, "read the Falls Village library dry." The breadth of her interests was a constant source of amazement to the librarian, Charlotte Kester, a Vassar graduate and a former English teacher. "Believe me, she was a brilliant woman with a razor-sharp mind. She knew her English literature. But she had a sharp tongue. She was impish. If she could say something satirical about someone she would. She loved to show how dumb people are."

Describing Barbara as a masculine-looking, short-haired woman with "smoky, very penetrating eyes" who enunciated beautifully, Mrs. Kester remembers Barbara joining the library ladies for afternoon tea. Then Barbara would go off and make fun of the little old ladies and their chatter.

"That's like Barbara," sighs Mrs. Kester. "She had a nasty streak. She really was a naughty person—without principle—but a lot of people didn't know her as we knew her in the library. Drink did not affect the workings of her mind, and it was a delightful mind. She might come into the library at ten in the morning and you could tell that she had been drinking, but she was coherent. She had a great deal of poise.

"Of course, she always spoke highly of Peter, except for his spelling, and she laughed about that. I remember her taking out *Tarzan of the Apes* in order to encourage his reading. The book was in bad condition and she said she was going to get Peter's godmother to buy a new collection of Edgar Rice Burroughs' books for the library, but I heard no more about it.

"There was never any hint that she didn't have love for Peter and take pleasure in him. I think she had built her life around him. It was a very happy relationship. She'd always say that she had to go pick up Peter somewhere or she had to go home because Peter was coming back to the house. She was devoted to him."

Few people in Canaan knew her personal history and they had good reason to doubt the few things that she chose to tell them. She was known to say things just to get a reaction. The greatest puzzle was her actual relationship to Peter Reilly. Was he really her son or was she raising him for another woman? Why did he have a different name? Who was his father? Was the father's name Reilly? Why had his rich Auntie B, his so-called godmother in New York, provided so much support to both Barbara and Peter? Why had that support stopped instantly and why were all appeals by Peter's friends and relatives rejected? And then the most crucial question of all: Had Barbara Gibbons and Peter Reilly enjoyed such a close, friendly, understanding and loving relationship that matricide was unthinkable, or was that relationship so sour, stormy and unbearable that mild-mannered Peter Reilly "exploded" during a sudden argument, as the State's Attorney would tell a jury, and savagely took her life?

At the time of her death, Barbara Gibbons was all the family that Peter Reilly had. He had never known his father or known anything about him. His grandparents were dead. His mother was shunned by her relatives. No one outside of the immediate community came to see them. Even his godmother maintained her distance, grudgingly mailing her checks to Canaan from New York, but no longer appearing herself. Peter's knowledge of family history and his mother's own upbringing was limited. Only after the murder would contact with his cousins and research for this book provide him with wider knowledge of his origins and his mother's own story.

In contrast to Peter's isolated and restricted upbringing in an obscure New England town, Barbara Gibbons—born in Berlin, raised in Britain, transplanted to America—was a transatlantic traveler as a child who had a swarm of relatives to visit on both sides of the ocean. Her early life was comfortable, stimulating and full of promise. She was bright, beautiful and resourceful. She was physically strong and courageous. The many dozens of photographs of her spirited girlhood and youth reveal the winsome, sometimes wild characteristics of a budding Amelia Earhart or Shirley MacLaine. The captivating images of young Babs, as she was known then, reveal a different woman from the pictures of an aging and careworn Barbara Gibbons in her final months.

A compact, well-proportioned natural athlete, she was a dark-haired brown-eyed girl. Her father, Louis Gibbons, was a well-traveled English businessman, living and working in his homeland at the time of Barbara's birth on November 20, 1921. She would have been born in England if her mother had not decided to visit her sister Rosa in Berlin to take advantage of a special form of child delivery performed in certain German hospitals. Or so goes the story Barbara related to friends.

Barbara Gibbons delighted in claiming that she belonged to three countries. Although born in Berlin, she came within the jurisdiction of the British Consul Service. The name on her birth registration in London is Barbara Consuelo Gibbons, though her middle initial on all other documents is V for Valerie. Louis Gibbons would address his daughter affectionately as "Barbara Valerie Consuelo." She automatically became an American citizen in 1939 when her father was naturalized some years after emigrating to the United States. Her Austrian-born mother was naturalized in 1954.

People in Falls Village remember Barbara's father was a classic Casper Milquetoast. Louis was "a gentle soul who had fallen on seedy days," says one acquaintance, whereas Hilda, in the words of a niece, "was a tough wife. She was tough on Barbara and she was tough on my mother and a lot of other people. She didn't hold anything back."

At the time of his death, Louis was a hotel night clerk. He died when he smashed his car into a tree. His employer suspected that "he had been nipping at my Irish whiskey." Hilda died a senile old lady in Florida who busied herself writing letters denouncing Barbara and urging Peter to avoid "rotten people, particularly women." She warned him, "Whatever else you do, for God's sake don't depend on people. They will let you down at the most critical moment." But in the early days of Hilda and Louis there were happy times and material success.

Louis Williams Gibbons was born in England in 1891, the son of Joseph Gibbons, a "general warehouseman," and Sarah Chapman Gibbons. He attended Owens College in Manchester and became so proficient in the Spanish language, eventually learning seven dialects, that he was sent for by the W. R. Grace Steamship Line in New York. He spent several adventurous years representing both the Grace Line and other British interests in Central and South America. A 1916 photograph taken in Guayaquil, Ecuador, reveals a trim, proper young Englishman complete with pince-nez, who had made himself at home in a foreign clime without, of course, stooping to go native.

Within the next few years, Louis Gibbons met Hilda King, a secretary at the Grace Line, during a visit to New

York. Four years his junior, she was an Austrian beauty, described by an old family friend as "a very feminine, Hedy Lamarr type." Her real name was Hildegarde Koenig, but it had been Americanized soon after her parents emigrated to the United States. She was a child of the times—one of seventeen children, but only three sons and five daughters reached maturity. Hilda's was an extraordinary family: talented and enterprising but quarrelsome and erratic. "To tell you the truth," says Cousin Victoria, "they were a little dotty. All of them. Wonderful people, of course, and some of them very successful, but they all had their peculiarities, every one of them."

Louis and Hilda married in 1920 and went to England to live. Barbara soon appeared and by the time she was ready for school they were comfortably settled in a fashionable residential section of Manchester, just across the road from a park and the exclusive Ladybarn House School. Barbara was precocious; she is said to have begun reading Shakespeare when she was four years old. Hilda and Louis enrolled her as a day pupil at Ladybarn House. The private school had just forty-eight girls and two boys. Uniforms were required and French was spoken. Soon afterward, Barbara's cousin on her mother's side, Victoria, came from America to live with the Gibbonses and go to school with Barbara.

"My aunt Hilda," Victoria relates, "was a tiny lady with a marvelous sense of humor and we had great times together—shopping and visiting antique and fashion shows. We were very close, Aunt Hilda and myself, but she and Barbara didn't get along at all. They were completely different, just as I was different from my mother. We should have had each other's mothers! Barbara was a very independent personality and anything she did was okay with my mother but not with Hilda. Hilda knew Barbara's capabilities and she was always carping at her to do better. That's the way it was. They kept the argument going for the rest of their lives."

The Depression brought an end to their affluent English life. Louis lost his job. They emigrated to America, taking only their best pieces of furniture, and moved in with Victoria's parents in Cresskill, New Jersey, a New York City suburb. Barbara was put in the fifth grade at the local public school. Hilda went back to work as a stenographer and Louis found employment in the city, humbling as it might be. For a while he ran an elevator in the British Empire Building in Rockefeller Center. He later became an export consultant and was able to resume his Latin-American travels.

For years, however, Hilda brought home the larger pay-check, especially during World War II when she became the treasurer of a boat company. Their marriage was unex-citing, and a member of the family recalls that Hilda, still good-looking, "had her own little escapades. She would go down the street to the telephone at the gas station to make her arrangements. She was no longer enamored with Louis and she was pretty bitter about the way his fortunes had gone down the drain, so I really think she ran around like a wild goddamn goose on the side."

Hilda and Louis dressed in style, set a good table, had friends over for bridge. In their new apartment in Engle-wood, New Jersey, and later on in the Bronx they kept things immaculate. Barbara rebelled against such a fastidi-ous and programmed existence. She hated the cleaning up, the shopping expeditions and the constant efforts to make a proper young lady of herself. In the family album there is a photograph of her dressed in a long print dress. She looks absolutely miserable. Then, as in middle age, she preferred to dress roughly for the outdoors. She was not an indoors person. When she was in the seventh grade she demanded that her mother buy her only boys' clothes.

Barbara Gibbons is remembered as someone who would take up any challenge—she swam across the Hudson River at age sixteen. "We were all buddies when we were grow-ing up," a New Jersey businessman relates, "and she was a devil. If there wasn't enough action she'd come down to my street corner in Cresskill with a .22 and shoot the goddamn street lights out, and then I'd get blamed for it. I remember the time she was holding a rifle and some idiot shot a bul-let right through the stock, but it never bothered Barbara at all. She was gutsy. You couldn't see her muscles because she was sleek-looking but, believe me, she was strong as an ox. She used to lift weights and put guys on her shoulders. At the same time she had a feminine build that you wouldn't believe. I mean, she was built! But as for sex, you never met anybody who was as standoffish as she was. You couldn't lay a hand on her. She just wanted to be one of the boys. I knew some guys who tried to make it with her; nothing doing. When we were seventeen or eighteen years old I introduced her to a friend of mine. We were all out swimming in a pond in the middle of the night. It was the perfect situation. I asked him what happened. Nothing. Then she met my nephew and they went out a few times together. I asked him how it went. No good."

Some members of the family say that Barbara had a physical problem, "a blockage," that made it impossible for her to engage in normal sexual intercourse, at least in her youth. The suggestion is that Barbara, although a tomboy, would have opted for a straight sexual life if she could have. Victoria's husband, who knew Barbara in her girlhood, believes that "she would have been positively ecstatic to have had a normal sex life, but when she found out she couldn't she went the other way." Later, when Barbara was a career girl working in New York in the 1940s, she would bring her girlfriends over to her cousin's apartment in New Jersey for overnight visits. "At first we didn't know what the story was," the husband says, "but when I realized what the hell was going on I took her aside and said, 'Hey, Barbara, nix on this jazz. Don't do it again.' And she never did." To which Victoria adds: "Every woman she came over with was well educated, well dressed, intelligent and interesting. There were many of them and they were wonderful to be with."

Barbara was placed in a special class for gifted children when she attended the Dwight Morrow High School in Englewood, New Jersey. The school even offered a course in photography. Barbara and a boyfriend saw their opportunity. They talked two girls into posing for nude pictures and then they sold the photographs. They were caught and given a scalding lecture. When Barbara graduated in 1939, a quotation from *Macbeth* was used as the caption for her yearbook photograph: "I dare do all that may become a man; Who dares do more is none."

* * *

The young Barbara Gibbons seemed to have the brains and the drive to carve herself an exceptional role in the world. In Peter's opinion, she could have excelled as a comedy writer for radio or perhaps as a photojournalist for *Life*. But she did not. Her thoughts and actions were often ahead of her time, but she never became a truly liberated woman.

"The drinking began when she was little," Victoria remembers. "My father was very, very angry with Uncle Louis because he would give Barbara sips of hard liquor. If only she had resisted alcohol and if only she had been able to get herself away from her mother, then I think she could have made a success of her life." The drinking did not become significant until many years later, but her inability to establish her independence was evident in her youth. She was a maverick by temperament, yet she remained at home with her parents for the first forty-four years of her life, even after Peter was born. They finally threw her out of the house in 1965, and even then she chose to live just a few miles away.

After graduating from high school, Barbara attended pre-medical courses at New York University, but dropped out after two years. That was the end of her formal education. She settled for a position with an insurance company.

Although the insurance business hardly seems the most exciting territory for a spunky young lady who would "dare do all that may become a man," the fifteen years that Barbara Gibbons spent with the Home Insurance Company were the most productive years of her life. They came to an end when she was raped in 1954 (if that is truly what happened), gave birth to Peter in 1955, and moved to Falls Village the following year to bring up her child in the country. Some good times, even idyllic times, were still to come, but Barbara's life had lost its promise.

She began work at the Home Insurance Company at its executive offices on Maiden Lane in lower Manhattan in July 1941 as a clerk in the Automobile Department. She did underwriting and accounting at the beginning, according to Barbara Sincerbeaux, a more senior Home employee who became her dearest friend and confidante. Barbara Gibbons found more room for her talents in the Public Relations Department a few years later. Sincerbeaux remembers that it was Barbara who suggested that the company's house organ, an employee magazine called *Homespun*, be revived. She won the editor's job and from then on she held a unique position within the firm. The job put her in touch with executives and ordinary employees at every level of the organization. She set her own schedule, moved about the company, wrote, edited, took photographs, found outlets for her sense of humor and helped organize parties and outings.

Barbara Gibbons' personal letters and papers include memorabilia from her *Homespun* days. They portray an image of a paternalistic insurance firm in the 1940s and 1950s, providing a way of life for its employees that extended well beyond office hours. The Home was home for many a white-collar worker. The social and athletic activities sponsored by the company's 59 Maiden Lane Club "for your enjoyment and participation" were numerous. The loyal, the lonely, the talented and the energetic could, for example, play in the company orchestra, sing with the glee club, perform in a drama, or play on the Home basketball team. Barbara's *Homespun* announced and reported the busy life at the Home as well as the routine business of personnel changes and social notes.

She would often make something amusing out of a routine item. For instance, "The Cashiers Department wishes a speedy recovery to Madeline Edson who was injured while vacationing in the Catskill Mountains. The area in which Miss Edson was hurt is spectacularly scenic."

For many of her friends, Barbara's sex life in those days remained a mystery. Her lesbian relationships, known to some, were tempered by her friendships with at least a few men. One was "Bobby" and for a while their romance seemed to be going somewhere. "Barbara and Bobby were part of a foursome and they all had great times together," an old friend relates. "They were very close, but it just didn't jell. That was the only time I ever saw Barbara's eyes even faintly glisten with tears."

She lives on in some memories as a lovely young woman who dressed neatly and smartly in slightly mannish outfits. She kept herself trim: "Barbara considered getting fat undisciplined." She was practical but spent her money freely—

perhaps so thoughtlessly that she could not afford to move away from her parents even if she wished to.

She was a versatile athlete, as much at home on the ski slopes and tennis courts as on a motorcycle. In later years she would often tell Peter about her motorcycling adventures. Her life on wheels had begun with bicycles and for a time she took part in long-distance expeditions, including tours of New England and a race from Long Island to Springfield, Massachusetts. When she graduated to motors, she began with a tiny paratrooper's vehicle and advanced to high-powered machines.

"She told me that she used to ride with a group of motorcyclists," Peter says. "They helped teach the Bronx police force how to hill-climb on ice. She once was with a group on a three-hundred-mile run in New York State that had her going through Sleepy Hollow at about two in the morning. She ran out of gas and they just left her alone in that place, waiting in the dark. There was a backup car with gasoline that was supposed to come along for emergencies. She wasn't scared, but she said she couldn't help but think of the story of the headless horseman. Another time on a motorcycle she had a front blowout. She flew across the handlebars and broke her nose. It was right across from some hospital so she dumped the bike and walked right over for treatment."

Louis, Hilda and Barbara Gibbons, while still living in The Bronx, had fallen in love with the small-town atmosphere of northwest Connecticut, perhaps during one of their Sunday drives into the country. In July 1950, Louis paid $7,500 for an old logger's cabin and one and a half acres of land on Johnson Road in Falls Village.

The dwelling was nicely situated on a dirt road, deep in the quiet of tall pines, only a few steps from a lake. Barbara, who seems to have been able to build anything, set to work expanding the little house and creating a rock garden. She was able to indulge her passion for automobiles. According to a local shopkeeper, "Barbara loved cars and she'd spend most of her weekends working on cars. When she first turned up around here, before Peter was born, she'd arrive in the village wearing a dress on a Friday night and she'd drive off wearing a dress Sunday night, but while she was in town she'd go around in coveralls just like a garage mechanic. She'd come into my place for coffee, all covered with grease and oil. She was anything but feminine."

By 1955, Barbara Gibbons was thirty-four years old, still single and still living with her parents. She preferred the company of women and she was a success at her job at the Home Insurance Company. Her weekends and holidays in the Falls Village countryside were times of pleasure and adventure, especially when her city friends came up to visit. Barbara Sincerbeaux, who would become one of the heads of Personnel at Home, not only was Barbara's best friend but she was liked and respected by Hilda and Louis. Barbara's business and social lives had become so entwined that Sincerbeaux would come to play the role of Lady Bountiful to the Gibbons family. Although she has since described the whole business as just "my favorite charity," her contributions as a kind of fairy godmother would, in time, provide the necessities of life as well as occasional luxuries to both Peter and his mother in their time of poverty.

To many people in Falls Village, Barbara Sincerbeaux was and is an enigmatic figure and the subject of much rumor and speculation. She is remembered as that handsome and refined blond lady of obvious breeding who periodically visited the Gibbonses.

Barbara Abbott Sincerbeaux was born seven years earlier than Barbara Gibbons, in New York City, as the third child of Frank Sincerbeaux, a wealthy Manhattan lawyer, educator and philanthropist. The Sincerbeaux family home was a mansion close to the famous West Side Tennis Club in Forest Hills, New York City, and Barbara Gibbons was a sometime house guest. Barbara Sincerbeaux continues to live on the same Forest Hills street but in a large apartment. For Barbara Gibbons of The Bronx, Barbara Sincerbeaux of Forest Hills, a patrician lady with a Parisian education, was a good friend to have.

She served as a kind of patron for Barbara at the company and as an adviser and problem solver in her private life. Their correspondence suggests that Barbara Gibbons needed help as far back as the early 1950s. A 1953 letter from Sincerbeaux takes Barbara to task for her spendthrift ways and unplanned life: "You are your own worst enemy. Don't hit me when I say that. I'd like to help you plan a *budget*, as I've thought your problem through and through these past two weeks. You will have no reason to fear anyone when you give yourself a feeling of *security*."

Two years later, Barbara Gibbons had a far more serious problem to contend with. She was pregnant. In the years to come she would give several versions of Peter Reilly's conception. She claimed that she had had a casual affair with a Fordham University student. She claimed to have been secretly married to a serviceman. This was her pretense at the time of the birth.

Barbara also told a few people that she had been raped and she gave Peter this account one evening when he was in his early teens. At the conclusion of a television program about rape that she had encouraged him to watch she spoke of the time that she had been attacked while crossing Van Cortlandt Park in The Bronx. She said she had kept on working until the time of his birth and that she had driven herself to the hospital, receiving a parking ticket for her trouble.

Hilda Gibbons had no desire to become a grandmother, at least in these circumstances. She is said to have urged Barbara to get an abortion but Barbara would not. After Peter's birth, on March 2, 1955, she announced that she would not be responsible for taking care of the baby while Barbara went to work. A solution was found at a foster home in Yonkers, just north of The Bronx, where the child would be taken care of five days a week, a routine that continued for the first year and a half of Peter's life. Every Friday evening his mother and his grandparents would pick him up and drive him to the cottage in Falls Village for the weekend. He would be returned to Yonkers each Sunday night.

Barbara Sincerbeaux paid the maternity costs at the Bronx-Lebanon Hospital. When asked recently why she had done so, she did not deny it, but said that she did not wish to discuss the matter. She paid for Peter's clothing and many other necessities and luxuries for the eighteen years of his life until the murder of his mother. The total cost ran into many thousands of dollars. To Peter, she was simply his rich Auntie B who once described herself on a Christmas card, when he was four years old, as "the Blonde in your life."

Despite the Yonkers foster home, Barbara Gibbons was a mother, like it or not, and it wrenched her life out of shape. She gave up the editing of *Homespun* to take another job in the Operating Department of the company, and then she resigned altogether in October 1956. The Gibbonses had planned to move to the country eventually; Peter's arrival speeded up the timetable. Barbara and her mother and the baby settled in Falls Village while Louis worked weekdays in the city and took the train to the country on weekends. Upon Louis' retirement, the Gibbonses, now four in number, became permanent fixtures in Falls Village.

Generations are required to win genuine acceptance in a rural area steeped in tradition and slow to change. The Gibbonses probably took longer than most to be accepted as part of the town's human scenery. "The whole family was nutty as far as I was concerned," says one Canaan old-timer. Hilda and Louis were obviously foreigners as well as city people, and Barbara, "Well, she was someone we never could figure out." Only little Peter made it into the hearts of the townspeople. One day they would go to his rescue.

10 ■ JOHNSON ROAD

PETER REILLY: I think she did a good job for what she was doing. I think she really tried. But, last year or two she told me that at this point she wasn't putting her all into taking care of me like she used to. That is, maybe three years.

LIEUT. SHAY: Maybe if your mother had a decent mother and father.

PETER REILLY: And, she didn't. She had a decent father but not a decent mother.

Peter Reilly was brought up in the kind of traditional small-town manner that might be envied by most American youngsters. He was not a child of city streets or of manicured suburbs. His world consisted of dirt roads, dark forests, sparkling streams and nearby mountains that provided a dramatic silhouette at sunset. There were lakes, swamps and hayfields all about. A huge stone fireplace helped warm his home in the snowy winters and he had a canoe and a treehouse outdoors for summertime fun. Each spring was spectacular and every autumn the woods would be carpeted with golden leaves. Peter had fish to catch, snakes to trap and furry creatures to chase. Good neighbors watched him grow, worried about him and hoped he was happy. In the village, everyone knew his name.

As the only child of an only child, he had no brothers and sisters, and he had no father. He was known as "that lonely little boy who is always looking for someone to play with." But his mother was as much a father as a mother to him and Peter will say today that "If you have to be brought up by just one parent you would want someone like my mother who was able to combine both roles at once." His grandfather was a kindly man who provided a certain male influence. Even his tyrannical grandmother was able to relax on occasion and let down her emotional barriers.

And his godmother often appeared at the pine woods cottage in those days, always bearing gifts. Good things would happen when Barbara Sincerbeaux arrived for a weekend or a holiday. The four Gibbonses had grown accustomed to her wealth. Her presence meant shopping expeditions, fancy meals in restaurants and some fun times in the house and outdoors. "Twice a year," according to an old friend of the family, "Sincerbeaux would outfit them all. She would take Hilda and Barbara to Gurley Eldred's shop in Lime Rock, which was a very fine and expensive dress shop, to outfit them for the season. She once took Hilda and myself to the Jug End Barn for dinner and Hilda had a ball up there. Hilda was always calling Barbara a bum for drinking so much, but she didn't mind a drink herself."

For Sincerbeaux, her Falls Village visits were an escape. "That's what I call a weekend!" she wrote Barbara Gibbons in 1959. "It was really terrific. I always meet my work with new vigor after a weekend on Johnson Road. I love to be spoiled and waited on and you do both for me. Peter never ceases to amaze and delight me. He is *so* bright and I adore his portrait on my bureau."

His Auntie B thought so much of Peter that she not only provided cash and gifts, but she made him the beneficiary, on at least one occasion, of a $30,000 flight insurance policy. To Peter, his godmother was that nice blond lady—high cheekbones, broad smile, very affectionate—"who used to bring a pile of gifts to me, always. I was really spoiled. My mother explained to me that Barbara Sincerbeaux was very, very interested in my well-being ever since I was born and that satisfied me. I had no reason to ask anything else. But ever since I was arrested for something I didn't do I've been curious to know why she dropped me like a hot potato and why all that money was paid for so many years."

* * *

In the wake of the death of his mother and with prison walls looming before him, Peter spoke of a very special, very personal ambition. He wanted, he said, to earn enough money someday so that he would be able to buy back his boyhood cottage and make his home in the woods once again.

"My grandfather was the only father I ever had and I was his only grandson. He used to spoil me something terrible. He would spend all his time with me. We did a lot of fishing together and I'd help him when he worked around the house. He was always fixing things, just like my mother, and putting up birdhouses. He was an excellent cook. My grandmother was a good cook too."

He remembers his grandmother making dill pickles. He remembers the hearty English-style Sunday dinners they used to have, especially the roast beef and Yorkshire pudding. He recalls the birthday parties and Christmas celebrations with at least one big gift like a bicycle or even a go-cart. "My godmother bought it all. The card on the present would say, 'From Mother and Auntie B.'"

Peter remembers best the things he did with his mother. "She taught me to shoot when I was about seven. We used to do a lot of target practicing with a .22. She taught me more about safety and firearms than about shooting. It wasn't so much getting good at it as doing it. We'd also go fishing together. She once hooked a snapping turtle that must have weighed sixty-five pounds. She taught me how to use tools and how to make things. She took an old 1936 Ford, cut out the rumble seat and built an extension in the rear that made it a little pickup truck for hauling wood. My mother always had time to do the things with me that I was interested in, but since I was an only child I was also very independent. I used to go off into the woods with my hatchet and my pocketknife for hours at a time."

His early sense of security as the youngest and best-loved member of a small family was enhanced by the presence of his uncle Jim and his aunt Margaret, who had bought a piece of land nearby. They built a vacation dwelling that they used on weekends and holidays for a number of years. The lawyer in Canaan who handled the legal details for them was a young man named John F. Bianchi. Two decades later, Jim and Margaret's daughter June would learn that Peter had been arrested and charged with the murder of his mother. She rummaged about the family papers in her New Jersey home to find the name of a Canaan attorney who could help Peter. She discovered John Bianchi's name and sought his help. Then she learned that he was the prosecutor who was seeking Peter's conviction.

Today Peter Reilly is, through no design of his own, the most widely known personality in Canaan. But even as a baby he garnered more than his share of attention from the townspeople because he had appeared so suddenly and bore a name that raised questions about his origins.

Marjorie Goerlich, a long-time Cornwall resident, tells of the crowds of weekenders on the 5:27 Friday-night train. "There were so many people that there were two stores at the West Cornwall station that would stay open late. Barbara's mother and father used to be on that train and she would meet them at the station with the car. One Friday night I was coming down the train steps and there was Barbara with a child in her arms. I said, 'Miss Gibbons, what a nice baby. What's its name?' And she said, 'Peter Reilly.' I was so surprised that I didn't know what to say. It seemed to be her baby, but it didn't have her name. I made some inane remark and that was the end of the conversation. There was great talk in the village, of course, that it wasn't her baby."

Although at birth the child's name was Gibbons, Barbara seemed to want to give the impression that the child had a father named Reilly, perhaps someone she had married and divorced or had married and buried. She said little to resolve the mystery. Some years before telling Peter the story of her rape in The Bronx she instructed him to say, in case anyone asked, that his father had been killed in the Korean War, though that war had ended more than a year before Peter was conceived.

Rosalind Ryan speaks of the day she introduced Peter's grandmother to a friend and then introduced him as "Peter Gibbons." Hilda Gibbons sharply corrected her: "No, it's Peter *Reilly*." When Mrs. Ryan asked where the name Reilly had come from, Hilda said, "Barbara pulled it out of a hat."

Hilda Gibbons tolerated little Peter. Though it is said that

"She really did care about the boy," Hilda would not accept him as a true Gibbons. Her daughter had disgraced the family. Other members of the family were confused; even when Peter was in his teens, letters from Barbara's aunt Steffie in Florida arrived, addressed to Mrs. B. V. Gibbons, Reilly."

"Even though I knew them all very well," Mrs. Ryan says, "and Sincerbeaux too, I cannot say for sure who Peter's mother was or is. I just don't know. I only know that everything was always veiled and that it was the most peculiar family. My husband used to get angry with me for even bothering with these people because he said they were all crazy. But I felt so sorry for this little boy because I had grandchildren that he used to play with and he wasn't allowed to have them come to his own house to play. His grandmother, who was a witch, wouldn't have them. They might get dirt on her precious rug or something like that. She once told me, gloating, that she never even knew that Barbara was pregnant. She said Barbara came home from the office one night and said to them, 'I'm going to the hospital to have a baby and I don't want you to come.' Well, no one else ever saw her pregnant either. I once saw a photograph of Barbara that was taken at an office party in the December before Peter was born in March. When she showed me that picture I said to her that she didn't look pregnant then. 'Oh, well,' she said, 'I wore a girdle.' I find that hard to believe, as a mother and a grandmother. You can see why there has been so much speculation that she had agreed to bring up another woman's child and was being paid to do it. You can put two and two together."

On the other hand, Leslie Jacobs of Jacobs' Garage is one Falls Villager who is sure that Barbara was Peter's mother. "I saw her pregnant in 1954, during the hunting season. She said some guy had broken into her house on Johnson Road and raped her."

The blood group of Peter's mother, as recorded by the Bronx-Lebanon Hospital at the time of his birth in 1955, was AB, one of the less common blood groups. Barbara Gibbons' blood group, as recorded by Sharon Hospital, was also AB. At Peter's birth, she called herself Barbara V. Bradshaw, wife of a sailor named Edward N. Gibbons, but she gave the hospital her correct age, birthplace and address in The Bronx. The baby is identified only as "Gibbons," without a first name, on both the hospital records and his New York City birth certificate. He arrived three weeks prematurely at 10:14 on March 2, 1955, weighing four pounds fifteen ounces and stretching seventeen and a half inches. He went home eight days later, a slight but thriving child.

The unwed mother's own itemized list of hospital costs was found among her personal papers after her death. In addition to the daily charge, for eight days, of "15.50—me; $5.50—Peter," she noted $20 for anesthesia and $1.50 for her baby's identification bracelet.

Barbara's cousin Victoria has always been convinced that Peter is Barbara's child. She believes that Barbara, by nature, would be very unlikely to burden herself with the care of someone else's infant. The mystery about Peter's origin, she suggests, can be credited to Barbara's lifelong habit of playing games with people.

Victoria recalls that Barbara did not even tell her that she was pregnant. "I remember that the phone rang when I was in the kitchen with Ellen, the colored lady who had taken care of our family for years. Barbara was on and she was up to her usual tricks. This time I decided I wouldn't fall for it. What she would do was call up and you'd lift the phone and say 'Hello,' and all you'd get was silence. She would just keep silent while you'd be saying, 'Hello, hello, who's there? Is anybody there?' and *finally* she would say something in the very sweet voice that Barbara had, a very delicate, lovely voice, and you'd say, 'Oh, Barbara, it's you!' And so, you see, you would already be defensive at the start of the conversation.

"Well, this time she finally got around to asking whether I had a high chair, crib, carriage or baby clothes that I could spare because a friend of hers was going to have a baby. I told her that I didn't have anything left. When I hung up I turned to Ellen and said, 'Barbara's going to have a baby.' Well, she was a very proper person and she told me that I'd better wash my mouth out with soap, but the next thing we knew Barbara did have a baby that was born out of wedlock and she didn't know what to do with it. She telephoned me when Peter was about three or four months old and asked me if I would be willing to bring him up. I said I would only if I could raise him with my twins like my own son, in my own way, without interference, but she said no. She wouldn't give him up. I just couldn't take care of him because if I did there would be no end to the harassment, especially from Hilda. Barbara finally did find Priscilla Belcher in Falls Village to help her with Peter. She can tell you how awfully Barbara's mother harassed her."

Priscilla Belcher was hired to look after Peter during the day, while Barbara went to work, until he was old enough to go to school. "When you took care of Peter you got Hilda too," Mrs. Belcher says. "Hilda was a very demanding person. She said she had shingles and gave that as an excuse for not being able to take care of Peter while Barbara was working, but basically she just objected to the whole idea." Barbara, too, "could be a very annoying person, someone who made a nuisance of herself in general," but less so at the beginning.

In the late 1950s and early 1960s Barbara Gibbons made an effort to support herself and provide a good life for her child. She came to live in northwest Connecticut and, with strong references from the Home Insurance Company, found a place with the Cole Insurance Agency at Cornwall Bridge. "She was a wonderful girl," says Mrs. Frank Cole. "She did a great job in the office for a number of years, before things started to go wrong. We relied on her very, very much. She was the best secretary in the world. She carried on with all the rules and regulations about the insurance. It became more and more complicated, but she kept great track of it all."

Barbara Victorien, a fellow employee, has a vivid impression of Barbara Gibbons in her first years at the agency. "She dressed very well, very tastefully, in good quality clothes—the whole thing: skirts, stockings, heels. She was interesting, smart and lively then. She was an excellent typist and she handled the insurance business with great ability. She was small in stature and built like a man, with her dark hair cut short. She squinted a lot because she needed glasses but wouldn't wear them. Her hands were rough because she did a lot of outdoor work at home. For example, she built a tree house for Peter. That's a very strong memory: the way she indulged that boy. She bought him a watch when he was eight, and it was a big thing for her to take him fishing. She always had German shepherds and I really think it was for his protection because they lived in a remote area. She would do anything for that boy."

One thing she did was to place him in a private school in Lakeville. She drove him there each morning and picked him up during her lunch hour. The exclusive Town Hill School, with classes from kindergarten through the fourth grade, is adjacent to Hotchkiss, one of the country's most prestigious prep schools.

"I went one year to kindergarten and two years to the first grade because I was left back," Peter says. "My Auntie B paid for it, five hundred dollars a year. There were two Buckley children in the school while I was there, so you can see that I was among the elite. But I didn't like it. I wanted to go to the Falls Village school with the rest of the kids." Barbara relented and placed him in the local school for the second grade, but she clung to the idea that he would go to Hotchkiss and on to Yale and a career as a lawyer. "She didn't know," Peter says today, "that I'd get an education in the law the hard way."

For at least five or six years after the Gibbonses arrived in Connecticut, the atmosphere in the little red house would have led a disinterested observer to conclude that these people were, on the whole, content with their lot. Hilda and Louis could savor the first years of retirement. Barbara had a good job and she kept in touch with old friends at the Home. She even attended some of the Home outings, especially those in Great Barrington, north of Falls Village in Massachusetts, where the company owned an estate. As for Peter, he was a healthy little fellow, easy to get along with, who was just starting school. Life was good.

Except that Hilda and Barbara would quarrel. Constantly. They had been snapping at each other ever since Barbara's childhood in England. Her mother was domineering and easily upset by anything that failed to conform to her idea of proper conduct. Barbara had to lash back at all the orders and insults or be reduced to utter slavery. But Hilda usually had the upper hand, the last word. Barbara would lose a little of her self-confidence with each encounter.

A near neighbor recalls a particular New Year's party: "The queen sat in her chair and she'd say, 'Lou, do this. Barbara, do that." She'd say, 'Barbara, get me a cigarette.' Barbara would not only fetch the cigarette, she'd light it for her too. Barbara and I would sometimes go bowling up at The Cove in Great Barrington and Hilda would come along too. I never could understand why; she couldn't bowl. They fought and yelled with each other all the way up and in the bowling alley and all the way home again. Barbara would say to me, if she could get me aside, 'I didn't want her to come with us.'"

The two women could not get away from each other in the small house. The walls were thin. Peter and his grandfather slept on bunk beds in one bedroom while Hilda, of course, had the larger of the two bedrooms to herself. Barbara slept on the pullout bed that doubled as the living room sofa. If she had a woman guest for the weekend or holiday they would share the sofa bed. Sometimes, however, her New York friends would stay in a tourist cabin in Falls Village or put up at the Wake Robin Inn in Lakeville.

In an undated letter, Barbara Sincerbeaux told Barbara Gibbons, "I know there is fault on *both* sides. It is not unusual for mothers and daughters to fight like cats and dogs. It is a real trial to have to continue to live under the same roof. I feel for you, but you both lack control at times. You are your mother's flesh and blood so this trait did not reach you out of 'thin air.' If you moved to Florida, they would be lost without Peter, but such a move might be worthwhile for all concerned. . . . Maybe just one year would make a difference. . . . Am sending the enclosure for your added expenses during the emergency."

The family atmosphere became increasingly destructive. Louis Gibbons, a sad little man in his retirement, became the family doormat. Hilda ruled the roost and Louis took his orders. He did most of the cooking and cleaning. "Hilda treated him like a servant," a neighbor says. "When I took her shopping she would buy some chocolate and say, 'I want Lou to make me a batch of brownies.' She loved brownies. Or else she'd buy a tongue and tell me that Lou would cook it for her."

The combination of Hilda's Prussian tactics, Barbara's prankish habits and their feuding served to isolate them from their relatives as well as many of their neighbors. Hilda's sister Margaret and her husband, Jim, no longer appeared in Falls Village. Margaret was mentally ill, and Hilda's interference in her treatment had strained family relations. Contact with either Hilda or Barbara was bound to be abrasive, Victoria states, "so we had as little to do with them as we could. They were just too much of a headache. We were sorry, though, that Peter had to be included in this because he was the sweetest child and we genuinely cared for him. Whenever we had news about him we would pass it along in letters to the rest of the family."

Barbara's coworkers at the Cole Insurance Agency noticed the changes in her appearance and behavior. She let herself go. She dressed carelessly, then unsuitably. At times they knew that she had been drinking too much the night before. She became less reliable and more unpredictable. She might, for example, bring her fishing equipment to the office and practice casting on the front steps when the boss was away.

Barbara would compensate for her problems, failings and frustrations by displaying her intellectual prowess. She was a mental exhibitionist. Her favorite periodical was the *Saturday Review*. She would fire off critical or complimentary letters to its editors and columnists. Her favorite book was *Parnassus on Wheels* and she tried in vain to persuade Bennett Cerf, the chairman of Random House, to restore it to the Modern Library series. He told her that there was too little interest, sad to say, in the works of Christopher Morley.

Barbara wrote to the *New York Times* about an editorial on President Kennedy. She objected not to the point of view but the grammar, punctuation and style. Using the proper proofreading symbols, remembered from her *Homespun* days, she made her corrections on a clipping of the editorial. Herbert L. Matthews of the editorial board sent it back, saying he agreed with at least some of her points, and admitted that he was "the culprit."

She wrote a long letter to the *Lakeville Journal* criticizing the widely respected principal of the regional high school, where Peter would one day be a celebrity, for his "strange report" of the last school year, written while he was on a summer tour in Finland.

Three paragraphs suggest her cutting style and her pretensions:

> *Perhaps my ability to appreciate Dr. Paul W. Stoddard's report on the Regional High School was hampered by the fact that, instead of being in a cottage facing the Gulf of Bothnia on the Finnish coast, I was merely sitting in our living room in Falls Village. I mention this; not to bore the reader with details of personal environment, but simply to set a familiar scene; I will not return to this theme again . . .*
>
> *There are many reasons why people enter the teaching profession: some drift in—others really have felt the call to teach and have a natural ability to inspire. The "call" cannot be very strong if a member of the profession abandons the problems of his own bailiwick to fiddle with vague topics which cannot possibly increase the dissemination of information in the manner in which it is most needed. He commits the sin of nonteaching that Milton denounces in* Lycidas . . .
>
> *I take the liberty of also quoting from whom I presume Dr. Stoddard meant to be John Donne, although by the spelling I could not surely tell, by saying: Sir, the bell tolls for thee.*

Dr. Stoddard wrote a gracious response. "I am delighted," he said, "that at last someone is really reading the town reports!"

Barbara did not spare her own kin. If her younger cousin June, for example, wrote her a letter with misspellings, she would send it back with corrections. Soon June stopped writing to her. Barbara said and did a number of things that seemed almost calculated to lose friends.

"Barbara had a dog," Priscilla Belcher relates, "and she used to get great enjoyment about the dog going over and frightening the little old ladies at Camp Freedman. That dog came over to our house and nabbed my husband." John Belcher continues the story: "She had it on a leash, but it jumped on my face, bit my arm and tore off my pant leg. Barbara's only comment was, 'I'll send my insurance adjuster.' I was furious but, as usual, she treated the whole thing like a big joke. Her idea of humor was to take that dog to the market, take it off the leash and watch the butcher standing there, unable to make a move."

Several former neighbors remember Barbara striding about the town wearing a hunting knife or a revolver. Leslie Jacobs of Jacobs' Garage in Falls Village recalls finding a number of tame ducks, whose wings had been clipped, lying dead alongside a beaver pond on Music Mountain Road. Someone had shot them. When he next saw Barbara Gibbons and mentioned the dead ducks, she claimed responsibility. "You've got to have something to shoot around here," she told Jacobs. He didn't know whether or not to take her seriously.

That Barbara Gibbons was a heavy drinker became more and more obvious. A local artist sometimes saw her Rambler parked at the edge of the woods some distance from her house. "I could see her sitting in the car by herself, raising a bottle to her lips. It was strange and pathetic."

The drinking fueled the fights between mother and daughter. Hilda, whose drinking was limited to a New Year's Eve whiskey sour, was a one-woman prohibition movement. Her husband was an alcoholic and she could see the way Barbara was heading.

In her old age, in 1971, Grandma Hilda would write to Peter from Florida to tell him that her life had been ruined by alcoholics. "Had I known thirty years ago what I know now, I would have put your mother out to shift for herself, not hang on to me for food, shelter and clothing, so for God's sake, work hard so you will amount to something."

Hilda, seeing herself surrounded by alcoholics, would not allow Barbara to drink in the house. She had to keep her bottle in the car. "Look at that bum," Hilda would say to visitors, "she has to run out to the car every five minutes."

That was her favorite word for her daughter: bum. She seemed to take malicious pleasure in denigrating Barbara to one and all. "Hilda would go into a temper tantrum," Rosalind Ryan recalls, "and scream and carry on like a maniac.

She would say that Barbara never went with a decent person except Barbara Sincerbeaux. She said Barbara was always attaching herself to people who were below their level, whatever that level was, and that some of those people were the world's worst."

Barbara would go to the neighbors and describe in detail how badly her mother treated both herself and Peter. She invited them to hear a tape recording she had made at the time that Hilda threatened to kick Peter if he did not move quickly enough. The State Police found the tape after Barbara's death. It was entitled "Kick Your Cock Off."

How constant this warfare between mother and daughter was is impossible to say. Surely there were quiet times, restful evenings, pleasant weekends and some display of fondness for each other. But clearly the bad times were frequent enough. Barbara would spend more and more time in her car with the bottle and then look for company.

"She would suddenly appear at the door," Mrs. Ryan relates, "let herself in, and then just stand there, without a word, for five or ten minutes. She was like . . . well, what would you call someone who is too drunk to move? A zombie? My husband would get disgusted and walk out and Barbara would still be standing there. Eventually she'd go away."

John and Priscilla Belcher, who speak in praise of her intelligence, sense of humor and devotion to her son, remember asking themselves whether Barbara was completely normal. "Like when she'd come in here at night," Mrs. Belcher says. "She'd walk in at any hour, walk around the room, not say anything, get in the car and drive away. Now that's not totally normal. It got to be an annoyance because she wouldn't just come in and have a good conversation. She seemed to be on edge and not knowing what to do with herself. I think it was probably that she didn't want to stay home and listen to her mother, and I wouldn't have blamed her."

Another Falls Village woman tells of the snowy night that Barbara arrived unannounced. "I offered her a drink which was a very bad thing, but that was before I knew that she drank so much. I said, 'My goodness, you can't even drive out there. What are you doing out on a night like this, Barb?'

She said, 'Oh, I had to get away from the house.' Well, she stayed and stayed and finally I said I had to go to bed. She said the weather was so bad that she couldn't drive home and asked if she could stay the night. I said that was all right and she could sleep in the guest room. When I offered her a nightgown she said, 'Oh, I don't wear a nightgown,' and she suggested that I get undressed and come in and sit on her bed. Well, look, all of a sudden I wasn't naive any more. I realized what was going on. I said, 'No, I'm tired, I'm going to bed,' and I went to the bedroom and locked the door. The next morning I woke her up as if nothing had happened. She had breakfast and she went home. Her parents never called anybody to find out where she was that night or anything. Apparently they weren't interested."

Peter was growing up and somehow coping with events in the house and with life in Falls Village. He was not a materially deprived child, but his emotional nourishment at home was clearly lacking. During the interrogation he was encouraged to feel sorry for himself and he agreed with the police that he had been treated like an animal: "I've been given food and I've been given my place where I slept but I've never been shown affection. . . . The problem was I was never shown the proper love and affection that parents should give." He also told the police that "I knew I didn't have the greatest, you know, home life," but at his grandparents' house he had learned all his manners. "You notice," he said, "how I always excuse myself and apologize for saying things."

During the interrogation Peter may well have dredged up some buried feelings of deprivation. Or he might have been saying anything that came to mind to please the authorities at that moment. Or both. He had always been a self-effacing and accommodating little fellow. He learned early in life that to get along you go along. To be accepted you try to fit in. He was quiet and harmless and colorless.

When the interrogation was described to Joseph Downey, who knew Peter in his Johnson Road days, he said, "He went through that every day when he was a boy. He wanted to please. When he came over to the house to play with our kids he'd do whatever they said. And he enjoyed it so much. He was a follower."

Priscilla Belcher had this to say: "Having known Peter all my life, I know he is too gentle a person to kill anybody. So much was made about his not crying about his mother's death, but Peter was not the type to show much emotion. Even as a small boy he was that way. Peter sometimes doesn't know himself and that's a fact. He's not sure of himself. He's always been that way. I remember when he stayed with us, or when he came to visit, and there would be an accident. Something would break and you'd wonder who did it. Peter would say, 'Did I do that?' as if he didn't know for sure. It's annoying to be around someone like that. If I asked my own kids, 'Did you do that?' they would know immediately, yes or no. Not Peter. If you thought he did something he would think he did it too, even if he didn't."

Peter was healthy enough in his boyhood, but he was not made for competitive sports. He never would pretend to be an athlete. He was mechanically inclined. He always wanted to know how things worked and what made them tick. He liked to build models and work with his mother on the car. Because his grandfather was not a strong male figure (Hilda, in time, would describe Louis to Peter in a letter as "a born shlemiel"), and because he was so much the object of attention for three females (mother, grandmother and godmother), Peter Reilly could have become the classic sissy. Since he did not, his mother must be given credit.

She was, as the neighbors say, "as strong as an ox," and she saw to it that there was plenty of rough and tumble in his life. He would never be the one to start a fight, but he learned how to take care of himself. (Peter during the interrogation: "I never had a fight, but I always told myself . . . that if I ever got into a fight where it's going to be a real fight, that I'm not going to fight clean. 'Cause when you get in a fight, you don't fight clean, you fight to win.") He was squeamish about some things—bumblebees, wasps and "creepie crawlies"—but Barbara had introduced him to life in the woods and there was nothing he liked better than camping out in the dark.

Barbara found a special drinking friend in Marge Downey, a troubled woman who claimed to be tired of being married to Joe, who was a good man but not the world's most exciting. Barbara and Marge began to spend a lot of time together in 1964 and 1965. "Barbara was a smart woman," Joe Downey says. "My wife admired her brains. She and Marge would start drinking in the evening and they'd keep on drinking after I went to bed. Friday nights, the two of them would take Peter and our kids shopping, then they'd come home and drink."

Barbara's relationship with Marge Downey was apparently the last straw for Hilda. She told her daughter to clear out. Barbara refused. Hilda and Louis, who did what he was told, called the police when the argument became a battle royal. On May 11, 1965, Barbara was arrested for "breach of peace" on a complaint made by her parents because, as the record shows, "They wanted her to leave their home" and Barbara would not leave. The case was scheduled to go to court on June 3 but the charges were dropped when Barbara agreed to move out. She was forty-four years old; Peter was ten.

"I remember my mother saying, 'if you want to stay with your grandparents, you can. If you want to come with me, you can.' I don't remember whether my grandparents asked me to stay, but my mother made sure it was my decision. I said I wanted to go with her so off we went. We loaded up the Rambler with her stuff and my clothes, my guitar and all my junk. We didn't have time to find anywhere more permanent where we could live so we went down to the Elms cabins."

For the first time in her life, Barbara was separated from her parents. For the first time in his life, Peter was truly alone with his mother. Their comradeship—the two against the world—would last for eight years and four months. They made an odd couple, Barbara Gibbons and Peter Reilly, but their love for each other was plain; the most luminous thing about them as they moved into an uncertain future.

11 ▪ ON THEIR OWN

PETER REILLY: Yes. But something else that I've noticed is that—
the first thing I thought of when I woke up—I don't know,
maybe it's just something that happened—was that, you
know, they're really giving me a rough time, it seemed like,
and I got to tell my Mom to help.

SGT. KELLY: Mm.

PETER REILLY: And, then, you know, I realized what happened.

SGT. KELLY: Right.

PETER REILLY: Because, if I ever got in trouble—like something
like this—she'd be right there.

The Elms Restaurant and its seven tourist cabins can be
found at the eastern edge of the town of Sharon on Route
7 near Cornwall Bridge. Barbara Gibbons and Peter Reilly
moved into cabin number 7 in June 1965 and stayed through
the summer months.

Moving day, as Peter remembers it, was also his last day
of school. As a special gift, Barbara drove him to Millerton,
New York, to buy him a parakeet. They named it Peanuts.

That summer, Barbara and Peter made a game of adver-
sity. Their cabin at the Elms was tiny, consisting of just a
single room and tiny bathroom. They shared the double bed.
With no kitchen, Peter says, "We had to eat out all the time.
We did a lot of barbecuing." They grilled fish that they caught
in the nearby river.

Peter remembers fondly their hikes and picnics, the way
they would drive around together, the shows they went to, the
summer fairs they visited, including the New York World's
Fair. Because Forest Hills was so close to the fairgrounds,
they stayed overnight at the Sincerbeaux mansion.

While sightseeing one day, Barbara and Peter discovered a small airfield near Great Barrington. Peter, who had never flown before, wanted to go up in a plane. A more conventional mother might have told her ten-year-old son that he was too young for such foolishness. Barbara was different. She treated him to flying lessons. With an instructor at his side, Peter flew a Piper Colt for thirty minutes over the Berkshire and Litchfield hills, doing "straight and level, and medium turns." He had two more half-hour lessons in the next two weeks, advancing to "climb and glide." His progress was marked in a pilot's log that he still has.

Barbara had time to spend with Peter because she had lost her job just a few days after moving to the tourist cabin. She had done a favor for her friend Marge Downey, who wanted to divorce her husband. As Joe Downey tells the story, he had been working on a piece of farm machinery one Sunday evening and was surprised to find Barbara and Peter sleeping on the living room couch when he arrived home. "Barbara stayed," he says, "and made supper for the kids because Marge had to go to a meeting or dinner in Sharon. Later on, Barbara left for the cabin while Peter stayed with us in the house. Then, after some time, Barbara telephoned and said Marge was coming over to the cabin for a drink after her Sharon meeting and they wanted me to join them. I wasn't too eager about going, but I went anyway. I was alone in the place with Barbara for a while. Nothing happened. Then Marge came in and she said something like, 'How long has this been going on?' She went home and called the State Police. She complained to them about me and Barbara. When they questioned me I figured I might as well say I had been there. If that's what Marge wanted, then she could have it. She later admitted to me that she and Barbara had set me up. Barbara and I were arrested and then the case was dropped. They didn't expect that much publicity. My wife moved out in September. I didn't contest the divorce because our marriage had been in trouble for a long time. We were divorced the following spring."

The headline in the *Waterbury Republican* of June 15, 1965, said: "COUPLE ARRESTED IN MORALS CASE." The one-paragraph story: "Sharon—Joseph P. Downey, 43, Beebe Hill Road, and Barbara Gibbons, 41, Rte. 7, were arrested Monday by Troopers Ralph Hazen and Walter Anderson, each on a charge of lascivious carriage."

Though the story was hardly earthshaking, it started tongues wagging in Canaan and Cornwall. Barbara was dismissed from her insurance job on the same day that the *Republican* story appeared. The bad publicity was not the only reason for the firing: her employers had already concluded that her "lack of good hygiene" was bad for business. Fortunately, a $1,000 check from Sincerbeaux arrived. Barbara told her coworkers, "I'll be able to get by with this," but at least one of them doubted it. "Barbara spent money like water," she told the police after the murder.

Peter had little realization of how bad things were, He cannot recall ever having heard of the "lascivious carriage" scandal. "I didn't take an interest in the newspapers until I was eighteen," he says. "All I can remember about the Downeys is that I went to their house with my mother many, many times to play with their kids, Joe and Sue. I'd go to sleep and my mother would wake me up at midnight to take me home."

Although she occasionally revealed to Peter her thoughts about suicide, Barbara usually kept her worries to herself. She gave Peter a sense of security because she seemed to be able to take charge, to get things done. "My mother told me that if there was anything I needed to just let her know and if it was within her power to get it she would." Even on the increasingly rare occasions when Barbara Sincerbeaux would visit, with all the advantages of wealth and position in contrast to Barbara's hand-to-mouth existence, Barbara Gibbons exuded strength. "I always felt that my mother was the dominant personality. She sort of called the shots when they were talking. Auntie B would do more listening than talking."

Barbara looked for another job. She tried the *Lakeville Journal* but they weren't hiring—and they knew her to be an erratic employee. She asked Mrs. Singleton Fish of Salisbury about working in her real estate office but, as Mrs. Fish says, "I knew she was a problem. Her drinking. She was not stable. I couldn't take her into my office under the circumstances."

Barbara and Peter went on the dole. With the exception of

six months in 1968 pumping gas at a service station, Barbara would never again have steady work.

In September 1965, they moved from their Elms cabin to an apartment in a renovated stone barn on Music Mountain Road in Falls Village. They stayed almost a year. Then in the early morning of August 5, 1966, Peter's grandfather lost his life in an auto crash. "My grandmother sort of fell apart when he died," Peter says. "My mother went back to the house to make arrangements, something my grandmother couldn't have done herself." They left the Music Mountain barn and settled again on Johnson Road. Hilda's sister Steffie, with whom she had often quarreled, moved in for a prolonged visit. Peter, now eleven years old, was an innocent bystander in a household heavy with argument.

"Barbara had broken her mother's heart," Mrs. Fish has said, and Hilda must have decided that there was no future for herself in Falls Village. Instead of a daughter who would take care of her in her old age she had a "bum of a daughter" who was hanging around her neck. Hilda wanted out and she set the wheels in motion to get herself out. She decided to sell the house and all the furniture, take the money and take off. All the way to Switzerland.

"There was a whole turn of events right there," Peter relates. "Everything happened at once. My mother was very bitter. I think this was part of the reason that she sort of, well, withdrew from everything. She'd spent years of work and a lot of her money on that house on Johnson Road, which was supposed to end up being my mother's and mine. She had put in a huge rock garden that went way down the slope, with hundreds of wild plants and stuff that she had collected on the mountain or bought. But my grandmother got the house and sold it. It was my grandfather's house, in his name. He had bought it. My grandfather left a will that never got filed. It was in a drawer and my mother told me that my grandmother burned it."

The house finally sold for $15,000 early in 1967. The furniture went to a dealer in Massachusetts. Hilda and Steffie packed their bags for Europe. "She telephoned me," Rosalind

Ryan says, "and told me they were going. I said, 'What about Barbara?' She said, 'I threw her out of the house.' I asked her, 'What about your grandson?' She said, 'He's gone with Barb and I don't care what happens to him.' I said, 'How can you say that about your grandson?' With that she hung up on me."

As the old ladies left for Europe, Barbara thought about going to Australia, but she and Peter had little money, just twice-monthly welfare checks and $100 to $150 handouts from Sincerbeaux. They moved into the tiny white house that has since become a Falls Village landmark as the murder cottage.

No larger than a two-car garage, the cottage was a former sandwich shop that stood between a small red barn and a large white house occupied by Mr. and Mrs. Fred Kruse. Some years before, Fred Kruse had put up partitions and installed enough equipment to make a living room, bedroom, kitchen and laundry room with toilet. The Kruses rented it unfurnished for a modest $35 a month.

Barbara wanted to buy back the family furniture that her mother had sold, so she persuaded Sincerbeaux to pay for the maple bunk beds and as many other items as the cottage could take. Sincerbeaux complained at the time to an acquaintance that she had bought the furniture originally and now had to pay for it a second time.

Their new home was comfortable except in the coldest weather. Barbara would one day plead with the Welfare Department for extra money to pay her electricity bill: "Please understand that I have needed to use available kitchen appliances, such as the stove, toaster and even the iron to keep this place warm enough to exist in, as the kerosene space heater is less than sufficient; many times this winter and last we have had to sleep in outer clothes in order to keep warm."

They were friendly with their landlord. Fred Kruse is a small, stooped but spry man in his eighties who used to be known to local children as "the lollipop man." He had moved from New York to Falls Village in 1946 with his first wife, who died six months later. "I was all alone," he relates, "so I started the gas station across the road. Then I married again. I had two pumps at the station and I had to run out of the house every time a car stopped. I was busy from 7 A.M. till 10 at night. It was the only place around here open at night. They called me the lollipop man because when a car came in for gas I gave the kids lollipops. Whenever they passed my station the kids would shout at their parents, 'Stop here! Stop here! It's the lollipop man.' I did a good business, believe me. Barbara used to bring Peter here for candy when he was a little fellow. He always asked permission before he touched anything."

Kruse, who came to the United States from Germany in 1911 and still speaks with an accent, took a kindly interest in Barbara and Peter. His belief in Peter's innocence rests on his knowledge of Peter's tender relationship with his mother, as he witnessed it for nearly six and a half years, and on the way the back screen door's bottom hinge was broken, at the time of the murder, as if the door had been kicked open from the inside by someone anxious to escape.

Kruse liked Barbara Gibbons. "She was a smart woman." But he did have a reservation: "I am German and I have worked all my life. Our family is a family of workers. She didn't work and that was one point that didn't suit me. She told me that she had worked enough."

At first glance, the neighborhood at the junction of Routes 7 and 63 looks nice enough. Except for the gas station and nearby billboards (which are banned in most other towns in the area), there is a picture-postcard appearance about the steepled South Canaan Congregational Church and the mixture of old colonial houses and modern dwellings. But the surrounding swamps give the place a feeling of isolation and the shabbiness of some of the dwellings, plus the peculiarities of some of the inhabitants, suggest a down-at-the-heels community that does not feel at ease with itself. When she was alive, Barbara Gibbons would occasionally be asked if she was afraid of living in what outsiders regarded as a remote location. And living, moreover, in a little house that was said to have been the scene of a shooting years ago, when a husband returned home to find his wife making love to a stranger. Barbara would say that she had a gun and was not afraid.

As a woman who had come down in the world, who was known for her drinking and zany behavior, and who lived on the dole instead of holding down a job, Barbara Gibbons was in her element. While most of her neighbors were respectable, hard-working citizens by any standards, there were others who were not exactly a credit to the community. Some were called "Raggies," a term that originally denoted the ragged charcoal burners who were a part of the area's iron-making industry in the last century. Nowadays in northwest Connecticut the Raggies, in common speech, are those members of the rural poor who seem unable to rise out of ignorance and indolence. Some are tenant farmers, others work indifferently, if at all.

The lifestyle of several of Barbara and Peter's neighbors was worthy of a Faulkner novel, northern style. They gave the community its undercurrent of violence. They fueled much of the gossip about incest, child abuse, early pregnancies, drinking, drugs and sex. Some of the teenagers, high school dropouts, had a knack for getting fired from their jobs, beating up their girlfriends and getting into drunken brawls. They accounted for some of the vandalism and petty thievery that went on in Canaan. The Falls Village recreation center was a favorite target. Once they moved up from their protected status as juveniles, their names appeared every so often on the police blotter, as published in the weekly newspaper. Several youths seemed to be excessively fond of guns and knives.

Kenneth Carter, who gave up the operation of the Texaco station soon after the Gibbons murder, remembers "one character who used to go around in some weird kind of Dickens outfit, then the next day he'd be dressed as a cowboy. I'd see him wandering in the woods with a shotgun. He'd stop by at the station and start shooting the breeze with me and I'd get rid of him as quickly as possible. Then one day he stole some cigarettes while I was outside pumping gas and I told him that I never wanted to see him around the place again. The next morning when I came to work I found the windshield smashed on a car I had left there overnight. It had been pushed against a gas pump hard enough to knock it down. It was obvious who did it. That whole place was a weird scene, believe me."

It was also the scene where Peter grew up during the more than six years that preceded his mother's death. Among the local kids, he played most of the time with Michael and Timothy Parmalee. Mike had gone to school with Peter since the second grade. He says that "I considered Pete my best friend until the tenth grade when I dropped out." Tim was a year behind them. The Parmalee brothers visited Peter at the cottage frequently. They often stayed overnight or else they would all sleep outdoors in the nearby woods.

Wayne Collier, three years older than Peter, was another boyhood friend. He lived within easy biking distance of Peter's house and visited frequently. He and Barbara Gibbons spent a lot of time talking together and she encouraged him in his schoolwork. One day he gave her a present, a used kitchen knife, little knowing that it would in time be portrayed in a courtroom as the instrument that Peter Reilly had used to mutilate his mother. Collier himself would eventually come under intense questioning about his murder-night activities.

Peter liked to work on model airplanes and tinker with old cars. He was getting interested in music and, much to his mother's surprise and delight, he taught himself to play the guitar. One thing his friends couldn't understand, just as the police and the prosecutor could not quite grasp it later on: He *enjoyed* being with his mother. Father Paul Halovatch would one day comment that "Peter had the greatest respect in the world for his mother, which is incredible."

They played chess together and he gave her what help he could with her crossword puzzles. They came to share an addiction for Ian Fleming's James Bond novels and they went to see every Bond film that came along. But Barbara was concerned about Peter's mediocre schoolwork, knowing that he had a higher IQ and a better mind than he was demonstrating. She had been a brilliant student herself, but, Peter says, "She wouldn't ground me for getting bad marks. She would just say, 'I'd like to see you do better.'"

She may have felt that her own intellectual interests and encyclopedic store of knowledge would rub off on him. She was right. Peter was an uncommonly well-informed teenager and he even learned to write in passable English. When he came home from high school one day with a high mark from a new English teacher for several short compositions Barbara was not sure she should be pleased. She doubted that the grade was deserved and she did not like to encourage any lowering of standards by the high school. So, as the teacher, Ellery Sinclair, well remembers, "Miss Gibbons telephoned the school and insisted on a meeting to make sure that Peter was not getting a higher mark than he deserved. I met with her and finally was able to convince her. She was the first parent who ever complained to me that her child was getting too high a grade."

Peter's sixteenth birthday in 1971 was celebrated in style. His mother gave him a card with this message: "DID YOU KNOW I WAS PUT ON THIS EARTH TO BRING JOY AND SUNSHINE INTO YOUR LIFE? HOW AM I DOIN' SO FAR?" She added, "After 16 years? What else can I tell you. Love, Mom." For a special treat she took Peter and his friend Ed Dickinson to New York City for a weekend of dinners and shows. Dickinson recalls that they were supposed to stay at Peter's godmother's place, but she managed to keep them at a distance by having them stay at a hotel. "Barbara had a $600 check," he says, "and we had a ball. We went to the Hayden Planetarium and the theater and all over. Barbara stayed in the room a lot while Pete and I roamed around. We had a supply of beer in the bathtub."

Peter's life began to change when he acquired his driver's license later in the year. His career behind the wheel began inauspiciously when he slid off an icy road and hit a telephone pole. Michael and Timothy Parmalee were his passengers. Mike was treated for cuts and bruises. Peter, unhurt, received a warning for speeding. He appeared on the State Police blotter, the only time before his arrest on suspicion of murder.

Having a car meant that he could visit friends outside of the immediate neighborhood and play his guitar in a rock band. He was able to drive to practice sessions and engagements. By playing at local dances and other events he could earn his own spending money. The bands had names like Departure, Subzero and Frosty Morning. The whole experience was so important to him that he had a tattoo, "SUBZERO," put on his left arm.

Largely because of his musical activities, Peter began to spend more and more of his time at the homes of Rick and Paul Beligni and Art and Geoff Madow. He would stay overnight frequently and often for several nights in a row. Like the Dickinsons, who lived closer to Peter's house, these families were always glad to see him, but his visits meant that they had to put up with Barbara Gibbons' phone calls. She did not try to stop him from seeing his friends, but she would become concerned about him, especially at the end of a day of drinking, and she would telephone to see if he was all right and find out when he would be coming home.

The Belignis and the Madows understood that these calls were a sign of her loneliness. They came to know Barbara Gibbons not through direct personal contact, which was most infrequent, but through her rambling statements on the telephone and the things said about her by Peter and their sons. They knew her reputation, but they also thought well enough of her to let their boys stay at her house just as Peter stayed at their homes.

Jean Beligni, for example, knew that Barbara could swear like a dockworker—"She had a mouth on her like nothing you ever heard; she could drive you bananas"—but she also knew that "she was very intelligent. Her trouble was that she talked over everybody's head. She'd call up and talk to you about some book she had just read and she would always make comparisons of a situation in very intellectual terms. Sometimes you wouldn't know what she was talking about."

To Marion Madow, Barbara Gibbons was "a strange person. She was very, very intelligent and had a vivid imagination. She was quite inventive. As far as being a mother, she was a good mother. Barbara took care of Peter. She saw that he was properly clothed and fed. Maybe his diet wasn't great. I mean, he drank a lot of Coke and stuff like that which some mothers object to and I don't allow, but he was taken care of that way. She was a good mother, but she was a weird lady. Maybe she had a split personality, which is not uncommon in alcoholics. One part of her was Mother Gibbons and the other part was fast, loose and whatever. Peter was exposed to her drinking and he lived with it and he accepted it. This is what Peter does. That's why he had no reason to kill her. He was not ashamed to bring boys into his home. He wasn't the kind of kid who was ashamed of anything. He just accepted what it was. He told me, and this is Peter's attitude, that he accepts what's handed down to him. This is his lot in life and this is the way it's going to be. He doesn't fight to change it that much."

While Peter took obvious enjoyment in the more conventional family life of his friends, and in their larger, more comfortable homes, he also had the satisfaction of seeing how much his pals liked coming to his house because of its uninhibited atmosphere and his mother's pleasure in their company. She could talk their language. She was a "gearhead" too; she had always been crazy about cars. She enjoyed games, horseplay and practical jokes. She was a middle-aged woman with a superior mind, but in some respects she had never really grown up. She was impulsive, disorganized and somewhat irresponsible. She would indulge herself today and face the consequences tomorrow. She acted on whim. So did Peter and his friends, and she enjoyed being one of them. Unlike their parents, she was no square.

She did not mind, for instance, if the boys did target shooting behind the house. They would fire rifles at targets nailed to the apple trees or hurl clay pigeons in the air and bring them down with shotguns. Barbara might even come out with her Uncle Jim's old pearl-handled Smith & Wesson .38 to join them. On one occasion, Rick Beligni picked up his brother's shotgun inside the cottage and fired it accidentally, a foot or so from Barbara's head, blasting out a window and knocking the top off the antique clock.

"Barbara wasn't too upset," Paul Beligni remembers. "It was just one of those things." Mostly because of his inquisitive mind and his interest in politics and other subjects that she was concerned about, Paul, who is a year and a half younger than Peter, became Barbara's best friend in the last two years of her life. He called her Babs. They would often talk together for three or four hours at a time.

"The police tried to make a big thing about their arguments," Beligni says, "but Barbara and Peter didn't really fight. They would yell at each other sometimes but it was like a couple of guys letting off steam. She was always monkeying with the car and it wouldn't work or else she'd get some imbecile to try to fix it. I was there once when he said, 'Mom, you make me so mad,' and he sort of zinged a flashlight at her. It hit her on the knee and you could see that he was sorry right away. The way she reacted was typical. She made a big joke out of it, crying, 'My knee! My knee! My poor knee! Call Dr. Bornemann!' But she also looked at him in a way that said he shouldn't do that again."

What Peter's friends, and Peter too, remember best are the pranks that Barbara enjoyed playing on any likely victim. She would telephone the State Police in her best little girl's voice to tell them about the mean man who had come by in his car and knocked her cat as high as the telephone wires. She would supply the number and description of a car owned by someone she was mad at. When a man who ran the Texaco station for a while annoyed her she would shout at him and play music through a loudspeaker hooked up to an amplifier. Once, after he accused her of stealing $50, she was not content to report the false accusation to the State Police. She and Peter went over to the station one night and put his trash cans on the roof.

Peter recalls the time that "she called me up at the Belignis and told me that the Falls Village Fire House was on fire. It's the only thing we've got for fires in the town so we immediately raced out. We went 110 miles an hour down the road to Falls Village. A cop had somebody pulled over on the side of the road and we just zoomed by him with the emergency flashers on. When we got to the middle of town we found that there was no fire after all. We drove over to my house. My Mom and Eddie Dickinson were sitting out on the front steps. They were in hysterics because they had seen us race by."

Another time she came upon the scene of an accident in Falls Village that was crowded with rescue crews and police.

She proceeded to race her engine and drive defiantly in circles.

Her everyday pranks were less dramatic. She once froze a $100 bill in an ice-cube tray and sent Peter across the road to ask the Texaco attendant to defrost it and give him change for cigarettes. On another occasion, after a friend of Peter's left his automobile running outside the front door and the exhaust fumes seeped into the house, Barbara took her revenge by creeping out to the car and spraying the interior with a can of Strawberry Essence. The fruity scent lasted for weeks.

Such zany exercises were "typical Barbara," according to Peter's pals, but it was her celebrated truffle-hunt hoax that said the most about her special turn of mind. It also greatly strengthened Peter's pride in her as an exceptional person. She simply decided one day to shake up the community by concocting an announcement about a social event that was bound to attract great attention. She was clever enough to deliver the text to the weekly newspaper so close to its press deadline that the editors had no time to check it out for authenticity.

And so, in its issue of June 8, 1972, underneath the headline "HOUNDS, PIGS COMPETE FOR TRUFFLES SUNDAY," the *Lakeville Journal* reported:

Mr. and Mrs. Miles Messervy of Sharon have sponsored a fully subscribed and most unusual sporting event for this area—a genuine truffle hunt—complete with truffle hounds and trained pigs, beginning June 11 in the late afternoon and ending at about 5 P.M., with a late tea on the Messervy terrace for participants, weather permitting.

Truffles are delicacies of a subterraneous tuber which grow on the roots of certain trees and are reproduced by spores, They grow underground, at a depth of several inches, in clusters.

The Messervys have taken great pains to cultivate the proper trees for a number of years, while introducing additional spores from time to time to assure a fine crop of truffles, which are usually eaten with *pâté de foie gras*.

Harvesting truffles is a rather unusual procedure; they

must be sniffed out by specially trained hounds and/or pigs. For this event all the entrants (hounds) have been brought by their owners from Belgium, West Germany, Southern France and the warmer parts of Italy.

There is a small group of very highly trained West-phalian pigs involved, considered by experts to be far superior in sniffing out the truffle delicacies than their canine competitors.

Each owner or handler must accompany his dog or pig, as the case may be, properly collared and leashed, so that the owner or handler may be prepared to dig out the truffles. This is especially important with respect to the pigs, which have been known to sniff a truffle cluster at 30 feet, dig it up and eat it in 30 seconds.

A dry run has already been held; all owners and handlers are familiar with the area, although the animals were not permitted to enter the truffle area. A.K.C. is handling all kennelling, including the Westphalian pigs.

All entries are in and the event is closed in this respect, but Mr. and Mrs. Messervy hope that the public may be interested in that a great deal of ecology planting, especially young walnuts, has been done.

Prizes will be awarded; first, second and third, to the owners of the animals discovering the most truffles during the allotted time.

According to the sponsors, a substantial amount of *pâté de foie gras* (plain) has been obtained from Fortnum and Mason in London to be eaten with the results of the truffle hunt.

Whatever the results are, the *pâté* will be very welcome, especially with the Beluga caviar, which Fortnum's are furnishing by air, in event of a hound-pig disaster or inclement weather.

As Barbara and Peter fully expected, the newspaper "was besieged with phone calls from readers wanting to know the Messervys' address," as the *Journal* ruefully reported in its next issue. The hoax was the talk of the towns in the paper's circulation area. Great efforts were made to locate the Messervy estate in Sharon. Someone finally figured out that Miles Messervy is the secret service chief "M" in the James Bond novels. In time, because she couldn't help bragging about it, Barbara Gibbons was unmasked as the author of the hoax that the editor of the *Journal* sportingly said was a clever prank and "all good fun."

12 ■ BARBARA AND PETER

SGT. KELLY: The only thing I can say to you is, it's not the end of the world.

PETER REILLY: It seems it, though, because she's gone, you know?

SGT. KELLY: Right. It seems it, Peter. But, as I say, there's nothing we can do about your mother now. All right? Absolutely nothing.

Many people in the Canaan area maintain that Barbara Gibbons was a notorious woman. Accounts of her conduct led *Good Housekeeping* to characterize her as "a self-destroying, alcoholic wreck of a once-beautiful, intelligent, high-spirited young woman who lived on welfare and entertained a multitude of men in the tiny four-room cottage on the edge of Route 63 that she shared with her son."

No multitude of men or women existed in Barbara's life, but she did, occasionally, accept money from men who appeared at her door. Both Peter and Geoff Madow speak of the truck driver who stopped by one day and dropped ten dollars on the table. She said something like, "Not today," and he left—and she kept the money. She did not sit outside the cottage, under a light, for the purpose of attracting customers, as even a few of Peter's supporters believe. However, because some stories of Barbara's wanderings and her bisexual activities were true, more fanciful and elaborate accounts of her behavior have fueled local gossip.

Barbara Gibbons had affairs with both sexes, but not many, and she had brief encounters with men that led her from the bottle to bed, but not many. The frequency of her sexual activities was less than popularly supposed, especially in her last years, and surely less than those of some other women, unmarried and married, in an area which has no monopoly on morality.

Barbara's affairs gave her a bad reputation. From this reputation the State's Attorney and the State Police might have thought that a promiscuous and contentious woman like Barbara Gibbons could have been killed by any one of a number of dubious characters. The murder was, after all, a sexual mutilation as well as a killing.

Although a different conclusion was reached when Peter was singled out as her attacker, Barbara's sex life demands examination. But it is a subject that has no sex appeal. Barbara's beauty was long gone. She was deteriorating physically. The most widely published photograph of Barbara and Peter together shows them dressed in identical pullovers and blue jeans, standing smiling next to the Kruse barn in the spring of 1973. Barbara appears attractive and happy as she looks at her smiling son. But another picture, taken moments later, shows a different Barbara—her face is tired, puffy, worn and defeated, and is not the face of a woman who seems interested in seeking or giving sexual favors.

By middle age her drinking began to take its toll. In October 1969 she was admitted to Sharon Hospital with a duodenal ulcer and impaired liver. Less than a year later Barbara was operated on for cancer of the uterus. The hysterectomy left her in a greatly weakened condition, but nothing, apparently, could dampen her sense of humor. She told a friend of Peter's that "they took out the baby carriage but they still left the playground."

Barbara had allowed her teeth to rot away. Peter says she was afraid to go to the dentist. He finally persuaded her to have her teeth fixed and all but four of her teeth were extracted. False teeth were fitted. Barbara was nearsighted and wore glasses. She was hard of hearing in one ear. This is not the portrait of a sexually attractive woman.

What did Peter think about his mother's affairs? The investigator for the Department of Adult Probation gave this report: "Regarding Peter's relationship with his mother, most people in the community feel that he was not embarrassed or humiliated by her activities. They seem to feel that he accepted her behavior."

Peter's own response: "She had a right to do what she wanted. She wasn't married. She was a mature woman. I don't blame her for trying to lead a life of her own."

Barbara did, from time to time, visit various bars—though more in the 1960s than in her final years. "As a matter of fact," one informant says, "she could clear out a bar pretty fast because you knew she was going to start an argument." She could, when provoked or just feeling ornery, swear like a hooker. She did do and say things that suggested a casual attitude to sex. One of Peter's best friends knocked at the cottage door one day, hoping to find him in, and was surprised when Barbara opened the door stark naked. She rushed to cover herself and explained that she enjoyed going about her own house with nothing on after a bath and forgot that she was undressed when she answered the door.

Barbara spoke freely about her lesbian inclinations. She did, by her own account to a neighbor, carry on an affair for a number of months with a young woman whose car was regularly seen at the cottage—someone she claimed to be blackmailing. A man lived in the cottage for more than a year. And not just any man but—of all things in a small New England town—a black man. Even one of Peter's staunchest supporters extrapolated from the situation and told an interviewer that "Peter was exposed to men living in the house with her—sexual relations in the same room with him."

This is not true, Peter says. He once heard some heavy breathing and squeaking bedsprings, as he told Lieutenant Shay, but he was not a witness to sexual relations. While the things he volunteers about his mother are apt to be the happier memories of the good times they had together, he has been forthright with his lawyers, the police and others who have questioned him repeatedly about his mother's habits. He speaks frankly of her drinking, her problems, the rough language she could use and even relationships of hers that distressed him. He also insists that his mother's dubious reputation is greatly exaggerated.

His friends who were in and out of the cottage constantly have no impression of Barbara as a "loose woman."

"I was there so often," says Paul Beligni. "Morning, noon and night for months. If you're at somebody's place that often, wouldn't you kind of notice that something was going on? Nothing was going on!"

Peter was present when some men came calling. One man, a near neighbor in his sixties, "used to come up constantly and ask my mom to go out with him." Peter says she did go out with him once for a horseback ride. The horse threw her and she cracked two or three ribs.

Yet another man—since moved to Florida—apparently saw enough of Barbara in the late 1960s to propose marriage. She asked Peter what he thought. "She was seriously considering it, but she didn't want to go ahead if it was going to affect me. I was fourteen or fifteen then. I said I wasn't so happy about the idea so she told the guy to forget it."

The only important relationship that Barbara had with a man in Falls Village, however, was her strange alliance with a black man who shall simply be called Gregory in this book because his former wife and children live close to Falls Village. He virtually moved into the cottage with Barbara and Peter for a year, in 1968–69, much to Peter's discomfort. The prolonged affair would prove to be the principal reason for the popular notion of Barbara as a sexual libertine.

The majority of Canaan residents, like all their neighbors in the Litchfield Hills, have little experience with other races. The percentage of blacks in northwest Connecticut, as in almost all of rural New England, is minuscule. In the 1960s, a number of concerned citizens in the area founded an organization called Concern to improve white-black relations. Many people could not see the point. Improve relations with *what* blacks? They didn't see many around.

Barbara's association with Gregory began one night in

1968 when she and Peter went to a tavern in Falls Village. They began to play billiards. Gregory, who had come to the bar for want of anywhere else to go, "really marveled at seeing this woman and her boy playing together. It really caught my attention. It was nice." Like Barbara, he needed someone to talk to, someone to drink with. He had many more personal problems than he could handle. Gregory and Barbara began to talk and they hit it off immediately. Gregory was intelligent enough to meet Barbara's exacting standards.

Although Gregory rented a house in a nearby town and had a job in Poughkeepsie, New York, an hour's drive away, he began to spend most of his time in the Gibbons' cottage. After he lost his job he was there almost constantly. During the Hartford interrogation Peter described Gregory as an alcoholic who had been "mooching off us and finally went a little bananas and my mom finally threw him out." One regular customer at the Texaco station recalls hearing "this awful row" just across the road from the station. "Obviously they were both drunk. Barbara was standing in front of the cottage and this colored fellow was on his knees with his arms wrapped around her legs. She was pounding the hell out of him with a magazine. He was saying something like, 'Barbara, I love you,' and she was saying, 'You no-good bastard, get out of here.' They were really going after each other, but I wasn't going to break up a lovers' quarrel." Gregory denies the incident, or cannot remember it.

Peter's friends also had difficulties with Gregory. "As I remember it," Peter says, "Mike and Tim Parmalee were over listening to records one night when Gregory started acting like the boss in the family. Mike pulled him out of the door and let him have it. Punched him five or six times. Gregory was in no condition to defend himself."

Peter himself finally got fed up with Gregory's presence. "I told my mother, 'Either he goes or I go,' and I went off to spend the night at the Parmalees'. She came down and said, 'He's going tomorrow.' I said, 'Then I'm staying here until tomorrow. I'll come home when he's gone.' She told him to clear out."

In the beginning, though, Barbara and Gregory, like two lame ducks, enjoyed each other's company. Someone who knew them both describes Gregory as "a well-spoken man and a gentleman, superior to Barbara in some ways. I was most surprised that he'd have anything to do with her." Gregory had many friends in the area who respected his involvement in liberal causes.

Unfortunately, Gregory's life had begun to collapse some time before he met Barbara. Due largely to his drinking and unpredictable behavior, his wife had started divorce proceedings. Her lawyer was Catherine Roraback, but Gregory refused to engage his own attorney as he resisted the breakup of his marriage because of his basic religious beliefs. He cannot even now accept that he is divorced because he took his marital vows "in the sight of God."

Gregory says that "I met Barbara at what was the worst time in my life. I was a desperate man. I needed someone to communicate with. Sex wasn't what I needed. It wasn't what I was interested in then. I was not attracted to her that way. But I was attracted to her quality. She was a very, very intelligent and compassionate person. She was someone you could really talk to because she was broad-minded and she had an amazing fund of knowledge. I would say about Barbara that she could be a wonderful friend, but also she was someone you would not want for an enemy. She was bitter about a lot of things."

As liberals, they saw eye to eye on the presidential campaign of 1968. Their common loathing for Richard Nixon and Spiro Agnew cemented their friendship in its first hours—and it would be the reason for their speaking again less than two weeks before Barbara was murdered. Although they had gone their separate ways four years earlier, both Barbara and Gregory followed the Watergate proceedings and the downfall of both Nixon and Agnew with great interest and glee. By mid-September 1973, Gregory says, "I felt that I just had to telephone Barbara to talk to her about Watergate. That was the last time I spoke to her."

Gregory insists that his relationship with Barbara was more circumspect than people think. They were just friends, and each had great need for a friend. "There wasn't anything furtive about it," he says. He even invited Barbara and Peter to his sister's house for Thanksgiving dinner. "I remember how nicely Barbara dressed up that time in a dress and every-thing. I once told her that I thought she could do a lot better with her life if she tried and she said, 'I can be anything I want.' "

Gregory slept on the green living room sofa when he lived at the cottage while Peter and his mother continued to share the bunk beds. Peter was away from home much of the time, however, and the inevitable happened—but only twice, Gregory insists.

"Look," he told me, "I'm no spring chicken. I've been around. But I didn't know anything about lesbians or what they do. I found out what Barbara was and I didn't understand it. Maybe it was a challenge. I don't know. All I know is that Barbara and I went to bed together just two times. That's all. The second time must have been because we had too much to drink. The first time was just curiosity. I had never known a lesbian. I guess it's a challenge to you as a man."

Gregory's has been a troubled life in the years since he knew Barbara Gibbons, but his fortunes have seemed better recently. "One thing that snapped me out of it," he says, "was the police investigation of the murder. When I realized what they were trying to do to Peter, the way they were claiming that he hated his mother or something, well, I stopped feeling so sorry for myself. First I was angry because they suspected me, until I proved that it wasn't me. Then I was more angry when they told me that Peter did it. You want to know some-thing about this boy who was supposed to have cut his mother all to pieces? I went to the hospital with him when Barbara was in there in 1969. We got as far as the doorway and we could see her lying in the bed with all these tubes running into her. Peter took one look and sank right to the floor. He just fainted on the spot. This is a murderer?"

Once Gregory left, Peter and Barbara developed more of a comradeship than a conventional mother-and-son relation-ship. When an interviewer asked Peter what living with a mother who spent the greater part of her days and nights reading and drinking and playing practical jokes was like, Peter shook his head and said, "Insanity. She used to come up with the ideas and we were like Ma Barker's boys. I always knew that I could count on my mother, though. If it was in her power to help me, she'd do it."

When Barbara tried to plead poverty to the Welfare Department, she was careful not to mention Barbara Sincerbeaux when asked about other sources of income. Once Peter got his driver's license, and especially after his godmother bought him a sports car, he would take his mother to the welfare office in Torrington and drop her off far enough away that the welfare people could not see what Barbara Gibbons and "Peter Gibbons," as he was identified, were driving. Meantime, Barbara was forever writing and telephoning Sincerbeaux for help. She referred to Peter's godmother as "moneybags."

Peter makes no claim that they were poverty stricken. There was always plenty to eat and they had what they needed to be comfortable. When he began to play the guitar in a rock band, Peter earned $20 to $35 for a night's performance. He was able to purchase several hundred dollars' worth of band equipment. One day when his band engagements conflicted with a part-time job he had at the Texaco station, he said that he wouldn't be able to pump gas on a Sunday. The operator told Peter that he would have to let him go. "It's too bad," the man said, "to lose a job like this. You could have used the extra money." According to Paul Beligni, "This got Pete kind of sore so he went to the bank and took out a few hundred dollars. He needed the money to buy a new guitar. Then he goes over to the guy in the station, reaches for his wallet, fans through the bills and pulls out a hundred. 'Sorry,' he says, 'I need some cigarettes but this is the smallest I've got.' You should have seen the guy's face."

Although Barbara Gibbons told people, without explanation, that Peter's godmother "had" to send them money, Barbara Sincerbeaux characterizes the whole strange business as an act of charity. Despite all the evidence of her intense involvement with Barbara Gibbons, Miss Sincerbeaux stated in 1965, "I hadn't really seen too much of her although we were employed by the same company. Our relationship was a business relationship. It wasn't a social kind of thing." As for being Peter's godmother, "It wasn't anything official; it wasn't exactly the role that people think." She said that "I've only seen Peter a few times in maybe fifteen years, something like that, so the contact has been very sketchy." (According to Peter, his godmother appeared in Falls Village only once every two years after they left Johnson Road. "The last time I can remember was when she came up by car to see my mother when she was in the hospital.")

"But as I said," Sincerbeaux continued, "this became my favorite charity. I enjoyed some wealth because of my family's success and these were people in difficult circumstances. I was glad to help. The only way that I could do it, with family problems to take care of, was to forward money to give Peter things he needed for his development and so forth, but I really kind of went overboard on my private charity and didn't expect it to be public property."

Barbara Sincerbeaux will not discuss her relationship with Barbara Gibbons and Peter Reilly or even help piece together the history of the "brilliant" woman whom she had known so well and had once admired. As for her reasons for declining to assist Peter after his arrest, she will say only that "Peter knows what I have done for him in the past. And, of course, I just became exasperated with Barbara's promises to look for work, promising to do better and get herself rehabilitated, and I gave her money for clothes and the means to get to work and so forth and so on, and nothing was happening, and I was tired, and my family situation changed. Really, this couldn't go on forever."

However gladly she gave help in Peter's early years, Sincerbeaux's aid was sent with ever greater reluctance as Barbara and Peter became a permanent burden to her. By 1964 her letters were becoming more businesslike and they concentrated on Barbara's financial problems. "Dear B," she wrote in September that year, "why don't you give me a breakdown of your salary and expenses? Why don't you speak to Cole [Gibbons' employer]?"

Barbara sent Sincerbeaux copies of her bills and the forms that she had to fill out for the Welfare Department. To one accounting of expenditures in September 1969, Barbara added the note, "I am at the post office now. This is where your money and all of mine went and I still have no brakes and absolutely no money, clothes or shoes." Another note a few months later reads like the next act in a melodrama; "Brakes are still holding out and I have the balance of your money at hand. The State has paid rent and most of hospital expenses. Obviously no rug yet. Keeping balance for Christmas. Peter wants a $140 amplifier. Hope you had a nice holiday. All my love, Barbara."

Peter says that "My mom was on the phone to Auntie B about once a week, but I'm not sure; I wasn't home all the time when she called. Sometimes they'd argue but not all that much. Sometime my mom had me call. She probably figured that my godmother might say no to her but couldn't refuse me so easily." The calls, of course, were collect.

"Dear B," wrote an exasperated Sincerbeaux in February 1970, "Kindly desist from phoning! What did the State say to do? What are you receiving monthly? Give exact amounts. Why don't you wash dishes? Or go to work like any decent person? No more funds to you after April 1. This is fair warning. How long must I suffer as a sucker? B."

Barbara's reply was pure Barbara—just a touch of sarcasm without going so far as to cut off the source of income. "This is the formal allowance schedule, monthly," she wrote. "As you can see, rent is included in the total. Heat and fuel cost more than double what is allowed. There is no allowance for clothes, per se, nor for car repairs, or anything over and above the bare necessities. In other words, even if one wanted to work, one is totally hamstrung for lack of clothing and transportation. As I pointed out, Peter has few clothes now, except for those he bought himself from what you sent him, besides the electronic equipment.

"Personally, the only shoes I own are a pair of classic ostrich pumps—hardly suitable for dishwashing, if there were a place to wash dishes. I suppose I deserve April 1, All Fools' Day—hadn't thought of that until now. Love, B."

Barbara Gibbons did do some part-time work, such as making Christmas wreaths or running the gas pumps across the road, and she did make an occasional effort to find a job. She applied in 1969 to the Welfare Department's Work

Incentive Program, giving her primary occupation as "editor of life insurance company magazine." She was later notified that "You are considered to be an inappropriate candidate for referral to the Work Incentive Program." On another occasion she received a "notice of rejection" from the State Personnel Department after trying for a job as a publicist.

No doubt there were times when Barbara was desperate. One entry in her notebook says, "I borrowed $200 from Peter, for which I'll never forgive myself." She and Peter lived well but not wisely. They certainly had great need of a car, but two sports cars were extravagant. Peter's godmother had told them most emphatically, "I cannot afford nor will I be able to support you as a two-car family." Nonetheless, Sincerbeaux wrote a $595 check in November 1971 so that Barbara and Peter could buy a red 1967 Triumph convertible. The following September she agreed to the purchase of a second car: a dark blue 1968 Corvette with a white convertible top for $2,395. Peter, now seventeen years old, had fastened his sights on this high-powered racer, and what Peter wanted, Barbara got.

The Corvette was a "beautiful, 435-horsepower machine," Peter says, that seemed a good buy, but many things required fixing or replacing. Barbara wrote in her notebook that "The labor on the Corvette is going to be astronomical." It was. Peter says that "We did over $2,000 worth of major repairs in the first year we had the car." Meantime, the Triumph went into a state of collapse so both Barbara and Peter had to use the flashy Corvette. As one neighbor groused, "It was bad enough paying taxes to support Barbara Gibbons on welfare but seeing her driving around in a Corvette was the last straw."

Fortunately for their financial situation, some money arrived from Florida. Hilda Gibbons had retired there after an ill-fated journey to Europe—she was knocked down by a trolley car in Switzerland and spent weeks in a hospital. She died in a Florida mental institution in December 1971. Her will left nothing to her daughter and only $854.60 to Peter. Two thousand dollars went to her brother-in-law Jim, a man Hilda considered "a saint." He must have been; he sent $1,000 to Barbara. To keep the Connecticut welfare authorities from learning of their windfall, Barbara opened a savings account in a Massachusetts bank.

Peter and his mother had a quarrel just before her last Christmas. She found that he had drawn a large amount of money out of his savings account and when he would not give the reason she berated him for handling his money foolishly. But all was forgiven on Christmas morning. He had used the money to buy her an electric typewriter. It was an act of devotion that she would rave about in a letter to her cousin June. Now, at last, she might be able to make some progress on a piece of writing she had been researching for years: an essay about Louisa May Alcott, the creator of *Little Women*. Peter and his friends would often see her at her desk, typing away, but no one read her work and no manuscript has been found.

By the end of Barbara Gibbons' life, Peter and his friends were the only people she cared about or who cared about her. She had her books, her bottle of sherry and whatever excitement her son could bring into her life. "No one would be there if I wasn't there," Peter says. "I think she was unhappy, in a way, just before she died. I wasn't home that much and she was alone a lot. As I look back, I really feel bad about that."

13 ▪ THE TRIAL BEGINS

SGT. KELLY: As I said to you, I don't think you're a vicious person.
PETER REILLY: I'm not.
SGT. KELLY: Basically. But last night—
PETER REILLY: Being pushed, and the tension and everything—
SGT. KELLY: Right. The animal instinct took over and you fought back to protect yourself. You see? You follow what I mean? This is the whole thing. But you got to get it out. If we don't get it out, you are going to have this inside of you and it's going to dig and dig at you, and—
PETER REILLY: There's something about me yelling, leave me alone.
SGT. KELLY: Okay.
PETER REILLY: I don't know, maybe I'm imagining it but it seems to be coming out of someplace.

The trial of Peter Reilly began a few days before his nineteenth birthday. John Bianchi and Catherine Roraback clashed even before the start of testimony. The press was upset because Judge Speziale was issuing the most stringent restrictions on reporting the case that the journalists had ever seen. Peter's friends suddenly found that they were forbidden to speak their minds. Security was tight. Everyone seemed on edge.

The brouhaha was in great contrast to the tranquil character of the old colonial town and the normally unruffled life of the Litchfield courthouse. Spectators able to squeeze into the second-floor courtroom found that the place looked strangely familiar. They had seen such a setting before in countless films and TV shows and on the pages of crime novels.

The big room is unpretentious and somehow reassuring in its absence of frills, including air conditioning. The walls are pale yellow. The white ceiling reflects the light of nine plain brass chandeliers. There is a fireplace, no longer used, at one end of the rectangular room and a great mahogany bench for the judge at the other end. A wooden barrier separates the working area from the rows of hard chairs for the press and public.

The Reilly trial, as one newspaper put it, got off to a "surprisingly sudden start" in late February, just a day after the Armentano decision permitting use of the confession as evidence and just as Peter was released from jail. Speculation had been that the trial would be put off for at least a month, but Judge Speziale wanted jury selection to begin immediately. Catherine Roraback did not object. She did not ask for more time to gather information to demonstrate the implausibility, if not the impossibility, of Peter's guilt.

She obviously felt that she had as much as she needed. Despite Judge Armentano's ruling, which demonstrated the risks of relying on constitutional arguments, she was going to put great emphasis on the questionable circumstances of Peter's arrest, interrogation and confession. Her style was not to play detective and find evidence to prove Peter's innocence. She did not choose to hire a private investigator, partly because there was no money, partly because she was suspicious of private detectives—they were usually ex-cops who had too cozy a relationship with the police. Anyway, strictly speaking, she did not have to prove her client not guilty; the State had to produce evidence to prove him guilty. She greatly doubted that the State could. She told friends, "I've got a winner."

Not surprisingly, Judge Speziale cleared the decks for the trial by denying Roraback's remaining pretrial motions. Then, he issued a warning to Peter, the attorneys, witnesses, policemen and others against giving interviews to reporters. He said that no cameras, TV or radio equipment or tape recorders would be allowed in the courthouse or its grounds. No sketching would be permitted in the courtroom.

When jury selection began, the introductory remarks by the two attorneys struck sparks. John Bianchi and Catherine Roraback clearly had different approaches and a different way with words. Bianchi tended to speak expansively, Roraback with more precision. The State's Attorney said that the trial would seek to determine who caused the death of

Barbara Gibbons. Not so, countered Roraback. As she presented Peter to the prospective jurors, and as they inspected the youth accused of a fiendish murder, she said that "We're not here to determine who caused the death of Barbara Gibbons, but to determine whether Peter Reilly caused the death of Barbara Gibbons."

When Bianchi said he would ask for a sentence of twenty-five years to life, Roraback called this "cruel and unusual punishment." Such a sentence would be "as final an act as death would be for a young man eighteen years of age."

Since Peter faced possible life imprisonment, both the State and the defense were permitted to dismiss as many as eighteen panel members of the more than sixty persons considered, without showing cause. Among those dismissed, by the judge as well as the attorneys, was a welfare worker who was familiar with Barbara Gibbons, a woman who said she was brought up to believe that the police are always right, and a twenty-two-year-old who admitted that it would be "a little tough" for him to return a guilty verdict against someone as young as Peter.

Roraback was looking for younger jurors while Bianchi, in accepting older persons, wanted to be sure that they would be able to set aside sympathies they might have for young people that might prejudice their view of Peter. One man selected, Edward Ives, an insurance agent from Litchfield, said that he could forgo such sympathies even though he was a scoutmaster and the father of three children, nineteen to twenty-five years old. He was named the jury foreman. He became one of the jurors most set on conviction.

Eight men and four women were chosen to serve as the Reilly jury. Of the twelve, four were in their sixties, three in their twenties and the rest in between. The first man selected was a New Milford bachelor who lived with his mother. He had once been a constable. Two men worked for the telephone company. Another was a commercial artist. Another was a maintenance foreman. One of the women worked in a factory laboratory. Another was the wife of a Congregational minister and the mother of three children.

The jurors looked like honest, decent, thoughtful people.

If there was any common denominator, apart from being residents of the same county, it was the fact that they had not noticed or taken any interest in one of the most fascinating crime-and-justice stories to come along in years. Catherine Roraback would remark that in her experience, "I was always shocked to discover how few people read the newspapers."

One prospective juror, a high school civics teacher, admitted that he and his wife had read about and discussed the case. He had even seen the *New Times* article. He had not made up his mind, he said, about Reilly's guilt or innocence, but he could see that this was "a very significant case, involving police procedures." It would produce "a very significant confrontation between two attorneys." He was absolutely right. And, of course, he was excused from duty.

Although Roraback had far more experience with trials, certainly controversial trials, her greater sophistication was less likely to be appreciated by a rural jury than Bianchi's chummier style. High-flown talk about her defendant's rights would make less of an impression than a graphic presentation of the details of the murder that somehow connected the defendant to the crime. Therein lay the danger for Peter Reilly.

Catherine Roraback was obviously less concerned about being liked. This was not a popularity contest. Her manner was direct and even brusque. In the male world of the law, and especially when she appeared in the clubby Litchfield courthouse, she had encountered plenty of antagonism and had overcome a good many obstacles. She was able to compete and more than hold her own. "But one of her problems," said a friend, "is that she refused to compromise on anything. That includes the way she interrogates witnesses, the way she approaches the judge and the prosecutor. She can be soft spoken but she comes on hard and she can alienate men who don't like strong women. I think she affected both Bianchi and Speziale this way. Maybe some of the jurors. She is someone who just doesn't take any crap from anybody and they could accept this approach better in a man. You could tell in the trial that there was an undercurrent of hostility towards her."

Judge Speziale has a mild and prim appearance and a

quiet, retiring nature, but he was clearly capable of keeping two tough lawyers in check. Off the bench he was amiable, courtly and easy to talk to. He wore a somewhat rakish tweed hat. As a fifty-one-year-old man of average size with a bland face, balding head and spectacles, he could easily be lost in a crowd. On the bench, however, wearing his black robes and his usual expression of intense concentration, he was a little larger than life and very much in command.

In Torrington, the old brass-making industrial town where he had grown up, he was a prominent citizen and a member of Italian-American and other fraternal organizations. He was proud to be a lifetime honorary member of local 514 of the American Federation of Musicians, having earned his way through college by playing the saxophone and clarinet in orchestras.

John A. Speziale is said to have been the kind of youngster who would be the only one to carry a briefcase to school. He was studious; he was going to be somebody. As one of five children in a family of modest means, the son of an insurance agent, he considered himself fortunate to get to Duke University on a music scholarship. His mother worked in a needle factory to help out. He studied economics, graduated Phi Beta Kappa, and earned his law degree at Duke after naval service in World War II. He survived twelve invasions in the Pacific Theater as well as kamikaze attacks, and he was one of the first Americans to reach Nagasaki after the atomic bombing.

Speziale became a Municipal Court judge at age twenty-six, just a year after passing his bar examination in 1948, making him one of the youngest judges in the country. He was active in local and state politics for thirteen years. He helped run Torrington, an island of Democrats in a rural sea of Republicans. When he was appointed to the Court of Common Pleas after three years as State Treasurer, the politician became the dedicated jurist.

According to a journalist who has followed his career, "Speziale's strength is that he's capable of growth. They say in Torrington that no man ever changed more drastically than he did when he became a state judge. He stopped seeing a lot of his old political friends and he told relatives that he could no longer give them legal advice."

The Connecticut Bar Association's first rating of the judiciary, announced in 1977, gave Speziale high marks. Peter Reilly's opinion, expressed after his trial, is worth something: "I think he's a very fair man. I don't know why exactly. It's just a feeling. It's my instinct." The Reilly case was the most difficult of Speziale's career. While it was underway, Speziale was named the chief judge of the Superior Court. He was later elevated to the Connecticut Supreme Court.

As Peter was preparing to go to court early one morning, he found Hannah Lavigne collapsing to the floor in a faint. Peter yelled to Art Madow to come and help. As Art revived his grandmother somewhat and helped her to the bathroom, Peter rushed to the phone to call the State Police because they were handling Canaan's ambulance calls. He told them to send an ambulance immediately.

Soon afterward, a neighbor, Elaine Monty, arrived to pick up Peter and drive him to Litchfield. She recalls that Art Madow came out of the house to say that he thought his grandmother was dying. When she went inside she found Peter standing by the stove in the kitchen. "Peter was shaking like he was freezing to death," she says. "That may be his ultimate emotion. He said to me, 'I don't think I can take this.'"

Nan was unconscious. A state trooper arrived and then the ambulance. Peter and Mrs. Monty moved furniture aside so that Nan could be carried out.

Then Detective Sergeant Fred Keller of the State Police, who had worked under Lieutenant Shay in the murder investigation, began to question Peter. He wanted to know: Were you alone with her? Did you touch her? Elaine Monty said to Peter he didn't have to answer anything. She told Keller that the judge was waiting for them in the Litchfield courthouse.

"Peter was very shook up about Nan's condition," Mrs. Monty recalls. He asked her to keep checking with the hospital. In the courtroom, as more members of the jury were being selected, the word came through that Nan was all right. Mrs. Monty gave Peter a signal. "He was really relieved," she says.

On the morning of February 26, while jury selection was still underway, John Bianchi came into the courtroom waving four newspaper articles that he considered prejudicial to both the State and the defense. He said he might call for a mistrial, which he did later in the day, but the judge denied it. While Bianchi was upset by Peter's comments to reporters at the time of his release on bail, as printed in three newspapers, an article in the *New York Times* upset him most.

The heart of the *Times* story was the quotations from an interview with Catherine Roraback, including this one: "It doesn't even rise to the level of a confession. They planted in his mind that he must have done it. They were holding an 18-year-old kid who had the shock of seeing his mother dead and then subjecting him to that type of grilling." Roraback did not deny making the statements, but she insisted that they had been made weeks earlier in what was supposed to be an off-the-record conversation. She apologized to the court and said that "it upsets me more than it does Mr. Bianchi."

During a long recess, Judge Speziale, worried about the possibility that the Reilly jurors would be influenced by press accounts, dictated an order that went beyond his earlier instructions to reporters.

He warned he would enforce the contempt power of the court against anyone who makes, reports or broadcasts any statement "that goes beyond the public record of this court, if the statement is reasonably calculated to affect the outcome of the trial." He cautioned the press not to "speculate, spread rumor or campaign for a particular result." He specifically prohibited Peter Reilly from granting interviews or making extrajudicial statements. Roraback allowed that it would not be "wise" for Peter to give interviews but she argued, unsuccessfully, against the restrictions on Peter's freedom of speech. Speziale said he was "impounding" the four newspaper stories that Bianchi had complained about; nothing in them could be reprinted.

The very next morning after the order, John Bianchi again moved for a mistrial. He complained about a four-man CBS

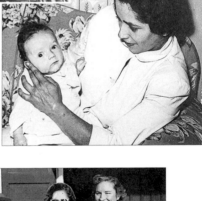

[LEFT] Barbara as a motorcyclist in New York in 1947, and [BELOW] with her child, Peter Reilly, a decade later in Falls Village, Connecticut. *Peter Reilly*

Barbara and Hilda Gibbons with Peter's godmother, Barbara Sincerbeaux. *Peter Reilly*

[ABOVE & LEFT] Peter, 18, and Barbara, 51, posing in look-alike outfits by the Kruse barn in the spring of 1973; two of their last pictures taken together. *Kenneth Carter*

Scene of the murder: Barbara and Peter's four-room cottage on Route 63, Falls Village. The Kruse house is to the right. *Donald S. Connery*

Peter and his high school friends at the graveyard memorial service for his mother. A jail official's overcoat covers the handcuffs. Lakeville Journal

Raising money for the Reilly Defense Fund. Peter, on guitar, playing with rock-band friends at a benefit dance. *From the author's collection*

Reilly supporters at Canaan railroad station: Donald Sager, Beatrice Keith, William Dickinson, Dorothy Madow, Marie Dickinson, Pat Sexton, and Mickey Madow. *Roger Cohn,* Register Citizen

The prosecutor, State's Attorney John F. Bianchi.
Roger Cohn, Register Citizen

State police lieutenant James Shay, who led the murder investigation.
Lakeville Journal

Superior court judge John A. Speziale, who presided over Peter Reilly's 1974 trial and his 1976 new-trial hearing.
Stephen Hawkins, Register Citizen

Grand jury prosecutor Paul McQuillan.
Mary Lou Estabrook,
Lakeville Journal

Defense Attorney
Catherine G. Roraback.
From the author's collection

Private detective
James Conway.
Joseph O'Brien, Hartford Courant

Attorney T. F. Gilroy Daly.
From the author's collection

Forensic pathologist
Dr. Milton Helpern.
Roger Cohn, Register Citizen

Psychiatrist
Dr. Herbert Spiegel.
From the author's collection

Peter's Falls Village neighbors
Michael Parmalee [LEFT] and
Timothy Parmalee [BELOW].
Stephen Hawkins, Register Citizen

Peter outside the Litchfield courthouse after
all charges against him were dropped.
New York Daily News

Peter at home in East Canaan
with Marion and Mickey Madow.
© Stephen Green-Armytage, 1976

Peter and Donald S. Connery in 1976 at the author's home office in Kent, Connecticut. Their collaboration on this book led to an enduring friendship and a commitment to assist in other cases of wrongful conviction. *Eric Connery*

Playwright Arthur Miller and Peter in 1995. As key speakers at a Hartford, Connecticut, conference on "Freeing the Innocent," they told of the dangers of police over-reliance on confessions to solve crimes. *Donald S. Connery*

television crew that had photographed the exterior of the police barracks and the courthouse. The TV people, he said, were taking pictures "as we all arrived in court." He said such coverage of the trial would "inflame the community of Litchfield County, either for or against the accused or for or against the State." The judge ordered an investigation of the CBS crew. County Detective James Bausch was dispatched and came back with a report.

Although Judge Speziale did not support Bianchi's motion for a mistrial and a two-month continuance, saying only that he would keep it under advisement, the State's Attorney did win a victory of sorts. The press was effectively intimidated from doing any reporting beyond the events in the courtroom. And, as the *Lakeville Journal* reported, "Friends of Reilly and other potential witnesses became much more guarded in their dealings with the newspaper, wire service and television journalists who have swarmed to the area."

"Swarmed" was too strong a word for the outside press interest in the case, but another immediate effect of the Speziale order was to discourage coverage of the trial by national media. The CBS crew, finding that even the local reporters shied away from being interviewed on camera, abandoned plans for a network feature on the case and left town. *New Times*, after having broken the Reilly story nationally, printed one more article, brief and innocuous, and then gave up its coverage entirely.

Only Connecticut newspapers, six of them, assigned reporters to the trial. Their stories were circumspect. One editor said privately that his paper was financially shaky and could not afford a court fight about the issue. The *Hartford Times*, at least, hurled an editorial brickbat at Judge Speziale "for an attempt to muzzle the press." Saying that "The charges of a coerced confession, whether ultimately sustained or not, should not be hidden from the public," the newspaper reminded the judge that he had the option of sequestering the jury if he thought the jurors would be influenced by press accounts. But "Judge Speziale has a unique approach: sequester the public."

What the editorial failed to note, however, was that Connecticut has no tradition of sequestering juries. Speziale felt strongly that locking up jurors in hotel rooms during long trials would ultimately prevent suitable jurors from serving at all.

"The trial went forward," says Marion Madow, "in an atmosphere of fear because we were afraid that they would put Peter back in jail if any one of us spoke to anybody that we weren't supposed to."

Given the bizarre circumstances of the Reilly case, it seems appropriate that testimony in the trial should begin on a false note. The very first witness for the prosecution would give vital testimony that was untrue. While some observers were suspicious almost immediately, it was not until two and a half years later that it became apparent that State's Attorney Bianchi knew then that the testimony could not be accurate.

"Kindly attend to the evidence," said a court official to the jury after reading the indictment charging Peter with murder. It was 10:47 on the morning of March 1, 1974, a wet Friday.

Roger Cohn, recalling his impressions as one of the attending reporters, says that "Peter seemed nervous, as though he was starting to realize for the first time just what was happening. He had been almost in a daze in the short time since his release from jail. He has a tendency to try to ignore things in the hope that they will go away. Now, seeing the jury seated before him, he knew that this was something that was not going to go away. It was only beginning."

The first prosecution witness was crisp and confident in her all-white uniform and white shoes. She was Barbara G. Fenn, a registered nurse and the wife of State Trooper Barry Fenn. Her testimony would give John Bianchi a foundation for claiming that Peter Reilly had plenty of time to kill his mother and dispose of the evidence.

As the evening supervisor at Sharon Hospital on the night of September 28, 1973, Mrs. Fenn testified, she had answered a telephone in the hospital's emergency room when it rang at "approximately 9:40 P.M." The hospital switchboard operator was putting through a call from someone who, Fenn said, had "a young male voice." (The caller was Peter; he had given his name to the operator but he did not repeat it when Fenn came on the line.) Fenn said the caller stated that "I am at the home of Barbara Gibbons. She is having difficulty breathing. There is blood all over the place." She said that she told him that she would dispatch an ambulance, but he explained that he had already called for an ambulance.

"Now, did you, in fact, dispatch the Falls Village ambulance," Bianchi asked, "and did you, in fact, notify the Connecticut State Police?"

"Yes, sir, I did," she replied.

Bianchi asked again for the time she received the call.

"I estimated the time at 9:40 and did that in correlation with the fact that there was another ambulance arriving in the emergency room at the same time, and I checked with the ambulance log in time, which was approximately 9:40— that's the closest—P.M., that I can place it."

If Peter had actually spoken to Mrs. Fenn at 9:40, on the fifth of the calls he dialed after rushing to the phone, then he would have had to begin telephoning some minutes earlier, say at 9:35, but that was just about the time that several people at the church meeting had seen Peter depart. Nonetheless, Catherine Roraback had only a few questions to ask the nurse. Mrs. Fenn said that the caller sounded "Soft spoken. I would say a little apprehensive, a little excited. This was my first impression."

Mrs. Fenn testified for less than five minutes and was dismissed.

State Trooper John Calkins was next. The prosecutor handed him a photocopy of entries that Calkins had made in the police log at the Canaan barracks on the night of the murder.

"Now, Trooper Calkins," Bianchi asked, "I would inquire whether or not you received a telephone call from Barbara Fenn in the evening of September 28, 1973?"

"Yes, sir, I did," Calkins replied.

"And is that telephone conversation noted on the photocopy of the log that I just showed you?"

"Yes, sir, it is."

Bianchi did not do the obvious and ask the time that the call from Fenn was logged.

Catherine Roraback asked the question, however, and the

trooper said that "2158" was the entry in the log. Calkins explained that the State Police operate on military time. Therefore the time of the Fenn call was 9:58 P.M. Having established that there was an eighteen-minute difference between Fenn's 9:40, when she claimed she took Peter's emergency call, and the police record of 9:58 as the time she reacted, Peter's attorney seemingly did not realize what was apparent to many spectators: that here, in the opening moments of trial testimony, was an incredible contradiction in the prosecution's case. Reporters who later joked about the Watergate style "eighteen-minute gap" could only imagine that the experienced Miss Roraback was saving her fire for another day. She never directly challenged the Fenn testimony. She made no use of Joanne Mulhern's statement to the police, received by Roraback just prior to the trial, which told of her arrival home from the Youth Center meeting at about 9:50 and her call to Sharon Hospital soon afterward. That call had coincided with the hospital's dispatch of an ambulance in response to Peter's appeal for help.

Defenders of Roraback's trial performance would point out later that she was working at a disadvantage that first day, because she had assigned Peter Herbst to deal with pressing business in her Canaan office. Thus she was on her own in the courtroom and lacked an associate to help her keep track of the testimony. And though Herbst would be on hand for most trial days, Roraback was at a further disadvantage because she was without the funds to order the all-important daily transcripts of testimony.

Trooper Bruce McCafferty, the next witness, told of being ordered to the murder scene at 9:58 and reaching the cottage at about 10:02. He spoke of being led into the cottage by Peter and Geoff Madow, seeing the body of the victim and radioing the barracks for a supervisor. Bianchi wanted to know if Peter was crying.

"No, he was not," said McCafferty, adding that "he was seated or standing at times, and he didn't seem that emotionally upset, either way."

After Bianchi learned from McCafferty that he took a statement from Peter at 10:45 P.M., Bianchi read the four-page statement in full. The jurors and others in the courtroom learned for the first time what Peter Reilly told the police less than two hours after the murder. His story about having come home from the church meeting, discovering his mother's body on the floor, and then telephoning for assistance, would have to be compared with the version in the confession he signed twenty-four hours later.

Among Bianchi's further questions for the trooper was this: "Would you tell the ladies and gentlemen of the jury whether or not he was in tears?" Again from the trooper: "No, he was not."

When Roraback questioned McCafferty, she got him to admit that he had never before seen Peter under stress and that he was not really observing Peter's reactions too closely. He said he did not remember Peter sitting in a chair in the living room and shaking.

Bianchi made sure he had the last word. He asked once again, "Did you see him cry, Trooper?" McCafferty said, "No, I didn't." He was the first of a parade of policemen who would be asked whether they had seen Peter Reilly weeping.

In the early days of the trial, Roger Cohn was trying hard to avoid becoming sympathetic to Peter. He thought the defendant could well be guilty and that the prosecution would probably introduce hard evidence against him later in the trial. He says that as he listened to the testimony, "It really disturbed me to see how effectively Bianchi was using his repetitive questions about whether Peter appeared emotionally upset that night. The police answers made a real impression on the jurors. It bothered me that Roraback didn't attack this line of questioning. All she did was question how closely the police observed Reilly and how well they knew him. But what she never got across to the jurors was that it didn't matter how Peter appeared. So what if he wasn't crying? If he had found his mother in that condition, he could easily have been in a state of shock. Maybe he just doesn't cry; maybe he holds back his tears until later. Yet Bianchi seemed to turn this into solid prosecution evidence when, in fact, it seemed meaningless to me. Instead of pointing that out, Roraback tried to challenge the police view of Reilly's condition with Marion Madow's testimony that Peter was shaking."

Marion Madow testified immediately after a civil engineer named Frank Desmond. He had drawn a precise floor plan of the Gibbons cottage for the State Police. To indicate the size of the house where Peter lived with his mother for nearly half his life, Desmond said that it would fit into the well of the courtroom.

That was one picture that stuck in the mind: the little white building in the center of the courtroom. Then Marion Madow described another: the telephone ringing in her home as she sat watching a movie called *Kelly's Heroes* on CBS. She recalled the segment as the one "when they were boarding a tank to go over the river to get into the town to get the gold, and some guy was jumping on the tank and said, 'I want to go with you,' and just about then the phone rang."

She was asked what the substance of the call was. "I answered the phone, and Peter said, 'Mrs. Madow, this is Peter. Is Mr. Madow there?' And I said, 'Yes, Peter.' And he says, 'I—I think—the reason I need the ambulance, something's happened to my mom. She is lying on the floor, and there's blood all over the place, and she is unconscious.'"

Yet neither of these mental pictures was so vivid and lurid as the photographs that were shown to the jury during the initial two days of testimony.

The first of the pictures was introduced while Trooper McCafferty was on the stand. It was a color photograph of the mutilated Barbara Gibbons as she sprawled on the bedroom floor. After McCafferty agreed with Bianchi that it was "a fair and accurate representation of the scene as you observed it," the picture was shown to Catherine Roraback and then to Peter. He glanced at it before turning away.

Dr. David Grendon, a radiologist who worked at Sharon Hospital, took the stand and described a set of five X-ray pictures of the victim as they were shown to the jury on a viewing machine. The X-rays revealed three bone fractures: of the left pubic bone in the area of the pelvis and both thigh bones, each halfway between the knee and the hip. Dr. Grendon noted that there was a difference between the two thighbone injuries. There was a simple oblique fracture of the right femur and a more complicated "comminuted" fracture of the left femur. Grendon explained that comminuted "means more than a simple fracture line. . . . If you take a bone and just crack it across like that, that's a simple fracture. If you crack it in more than one place and [there is] an intermediate piece, that's comminuted."

In his confession, Peter had said that he remembered "jumping on my mother's legs." The obvious question was: Could a 121-pound youth wearing sneakers have cracked the femurs, two of the toughest bones in the human body, in two different ways? It was not asked by either the prosecution or the defense.

Although the murky X-ray photos could be studied dispassionately, the color photographs and color slides presented during the testimony of the next two witnesses were stomach-churning pieces of evidence. In the photos, Barbara Gibbons was bloodless and bloodstained, almost too white to be real.

Sergeant Richard Chapman, a police photographer, was on the stand as his pictures of the victim were passed around, first to the attorneys and then to the jurors.

"I don't know if I was just viewing the whole scene melodramatically," Roger Cohn relates, "but it seemed as though Roraback was deeply disturbed by the photos of Gibbons' body. She almost had tears in her eyes." She objected to them as "highly inflammatory and prejudicial." She suggested that the State was just trying to "pile up the record with inflammatory material."

Roraback appeared to be concerned that the jurors might be so shocked by the horrible details of the murder that they would look more harshly on the accused murderer. Bianchi insisted that the photographs were material and relevant: "Certainly, they show the crime scene, which . . . I have a responsibility and an obligation to show them."

The real horror show began after the lunch recess when

the courtroom lights were dimmed and nineteen color slides of the victim were shown to the judge and the attorneys by Sergeant Chapman. The jury was out of the room for this preliminary screening.

Explaining that the shots had been taken while Dr. Izumi conducted the autopsy, Sergeant Chapman intoned the details of the pictures: "The neck. . . . The face of the victim as we started our operation. . . . The right hand with a probe through it. . . . The stomach. . . . Right leg. Left leg. Vaginal regions. . . . Close-up. . . . This is the vestibule of the vagina. . . . This is the hyoid bone. That's the conclusion."

Peter's lawyer told Judge Speziale that she objected to several of the slides. She described these as "highly inflammatory, especially to the women on the jury." The pictures of the great gash in the neck were bad enough, but, "when we get to the interior of the victim [these are] grossly inflammatory photographs." She felt that some of them were simply repetitious: duplications for shock effect. Bianchi disagreed.

Roraback would not drop it: "I quite specifically objected, Your Honor, to the photographs of the vagina. . . . I mean that perhaps I have reacted to these photographs quite differently than anyone else in this—Your Honor, or Mr. Bianchi, or Mr. Chapman, or indeed, Dr. Izumi. I am a woman, after all, and I must say that some of these photographs of the vagina and the so-called exploratory operation in the vagina area are, to me, the most disgusting thing and violative of my own sense of dignity as a woman that I can think of—and I just can't think that anyone on that jury is not going to react in a similar way." She added that "I object, highly, especially as to the women who are on that jury who I think would react exactly the same way I have."

One reporter felt that Roraback was reacting with a feminist view that seemed naive under the circumstances. "If a man was murdered and found nude, wouldn't the prosecution present pictures of his body, especially if his sex organs had been cut as part of the killing?"

Bianchi said to the judge that "counsel is here as an attorney" and the murder photos "are necessary and vital to the proof of the State's case." Bianchi then put Dr. Ernest Izumi on the witness stand to say that the color slides are essential to his description to the jury of the injuries sustained by the victim.

Judge Speziale ruled that the slides would be shown—but not that day. Before adjourning the court he reminded the jury, as he did throughout the trial, that "You are not to discuss this case with anyone, not even amongst yourselves, not to discuss it with any friend or members of your family or anyone else. Don't seek out any information about this case. You are to completely ignore any of the news media or any other source if they refer to this particular trial. Should anyone attempt to speak to you, ladies and gentlemen, in any manner, shape or form, that must be reported to me."

14 ■ PROSECUTION

SGT. KELLY: That's what I'm asking you for now, the details. Do
you think the razor is behind the barn?
PETER REILLY: Either that or behind the gas station.
SGT. KELLY: All right. Either one of those places.
PETER REILLY: They will be the two places I would think quickest
to throw it.

Judge Speziale said after the Reilly trial that "Dr. Izumi
went through the courtroom like a bulldozer." The pathologist's three-day testimony revealed all the gory details of the
murder. It stood as the authoritative last word because the
defense—even though warned by Speziale halfway through
the trial that the testimony would powerfully influence the
jury—presented no medical expert to challenge Izumi or his
conclusions. One juror was so impressed by Izumi's presentation that he called it "the real meat of the trial."

The pathologist took the stand Tuesday afternoon, March 5.
A screen was set up in the well of the courtroom so that the
jurors as well as the judge, the attorneys and the witness
could see the color pictures.

Dr. Izumi, a heavy-set man of fifty-six years, outlined
his personal history at Bianchi's request. A native of San
Francisco, he had studied at Stanfrd and the University of
California, served in the Army Medical Corps for four and
a half years and earned his medical degree at the University of Texas. He had gone on to Yale Medical School before

beginning his career in pathology. He was involved in the Reilly case as an assistant state medical examiner.

Not mentioned was the fact that Dr. Izumi himself had been in serious trouble with the law in 1972. The Internal Revenue Service had charged him with income tax evasion—failing to report more than $127,000 in taxable income for 1965–68. Maximum penalty: five years in prison or a $10,000 fine, or both. He had pleaded not guilty at first, then switched to a plea of no contest to a lesser charge. Finally he was fined $5,000 and given a one-year suspended sentence.

Roger Cohn remembered interviewing Izumi about a murder in Torrington. Izumi, after the autopsy, had said that he could not state the cause of death until he had "all the results of the police investigation on hand. I have to have their information, and they have to have my information, then we have to piece it together." Cohn wrote down the declaration "because I was so surprised. I always thought that a medical examiner gave an independent expert opinion without checking things with the cops."

Although Roraback said privately after the trial that she considered Izumi a hostile witness, she did not bring in her own medical authority for at least two reasons. She had submitted Izumi's findings and conclusions to an expert for review and he could not fault them. She feared that additional medical testimony, even by her own witness, would simply deepen the picture of the horrifying murder in the mind of the jurors.

With the courtroom darkened, Dr. Izumi gave thumbnail descriptions of the nineteen slides as they were shown. When the lights were turned on again and the blinds opened, Izumi related his actions in the Gibbons cottage after the murder.

Rigor mortis, "stiffness of a body," had already set in by the time he began his external examination at 4:40 A.M., Izumi said. He had found no signs of liver mortis: the redness of the skin in a part of the body where blood had gathered, because the severe lacerations, "the deep, penetrating wounds," in the neck area had caused an almost complete pumping out of blood—four quarts in all.

Izumi estimated that the blood would have gushed out within sixty seconds, although, he said, Barbara Gibbons did not die, biologically speaking, for another five minutes. He explained:

> Clinical death is described as how an individual or a doctor sees that patient. That is, in a period from one minute to five minutes, there may be no pulse. It is during that time that the patient has no heartbeat. He appears dead, but he is really not because it is only the clinical judgment of the observer during this time. It is during the zero to five minutes when no artificial resuscitation or no oxygen is gotten to that brain, then, death occurs because there is cellular and tissue death. The patient is biologically dead at the end of five minutes.

Izumi concluded that the slashing of the neck had occurred first and that the wounds on the lower parts of the body "were inflicted after the patient had died." This testimony was crucial because it was the State's contention that if Barbara Gibbons was still breathing when Peter found her, as he had stated in his telephone calls, then Peter had to have inflicted the wounds that were made after she stopped breathing. This, with the confession, was the essence of the case against Peter Reilly.

How could the victim breathe if the neck had been slashed so severely that the head was almost detached, and if all the blood had gushed out in a minute's time? Izumi had an explanation but would take a while before he gave it.

In the darkened courtroom, he showed the color slides in slow order and gave a narration. He used a wooden stick to point out details. The slide show was like nothing the jurors had ever seen. A reporter would write at the end of the day that "As they left the courtroom, several jurors looked emotionally drained by the sights they had just witnessed."

The first slide was of the battered face of Barbara Gibbons. The fractured nose and black eyes, Izumi said, were the result of "a direct traumatic blow in this area." The murderer, he believed, had first smashed the victim's face before killing her by slashing the throat.

Izumi told of discovering a bruise in the back of the head. Then, having worked his way into the brain cavity, he had found evidence of a small hemorrhage in the soft tissues of the brain. He speculated that before death, "the victim either fell to the floor or was knocked to the floor or else backed up against the wall and the back of her head hit the wall."

The second slide flashed on the screen. "This is a very deep wound to the left side of the neck," he said. It went almost from ear to ear. "The deep-cut wound was brought across the voice box someplace in this vicinity, completely separating and opening the voice box so that the vocal cords could be exposed and could be clearly seen." He described three other cuts. Peter had said in his confession that he had slashed only once at his mother's throat. The severing of the windpipe and the voice box was caused by a sharp instrument, the doctor said, and they could not have been self-inflicted.

Izumi stated that "This victim could neither speak nor scream because, to all intents and purposes, there is no mouth because these openings communicate directly with the outside. This, now, provides the main source of any breathing." Peter, of course, had said in his emergency calls that his mother was still breathing. As for the lungs, Izumi said that he found clotted blood in the main windpipe. The jurors and audience could imagine the scene in the cottage: the killer slashing away, the nearly headless victim unable to scream for help.

Nothing more was said about any possible breathing until this dialogue between Bianchi and Izumi the next day:

Q: Now, Doctor, yesterday, when you were testifying about cuts about Miss Gibbons' neck, I believe you testified that with such cuts, the location of those cuts, that she could not talk or scream immediately after their occurrence, is that correct, Doctor?

A: Yes, sir.

Q: Now, I would ask, during that period of time, would there be any indication of her breathing or gasping or any such activity as that and, if you feel there could be, would you describe it to the ladies and gentlemen?

A: At the time that the windpipe is cut, the air now comes from these openings, the mouth plays no

part in breathing, at all. The intake and output of
air comes from these openings in the windpipe. At
these times, the victim could continue to breathe
until the time of death.

Q: And would that—how would you describe that
breathing in laymen's terms, Doctor?

A: It would be labored or forced breathing.

Q: So that, as you indicated, yesterday, I believe you
said it was some four to six minutes after this cutting before this person was biologically dead, is
that correct?

A: Yes, sir.

Q: And so there would be, during that span, some evidence of breathing, Doctor?

A: Yes, sir.

Q: —in this gasping or labored manner, is that
correct?

A: Yes, sir.

Half a dozen color slides were shown to reveal cuts, bruises
and fractures that were inflicted after death, in Izumi's opinion. There was a before-death "defense wound" in the right
hand that went right through the hand. Izumi said that when
he opened the partially clenched hand he found "four to six
small objects which had the appearance of hair."

The "deeply incised" stomach wound, he said, was
apparently done with "a very small, sharp, cutting-edged
instrument."

Bianchi asked whether the doctor was aware before the
autopsy that both femurs were broken. "I was completely
unaware that her thighbones had been fractured until I lifted
the body from the carriage over to the autopsy table. It was
then that the grating sensation and the deformity due to the
moving was clearly shown." He concluded that both femurs
were broken after death, but could not say how they were
broken, only that "it would take a great deal of force."

Dr. Izumi's slide show was interrupted by the judge at
close to five o'clock in the afternoon when he adjourned the
court. Next morning, before the doctor resumed testifying,
John Bianchi sought to introduce a certain knife in evidence

because "I can show through Dr. Izumi that this instrument, here, will coincide to some of the markings on the body. These wounds would not, of themselves, have caused death." In other words, he had a weapon to show, but he was not claiming it to be the murder weapon.

With the jury absent, Trooper Marius Venclauskas identified a wooden-handled, broken-tipped knife as one that he had found, with two others, in a brown pouch hanging on a kitchen cabinet of the cottage. He had marked it with his initials on a brass portion of the handle. This was the knife that Wayne Collier had given to Barbara Gibbons.

Catherine Roraback objected strenuously to the attempt to place this knife in evidence because it "was seized during the course of a warrantless search."

After the lawyers discussed the matter in chambers with the judge for an hour, Bianchi returned to the courtroom carrying the plastic bag containing the knife. He threw it on the evidence table. "At this point," Bianchi said to Judge Speziale, "I will withdraw the offer and go back to it at some later date, perhaps."

Dr. Izumi continued his narration as Sergeant Chapman showed the remainder of the nineteen slides. He spoke of the cuts and punctures on the stomach and the back of the victim as having been inflicted after death. A large interior tear, two to three inches long and "right in the pit of the stomach" was the result of "a direct blow." His description of a cut up to two inches long inside the pelvic cavity and several wounds at the opening of the vaginal canal painted a clear picture of the murderer thrusting some large object deep within the victim.

The lights were turned on again and the screen was moved to one side. Answering Bianchi's questions, Dr. Izumi said that the victim's rib cage on the left side had revealed three fractured ribs. "These occurred after death." He said that no male sperm was found in the body. Bianchi read to the jury the full texts of Izumi's initial report and his autopsy report.

Roraback began her cross-examination, saying, "I just have a few brief questions." She was curious about the wet dungarees and underpants. Yes, Izumi said, these articles of clothing were wet, but there was no water on the floor around them. The two shirts on the body were wet on the bottom but not on the top. The rug was wet but only underneath the body.

"Did you ever determine what was this dampness that was underneath the body?" Roraback asked. "No, ma'am," he replied.

Roraback continued her cross-examination. Izumi said "tremendous" blows were required to break the thighbones. And "it would take a good deal of choking force" to fracture the hyoid bone in the neck. He said that he judged that the T-shirt had been pushed up over the neck wounds after the slashing of the throat.

> Q: Let me ask you this, Dr. Izumi. A good deal of blood came out of those wounds. Would the blood have come out almost immediately as the wound was inflicted?
> A: Yes, ma'am.
> Q: Would have spurted out?
> A: Yes, ma'am.
> Q: And the person who inflicted the wounds would probably have had blood upon him or her, is that correct?
> A: Not necessarily. It would depend on the position of the assailant. If he were directly in front or on the left, the blood would spurt toward the left side. If, also, the T-shirt were pushed up in this area, the spurting could be decreased.

An important part of Peter's defense was that not a drop of blood had been found on his person or his clothing. Could he or anyone have carried out such a gory and complicated killing and emerged without showing any sign of blood or bruises? The prosecution chose to believe so and Dr. Izumi's testimony was most helpful. Some of the court spectators shook their heads in disbelief. Cousin Victoria's husband, John, an experienced deer hunter, remembers that he had to restrain himself from leaping up and shouting at Izumi. "Christ Almighty, when I heard what that guy was saying I couldn't believe it. I was ready to jump on him. He was actually saying that you could do that kind of job on Barbara without getting any blood on you. It's insane. Anybody who has ever used a knife on an animal knows what happens. You can't even cut your finger without getting blood on you! We had to sit there and listen to all that garbage. And Roraback didn't even pick it up."

Roraback quickly ran out of questions. Izumi was excused—but he would be back in three weeks as Bianchi's final witness before the State rested its case.

In eight days of testimony over a period of nearly four weeks—much time was lost because Peter became ill—the State put nineteen different witnesses on the stand. Several, like Izumi, appeared more than once. Eleven were state troopers and two were FBI agents—the prosecution built its case largely on the word of thirteen law-enforcement officers.

Bianchi made points by sheer numbers. In the absence of hard evidence proving Peter's guilt, he was making much of the fact that Peter had expressed or confessed his guilt to four different officers, in informal remarks as well as the formal interrogation, and had appeared to be remarkably calm and unremorseful to two more officers.

From late afternoon of Saturday, September 29, until mid-morning of the following day, when he began talking in the Litchfield jail to persons other than policemen, Peter Reilly either thought that he had killed his mother or thought that he might have. He believed that he had experienced a memory lapse. If he had agreed with his interrogators about his guilt, then it was consistent for him to have spoken of his guilt to other officers in informal conversation. For that certain period of time he was capable of telling hundreds of people that he was his mother's murderer, believing it to be true.

Six officers were from the Canaan Barracks. Only Percy Salley and John Calkins testified without evident hostility to Catherine Roraback. Lieutenant James Shay and troopers Mulhern and McCafferty made obvious their resentment of Roraback's questions.

In her questions to Sergeant Salley, Roraback brought out details of the four hours that Peter had spent with him in the barracks kitchen. She asked if Reilly had slept at all. "He just rested his head on his folded arms at the table," Salley said. He could not remember Peter asking if he could go somewhere to sleep, but he did recall Peter asking to go to the Madows'. "I told him that Lieutenant Shay wanted to speak to him before he went." Salley admitted that the police knew all along that there was a home for Peter to go to and friends who were waiting for him.

Shay's testimony required two days. As the commander of the Canaan Barracks, he had taken charge of the police activities in the cottage. He had questioned Peter Reilly initially, then, in partnership with Tim Kelly, he ran the Hartford interrogation. Shay fixed on Peter as the prime suspect, ordered his arrest, and sold the case to John Bianchi.

On the stand, Shay's strong facial features, neatly combed dark hair, trim physique and quality suits gave him the appearance of a headquarters officer rather than a "cop on the beat." The calm, articulate Shay is, according to some of his colleagues in Hartford, a "guy who knows how to put it down on paper."

When questioned by Bianchi, Shay told of reading Peter his constitutional rights and of being "struck by the fact that he was very calm, very poised and showed no emotion." He said his conversation with Peter early Saturday morning lasted some fifty minutes. He next saw him in Hartford that afternoon and questioned him further. Before Shay could relate what admissions Peter had made to him, Roraback sought to prevent his doing so on the grounds that Peter's statements were uttered in a totally coercive situation. Judge Speziale, after referring to Judge Armentano's decision not to suppress Peter's statements, overruled Roraback's objection.

Bianchi then asked Shay to report what Peter had said in Hartford. The jury heard for the first time the police gleanings from the prolonged interrogation.

> He told me he came home, walked into the house, looked to the right into the bedroom and saw his mother in the top bunk. He said that, at this point, he did what he called a "double take," and then saw her on the floor with blood

on her. He told me that they had argued about a car and that he recalled telling his mother to leave him alone. He told me that he remembered picking up a straight razor and that he slashed his mother's throat. He told me that there may—there might, also, have been a knife involved. He told me that he remembered jumping on his mother's stomach, and he told me that he might have washed his mother down.

Roraback's questioning of Shay was a dazzling piece of courtroom work. Some observers thought it the high point of her defense effort. Reading notes made of the taped dialogue between Shay and Peter, in both Canaan and Hartford, she repeatedly asked the lieutenant if he could remember asking a particular question or hearing Peter give a particular answer. As Shay more and more often said that he could not remember, he sounded increasingly evasive. He claimed that he could not recall asking a number of questions that seemed to have put ideas into Peter's head.

He was asked, "Do you remember saying to Peter Reilly, 'We have proof positive that you did it'?" Shay said that he did. "Do you remember Peter then saying, 'Then I might as well say I did it'?" Shay answered, "I don't recall that, no."

Shay could not remember Peter saying, "Should I really come out and say something I am not sure of?" Shay often responded to Roraback's questions by saying, "I may have." When Roraback read a long passage from the tapes that included his threat to lock Peter up and treat him like an animal, Shay responded, "I said part of that . . . I didn't say that we were going to treat him like an animal."

By this time Roraback's questions had become more and more sarcastic in tone, implying that Shay's was a highly selective memory indeed. She might have wished to continue her grilling, but it was now five o'clock on a Thursday night. The court was adjourned. The trial did not resume until twelve days later—Peter was suffering from strep throat and a high fever and his doctor advised him to stay in bed.

The delay was regrettable because the participants in the trial and the regulars among the press and audience were just getting used to the rhythm of the proceedings.

The action began again on March 19. Lieutenant Shay arrived in the courtroom with a large transparent bag containing the blue jeans, brown shirt and sneakers that Peter had been wearing when he was taken into custody by the police. They were admitted as evidence. With Shay again on the stand, Roraback in her questions put emphasis on Barbara Gibbons' injuries that Shay had known about as he interrogated Peter. He acknowledged he probably had told Peter about the cut in the abdomen and the broken legs, but he said that Peter had first referred to the slashing of the throat. Under redirect examination by Bianchi, Shay said that definitely neither he nor anyone else had told Peter about the throat wounds. "I know that," Shay insisted, "because we went to great pains to see that that didn't happen."

Following Shay's testimony, Bianchi, over Roraback's vigorous objections, succeeded in placing into evidence the straight razor and the six-inch, broken-tipped knife found in the cottage. Although Peter had spoken of slashing his mother's throat with a single swing of this very razor, Bianchi did not claim that either it or the knife was the murder weapon.

After Sergeant Timothy Kelly made a brief appearance to tell of giving Peter his constitutional rights before the Hartford interrogation, Trooper Mulhern took the stand. He told his tale about entering the interrogation room with the sandwich and hearing Peter say, "I killed her"—the words that were never said. Roraback tried to shake the story, but he stuck to it. He denied that Lieutenant Shay had sent him in to ask further questions because he was a friend of Peter's.

> **Q:** Do you remember Peter Reilly saying to you, "I don't know what to do, Jim, I am still not positive any of it happened. The only things I am positive about, she was on the floor, and calling the Madows and what I had in my original statement."?
>
> **A:** I believe he said something to that effect.

Peter's comment to his friend Jim sounded like a cry for help, but Mulhern's testimony made clear that the trooper had been given his instructions. His job was to write out the confession. The jury now learned that this had been a most complicated process. The result of Mulhern's work was not a single, clear statement but three separate pieces of paper (State's Exhibits Z, AA and BB), written between 8:30 P.M. and 10:45. The messiness of it all is seen in the declaration by Peter, according to one of the exhibits, that "when I slashed at her with the razor, I swung with my right hand from left to right, and I cut her throat." But Peter, saying that "It's almost like a dream," had actually told Mulhern that "it seems" he swung his right hand from right to left.

While writing the statements, Mulhern had done a little adding and subtracting of his own, though it was not the professional thing to do. "In the preparation of the written confession," say Inbau and Reid in their textbook *Lie Detection and Criminal Interrogation*, "no attempt should be made to improve the language used by the subject himself. It should represent his confession *as he tells it*." Roraback established in her questioning that the confession was not in Peter's exact words but a Mulhern-edited document. Some words, he admitted, were "changed to make sense."

Mulhern's credibility was particularly damaged after he claimed he had no knowledge of Barbara Gibbons' throat wounds when Peter spoke to him about slashing her throat. Roraback was exploring the extent to which ideas might have been put into Peter's head.

Q: I believe you said, Trooper Mulhern, that you had no knowledge of the victim's throat being cut, in response to one of Mr. Bianchi's questions?

A: Yes, ma'am, to my knowledge, I had no knowledge whatsoever of this.

Q: Isn't it true, Trooper Mulhern, that you heard in the course of questioning of Mr. Reilly by Sergeant Kelly references to the slashing of the throat?

A: I don't recall any, ma'am.

Q: Well, let me show you this report which you

filed—a copy of it, and ask you if that refreshes
your recollection.

A: (After reading.) I must have heard it, then.

Mulhern was followed to the stand by thirty-year-old John
McAloon, a thin, small, nervous man of various aliases who
was introduced by Bianchi as "presently a prisoner of the
State of Connecticut." He was serving two to five years for
auto theft in 1971. He was also under indictment in the Litchfield Superior Court for escape from the Litchfield jail, auto
theft and burglary. His "rap sheet" was a long one after a
dozen years of mischief, thievery and assault.

McAloon had been in the Litchfield Correctional Center when Peter became an inmate on September 30, 1973.
McAloon testified that "when a guy brang him in" he had
asked Peter "what he got busted for, what he got arrested for."
Bianchi asked McAloon to relate what Peter said.

A: He said for killing his mother, but, at first, I thought
he said his grandmother, when he said it.

Q: But, later on, he said it was for killing his mother?

A: One of the guys who was standing there told me,
said he just said his mother, he says.

Q: Not his grandmother?

A: I thought he said his grandmother, at first.

When Bianchi asked for more details McAloon told this
story:

He said his mother was getting—was drinking a lot and
that she was making him stay home all the time and that
the night it happened, that he wanted to go out, meet some
friends somewhere and that his mother threatened him
with taking the car or the plates off the car, and he just
went crazy, went berserk and started hitting her; and the
next thing he knew, he had a knife in his hand and she
was on the floor.

He said that she was always trying to make him stay
home, she was ashamed of him or something, that he
didn't have a father, he was an illegitimate, there was

illegitimate—his mother had been ashamed of him all his life and that she had been drinking a lot, and then she had an operation of some kind lately, and she was supposed to take some kind of shots, and she didn't take them. It made her worse by not taking these shots. . . .

He said that after he realized that he killed his mother he was all bloody in front, and he took the clothes off, rolled them in a ball, got in his car and drove somewhere through the—he drove somewhere and got rid of the clothes and came back to the house.

McAloon added that Peter had a pair of Hush Puppies on his feet when he appeared in jail. In response to a question by Roraback, who spoke of Peter wearing sneakers when he was brought to McAloon's section of the jail, McAloon insisted that "the morning I seen him, he had a pair of Hush Puppies on." He said that Peter had admitted his guilt within half an hour after being placed in the cell. "When he first come in, he asked if this is where they keep all the murderers, this section, here; and I told him, 'You are the only guy here for that.'"

Although several jurors said after the trial that they simply discounted McAloon's testimony, along with that of Robert Erhardt, who appeared as a defense witness, the jurors seem to have taken seriously the idea that Peter could have driven away from the cottage to dump his bloodied clothing.

"I didn't speak to him," Peter says of McAloon. "The only time I ever saw the guy is when I watched the World Series [on television]. He was there with the other guys. I was told by one of the other inmates when I first got there to watch out for this guy—he's a creep."

His own brother would state long after the Reilly trial that McAloon is a pathological liar who has made a practice of informing on fellow inmates. On his way to court one day, two weeks after Peter's arrival in the jail, McAloon volunteered to a state trooper that he knew Peter Reilly had killed his mother. He said he knew it because Peter had told him so. The trooper reported this interesting news. McAloon was soon telling his story for a statement that he signed on October 15, 1973.

His statement is inventive, if jumbled. He quotes Peter as saying that he killed his grandmother and that he told the police that a burglar must have done the murder. "Then he started talking about his mother and how she put him in a picnic basket and tried to hide him." According to McAloon, Peter said he drove away from the house and threw his bloody clothes into "an open field." As for blood on himself, "He said he cleaned himself off before anyone knew what happened. He took a long shower later in the day."

Needless to say, Peter, who was under police guard within minutes after telephoning for help, took no shower. Nor had he killed his grandmother. John Bianchi had to know that these portions of the statement were false but he apparently considered other parts believable.

If he did believe the key element of McAloon's story, about the disposal of the clothes, and if he did believe in the rest of his case against the defendant, then Bianchi had to think, against all common sense, that Peter Reilly had done the following:

1) Attacked his mother and slashed her throat before 9:40 P.M., getting blood on his clothes and perhaps on his hands.

2) Telephoned three different places for help, including Sharon Hospital where Nurse Fenn heard him tell, at about 9:40, that his mother was on the floor and breathing.

3) Returned to his now dead mother to break her legs, cut her stomach and back, mutilate her genitals—even though he knew the police, and at least two ambulance crews were on their way.

4) Taken off his bloody clothes, washed himself, and put on an identical set of clothing.

5) Gotten in his car, driven away, and thrown the clothes in an open field although several sweeps of the area by police investigators failed to find them.

6) Returned to the cottage in time to receive the police and others who had responded to his emergency calls.

John McAloon, already in jail for other crimes, faced more time behind bars for having escaped from the Litchfield jail (on the very day of the Gibbons murder), breaking into a construction company and stealing clothes, money and an automobile before being captured. He pleaded guilty on April 16,

1974, to all of these offenses. Bianchi, not known as a man soft on crime or easy with criminals, appeared in Litchfield Superior Court soon after the conclusion of the Reilly trial to ask that McAloon be set free. He said threats were made against McAloon in the Litchfield jail. Bianchi recommended concurrent one-year sentences for the several crimes, and that they be suspended. Judge Robert A. Wall did what Bianchi wanted. John McAloon was last seen heading for Florida.

March 20 was an all-police day on the witness stand. The prosecution presented five state troopers and one FBI expert. Trooper Donald Moran told of finding a black-handled straight razor in the cottage. Although during the interrogation Peter had spoken of hurling his straight razor behind the gas station or over the barn, Moran, when cross-examined by Roraback, said that he had come across it on the top of a bookshelf.

Sergeant Timothy Kelly—a stocky, square-jawed man with a graying crew cut and black-rimmed glasses—made an impressive witness. In his slow, soft-spoken way he seemed to be trying to think through his answers and give honest responses to the questions asked.

Kelly told of Peter speaking about his poor home life, his fear of having a mental problem, his memory of slashing his mother's throat, his feeling that he might have jumped on his mother's legs, and, finally, his remark about doing a sexual injury. Said Kelly:

> At this time, we had been in touch with the Canaan Barracks and had been informed as to some of the results of the autopsy; and one of the indications that we were given was that there was damage done to her sexual organs. So I went back into the room and started talking to Peter about what he considered the worst thing he could have done to his mother, last night, and . . . he says, well, the worst thing he could think about would be slashing her throat. I said, "No, Peter, besides that." And we sat there and we talked, and he said the only thing that he could think of, he raped his mother the night before. I indicated

to Peter that there was no indication of male sperm and that I didn't think that he did this act of rape, and he says, "Well, what did I do?" I says, "Peter, I don't want to tell you. I want to hear it from you." And at one point he says to me, he said, "I think I could have tried to cut out her sexual organs," and I said, "Why do you think that?" He said, "Well, that's the worst thing I can think of." And I said, "Why would you want to do something like this?" He says, "I don't know." I said, "Could it have been because this is where you came from?" And he said, "Yes." And that was the gist of our conversation.

Since Peter had apparently not been told by the police that the autopsy had revealed sexual injuries, a reasonable conclusion for a juror would seem to be that Peter's statements to Kelly indicated knowledge that sexual harm had been done. Consequently, Roraback, early in her cross-examination, brought out that Peter had said to Kelly, when first recounting the events of the murder night, that Geoffrey Madow had mentioned the possibility of rape. Her suggestion was that this was an idea already lodged in Peter's head. (Lieutenant Shay had also put sexual questions to Peter in his Canaan questioning.) Roraback also managed to show that Peter's notion that he might have had a memory lapse, thus failing to remember attacking his mother, was implanted during Shay's earlier interrogation.

In a skillful series of questions Roraback succeeded in establishing that Peter had said a great many things in addition to the incriminating statements—things that indicated his confusion, his qualifications of his admissions, and his questioning of his own confession. Kelly said he could remember Peter speaking of "jumping up and down" on his mother's body, but he could not recall the next phrase: "If it was me."

Q: Did you say, Sergeant Kelly, "I want to hear it from you. What else did you do to your mother?"

A: Yes.

Q: And do you remember Peter saying to you, "You keep asking what I think I did, but I don't know what I did."?

A: We had conversation like that. I don't know exactly when, but we did have conversation.

Next, Trooper John Calkins spoke of driving Peter to the Litchfield jail and hearing him say that "He entered the house, looked to his right into the bedroom, and his mother was in bed; and from this particular point, his mind went blank, and the next thing he knew he was standing over her, and she was lying on the floor with blood on her." And, furthermore, "He told me he realized that the act itself was wrong but, somehow, he was not sorry."

After Sergeant James McDonald and Trooper Walter Anderson testified about the broken-tipped knife and hair samples taken from Peter's head, FBI Agent Robert Neill was introduced by Bianchi. A hair and fiber specialist, he said he testified about his hair findings from 200 to 250 times a year. The Connecticut State Police had sent the FBI, for analysis, the hairs found in Barbara Gibbons' clenched fist as well as samples of Peter's hair. Neill had examined them and reached some conclusions. But all he could say was that two of the five or six hairs in the victim's hand (he did not specify either five or six) were either Reilly's or from a person of the same race with similar microscopic characteristics; one of the hairs might have come from the victim herself; one blond Caucasian head hair was "dissimilar to the accused and to samples of the deceased." The remaining hairs could not be linked to any particular person.

The information pointed in different directions. The FBI man said he had found no roots on the hairs that might have been Peter's; they had not been pulled out in a struggle. If they had come from Peter, they could have come into his mother's hand in various ways, perhaps as she clawed at the dirty rug. The hairs that clearly belonged to neither the victim nor her son remained an enigma.

A similar inconclusive quality characterized the testimony of a second FBI agent who appeared the following day. James A. Porter, Jr., flown in from Washington, said that he had determined that the "light smear" found on both sides of the six-inch blade of the broken-tipped knife—Exhibit X—was human blood. But he could not identify the blood type. Nor could he say how long the blood had been on the knife. Porter said he had found no blood on the knife's four-inch handle and no blood on three other knives from the cottage submitted for examination by the Connecticut State Police. Peter's brown shirt and one of his sneakers had also gone to Washington for testing. No blood was discovered.

The police had not sent the straight razor to the FBI for examination. They knew it had no blood on it and probably neither they nor Bianchi believed that it was the murder weapon. If Peter had used it and then washed it off before placing it on the bookshelf, there was no evidence of that action, as the sink traps in the cottage had been carefully examined for signs of blood, without success. Even so, the prosecution placed the straight razor in evidence. As it happened, the kitchen knife made more of an impression on the jury. One juror said privately after the trial that the jury figured that Peter had used the knife for *all* the wounds, from the throat to the vagina, and then returned it to the pouch in the kitchen.

John Bianchi could thank Dr. Izumi for fixing the importance of the kitchen knife in the minds of the jurors. When the pathologist returned to the stand as the final witness for the State, he said in reference to the abdomen cut, "My opinion would be that this knife is the instrument that caused this type of wound." And again, after showing another slide, he said, "The same knife had caused these wounds on her back."

Dr. Izumi spoke of "this weapon or knife" as a "sharp, cutting instrument" whose blunt end matched certain characteristics of Gibbons' abdomen and back wounds. When asked by Bianchi if he had formed an opinion about the cause of the so-called defense injury in the right hand of the victim, he said, "This knife could, also, cause the defense wound."

Since it seemed to be the assumption that another instrument had caused the fatal throat wounds, Izumi's version of events presented a puzzling picture of a killer in action:

1) The murderer, with the kitchen knife in hand, struggles with the victim and stabs her in the hand.

2) Switching to a different weapon, he kills her with vicious throat slashes.

3) Switching back to the kitchen knife, he inflicts wounds on both sides of the body.

4) The murderer goes to the trouble of leaving the slightly blood-stained kitchen knife in its usual place in the house, where it is sure to be found, while disposing of the murder weapon so successfully that it is never discovered.

5) All of these actions could have occurred without the killer getting a drop of blood on him.

Dr. Izumi had been holding the broken-tipped knife in his hands during Bianchi's questioning. Now Catherine Roraback approached him, took away the knife and stepped toward the center of the courtroom. With her back to the witness, she asked whether the pathologist had examined "any other knives or instruments" to see whether they matched the wounds. Izumi admitted that he had not. She turned to face him and asked, "If there were a knife on which the tip had not been broken off and that knife had the same width blade, could it have caused the defense wound you saw?"

Said Izumi: "Yes, it could." But he thought it unlikely because of a "double scratch" shown on a slide.

Roraback said she had no further questions to ask Dr. Izumi. Neither did Bianchi. When the doctor left the witness stand the State's Attorney announced, "May it please the Court, the State of Connecticut rests." It was 12:26 P.M., March 26.

15 ■ DEFENSE

SGT. KELLY: But you still—Peter, you don't trust me! This is the whole thing. You still don't trust me. And, I don't know what I can do to make you trust me, other than saying I've helped other people before, and I don't lie about it. So, what I want you to do is tell me how it happened and then we're home free, you're halfway through the battle and you're on the hill coming back to being yourself again.

The sudden end of the prosecution's case surprised many of the journalists and spectators in the courtroom. "I was amazed," says Roger Cohn. "I had been expecting the State to drop its big bombshell: the single, conclusive piece of evidence that would tie Reilly to this crime—his bloodied clothing found behind the barn, perhaps, or his fingerprints on a murder weapon, or something. But there was no bombshell. Incredibly, the State had done exactly what I believed it would never do, which was to base its case almost entirely on Peter's confession. One of the court officers told me privately as we sat downstairs in the sheriff's office just before the defense began its case, 'To tell you the truth, I was surprised a State's Attorney would even walk into a courtroom with a case like that. I didn't see one shred of material evidence.'"

Nonetheless, each day of testimony had been an ordeal for Peter. Marion's sister Vicky remembers that "Peter was very withdrawn during the trial." He went to sleep early and slept away most days he did not have to appear in court. Marion would sometimes go into his bedroom and give him back rubs at night to help him feel better and assure him that he was loved.

Fortunately for Peter's state of mind, the end of the prosecution's case brought a sharp change in the atmosphere in the courtroom. There had been something ominous about the first weeks of testimony: a marshaling of forces to push Peter into prison. Suddenly the worst was over and it had not been so bad after all. The time had come to tell the other side of the story. His supporters were optimistic about Peter's chances.

More people from Canaan came to the courthouse because their friends and neighbors were scheduled to testify and because they hoped to be there when and if Peter took the stand. A number of young people of Peter's age attended the trial.

As far as Peter's attorney was concerned, there was no need to go ahead with the trial at all. Immediately after the State rested its case, she asked if the jury might be excused and then made a motion to dismiss the charges. She said that the prosecution had only established that "a very gory and horrible murder" had taken place and that Peter Reilly was present when the police arrived at his home on the night of September 28. They had held him in custody for twenty-four hours, allowing him little food or sleep. During prolonged questioning he had remained uncertain about what had occurred the previous night.

John Bianchi, objecting to the motion to dismiss, maintained the evidence against Reilly was "overwhelming." He was an "alert" and "able" young man who had willingly confessed his crime to the police after having been informed of his legal rights four times. Bianchi said that the State had established that the defendant was in the house while his mother was still alive, thus the defendant must have inflicted the after-death wounds. Roraback countered that the medical testimony indicated the victim could have shown signs of breathing for up to five minutes after receiving the fatal neck wounds. She claimed that this would account for the gasping sound that Reilly said he had heard when he arrived home.

Judge Speziale denied the motion, as Roraback fully

expected, but at least she had protected herself in the event of an appeal. The trial would go on.

The jury had undergone a change in composition. One man had become ill and was replaced by an alternate: the wife of an aircraft plant worker and the mother of four children. Now there were seven men and five women on the jury.

Catherine Roraback's first witness at the start of the defense case in the afternoon of March 26 was the Reverend Peter Dakers of the Canaan Congregational Church, the first of eight witnesses to testify about Peter's presence at the Youth Center meeting in the Methodist Church basement not long before the discovery of the murder. Roraback wanted to demonstrate that Peter was telling the truth about his movements that night and to indicate that the time of his departure from the church after the meeting would have left him with no time to have carried out the killing and the other actions described in prosecution testimony. She also wanted to establish that Peter had been wearing the same clothes at the meeting that he was wearing when the police arrived at the cottage.

Just as the prosecution had made an impression on the jury by sheer weight of numbers—the parade of policemen—the defense was making a point by the quantity of its own witnesses. The message was that these ordinary, small-town citizens, young and old, surely could not all be mistaken or willing to tell untruths. Clearly Peter Reilly had been at the Canaan meeting, and, from the accumulation of testimony, a juror could believe that Peter had driven away from the church between 9:30 and 9:40. Unfortunately for the defense, the imprecision about his departure time left open the possibility that Peter had time enough to do what the State said he had done.

Similarly, the testimony indicated that Peter had worn the same brown shirt at the meeting that he had on when the police first saw him at the cottage—he had not changed his clothes. Yet, most witnesses were not positive about Peter's clothing. The testimony about the brown shirt was virtually negated by a few words spoken, in good faith, by Peter's young friend, John Sochocki, who was familiar with Peter's wardrobe. He said, when asked about Peter's clothing, that he recalled Peter wearing a brown plaid jacket.

That was something that stuck in the minds of the jurors and Bianchi made the most of it. Despite knowing that the jacket had no significance—the police had found the jacket in the cottage and decided that there was nothing suspicious about it and returned it to Peter—Bianchi proceeded to give the impression that it did. If the jurors wondered how Peter could have emerged from the slaughter without any blood-stains, well, perhaps they could imagine that the jacket had blood on it and perhaps Peter had disposed of it somehow. Bianchi periodically mentioned the jacket when questioning witnesses. The jurors, after retiring to reach their verdict, sent out a note asking, "The plaid jacket . . . where is it?"

The jacket had been in the courtroom since the Sochocki testimony, stuffed in a bag. Roraback did not attempt to introduce it as evidence or even let the jury know that it had not been thrown away. It seems that she had noticed a dark stain on the jacket and feared that Bianchi would lead the jury to believe that it was blood. She could not be certain herself that it was not blood because she did not have the jacket analyzed by an independent laboratory.

The most impressive witness on Peter's behalf on the first day of defense testimony was Joanne Mulhern. Her husband had testified for the prosecution, but Mrs. Mulhern testified in support of Peter's story of the murder night. She had seen him at the Youth Center meeting and she remembered him driving away at about 9:30. She said that she had seen him the following morning at the police barracks wearing the same clothing.

Ten witnesses testified the following day: three Madows, one convict, a friend of Peter's and five policemen.

Geoffrey Madow's story was important because he had been with Peter much of the day of the murder and had arrived at the scene of the crime before his parents, the police or anyone else except Peter. He had been under police suspicion initially because they had found him at the cottage with Peter and the corpse.

Geoff Madow told the jury about the events of September

28, 1973, as he knew them: from his daytime activities with Peter to his conclusion, after seeing Barbara Gibbons dead, that she must have been raped. When Bianchi questioned the young man he was interested in the way Peter and his mother carried on in what he referred to as "the Reilly homestead." Geoff agreed that there were frequent arguments. When pressed, he said they were about such things as Watergate, the car and Peter coming home late. "She was always picking on Peter Reilly, wasn't she?" Bianchi asked. "Not all the time," Geoff said.

> Q: Not all the time. And they would use profanity when they would argue back and forth, wouldn't they?
> A: Occasionally.
> Q: Would you tell the ladies and gentlemen the type of language that went on between Miss Gibbons and Peter Reilly—it may be embarrassing but I think it's important.
> A: Well—well, they would swear at each other and sometimes they would say, "fuck you," something like that, "shut up," couple of other things.
> Q: Back and forth at each other?
> A: Yes.
> Q: Peter would say that to his mother and she would say it to him, isn't that so?
> A: Yes.
> Q: In your presence?
> A: Yup.
> Q: Isn't it true they would use the term "shit"?

At this point Judge Speziale intervened because of giggling among the adolescents. "Sheriff," he said, "I want to caution those lads down there. Any outbursts by any spectators in this courtroom and the spectators will be actually thrown out of this courtroom."

Bianchi then wanted to know whether Peter and his mother had used terms like "bastard" and "bitch." Only when they were referring to other people, Geoff said, not to each other. He estimated that Barbara Gibbons was drunk about half the time when he visited her house and "sometimes she was nice, sometimes she was bitchy, depending on how she was feeling, I imagine."

By extracting such testimony from Geoff Madow and later from Peter himself, Bianchi was able to suggest to the jury that there was bad blood between the defendant and his mother and that her life had been taken because of a sudden, violent argument. What was never said at the trial was that the arguments and the use of rough language—shocking as some rural New England jurors might find it—could be regarded as a sign of the unlikelihood of Peter killing his mother. Studies of children who have killed their parents reveal a pattern of suppressed feelings. "It's like a teakettle," says the psychologist Dr. Joyce Brothers. "If you don't allow the steam to escape, you'll eventually have an explosion." However courteous and deferential Peter Reilly may have been in other people's homes, he appears to have been free to let off plenty of steam in his own house.

Next, Marion Madow took the stand. She is an energetic woman with warm brown eyes and dark brown curly hair. Though she would often speak of herself, her family and her neighbors as just ordinary people who had rallied to Peter Reilly's side, she had done an extraordinary thing in making a home for a youth who was accused of murder. She would say, long after the Reilly trial, that "It's hard for anyone else to understand the tension we all lived with." The normal family life of the Madows was wrenched out of shape by the problems of the Peter Reilly case. But when a reporter asked if there was ever a time when she and her husband felt that the job was too big for them, she replied, "No, there really wasn't. You know, it's maybe only once in your life that you are given a chance to do something that really matters. We felt Peter was ours."

In the courtroom, answering Roraback's questions, Marion Madow said that Peter had telephoned her house between 9:40 and 9:50 P.M. and she described the way Peter was shaking when she saw him in the murder cottage. She spoke of his request to be allowed to go home with her.

Cross-examining, Bianchi began by asking, "It was cold that night, Mrs. Madow?" He was sharp and sarcastic.

Q: I am asking you the reason that he was shaking. Because it was cold?
A: It wasn't that kind of shaking.
Q: Oh, there are different kinds of shaking?
A: Yes, there are, with children.
Q: He is 18 years old, isn't he?
A: He is still a child.
Q: State of Connecticut says he's a man.
A: Mm-hmm. But a mother says he is a child.

Mickey Madow followed his wife to the witness stand. Most of the questions put to him were directed to his activities as a volunteer ambulance worker who had responded to Peter's call for help, but before he was dismissed Bianchi asked him the same question he had put to Mrs. Madow and to other witnesses: "Was he crying?" Madow said he was not. To offset this, Roraback drew from him the observation that Peter was shaking as he stood in the murder cottage. Bianchi had the last question: "It was a cold night, wasn't it, Mr. Madow?" Answer: "Yes, it was."

The appearance of Robert Erhardt provided a balance to McAloon's testimony. Dressed in a black suit, black shoes and white socks, Erhardt looked the part of the convict who had been let out for the day and had slicked himself up as best he could for the occasion.

He told about his first talk with Peter in the jail and his surprise at learning that the boy was charged with killing his mother. "He was really talking in circles. He really didn't know what to do. . . . None of his statements were coherent." Roraback was putting the questions:

Q: Did he, at any time, that morning, Mr. Erhardt, say that he had killed his mother?
A: Not directly, no.
Q: When you say, "not directly"—?
A: I mean, in the term that he—the only thing he told me was about the interrogation and that, due to the

fact that he was kept on his feet for this X amount of hours, that he was willing to sign anything or do anything just to get relief from the immediate questioning.

Both Roraback and Bianchi extracted details about Erhardt's life in crime. He said he was forty-five years old, and when asked how many years he had spent in prison, he stated, "Well, I have been very fortunate in that respect, I guess, in comparison to my record. I would say the total years spent in prison would be sixteen." Bianchi wanted to know whether Erhardt had said to Sergeant Norman Soucie, during a conversation in Somers prison on November 15, 1973, that "There are going to be a lot of disappointed people," meaning Peter's supporters, when the truth about the case comes out. Erhardt vigorously denied saying anything like this. "I don't know where you are getting this information from." He said that he had spoken of the way the State was going to be disappointed "because Peter is not guilty."

The jury learned that Erhardt had refused to give a statement to Sergeant Soucie. He said that he only puts his signature on a statement when he writes it himself. He had, in fact, after the Soucie interview, typed out and signed a statement of his own, very supportive of Peter Reilly, and had mailed it to the State Police, Peter and Roraback. "I signed that. It was my own." Roraback sought from Erhardt more details from his conversation with Sergeant Soucie, especially the things the officer said to him, but Bianchi's objections were sustained.

Erhardt went back to Somers a bitterly frustrated man. He felt that he had not been given a chance to tell all he knew. That night he typed out a letter to Peter that said in part:

I wasn't permitted to tell from the stand the facts concerning that interview! But when the police were here on that interview they offered me a "time cut" and also a "transfer to another institution" if I would testify for the State. I was burning up when this type offer was made and in my own way I did manage to tell the policeman what I thought of him and his offer. I'm sorry that I was unable to get this before the court. I'm also sorry that I couldn't clear up the air concerning Connecticut's prime informer McAloon.

If it's any consolation at all, Pete, we who know you still believe in every way that our friend Pete will be found innocent. As you know I have a terrible past record but on the other hand I have never hurt or in any way assaulted another human being, and I know that if this is true in respect to myself, then there is no one in this whole wide world that can convince me that you could harm anyone.

If you were my own son, and I had no record, I couldn't believe in you any more than I do already. I appreciate the "good and decent people" who have come to your aid. I think that, in itself, is going to hold an awful lot of weight with the jury.

Paul Beligni's testimony was interesting because he was familiar with the knife that Dr. Izumi said had caused most of the wounds on Barbara Gibbons' body. He had used the knife early in the summer of 1973 to dig a bullet slug out of a tree behind Peter's house. He broke the point of the knife while doing so. He also recalled that Peter had cut himself some time earlier while carving the handle of that very knife. The suggestion was that some blood could have gotten on the blade at the time.

Beligni, who had a part-time job at Bob's Clothing Store in Canaan, also testified that he had sold Peter the brown knit shirt he had worn on the day of the murder. Being familiar with Peter's wardrobe, he was sure that Peter had no other brown shirt and no other sneakers like the ones he had been wearing on September 28. Bianchi, however, was interested in the brown plaid jacket. Beligni agreed that Peter did own one.

Roraback finished the day by putting five police officers on the stand in quick order: McCafferty, Salley, Shay, Moran and Mulhern. Her purpose was to show that Barbara Gibbons had been robbed as well as murdered. If she could portray the events of September 28, 1973, as including robbery as well as murder, the jurors could more easily envision some-one other than Peter Reilly assaulting his mother.

Shay remembered the 11 cents lying near the victim's feet. He said the police had found an empty wallet in a living room drawer (after Peter had told him about it), but no other wallet and no money other than the coins by the body and a nickel on the living-room floor.

Jim Mulhern, on the stand once again, spoke of the time he had been "sent down there to speak with Miss Gibbons concerning the harassing phone calls she had been receiv-ing." Roraback then wanted to know if he had investigated whether Barbara Gibbons had cashed any checks on the day of the murder.

Bianchi objected and then successfully moved to have the whole of Mulhern's testimony stricken from the record. While faulting Judge Speziale for his decision, some report-ers felt that Roraback had failed to do more with the whole business of the missing wallet and money. They wondered why she had not brought on as witnesses bank personnel and store owners who might have seen the victim handling money just hours before her death.

The following day, March 28, was a strange one. First there was a bit of comic relief when eighty-four-year-old Fred Kruse, the Gibbons landlord, took the stand. When asked to identify Peter Reilly, he said he could not see him in the court-room. Maybe he could not but he seemed to be pretending. He left the stand and walked about the well of the courtroom, peering at Bianchi, Peter Herbst, then Peter Reilly, saying, as if surprised, "Oh, there he is. What'd you do, dye your hair?" (Bianchi took this seriously and later asked if Peter's hair was the same color as it used to be. Kruse said it was.)

Kruse remembered that he had seen Barbara Gibbons reading outside under a light at about 8:30 on the night she was killed and still sitting there at 9:00 to 9:30. Then, before retiring himself, he had noticed that the outside light was off and that she had gone inside.

Sergeant Jack Schneider testified about the tapes of the Reilly interrogation: where they had been kept, who had used them, who had access to them and so forth. The authenticity of the tapes was at issue and there was discussion whether they should or should not be played in their entirety. As Bianchi pointed out, long passages concerned the lie detector test. Such testing "is inadmissible under our rules of evidence." Judge Speziale called for a recess so that the matter could be discussed in chambers.

The recess lasted five hours, partly because John Bianchi was offering Peter a chance to plea bargain and get off with a light sentence.

Bianchi first broached the deal to Roraback, offering a sentence of from two to five years if Peter would plead "no contest" to the murder charge. It would amount to an admission of guilt. When Roraback took the offer to Peter, he asked if Mickey and Marion Madow could be asked to come to the courthouse to help him decide what to do.

Mickey remembers arriving in Litchfield and asking Roraback what was going on. She said the offer had come as a complete surprise to her. He asked her, "Do you think he's guilty?" He recalls that she replied, "No, absolutely not."

Peter was absent when Bianchi, in the lawyers' lounge behind the courtroom, explained the offer to the Madows. Bianchi went out and Peter came in. The terms were outlined to him. "Peter looked at us," Mickey recalls, "and we said that he was of age and that it all boils down to being his decision." Then Marion said, "Did you do this, Peter?"

He replied, "No, I didn't do it. Why should I plead guilty to something I didn't do?" He felt that he should turn down the offer.

The Madows agreed and told Bianchi of the decision after Peter left. Mickey suggested to Bianchi that a fair sentence, if Peter were to agree to "no contest," would be the four and a half months he had already spent in jail, plus probation. "How about showing a little compassion, John?" he said. Bianchi said that there was no possibility of such a sentence. "He's innocent, John," Mickey said. "No, he's not," said Bianchi.

According to Marion Madow, "Catherine came over to me just before the court convened again and said, 'Marion, the judge says, are you sure that this is the way you want to go?' And I said, 'Yes, that's the way we want to go.

Peter's not going to plead guilty or no contest to something he didn't do.' "

When the court resumed after four o'clock, Judge Speziale announced that the State's Attorney had affirmed the authenticity of the tape recordings that the defense wished to present as evidence. Bianchi and Roraback had agreed that "It won't be necessary to call a panel of experts to be certain the tapes were not tampered with."

The tapes would not be heard right away, however, because Roraback had decided that Peter would take the stand to tell his story in person.

"Peter Anthony Reilly" was sworn in at 4:21 that Friday afternoon, standing erect with his left hand held tightly at his side. Joe O'Brien would write in the *Hartford Courant* that "A shock of light-brown, shoulder-length hair fell across his right eye. . . . He spoke in a soft, firm voice." He seemed surprisingly relaxed. Perhaps the experience of turning down the State's offer of leniency had buoyed his confidence. The jurors examined him carefully. Was this a cold-blooded killer or an innocent lad falsely accused?

Roraback wanted to get certain aspects of Peter's relationship with his mother out in the open before Bianchi could make too much of them. Peter described how he had spent a lot of his time away from home in the months before the murder, in the summer of 1973, visiting the Madows and the Belignis. He once stayed at the Belignis for nearly two weeks. He had helped them put in a swimming pool. But while staying there he would return to his own house every day or every other day. "I would use Mrs. Beligni's car. She would lend it to me. I would drive down and see my mother for an hour or two."

> Q: Now, Mr. Reilly, you have heard some testimony about conversations that you had with your mother?
> A: Mm-hmm.
> Q: Can you tell me what sort of language you and your mother used to use in your conversations?

A: Well, we did use bad language. I guess you would call it profanity. We used such terms as "fuck you," "bastard" and "bitch," things like that. . . .

Q: And what were the occasions when you did use such words?

A: Oh, when we'd have an argument about something or arguing about something—whether it would be the car or—anything—anything that happened to be of interest at the moment.

That ended the day's testimony. The courtroom was packed the following Tuesday. The press had reported that Reilly would return to the witness stand. The Litchfield courthouse had not seen such crowds in years. A makeshift cardboard sign saying "COURTROOM FULL" was put up. People were lined up in the ground-floor corridor hoping that seats might become available.

Roraback's questions to Peter were designed to take him through the day of the murder. He spoke of the "brown shirt, blue jeans and gold sneakers" he had put on that morning. He identified several State's exhibits as the same clothing. He told of coming home that afternoon and learning from his mother that she had cashed a $100 check and had purchased a new wallet. She had done so, he said, because a wallet containing $120 had been stolen a week or two earlier. Peter said that his mother had shown him the wallet and then had put it back in the right rear pocket of her dungarees. He also described the back door of the house and its two inside locks, saying the door was seldom used and usually locked.

Peter described his movements on the night of the murder, his telephone calls for help and the actions taken by the police once he was in their custody. He said that he and Sergeant Salley had "talked small talk" while seated in the barracks kitchen, "but I remember him telling me about a wound my mother had in her abdomen." Roraback wanted to know about the interrogation in the barracks.

A: Lieutenant Shay started questioning me, asked me what my activities were up until that point; and then, when he got done, he went out, and I remember asking him to get me a cigarette; and then Sergeant Salley came in, and he sat down, and he started asking me the questions, again. So I went through the questions again. At this point, I was exhausted, and we got done, and I asked him if he would get me a cigarette. He said he would see what he could do. Then he went out, and then Lieutenant Shay came in and started asking me questions again, a third time, and—

Q: Do you remember what you said, at that time, Mr. Reilly?

A: Well, I—I asked him—I don't know, something—I told him that I had already been asked these questions twice in a row; and he said, "Well, we'll ask them to you one more time and then we'll get you some sleep." So, he asked me the questions.

When he finally was led to a bedroom, "I tossed and turned, I would say, for an hour and a half, two hours before I started to go to sleep . . . and then the next thing I knew, Officer Mulhern was waking me up." After that brief sleep, he related, he was taken to Hartford, and then there were conversations with the police "from around two that afternoon until around 11 P.M." All he had to eat was a quarter of a ham-and-cheese sandwich.

Peter said that when he woke up in the Litchfield jail that Sunday morning and was taken to the boundover section, he met several prisoners, including Robert Erhardt, but not John McAloon. He didn't even see McAloon. "If I am not mistaken, he was locked up that day."

During a late-morning recess, Peter stood chatting with his friends and smoking a cigarette in the upstairs hallway, as he often did, when Trooper Jim Mulhern came up the stairs. He was heading for the State's Attorney's office with a carton filled with cups of coffee. "Morning, Peter," he said. "How are you this morning?"

"Good, Jim," Peter said. "And you?"

"Good, Peter, good," Mulhern replied. And he moved on down the hall.

Back on the witness stand, Peter touched off a few smiles

in the solemn courtroom when he described how he and his fellow inmates had tried to find a lawyer for him. "The name Roraback rang a bell," he related, "and I said I would like Catherine Roraback. They told me I probably couldn't afford her, but that's who I said I wanted."

The jurors watched with fascination as Roraback showed Peter Exhibit X, the broken-tipped knife, and then Exhibit CC, the straight razor. He said that the knife was one of several knives that his mother kept in the kitchen. A friend of his, Wayne Collier, had given it to her a year and a half ago. Peter said that he had put the carving on the handle a year before, using another knife, and had cut himself in the process. As for the broken tip, Peter recalled the time that Paul Beligni used the knife to dig a bullet out of an apple tree. "I said, 'You better watch it, you are going to break the tip of the knife,' and just as I said it, it happened, the tip of the knife broke off."

The straight razor, Peter said, had come from Mario's barbershop in Canaan. His mother got it for him "because I was always running out of razor blades when I was building model airplanes, balsa models, so she got it so I could have something with a handle on it or whatever so I could work on it without carving up my fingers."

When Roraback asked him about the Hartford interrogation, Peter had difficulty recalling the things that had been said. About Lieutenant Shay: "He said something to the effect of 'Don't be afraid to say that you did it,' and that was—I think that's about the only thing I remember." At the prosecution table, John Bianchi laughed to himself just loudly enough for the jury to hear. It was a device he often used to indicate his disbelief. Peter said that he remembered signing several pages of the confession, "but it's very vague to me." When Roraback pointed out his name at the bottom of one document, he said, "I imagine that's my signature. It does have my signature on it." Shown another paper, he said, "I don't remember specifically signing this document, no."

The trouble with such responses was that Peter sounded evasive when it was important for him to come across to the jurors as a totally honest and believable young man. Judge

Speziale, among others, felt that he made a poor witness. Roraback ended her examination by asking two questions:

Q: Did you, in fact, slash at your mother's throat?
A: No, I did not.
Q: Did you, in fact, kill your mother, Mr. Reilly?
A: No, I didn't.

Peter had appeared calm and collected during his law-yer's questions, but lost some of his composure when facing the prosecutor. Bianchi asked only a few questions this day because he had a fever and was feeling sleepy because of the medication he was taking. "I really do feel pretty poorly," he told the judge. The proceedings were suspended until the following day.

The defendant appeared in a red-and-white-checked sport shirt and red corduroy pants. The bulky prosecutor wore the beige suit that he often put on during the later, warmer days of the trial.

Roger Cohn remembers Bianchi's cross-examination this way:

"Just as Roraback displayed a contempt for some of the police, so did Bianchi display the same type of contempt for Reilly and a few other pro-defense witnesses. Since I feel the jurors identified more with his outlook and values than with Roraback's, I feel they responded much better to his displays of contempt. Bianchi was very effective in his cross-examination of Reilly, probably his most impressive moment at the trial. He handled Peter with just the right amount of skepticism and disgust, without bearing down so hard that he made the jurors sympathize with the defendant. Bianchi was able to prod Peter just enough to put him on the defensive. The prosecutor would pace back and forth before the jury box before turning and firing his questions. His slow, deliberate manner seemed to throw Peter off guard. Peter frequently sipped water from a styrofoam cup, probably more out of anxiety than thirst."

After asking about Peter's school history, Bianchi framed an odd question; "So, Mr. Reilly, would it be safe to say that you have been and are an intelligent, articulate, calm, alert individual?" All Peter could say was "I guess."

Bianchi wanted to know about his eating habits. Peter said that he had not eaten breakfast on the morning of the murder. In fact, "I don't think I have eaten breakfast in three years." He admitted that he had declined breakfast in the barracks when it was offered to him by Mulhern. This was handy testimony for the prosecution. The defense could not make too much of the argument that Peter lacked food as well as sleep while in the hands of the police.

Bianchi asked, "Do you know a lady by the name of Barbara Sincerbeaux?" The jurors learned that this was Peter's godmother. She had bought the Corvette for him and his mother, Peter agreed, and had sent funds regularly to them. "Was your mother a welfare recipient?" Bianchi asked. Peter replied, "I believe so, yes." He said he didn't know for sure if the check his mother had received September 28 was from his godmother. He did know that he had not seen Barbara Sincerbeaux since that date.

The prosecutor wanted to know about Peter's arguments with his mother.

Q: Your mother would bug you about the car, threaten to take the car away from you if you didn't do what she wanted at all times?

A: She never threatened to take it away.

Q: To put it away from you and not let you use it.

A: No.

Q: Or to sell it because you couldn't afford to keep it?

A: No, she didn't.

Q: She never did that?

A: No, she didn't.

Q: What was it you did argue about?

A: Well, we argued about the car breaking down all the time, and we argued about the fact that maybe we should get rid of the car which was my idea; and that the car was costing us a lot of money, and it wasn't worth it, and she liked the car. She called it a—what's the word—I don't know, kind of a—something fancy that you would own or—I can't

think of the word she used—I don't know, something special, you know, like if you are driving it
around, people would say, "Wow, look at the car."

After getting Peter to talk about his friendship with
Trooper Jim Mulhern, Bianchi asked about the confession
and whether Peter was saying that "your friend Jim Mulhern wrote down on that paper something that wasn't true
or something that you didn't say, is that what you are telling
these ladies and gentlemen?".

Peter protested that "I never said that. What I said was
that I wasn't sure if I said this or not."

"So you may have said it?" Bianchi asked.

"I may have," Peter replied.

At this point, Bianchi threw the confession papers down
on the evidence table in a dramatic gesture of disgust. When
Peter said that he could not remember whether he had read
the confession that Mulhern had written for his signature,
Bianchi asked if he was sick at the time. Peter said, "I wasn't
sick, I don't think" but "I was just totally exhausted." Bianchi
then proceeded to show that Peter had not been too tired to
remember any number of things, like the drive to Hartford
and accepting a ham-and-cheese sandwich from Mulhern.

Peter denied having seen John McAloon on the day he
was put into the boundover section of the jail. In which case,
Bianchi wanted to know, how could McAloon have known
some of the intimate details of his mother's medical history.
Peter figured that he had picked up the information from
someone that Peter did talk to.

When Bianchi turned to the "breathing" that Peter had
reported in his phone calls, and spoke of Dr. Izumi's testimony that his mother's legs were broken after she died,
he asked, "And there was nobody there but you?" Peter
responded with a soft "Mm-hmm."

Q: And you heard Dr. Izumi say that the cuts on abdomen and on her back and in her vagina area were
   all done after death?
A: I heard him say that, yes.
Q: And there was nobody there but you?

Roraback objected to the question and was overruled. Peter said, "Yes."

After a midmorning recess, Bianchi wanted to know about the man who had lived in the cottage with Peter and his mother for some time in 1969 or 1970. "And was he black?" Bianchi asked. Peter said, "Yes, he was." Bianchi continued, "This was a pretty trying thing for you, was it not?" Peter agreed that it was.

The prosecutor ended his cross-examination by asking why Peter had not broken down and cried about the death of his mother.

A: Well, I held it back.
Q: Did you make any attempt—any attempt at all, to assist your mother when you saw her laying there on the floor?
A: No, I didn't.
Q: You didn't rush over and attempt to stop the bleeding or do anything to assist her?
A: No, I didn't.
Q: Do you recall saying to Sergeant Timothy Kelly in Hartford, "What right did I have to take her life?"
A: I may have said that.
Q: Lieutenant Shay, Trooper Mulhern and Sergeant Kelly certainly were most considerate of you when you were in Hartford, were they not?
A: I guess, yes.
Q: They didn't hurt you, did they?
A: No, they didn't hurt me.
Q: And, in fact, near the end of the interrogation, didn't you ask Lieutenant Shay if you could go home and stay at his home until this was all over?
A: Mm-hmm.
Q: You did?
A: I believe I did, yes.

In her redirect examination, Roraback drew from Peter the memory of Lieutenant Shay yelling at him. "I remember, at one point, he said something about locking me up and treating me like an animal."

Roraback had two final questions. One was about the percentage of time that he and his mother argued when they were together. He guessed "one fifth, one fifteenth, one tenth of the time." And, "Could you tell me what you thought your relationship was with your mother." Peter said quietly, "She was my mother, I loved her."

In his final questions, Bianchi suggested that "they were pretty violent arguments, weren't they?" Peter replied, "Orally, not physically."

> **Q:** And even though you loved your mother, and I don't doubt that for the slightest minute, her actions left you pretty sad at times, didn't they?
> **A:** Well, at times, but you had to understand my mother.
> **Q:** Living with [a man] who was of another race in your house, in that tiny little house with your mother and you, that had to be a pretty sad thing, wasn't it?
> **A:** I guess.

After Peter's testimony, Roraback moved for the admission as full exhibits of the five tapes of the Hartford interrogation "except those portions of those tapes which refer to the taking of the polygraph tests." Bianchi's response was that "the State has absolutely no objection, whatsoever, to those tapes coming into existence as they are although I cannot see any reason for them." The single tape of Lieutenant Shay's interrogation of Peter in Canaan was refused as evidence by Speziale because it was too garbled.

The judge's decision was that the whole of the tapes should be heard by the jury because the polygraph parts were so interrelated; removing them would give a distorted impression of what had taken place. He told the jurors that they would be hearing the interrogation tapes and said they should put out of their minds any references to the polygraph test results. It is doubtful, of course, that even the most conscientious juror could avoid concluding from the dialogue on the tapes that Peter had failed the lie test.

The tapes were played that afternoon and the next day. Fatherly Sergeant Kelly, in civilian clothes, operated the tape machine instead of a court functionary. Several observers have since commented that Kelly's presence neutralized the interrogation passages that sounded like police browbeating of the suspect. "Kelly just looked like too nice a guy to do anything like that," a reporter said.

The tapes were difficult to hear. The jurors had to strain to make out much of the dialogue. As the hours went by they seemed occasionally to lose interest. They often appeared to be barely listening, but would perk up when the conversation suddenly became louder or clearer.

The early parts of the tapes seemed to make the jurors sympathetic to Peter. He sounded so eager to take the polygraph test and so sure that he would soon be found to be telling the truth. One juror smiled at Peter as she heard him asking the cost of the lie detector. Two of the men beamed at him when he spoke about his bicycle and how long it had been since he had gone for a bike ride. Hours later the dialogue focussed so much on the various ways that Peter might have harmed his mother, and the weapons used, that the jurors no longer looked at him kindly.

During the final hour of the tape playing, late on a Friday afternoon, the jurors could hear Peter saying, "I don't remember the details of what I did" and asking, "Does it sound in the facts that you get—does it sound like a cold-blooded killer?" Then, as he demonstrated to Mulhern how he might have used the razor on his mother, he could be heard saying, "It's almost like in a dream." The jurors had to decide whether they were hearing the truth or things dreamed up.

Earlier in the trial, Judge Speziale encouraged Catherine Roraback to introduce psychiatric testimony to shed light on Peter's confession. He eventually took her to task for not having done so, as did others. She was bitter in her denunciation of those who criticized with all the benefits of hindsight.

Roraback had arranged for two days of psychological testing of Peter while the trial was in progress, on March 22-23, and then must have agonized about whether to introduce the conclusions of the psychologist and put him on the stand. He was Dr. C. Brooks Brenneis of Yale University's School of Medicine. Portions of his report could have been used to argue that Peter was peculiarly susceptible to police suggestions. Thinking of himself as a misfit, Peter was said to have a "weak, fragile and vulnerable" image of himself, and thus "He does what he is told, and what he has learned others expect of him."

On the other hand, the psychologist wondered "How much craftiness or cunning is associated with this posture" and said that "Behind his shyness and compliance, there are feelings of profound mistrust and vigilance." Roraback could imagine what John Bianchi would do with those passages if she should introduce the report as evidence. "From the tests," Dr. Brenneis wrote, "I would anticipate that Peter would have moments of suspicion, of unrealistically feeling mistreated and exploited, and of bitterness towards others. Clearly, also, he would at such times be especially guarded, reluctant to be open, and perhaps contentious. Peter's intellectual functioning on well-defined tasks is quite good and free of vigilance and mistrust. His WAIS (IQ) scores (FS 115, V 115, P 113) are in the bright normal range and seem relatively stable."

Roraback decided to withhold the Brenneis report. Whether or not her decision was sound, it meant that the jurors were left in the dark about Peter Reilly's personality, They would not even hear character-witness testimony from such individuals as the Reverend Paul Halovatch, Jean Beligni and Kenneth Carter.

The overall impact of the Brenneis report is a sympathetic portrayal of a distressed youth. It says in part:

> The test picture is of a shy, withdrawn, somewhat immature young man struggling to maintain his balance in the face of massive depressive feelings of loss, emptiness and uncertainty. . . . Peter's current state is akin to whistling in the dark. While aware of intense depressive feelings, he seems to sense that experiencing these feelings fully is an invitation to disaster. He senses that he simply cannot cope with how discouraged and disheartened he feels with his life without also feeling without hope and empty, as if he has lost everything. Presumably, being more fully cognizant of such feelings would also give rise to a bitter and angry sense of victimization.
>
> To protect himself, Peter has assumed an attitude of

forced courage and optimism. Thus, he comments quickly after confiding that he has "lost everything [he] ever had," that "you can't keep a good man down." This refusal to let the impact of recent events fall upon him with their full weight may be resourceful to the extent that he is not yet capable of coming to terms with them. It may also partially account for his air of apparent calm and stated lack of anxiety about his fate: he has yet to react fully and, in fact, does not react for fear of drowning in his despair and bitterness. . . .

It would be mistaken to suggest that what Peter is struggling with is merely a reaction to recent traumatic events. Most likely, these recent events have aggravated long-standing concerns *and* exaggerated long-standing ways of coping. This is a lonely young man, hesitant about human contact, with intense feelings of emptiness and needfulness. . . . He feels uncertain of his connectedness to others, regards himself as too vulnerable to take chances, and may view his own hunger and needs as destructive or extravagant. Nonetheless, Peter seems capable of tenderness and regard, although, because of his readiness to be disappointed, he must have very mixed feelings about expressing his own tenderness and caring.

The remaining two days of testimony came as an anti-climax. The defense had six more witnesses, then the State brought forward eight people on its own, some of them familiar, for its rebuttal.

Trooper Walter Anderson spoke about what had appeared to be a footprint on the carpet near the body of Barbara Gibbons. Tests had been made, he said, but there was not enough detail to be of any value for comparison purposes. In short, it probably was a footprint but it would remain a question mark. Bianchi could not resist asking, "In other words, Trooper Anderson, it might have been a footprint of Peter Reilly, might it not?" The trooper's response was commendable: "I didn't know whose footprint it could have been. I have no idea of knowing whose footprint it was."

Sergeant Gerald Pennington told of finding an identifiable fingerprint on the rear screen door—a print that belonged neither to Peter nor his mother. The State Police did not know whose print it was and seemed unable to find out. The sergeant spoke of the difficulty of it all, even when working with the FBI: "It's a time-consuming job. I mean, takes years to go through all of them. They have a single fingerprint file, but in that file at the FBI are only the notorious persons who may turn up, from time to time."

Dr. Abraham Stolman, Connecticut's chief toxicologist for nearly a quarter century, testified for the defense and said he had found no blood on the straight razor. He was not asked a similar question about the kitchen and sink traps that had been removed from the cottage for analysis. Stolman then testified for the State about how drunk Barbara Gibbons had been when she was murdered. He said that he had found an alcoholic reading of .22 percent in the blood of the victim: "The individual was definitely under the influence of intoxicating liquor."

Roraback's last two witnesses were Barbara Gibbons' cousin Victoria and her husband, John. Although Victoria knew more about the personal history of the victim than anyone else, she said she had never seen Peter until the murder brought them together. She and her husband had rushed to northwest Connecticut as soon as they were notified of the tragedy.

Roraback asked Victoria what had happened when she met Peter for the first time in the law library at Torrington City Hall three days after the killing. "He started to cry. . . . I comforted him the best way I knew by saying that he was welcome to come to stay with us, and I talked to him and assured him that he would always have a home with us. . . . I held him in my arms about six to ten minutes."

Then her husband's account: "We were told that my wife could be with Peter and visit with him a little longer, and she went in with him, and he was in there for a while. And, finally, I went in with this officer and she was holding Peter and she was crying and I was crying and he was crying."

Catherine Roraback announced: "Your Honor, the defense rests."

16 ▪ THE VERDICT

PETER REILLY: The thing I'm really scared of is being thrown in
  jail or something.
SGT. KELLY: Oh, Pete, don't worry about things like that.
PETER REILLY: I mean I—that's not going to happen, is it?

Thursday, April 11, 1974. Peter Reilly knew when he awoke
that he could be a free man by suppertime. Or, if the worst
happened, he could be condemned by a jury as the killer of
his mother.

Peter, of course, expected to be found not guilty. He still
believed, despite everything, that his innocence was his
shield. He could not imagine that the jurors would think him
guilty, not after listening to the tapes, not after seeing that
the prosecutor had no real evidence against him. He knew
a guilty verdict was possible, but it was something he had
pushed far out of his mind. Besides, all his friends were telling him that he was sure to be declared innocent.

Mickey and Marion Madow drove Peter to the courthouse.
Art and Geoff went with them; it was Geoff's eighteenth
birthday and they expected to have more than enough reason for a celebration that night. Many other Reilly supporters
made their way to Litchfield. Jacqueline Bernard, who had
put up most of Peter's bond, came up from New York.

Catherine Roraback was worried, and not only about the

verdict. She had just learned that her only brother, Albert, an ocean away in Holland, was dying of cancer. Her father had died only a few months earlier just as she was starting work on the Reilly case. After the trial, when some people spoke of the rambling and disconnected quality of her summation this day, they would be reminded of her distress.

The trial had taken place at the end of a long winter. There had been some days of bitter cold. Even now, close to mid-April, there were pockets of snow in the Litchfield Hills. As Bianchi began his summation, he commented, "We had illness interrupt our matters; we lost a juror because of illness; many of us became ill while we went through this case; and we had a surprising ice storm." It was appropriate, then, that Bianchi should use a wintry scene to make his point that circumstantial evidence, "many times, is much better than direct evidence."

> If you came upon a house with your car, one snowy evening, just as it stops snowing, and you look at the front walk of that house and you saw some footprints come from the front porch, you followed them around the house and they came back in the front door again; you rang the bell, and inside the door were a pair of wet rubbers. There is one person. You search the house completely. There is one—only one individual in that house. The rubbers fit his feet. The rubbers' tread marks are the same as the footprints that go around the house; and you ask the individual, "Have you been out of the house tonight?" and he says, "No," he hasn't.
>
> I am sure you can clearly see that the circumstances of that particular case show that the man was not telling the truth. It's extremely strong that he was the only person that could have walked around that house. That's the illustration of circumstantial evidence and we will claim, ladies and gentlemen, that besides having a tremendous amount of direct evidence that this young man committed that murder, that there is also overwhelming circumstantial evidence that he did so.

Having spoken only a few minutes, Bianchi sat down. Roraback was surprised and unsettled by the brevity of the prosecutor's opening remarks and she complained to the judge about it. She said that "I am taken aback by Mr. Bianchi's summation because it seems to me that he has not, in fact, done his summation. He has merely done an outline of what he plans to have in his summation after I have finished speaking; and that seems to me a reversal of the usual procedure in a criminal case." Judge Speziale's curt reply: "Might be unusual, Miss Roraback. I see nothing improper in it."

Roraback, who had only just begun making notes to answer the points in Bianchi's argument, had to start cold. She reminded the jurors about the original presumption of Peter Reilly's innocence. She said that their decision would simply be "a question of whether the State had proven that he committed a crime, not whether he, himself, proved his innocence. We don't have that nice, neat formula that you may have seen on *Perry Mason* or some of the other television programs. I won't be able to, at some point in my final argument, point out to somebody sitting back there in the spectator's section and say, 'That's the person that really did it.'" She spoke of the old Scottish tradition of the jury bringing in a verdict of "Not proven" and said, "I think that's really what we are talking about here. We are not talking about a verdict of innocent but a verdict of not proven. . . ."

Roraback disputed Bianchi's claim about the State having "a tremendous amount of evidence" against Reilly. "I think it's really a very small amount of evidence in total sum." She said that the State had proven that Peter had said on the telephone that his mother was breathing, and that this had been tied in with Dr. Izumi's comments about the postmortem wounds.

However:

I would suggest that you might read his autopsy report, if there is any question in your mind, because that autopsy report refers to most of them as contributing to death which seems to me to be a slight contradiction.

In any event, Dr. Izumi did say that there was a period of, perhaps, five minutes or so when a seeming breathing could be observed by an individual looking at a person who had been subjected to the sort of brutal murder that Barbara Gibbons had been subjected to, even though she—there was the distinction between clinical death and the other death, that just gasping could occur after technical death.

She read Peter's original statement to Trooper McCafferty, saying that this "is what he best remembers, now, actually happened." She reminded the jury of all the people, including the wife of Trooper Mulhern, who had seen the clothes that Peter was wearing before and after the murder—the clothes he had never changed. She spoke of the police inspections of Peter's clothes and body that revealed no bloodstains and no bruises except a red knuckle. She mentioned the bloody footprint on the rug by the body: "They had the shoe, they had the rug, and they were unable to tie in Peter Reilly's shoe with that rug and, indeed, they couldn't even find blood on that shoe."

Roraback was least impressive when she came to the murder-night time sequence. She did not challenge the State's version of events by pointing out the peculiar eighteen-minute gap between Barbara Fenn's supposed 9:40 talk with Peter and her emergency call to police at 9:58. She simply said that "There is a general consistency about the time elements in this case, and I think that we may assume that sometime between— sometime around 9:45 or 9:50 Peter Reilly got home."

Roraback gave a vivid description of the Hartford interrogation:

He was there in isolation and in a topsy-turvy way, his world got turned upside down; and I submit, most shocking to me, although it is for you to determine whether or not it's shocking, that State Police of Connecticut created in Mr. Reilly's mind the feeling that it really wasn't so bad to have killed his mother and, in fact, he had killed her; and, yet, you remember, through it all, right up toward the end, Peter Reilly is still saying, "I don't think I did, I am not sure I did it, it seems I may have done it, it's like I am dreaming, it's as though I remembered it." And at one point he said to Trooper Mulhern . . . "I am really not sure of what I am saying, Jim, will you put that in the statement, I am not sure of anything I have said?" And you remember Trooper Mulhern saying, "Sure, sure, that will be in the statement," but it never got in the statement.

Roraback set up and knocked down the razor, knife and other pieces of State's evidence. She reminded the jury of the missing wallet and money, the open back door and the "unidentified but identifiable fingerprint." As for the hairs in the victim's hand, "Only two of the hairs of those five or six were Peter's." (As a matter of fact, the FBI expert had not gone that far. He had not said they were definitely Peter's.) "Certainly," she said, "in a house which we know was not exactly clean—in fact, a little dirty—such hair could have been picked up on the palm of almost any surface and since it is a mixture of various hairs, it seems to me it is not the thing you can claim or consider to have been pulled from the scalp of Peter Reilly. . . ."

As Roraback came to the end of her argument, she said that she wished to speak briefly about Peter Reilly who "lived with his mother in that little house in Falls Village." She questioned the likelihood of Peter committing murder over a "rather petty issue" like the car: "I would say that that's probably the major argument in the American household, frequently." (It had not been established, of course, that there had been an argument. That was only something the police and Peter had speculated about in the interrogation.)

She said that Peter could not possibly have killed his mother, cleaned himself up, and then put on "a duplicate of that brown shirt, a duplicate of those rather unique sneakers, put them on and hidden his offense from the public." She went further:

I submit that that's impossible, and I submit to you that, if nothing else consonant on that state of facts with Peter Reilly's guilt, there is certainly reasonable doubt—as His Honor will tell you—that Peter Reilly did not do this really awful crime. I would submit that there really is—and I trust you will agree with me—so—no other verdict to return than one of not guilty.

Roraback's argument, which lasted exactly one hour, came to a lame conclusion when she betrayed again how unnerved she had been by the brevity of Bianchi's opening statement. "Mr. Bianchi," she said, "is about to get up and make an argument to you, and I won't be able to answer him, now. I won't be able to—I have been trying to anticipate what he might say but I have not been able to answer what he might say. . . ." She asked for a just verdict "and I would hope, most sincerely, that that be a verdict of not guilty."

Peter's defense attorney was sincere, soft-spoken and obviously deeply concerned about the fate of her client. When she talked about his life she had stood behind him, her hands on his shoulders, and it was a maternal scene—this lost boy and this formidable but comforting middle-aged woman.

John Bianchi seemed to be more conscious than Roraback of the trial as theater and the courtroom a stage. He had not been shy about saying that he had been trying criminal cases for twenty years, a statement that was bound to give an exaggerated impression of his actual experience in these matters. He had seldom dealt with homicides in his career and this was his first murder trial as a prosecutor. He exuded confidence. Whereas Roraback had spoken of reasonable doubt, he virtually shouted that there was no doubt about Reilly's guilt. Over and over again he asked, who else but Peter Reilly could have killed Barbara Gibbons? He stressed Peter's unfortunate life with an alcoholic mother in order to say that it was no wonder that he ended up killing her.

The fact of the relationship between Peter Reilly and his mother had been denied on the stand by him, as I recall; but recall the tapes that were played for you where he indicated that she was "on his back," that she was calling him constantly, that he was finally free of her apron strings, that she harassed him about the car, that she would threaten to take the car away from him. . . .

It had to be a pretty unhappy place to grow up. . . . This had to be a very, very unhappy arrangement for Peter Reilly; and, thus, it's not strange to me that when he finally began to tell what happened, that night, in Hartford, to the officers, he felt free at last. His burden was gone; and with this happening, does it surprise you, ladies and gentlemen, that he had difficulty, after this horrible experience, in remembering each and every detail? It doesn't seem strange to me at all. Think of serious automobile accidents that, perhaps, you may know of, yourselves. Do the victims of those accidents recall every detail of that terrible traumatic injury? It is not surprising that he doesn't remember every detail of this thing; and that only after questioning would the fact begin to come back to him, that he was finally free of this horrible life that he had been living.

Bianchi then discussed the circumstantial evidence. He said not one word about time—when Peter might have arrived home, how many minutes he had to kill and conceal evidence—but he put great emphasis on Dr. Izumi's testimony. He described the terrible blows and wounds suffered by "this little woman." Slashing at himself with his hand, he described the various postmortem cuts and injuries and said that "Peter Reilly was the only one in that house at the time." He spoke of the knife that had a film of human blood on the blade, according to the FBI agent. He spoke of Dr. Izumi, "who is here as a technician and no other," who said "that that knife caused that wound in her hand, and that that knife caused the wound that she received after she was dead." Who, he wanted to know, "committed that murder but Peter Reilly?"

Bianchi quickly disposed of the idea "that this might have been a robbery." He ridiculed the idea that a robber would have bothered to carry out such a mutilation of the victim. "The robber would strike out, perhaps, cut her throat and escape. There isn't any evidence of a robbery."

He described the interrogation of Peter Reilly as an entirely voluntary proceeding. Peter had been read his rights many times. He was known as "an intelligent, articulate, calm and alert individual" and "he wanted to go to Hartford." He was taken there by "his good friend, Jim Mulhern."

Bianchi pointed out that "Jimmy Mulhern" simply wanted to write down the truth in the confession, but "they would have the unmitigated gall to stand in front of you and say that that young man altered that statement and put down something that this boy didn't say." Bianchi's opinion was that Reilly's off-the-tape statement "I killed her" was the clincher: "If there ever was a confession, that, ladies and gentlemen, was it, right then and there. 'Because I killed her' to his good friend, Jim Mulhern."

Bianchi mentioned other comments made to Mulhern and Calkins. He singled out the remarks Peter made (according to Calkins) on the drive to the Litchfield jail.

"You had an opportunity to view the trooper. Was he telling you a falsehood? Are all of these troopers in here with one big lie simply to convict this young man? Ladies and gentlemen, nothing could be further from the truth. They are in here telling you what happened as they heard it from this young man's own lips."

After urging the jurors not to overlook the statements of John McAloon, even though "he's got almost as bad a record as Mr. Erhardt," Bianchi spoke again of the truthfulness and trustworthiness of the Connecticut State Police. He ended his forty-one-minute summation with these words: "He is guilty as we have charged him, and I recall, once again, the end of those tapes where he was seated with Jim Mulhern, his good friend, and he said, 'Jim, everything I said I mean, and it's the truth.' Thank you, ladies and gentlemen."

The judge charged the jury for an hour and a quarter. For those who were unfamiliar with the finer points of the law it was an opportunity to hear the equivalent of a law-school lecture.

The jurors were told that they were entitled to believe the witnesses they trusted and to discredit the statements of those they distrusted. "The testimony of a police officer is entitled to no special or exclusive sanctity merely because it does come from a police officer." He said that when considering McAloon's testimony they should keep in mind that he may be "looking for or hoping for some favors in the disposition of his own cases." He said of the confession that there must be evidence to "substantially corroborate the admissions of the accused." He told the jurors to forget about the lie detector:

278 DONALD S. CONNERY

"The polygraph is just simply not reliable enough for you to
give any consideration, at all, to the test results."

Given the dearth of direct evidence against Peter Reilly
and the State's reliance on circumstantial evidence, Judge
Speziale's remarks on the difference between the two were
probably the most important element of his charge. He said,
in part:

> The law raises no distinction between direct evidence and
> circumstantial evidence. Your own common sense will
> tell you that the conclusions to be drawn from a chain
> of proven circumstances are often stronger than the tes-
> timony of a person who claims to have seen an act; and
> your own good sense will also tell you that, if the law
> were to impose upon you the duty of regarding circum-
> stantial evidence as insufficient or if jury men of their
> own volition should impose upon themselves such a duty
> without sanction of law, the execution of criminal laws
> would be practically paralyzed as would be, also, the pro-
> tection of civil rights.
>
> Therefore, it is your duty to consider circumstantial
> evidence in the same way as you consider direct evi-
> dence. . . . The only practical difference between direct
> and circumstantial evidence is that, when you have direct
> evidence of the commission of a crime, the only thing
> the jury has to do is pass upon the credibility of the wit-
> nesses and decide whether the facts testified to did exist,
> and then they have to decide whether the happening of
> those events or the existence of those facts forces them,
> logically, to the conclusion that other facts existed and
> other events occurred, and, ultimately, that the crime was
> committed by the accused.

The judge said that "The law does not require that the
State, in order to get a conviction in a criminal case, must
prove a motive." However, "In any case in which it appears
that there is no adequate motive on the part of a particular
accused to commit the crime, that fact tends to raise a reasonable doubt as to the guilt of that accused."

There are three possible verdicts, said the judge: guilty

as charged, guilty of manslaughter in the first degree (if it is felt that the accused did not act with the intent to cause death), or not guilty. "When you have reached your verdict, which . . . must be unanimous, you will then notify the sheriff by knocking on the door, and then you will be brought back into the courtroom, and you will report to the court."

At 12:56 P.M., the jurors stepped down from their seats in the jury box, walked across the courtroom and disappeared behind the thick door of the jury room. The court clerk followed them in with a large cardboard box containing the evidence.

Although Peter and his friends expected an early jury decision in his favor, the jurors themselves knew that they might take a long time making up their minds. Their first poll revealed five who believed Peter to be guilty, four who said not guilty, and three undecided.

The jurors debated all the rest of that day and well into the night. During the long wait, the crowd in the courtroom gradually thinned out until only a few people remained with Peter, his closest supporters, the lawyers and the reporters. During much of the afternoon Peter sat in the courtroom holding hands with his girlfriend. There were several false alarms: Each time the jurors knocked on the door the word spread that the verdict had come. But the jurors only wanted more information. When they sent out a note asking, "Plaid jacket—where is it?," the judge called them into the courtroom to tell them it was not part of the evidence. "You are not to surmise or conjecture as to its whereabouts."

The jurors came into the courtroom twice more to hear, at their request, key passages of Dr. Izumi's testimony—particularly those explaining the difference between clinical and biological death—and portions of the taped interrogation. Finally, at 10:38, Judge Speziale said to go home, sleep and come back in the morning.

Good Friday, April 12. The jurors still couldn't reach unanimous agreement. At 2:39 P.M., Judge Speziale instructed the sheriff to summon the jury. He had something to say to them.

All right, ladies and gentlemen, you have been deliberating for some time in this case, and I want to address you briefly, at this time.

I kept all of you here until about 10:40 last evening, and it is now about nineteen minutes to three. And, first of all, let me assure you, ladies and gentlemen, that I have no criticism to make of the length of time that you have been in conference. In fact, it indicates the earnestness with which you are considering the matter. However, I feel it is my duty to give you ladies and gentlemen whatever aid I can in assisting you in arriving at a verdict, if you are having a problem.

Although the verdict to which each juror agrees must, of course, be his own conclusion and not a mere acquiescence in the conclusions of his fellows, and although each juror has the right and duty to retain his own opinion, yet, in order to bring 12 minds to a unanimous result, each juror should examine with candor the questions submitted to them with due regard and deference to the opinions of each other, bearing in mind that the other jurors have heard the same evidence with the same attention and with equal desire to arrive at the truth, and under the sanction of the same oath.

I want you to bear that in mind, ladies and gentlemen, and I am going to ask you to return to the jury room.

The judge's little speech is known in the trade as the "modified Chip Smith charge," stemming from a Connecticut case in 1881 (*State v. Smith*) and an 1851 Massachusetts case. The idea is to give the jurors a little shove toward reaching a unanimous agreement while pointing out that a juror should not give up a personal opinion simply for the sake of agreement. It can be argued—as Roraback did argue after the verdict—that the judge should not have pushed the jury to come up with a decision when he did, because the jurors had not said that they were deadlocked.

The Reilly jurors retired at 2:43 P.M., after Speziale had spoken to them. Twenty-one minutes later they knocked on the door and sent out a note: "We have come to a unanimous decision." They had taken a vote just after lunch and found ten for conviction, one for acquittal and one undecided. Now, on the last vote, the two holdouts went with the majority.

The half-empty courtroom filled up quickly as spectators

rushed in from the hallways and the sidewalk. The jurors took their seats in the jury box for the last time. They looked tired and somber. Peter Reilly rose from his chair at the counsel table. With his attorney at his side, he stood facing the jury.

The assistant clerk of the court stepped forward. "Ladies and gentlemen of the jury," he said, "look upon the accused. What say you, Mr. Foreman, is he guilty or not guilty of the crime with which he stands charged?"

The foreman, Edward L. Ives, Jr., the Litchfield insurance man and scoutmaster, said in a strong voice, "We find the defendant guilty of manslaughter in the first degree."

His words fell like great stones in the hushed courtroom. A spectator gasped, "Oh, no." Peter closed his eyes and seemed stunned for a moment before looking down at the floor. The color had gone from his face. Marion Madow and other women in the gallery began to weep.

The jurors were dismissed. They left the jury box and the courtroom in single file, passing close to Peter. The day for sentencing was announced: May 14. Then the attorneys went to the judge's chambers to discuss the presentence investigation and the continuance of the bond. Peter sat with Peter Herbst in the center of the courtroom, his face in his hands, his elbows on the table. Like so many others, he seemed paralyzed by the turn of events.

Very slowly, Reilly supporters like Bill and Marie Dickinson, and Murray and Dot Madow, shuffled out of the courthouse and into the inappropriately bright sunshine. "Now all we have to do is find the killer," Murray Madow bellowed. A woman who had sat through most of the trial said bitterly, "It seems like the State's attitude was, 'If Reilly didn't do it, then who else did?' If that's American justice, then I sure hope I never get in any kind of trouble." The wife of a deputy sheriff told a reporter, "One thing this trial has taught me—if I'm ever questioned by the police, I don't care what it's about, I'm not going to say anything or sign anything until I see an attorney."

Joan Barthel wept. Farn Dupre, a young reporter for the *Winsted Citizen*, broke into tears and fell to her knees on the sidewalk, crying hysterically. Even a burly deputy sheriff, Joseph Battistoni, a retired Torrington fireman, had been seen wiping his eyes after the verdict was announced. He said to Marion Madow that he would like to help Peter get through the crowd outside: "It's the least we can do."

Peter came out of the courthouse. His face was blank; his long hair was flopping in the breeze. He held onto a package that he had stuffed into a pocket of his tan bush jacket. It was a statuette of the Virgin Mary, given to him by a woman in the courtroom. Reporters, photographers and television cameramen rushed up, but Peter said he had no comment.

The press turned to Catherine Roraback. She growled that she had nothing to say. John Bianchi, wearing a Cheshire-cat smile, announced that he was satisfied. It had been a "just" verdict. "That's all it was—manslaughter. I believed that from the very day it happened."

His is a comment worth thinking about. Judge Speziale was shocked when he heard it. If a prosecutor believes that a defendant is guilty only of manslaughter, should he go all out to persuade a jury that he is guilty of murder? In any event, the jurors had obviously settled on manslaughter as a compromise in spite of the prosecution's elaborate description of a sustained murderous attack.

In an interview long afterward, Bianchi said it was the grand jury, not himself, that had originally charged Peter Reilly with murder. He was simply the tool of the grand jury. "Actually, it's the reverse," said an attorney who was told of Bianchi's comment. "Before a grand jury is ever convened, as a matter of universal practice the indictment is typed in the prosecutor's office and handed to the foreman to be signed by the foreman upon the vote in the grand jury room. So to say that that was the grand jury's doing is a lot of nonsense."

According to those jurors who were willing to talk about the case after the verdict, the most persuasive evidence was the knife and the Izumi testimony about the wounds and the length of time the victim could have been "breathing" after the throat had been slashed and all the blood had gushed out. Peter's stated belief that his mother was breathing when he discovered her body was his undoing. The jurors had worried about whether Peter would have had time enough to carry out the complicated killing, but after using stop watches and acting out the murderer's actions in the jury room they had concluded that the whole business could have been accomplished in less than four minutes.

The idea that an unknown robber had done the killing was dismissed as "strictly innuendo." It made more sense to believe that Peter Reilly had done this horrible thing and then had blocked it out of his mind. "He never told the police that he definitely didn't do it," said one juror who must not have listened closely to the tapes. "If I was in that position, I'd have said I didn't do it no matter how tired I got." Another juror said, "I don't think Peter's mind will ever let him recall the killing."

The jurors had quickly agreed that this was a matter of manslaughter, not murder. They felt that Peter had not planned to kill his mother, but they believed in Bianchi's portrayal of hostility between mother and son. As one juror said, "There was no love lost between those two. In fact, I think there was a deep-seated bitterness." The sexual mutilation of Barbara Gibbons "sure as heck was a big factor" in the guilty verdict, a juror said. Another stated that "I couldn't picture any robber doing all of that."

By all accounts, the jurors did their work calmly, deliberately and without great argument. Charles Kochakian of the *Hartford Times* was told by one juror that "I think we were as fair as any twelve people can be. I don't think anyone wanted to find him guilty, but we didn't have any choice."

Kochakian wrote: "The judge's instruction [the modified Chip Smith charge] in no way influenced the decision of a single woman juror who continued to have some doubts about Reilly's guilt, jurors said. The jurors told the woman that they would support her decision if she were unable to return a guilty verdict."

On the night of the verdict, reporters, TV crews, Peter's friends and adults from the Reilly Committee crowded into the Madow house. Father Paul Halovatch was present as well and there was much talk about Christianity and hope. Peter found comfort in the thought that "Jesus Christ was also sentenced on Good Friday," and he made it a point to go to Easter mass Sunday morning at St. Joseph's Church. Roger Cohn was present and he says that "It was strange for me to hear Peter talking about Christ while Marion's mother, Nan, the perfect Jewish grandmother, sat beside him and agreed with everything he said."

The telephone rang constantly. Peter said what he thought and his comment was sent across the country by Associated Press: "There is a murderer walking around the streets right now. I have no idea who he is. But I didn't murder my mother." He said of the jury's verdict that "I'm just shocked because I didn't feel they could find an innocent person guilty."

The telephone kept ringing that Easter weekend. Some of the more than one hundred calls came from as far away as Michigan and California. "We all walked away from that courtroom," Marion Madow said, "with the feeling that something is terribly wrong here. I've gotten many calls from people who've never met Peter, but whose voices are trembling. They all say they can't believe something like this can happen in this day and age."

Many others, of course, believed that justice had triumphed. People who had not followed the Reilly case closely had no reason to doubt Peter's guilt. Many probably shared the opinion of a man in Canaan's Colonial Restaurant who thought that Reilly "got off easy" with a conviction for manslaughter rather than murder. "If he didn't do it, then who the hell did it?"

As the national headlines told of the Watergate exposures of wrongdoing at the highest levels of government, so did the headlines and editorials in Peter's corner of New England reflect the widespread feeling that something was amiss about the Reilly case. "REILLY MANSLAUGHTER VERDICT STUNS AREA," said the *Lakeville Journal*. "VILLAGERS SHOCKED BY JURY'S VERDICT," said the *Hartford Courant*. "REACTION TO REILLY VERDICT: DISBELIEF IN MANY QUARTERS," said the *Torrington Register*. The stories told of the determination of the Reilly Committee to continue fighting for his vindication. Editorials took the police to task for their interrogation techniques and the prosecution for relying on a confession that, as one paper pointed out, "consisted of ideas planted by police during protracted questioning rather than of Reilly's own thoughts."

Perhaps the most powerful indictment of the performance of the State Police and the State's Attorney for Litchfield

County was an analysis of the case by Stewart Hoskins, the editor emeritus of the *Lakeville Journal*. "According to the police," Hoskins wrote in the *Journal*, "Reilly transformed himself from a teenage kid coming home from a carefree gathering into a fiend incarnate." Reilly was supposed to have carried out a number of incredible acts, and then "this arch fiend stayed quietly and waited for Justice to take its course."

Hoskins spoke of "big, friendly John Bianchi, gluing together a flimsy case for the State with his masterful manner, well known in Canaan. His big moment came on accusing Reilly of tramping on his mother's legs and doing sundry other things *after* calling for an ambulance. So logical." Hoskins concluded:

"The short time factor stuns me; the police interrogation disgusts me; the State's Attorney's participation as an adversary rather than as a public defender of truth and justice saddens me; the judge's ruling or lack of rulings worries me.

"The simple fact remains (and even the 'law' concurs), the door of the Reilly home was open to all types of people and many came and went. That night the door was unlocked as usual and the one person inside nearly helpless with drink (authorities report); and no one knows or has really tried to find out who, besides Peter, entered it—and did not stay."

17 ▪ THE SENTENCE

SGT. KELLY: You're tired and I'm tired. We on the State Police are
not your enemies. We don't—
PETER REILLY: I know.
SGT. KELLY:—we don't look with happiness on other people's
misfortune. If we can help you and I know we can help you,
we will help you.

The Saturday night teenage dance could have been anywhere
in America. But something was different about this lively
happening at the Cornwall Consolidated School. The lead
guitarist, playing his glistening Gibson electric, was a skinny
nineteen-year-old from a neighboring town—a young man
recently convicted for the death of his mother. Within a few
days he would be sentenced to years in prison.

The name of the makeshift band was Reilly's Raiders.
The aim of the dance was to raise money for the Peter Reilly
Defense Fund, and a grand total of $146 was added to the
more than $3,000 that had been collected in the month since
Peter's conviction. The dance in Cornwall was just one of
many such efforts made in the weeks following the verdict
to arouse support for Peter Reilly and raise money for his
appeal. Peter's most fervent supporters would not accept the
guilty verdict. Marion Madow said, "We're not going to stop
now. We're going to keep fighting this thing."

The Reilly Committee met in the Canaan Methodist
Church parish house on a cold Tuesday night, four days after

the conviction, to decide what to do next. Twenty-eight people attended, a larger gathering than usual. It was, however, typical of the often stormy and overlong meetings during the most critical months of the Reilly case. Few of the participants had had any experience at crusading for a cause. They would sometimes ask the reporters covering their meetings for advice, but the reporters felt uneasy about becoming active participants and tried to keep their distance.

At this April 16 meeting the Reilly supporters discussed the seemingly naive proposal for a campaign to persuade Judge Speziale to release Peter to the community instead of sending him to prison. Given the seriousness of the crime, the judge was unlikely to do any such thing, but, as Roger Cohn observed, "There was something refreshingly bold about the Committee's attitude. They weren't going to sit by and allow what they regarded as an injustice to occur. And they were prepared to seriously question the authorities even though it was not the kind of thing they were used to doing."

The idea of writing letters to the judge had the endorsement of Catherine Roraback. Although she kept apart from the Committee's activities, she had told Mickey Madow that letters might help. Mickey explained to the others that "The letters should say that enough has been done to Peter already, and that it would be to his benefit and to the benefit of the community to have him with us—rather than have him put away in jail."

Murray Madow, who was always more of a firebrand than his more even-tempered brother, interrupted to say that "They'll just be thrown away."

"We don't want to say anything too rambunctious," Mickey cautioned.

"Dammit, Mickey," snapped Murray, "we just can't go out and not say anything. They've got to know that we're unhappy about this. Otherwise, we're going to end up in the same place we started from."

The meeting finally settled down to such practical matters as tag sales, bake sales, auctions and other money-raising events. And they agreed that Mickey Madow and Father Paul should try to meet with Police Commissioner Cleveland Fuessenich to ask him to reopen the investigation into the Gibbons murder.

Fuessenich, who retired the following year, lived nearby in Litchfield. He was known, at least in the immediate area, as an exceptionally considerate and open-minded police officer. As a onetime commander of the Troop B Barracks, he was familiar with Canaan and its inhabitants. A decade earlier he had been a central figure in a sensational murder case that had produced charges of psychological coercion and police bungling. A nineteen-year-old high school senior, accused of the gory slaying of a Barkhamsted housewife, had confessed after a lengthy taped interrogation. ("I killed her, that's what you want," said the youth, but—"I just can't remember what actually took place. I don't actually remember what happened.") There had been a hung jury and then a conviction on a lesser count. The story was told in great detail in Mildred Savage's *A Great Fall*.

Fuessenich agreed to talk with Madow and Halovatch, and the three men met at St. Joseph's rectory. Afterward Fuessenich reviewed some of the police files and talked to John Bianchi. His conclusion, after his cursory examination, was that the Reilly supporters had nothing substantial to offer that had not been thoroughly aired in the courtroom. He said that the case would, of course, be reopened if new evidence was discovered, but, now, "there is no basis for further investigation."

The next Committee meeting, described in the *Hartford Courant* as a cross between a town-meeting debate and a social club planning session, attracted fifty people. Bea Keith announced that Catherine Roraback had been paid about $1,000, even though she had made no demands on the Committee. (Roraback never did send a bill for her services. Ultimately, she received $3,500. She suffered a heavy financial loss in taking the Reilly case and had turned down considerable business while engaged with it for over half a year.)

Mickey Madow told the audience that at least $15,000 would be needed for Peter's appeal. The trial transcript alone, a necessary tool, would cost at least $1,500. Again a vigorous debate ensued about how to approach Judge Speziale to appeal for clemency and whether to go beyond letter writing and organize demonstrations.

Peter's supporters wrote a petition: "We the undersigned

ask that Peter Reilly be allowed to remain in our community. In this case a prison sentence would serve no useful purpose. Peter is a fine young man and we want him to live among us and resume a normal peaceful life."

The result of the several meetings after the verdict was a flurry of activity that raised $2,000, produced several thousand names on petitions and sent dozens of moving personal letters to Judge Speziale. Peter spent one Sunday afternoon at a Canaan rally that he described as "fantastic." An even larger affair was held at a huge cocktail lounge in Torrington (after the organizers failed to persuade the local churches to provide a meeting place). The sound of crashing bowling pins could be heard below as some two hundred people sat on folding chairs in the Starlite Room of the Sky-Top Bowling Lanes and munched on cookies and cake. Peter shook hands, served soft drinks and answered questions. "Do you pray to God a lot?" asked a girl interviewer from a high school newspaper. "Oh, yes," said Peter. He would be back in Torrington two weeks later, playing his guitar at a Reilly benefit dance with another makeshift band, the 101st Southern Berkshire Artillery.

Judge Speziale eventually became annoyed by some of the pro-Reilly activities, especially when the press reported plans for a mass rally in front of the Litchfield courthouse on the day of sentencing. He felt his decision should not be made under pressure from pro-Reilly partisans. He told Peter Herbst to contact Catherine Roraback and let her know that he did not approve the campaign the Committee was mounting. Roraback was in Europe looking after her dying brother. The sentencing date had been delayed for a week because of her absence.

As the day for sentencing drew closer the plans for a major demonstration were put aside. The Committee hoped that enough people would go to the courthouse on their own to show the judge that there was great concern about Peter's fate.

Peter's life in limbo was both prosaic and extraordinary. To judge by outward appearances, he lived like any other teenager who had dropped out of high school. He worked part-time at a gasoline station. He raked leaves and did other odd jobs around the house. He was clinging to the normal life as much as he could, but he could hardly forget his predicament. He seldom went anywhere alone. Art and Geoff Madow made a point of being with him, almost as bodyguards.

Peter said little about his feelings. Dr. Ellis A. Perlswig, a New Haven psychiatrist who examined Peter at this time at Catherine Roraback's request (she wished to furnish Judge Speziale with a psychiatric report before sentencing was pronounced), concluded:

> Peter is a nice-looking youth with a warm, quiet and pleasant manner. Throughout the sessions, he maintained a sense of control and denial of feelings that was perhaps intended to show maturity in the sense that a man does not show how deeply he is affected by adversities. . . .
>
> Peter has not yet mourned the death of his mother. He denies the sadness, yet reveals a considerable amount of clinical depression: ideas of loss, loneliness, emptiness, and abandonment. External factors have undoubtedly played a part to prevent his experiencing the depression of his mother's death. He has no close person with whom to share his grief. He is a boy who is literally alone, without close relatives to comfort him as a child needs to be comforted. The Madows are too new in his life to have that role yet. He must also live with and defend himself against the public implication of his involvement in his mother's death. . . .
>
> Peter is an appealing young man. He is not a delinquent youth, nor do I find evidence of psychosis. He is a troubled adolescent who can mature into a good and productive man. I hope that Peter will not be sent to prison. I do not see confinement in any correctional center as helping him to discover himself in any corrective way.

Peter let himself go one day, soon after the verdict, when he said in an interview with Roger Cohn that "The police conned me and tricked me into saying something I wasn't sure of. I wonder how many people have been railroaded like this. It makes you wonder whether the police are really out to help people. They knew they were dealing with someone who had never been in trouble before. If I had been, I would have known better than to go with them. If it happened today and they asked me to come out to the car to sign a statement, I wouldn't say a word until I had an attorney. That way I wouldn't have spent 143 days in jail and the police would have kept looking and maybe caught the person who did this.

"I really had plans for the next few years of my life. I wanted to settle down and make some good out of my life. I wanted to make myself into a decent human being. It just doesn't seem right that they're going to take this away from me. Someday I want to hold a job, own my own home and raise a family. This whole thing is just throwing a wrench into my plans."

Catherine Roraback and Peter Herbst appeared before Judge Speziale in Hartford Superior Court to argue her motion to set aside the guilty verdict. They said that there was "undue interference by Your Honor" when he told the jurors, minutes before they reached a verdict, that they should consider the opinion of the majority. They contended that the State had produced no motive for the killing "other than arguments . . . of an adolescent with a parent." They attacked the interrogation statements as involuntary. John Bianchi, in his response, said that Reilly's confession had been "argued ad nauseam." He called the interrogation "a surprisingly gentle handling of a man who was a suspect in a murder case." The judge denied the motion.

One of the defense complaints in the motion concerned Judge Speziale's failure to instruct the sheriffs to keep the jurors together and away from contact with "third parties" when they went to lunch soon after beginning their deliberations. They had scattered to different restaurants. When Roraback protested to the judge that afternoon, Speziale said, "Maybe if you had stopped me at that time I might have sequestered them." She replied, "You were off the bench before I knew what was happening, Your Honor."

The incident suddenly became crucial immediately before the sentencing was to take place. Joe O'Brien reported to the judge that the jury might have been contaminated by a third-party influence. If so, the whole trial was in jeopardy. O'Brien said that soon after the unsequestered lunch by the jurors he had spoken to the remaining alternate juror, who had been released from duty at the end of testimony, and learned from him that Reilly probably would be found guilty because there had been a 5-4-3 first ballot by the jury. Either the alternate had made a shrewd guess about the vote or he had been discussing the case with at least one juror, against all the rules.

Speziale personally conducted sixteen hours of closely guarded hearings over three days to determine the truth of this matter and of a separate charge of a jury impropriety raised by the defense. A juror was said to have publicly expressed his feelings about Peter's guilt midway through the trial.

Announcing the results of his inquiry in the courtroom, the judge simply said that there had not been any "extraneous influence" on the jurors and ruled that Peter Reilly had been "duly tried by a fair and impartial jury." He then ordered the record on his inquiry to be sealed and impounded by the court and all participants to remain silent.

Peter Reilly was sentenced on May 24, 1974. "I didn't take anything extra with me that day. I just had the clothes that were on me and maybe a dollar in my wallet. I didn't want to take a Bible or a toothbrush or anything because I was making myself think positively. I realized that I could be going to prison, but I didn't want to prepare for it. I was thinking positively. I wanted to go to court in the morning and be home again in the afternoon. I didn't want to think about going to prison."

Soon after 8:30 A.M., Mickey, Marion, Geoff and Peter piled into the Madow family's blue Chevrolet Impala for the drive to Litchfield. Art would follow in his own car. Nan kissed Peter good-bye.

On the gray and misty May morning, the family had little to say. They would soon know the sentence. Probably the judge had already made his decision, but there would be a last-minute chance to appeal to him. As Peter looked at the soft contours of the Litchfield Hills, he thought of the view in a prison cell, behind bars, behind walls.

They parked in front of the jail. Peter looked up at the jail windows, perhaps expecting to see convict friends, then walked with the Madows toward the courthouse. Peter's expression kept changing: a look of sober apprehension gave way to bemusement as he noticed that someone had hung the American flag upside down in front of the courthouse.

"He clearly was struggling to keep himself composed," Roger Cohn remembers, "as the photographers and reporters moved in on him. To question him now seemed somehow offensive, an invasion of his privacy. Several of his supporters wished him good luck as he headed up the courthouse steps. We watched as he held the door open for the Madows and then disappeared inside."

The courtroom was jammed. Extra seats had been added. Most of the spectators were members of the Reilly Committee and their friends. Judge Speziale entered at exactly ten o'clock, and promptly left again when Catherine Roraback asked for and was granted a short recess. Peter had a few minutes more to lean over the railing and chat with friends. Judge Speziale returned to the bench at 10:10. "All right, Mr. Bianchi," he said, "you may proceed."

John Bianchi, smooth as ever, low-key in his presentation, described the bare facts of the case against the convicted Peter Reilly. Eight months had passed since the brutal slaying of Barbara Gibbons. Bianchi said it was an "unusual circumstance" for himself as State's Attorney to have known the victim.

"I had known her for nearly twenty years, I would say, in my general practice of law, and . . . I do know that the victim had certain problems, Your Honor. The evidence in the case showed that she was under the influence of alcohol at the time of her death. There are some things that the State knew, also, that did not come into evidence. Namely, a benefactor of the family had, just that day—a letter had been received, just that day, indicating, as I read this letter, that her assistance was finished, that the family was going to have to go it by themselves; and I think it's been evident to me that this benefactor has been completely out of this matter since that very day."

No one in the courtroom needed to be told that the State's

Attorney was speaking of Peter Reilly's mysterious New York godmother, "the other Barbara," who had helped him financially since the day of his birth. Neither the prosecution nor the defense had called Barbara Sincerbeaux as a witness in the trial. Now, for whatever reason, the State's Attorney thought it pertinent to introduce the interesting information that the murder of Barbara Gibbons had followed, in a matter of hours, the receipt of a letter that seemingly contained a threat to cut off support. In truth, the letter was not unusual; Sincerbeaux from time to time would express her exasperation about supplying funds to Barbara.

John Bianchi continued, "I have felt, always, in this case, Your Honor, that this was a matter of manslaughter and not murder under our statutes. This was an explosion by this young man, in my opinion. The end result took just seconds to accomplish; but, regardless of that fact, certainly, Your Honor, Barbara Gibbons had a right to live."

The State's Attorney concluded by recommending "a minimum sentence of seven years and a maximum of sixteen."

"Miss Roraback?" said the judge. Catherine Roraback knew that this was no time for any dramatic assertion that the wrong man, or boy, was about to be sentenced. She hoped for a light sentence, perhaps even a suspended sentence. She had told the Madows an appeal would depend on the sentence and accepting a truly lenient decision, one that took account of the months Peter had already spent behind bars, might be better than the arduous and expensive process of an appeal. Peter would bear the brand of guilt, but at least would be able, in a short time, to start making some kind of normal life for himself.

Roraback began by noting the information available to the judge in addition to the trial evidence. A thorough report on Peter's background had been prepared by the Department of Adult Probation, and many letters of support from persons in the community had been gathered. The reports of the psychiatrist and psychologist who had examined Peter at her request had been made available "with Mr. Reilly's permission," she said.

"Apart from that material, Your Honor, I would like to speak, not to the facts of the case. Mr. Bianchi has again reviewed what he considers to be the evidence in the case, and, indeed, refers to some evidence that was not evidence in the case. Defendant has denied his guilt of this—these charges, and he continues to do so; and that is always a difficult situation to be placed in on a hearing on a sentencing.

"But I would urge Your Honor to consider the total background of Mr. Reilly, the fact that he has, since he was approximately one year old, or for the last eighteen years, lived in the hills of Litchfield County, grown up in the township of Canaan in Falls Village, gone to school here, had his friends here, had his roots here. And he has, throughout that period, as is attested by all of the various people to whom the probation officer spoke—and, indeed, the various persons who wrote letters to Your Honor that I submitted yesterday, the ones who knew Peter Reilly—he has always enjoyed a very good reputation within his community.

"He has been polite, respectful, sincere; he has a sense of humor; he enjoys the outdoors. He enjoys, also, the companionship of his friends. He has been an adequate student, not an outstanding student, but he is presently a senior—or was a senior at the time of his arrest. It is his desire to go back and complete his high school education and to stay in this community."

Cautiously mentioning the "correctional" facilities of the State of Connecticut, she suggested that "they fall a good deal short of the ideal situation," especially for a young man without a prior criminal record. "I, myself, observed Peter when he was in jail. I only first met him the day after his arrest, and I watched a continuing period of what I can only characterize as a combination of withdrawing from ordinary society and being highly skeptical of it and also—even almost a slight sense of cynicism about it, a feeling, I think, that was inculcated in the confines of Litchfield, which . . . is, perhaps, the best of all our institutions. I would, myself, quite literally, hate to see what might happen to Peter Reilly if he were to be incarcerated anywhere else than Litchfield."

Roger Cohn, sitting in one of the press seats behind the wooden barrier, felt that "Judge Speziale could hardly conceal his agony as he listened to Roraback's plea. It was clear that he was facing a struggle in his own mind."

The judge spoke. "Miss Roraback, I really don't intend to divert your train of thought here. You mentioned, correctly, 'rehabilitation,' and, earlier in your presentation, you did mention the fact how the defendant is proclaiming his innocence, and you properly put your finger on a point that makes it extremely difficult for this court because, even in terms of rehabilitation, the first step is remorse; and that is one thing I do not find anywhere through all of these—I have the report from the Adult Probation Department; I have all of these letters that you gave me yesterday; I spent a good part of the evening just going over them, over and over again; and I just don't see remorse anywhere here at all, Miss Roraback."

Measuring her words carefully, Catherine Roraback suggested to the judge that "remorse" might not be the proper word to apply here. "Mr. Reilly," she said, "is fully cognizant of the horrible thing that happened. He does not condone that. I think Your Honor heard the lengthy interrogation of him by the state troopers where he did, in fact, talk somewhat about—you know, who has the right to take someone's life. . . . And I would not think, Your Honor, most respectfully, that remorse is going to be created in Peter Reilly by incarceration."

She suggested he be given a suspended sentence. Admittedly, she said, a suspended sentence with probation would be "a highly unusual step, but this is an unusual case; Mr. Reilly is an unusual young man; and, indeed, his situation in a community which does not, indeed, reject him but, in fact, supports him so fully" is still more unusual.

Roraback asked for and received permission to present several persons who wished to speak briefly in Peter's support. They stepped forward, one after the other, and addressed the Court. Mrs. Rose Ford of Falls Village, one of his grade school teachers, said that he would become "a decided asset to our community" if the Court would "return him to us as soon as possible." Two cousins of the murdered Barbara Gibbons spoke of their own children at their homes in New

Jersey and New York and of their readiness to make a place for Peter. The Reverend Paul Halovatch told of the value of a good family situation for Peter, "knowing that he is easily influenced." The Madows spoke last.

"Your Honor," said Mickey Madow, "Peter has lived with us since the situation arose, and he has been a model as far as him being in our home, behaving properly, showing respect, and Your Honor mentioned the word 'remorse,' sir. I believe my wife and myself would be the only ones that would possibly observe him at the time when he is the most quiet, when he has a chance to sit and reflect, and all I saw in his eyes and all my wife saw in his eyes was sorrow. And in all the time he has been at the house, the only thing I have ever heard him say was 'my mom,' 'my mom did this,' and 'we used to do this,' and 'we did that.'

"Now, if this was someone who he hated, I am sure he would not use that type of language and would not refer to her in that particular type of address.

"I believe the best thing that could possibly happen to Peter would be to leave him in the community where he can be guided and shown the proper way, and he is—he could be a very good citizen. He has worked for Mr. Houston of Falls Village. When he received his paycheck, he came back, handed it to Mrs. Madow, three quarters of it, and had her put it in the bank for him, and he has a little small sum in the savings bank. He has used the rest for his own expenses and wherever he could, he tried to pay his own way.

"It would—if we went somewhere and had to buy something, a drink or sandwich, he always tried to pick the check up, such as it was; and to my mind, a boy like this deserves a real good break. Thank you, Your Honor."

Marion Madow took her husband's place at the table. She said she might break up a little while speaking and apologized. "I just feel that having Peter go back to prison won't serve any purpose at all. He certainly is not a threat to society and we in the town want to keep him there.

"I remember when we used to go visit Peter at Litchfield, and we went every Saturday. It would take us fifteen or twenty minutes to get him back to our world. By the time the visiting hours—the half hour was over—that Peter was Pete

again, and the boy we saw when we first walked in there was
Peter again, and we could feel this sure difference in him as
soon as you saw him there; and then, when we got him home,
it took two or three weeks before Peter could really relate to
us as he used to before.

"He was guarded and suspicious and was not sure of anything we said. Sometimes we joked with him, and he kind of
sat back, and then would laugh and realize it was just a joke;
we weren't being mean or nasty. And I know he probably—
he has been convicted, and I guess he has to be punished,
but I feel that conviction is punishment enough for a young
man. Wherever he goes, it's always going to be with him.
And if feeling remorse has to be outwardly, which I seem to
be doing now, I think Peter's is very deep inside, something
that, if he is left in a loving family with his cousins and us,
it will come to the top. And I think it will be a good day for
Peter if it does."

Mrs. Madow concluded by saying that "he is welcome in our
home for as long as he wants, and if the Court would release
him to us we would take care of him and see that he is always
taken care of and never cause any problems because Peter does
listen, and he is a very good boy, and we love him."

Catherine Roraback said that she had nothing further to
say. John Bianchi had a final word. He reminded the Court
that "this was a horrible homicide. . . . There have been thousands and thousands of words written about this case. The
expressions for this young man by his friends in the community at the time of the bond hearing and this morning are
very laudable, but I have not heard one word of Barbara Gibbons, who lies dead in her grave in Falls Village."

Then Judge Speziale turned to the defendant to ask: "Peter
Reilly, before this Court imposes sentence, have you anything to say to the Court?"

It was 10:47 A.M. Peter Reilly rose to speak. He seemed to
be fighting to keep control of himself. His hands were stiff
at his sides; his voice barely carried to the rear of the courtroom. "All I can say is that I will not be a threat to society,
and I just want a chance to live a decent life."

Peter sat down. The courtroom was still.

"I have devoted a great deal of time to this trial," the judge began. "I think this is, perhaps, the longest trial that I have had in my whole judicial career; and this is an extremely difficult case for this Court to impose sentence.

"This Court is impressed by the outpouring of the defendant's friends in the community, all of these letters that have been presented in behalf of the defendant that I have read through very, very carefully.

"However, this Court cannot lose sight of the fact that a human being has been killed as a result of a very vicious and horrible homicide.

"Taking everything into consideration, Peter Reilly, it is the sentence of this Court that you be imprisoned in the Connecticut Correctional Institution at Somers for a term of not less than six nor more than sixteen years."

Two deputy sheriffs moved up from the bar railing and stood at either side of Peter. He remembers "that I felt a kind of rage when I heard the sentence, but it was something cold in me, because I decided right then that I was not going to accept this; I was going to appeal it no matter what my lawyers or anyone else said."

The weeping in the courtroom was unmistakable: the high school girls, Peter's cousins, the women of the Reilly Committee—all crying. The judge moved briskly to conclude the morning's business. He spoke of his willingness to help place Peter in a facility best suited for a young person. There were some documents to be signed and bond to be set. The State's Attorney recommended a bond "in the vicinity of $100,000," but to the great relief of Peter's supporters, the judge decided on $60,000. That would mean raising an extra $10,000 but it could be done, and perhaps that very day. After the court recessed at 10:55, Peter remained for a quarter hour longer while his attorneys prepared the appeal forms. Then it was time to go to the penitentiary.

"The sheriffs took me to a room at the rear of the courtroom," Peter remembers, "and Catherine Roraback asked them if she could speak to me privately for a moment. She asked if I had any money and when I said I didn't she slipped me a ten-dollar bill. She thought there might be some things

I could buy in the prison. I really appreciated that. Then I was taken to another part of the building, downstairs, where they handcuffed and shackled me and everything. There's a chain they put around your waist and it's got two cuffs that come off it and go on your wrists. Then I was taken out to a police car at the side entrance. It was a sheriff's car, I think, tan or gold, I believe a Plymouth, and there was a blue police cruiser in front of us with the lights going. I was in the back seat between two big guys in plainclothes. The guy in front drove like a maniac. We zoomed out of there and made a fast right turn. I could see the crowd outside the courthouse and some of my friends. Paul Beligni was there, giving me a thumbs-up sign, and all I could do was raise my hands just up to the window to give my own sign. We took the back way over to Route 8, heading for Somers, and they seemed to be making sure that nobody would follow us. The police cruiser went along for about three miles and then we kept going on our own."

Peter was later asked what going to prison was like. "Well, at the time I wasn't so happy about it, but I have to admit it was interesting. Really. I'm glad I know it today. Because I think I would have lived my entire life without knowing what people go through when they go to prison, not understanding them. It was definitely a learning experience, like everything else in this case.

"I remember it was very flat up there in the Enfield area. It's tobacco-producing country and they still have those long red barns. We went by the prison farm and then I saw the fence and what I figured were machine-gun towers. I didn't know whether it would be like the prisons you see on TV or those stalags in Germany, but I could see the buildings behind the fence with the barbed wire on top and it looked fairly new. I remember hobbling out of the car with those chains on. They were hurting my legs. The sheriffs took me into the place where they book you. They asked who I was. I couldn't remember what my number had been in the Litchfield jail. Then there was this whole routine about my clothes and getting the stuff I needed in the prison. They asked me whether I wanted my clothes destroyed or sent home. 'Send them home,' I said. They took my belt, the wallet and money. It was all listed on a form. I got a receipt. I had to take a shower and they gave me some kind of disinfectant. I had already washed my hair that morning. I thought: twice in one day! I got into my prison uniform and I was taken to a cell block, a row of cells. They put me into a cell and closed the door on me. I was behind bars!

"There was a window, bed, sink, open-bowl toilet. I could see the other prisoners in their cells. I asked if anybody had a cigarette. They said the doors would be opened pretty soon and they'd bring over a pack. Someone asked me what happened, so I said I had just been sentenced in the Litchfield court. And this one guy says, 'Oh, yeah, we saw that on television.' Maybe he meant that he had heard about the case on television. I started to read the booklet they gave me on prison regulations.

"I think I was in the cell about twenty minutes when somebody came by and said, 'Reilly, your door's open. Come on out front.' He was some officer whose job was to make sure I was okay, not holding grudges. He wanted to get my side of the story. I told him I had been accused and convicted of something I didn't do, so how can I be okay? We talked for a while and then I went back to the cell. I was just starting to throw some blankets on the bed and make it when they called me and said, 'Reilly, grab all your stuff and come down front.' I walked down there and found out that someone was coming to get me. The money had been raised. I was going home.

"I had to take off the uniform and put my clothes back on again, everything except the underwear. I asked the prisoner who had measured me for the uniform if I could keep the underwear—they've got numbers on them. I figured they could make a good conversation piece, though I suppose it depends on who I'm with. 'Go ahead,' he said. I also kept the toilet kit, another souvenir of Somers.

"The guard walked me out of there and I saw Mom and Dad—the Madows—and Joe O'Brien of the *Courant*. The captain of the guard said to them, 'I'm glad you came to get him out of here because a kid like that would have been lost in this place. He would have disappeared in there.' " Mickey and Marion told him about the raising of the $10,000. Despite the size of the gathering outside of the courthouse just after sentencing, there had been a strange quiet, but something had to be done about the bond and fast. An impromptu meeting of the leading Reilly Committee figures was held on the Litchfield Green and six persons quickly pledged enough money to make the $10,000. They scattered to banks in Canaan, Winsted, Torrington and Great Barrington to pick up checks that ranged from $1,000 to $3,000.

Father Paul kept count as the checks began arriving. He scribbled on a piece of paper resting on his Bible. In less than two hours, $7,000 had been raised. At 1:48 P.M., Murray Madow arrived on the Green with the remaining $3,000. Peter's lawyers filed his appeal and Mickey and Marion, on behalf of the Committee, presented the court with a $60,000 certified check for the bond. Then they rushed to the penitentiary.

Peter returned home that night at seven. He received an emotional greeting from Nan and the cheers of friends who had dropped by to hear about his brief brush with prison life. It was part wake; part celebration. The sentence was six to sixteen, but at least Peter would be living at home during the appeal struggle.

18 ▪ TAKING THE OFFENSE

LIEUT. SHAY: We know—Pete, I'm going to tell you right now. We know by time now, that when your mother became deceased—when she died—

PETER REILLY: Ya.

LIEUT. SHAY:—you were in the house. We know that. We can prove that.

PETER REILLY: Oh, yes.

LIEUT. SHAY: Okay. So, *this* is academic, I know. What I want you to do, Pete, I want you to understand that, you know, this is the best for you. There's no question about this. I want you now to sit back there and recite for me in a chronology of what happened now. I know this may be painful to you—

PETER REILLY: It is.

Jim Conway grew up in a tough Manhattan neighborhood. He saw combat during World War II as a navy gunner's mate. He won citations for bravery as a New York policeman in the violent 41st Precinct of The Bronx. In 1956 he took his family to Connecticut "because New York was becoming a disaster area." He worked as a bail bondsman and as an investigator before becoming a private detective. In the autumn of 1974, operating out of his home in the small town of Rockville, near Hartford, Conway had several jobs to do, but his thoughts kept turning to someone he had never met: Peter Reilly.

One year after the death of Barbara Gibbons, Jim Conway knew nothing about the case except for the facts he had seen in the newspapers and the speculation he had heard during conversations with attorneys. But the Gibbons murder preyed on his mind. He had a "gut feeling" that something was wrong with the prosecution of Peter Reilly. He was troubled by the evidence that the State had produced against him. Conway respected some of the State Police officers, but was often at odds with them on his assignments. He had seen "too many screwed-up investigations." He had written to Catherine Roraback urging her to engage a private detective, not necessarily himself, on Peter's behalf, but "I never heard from her." He had tried to forget about the Reilly case, but it kept nagging at him.

"I'll tell you what bugged me about it," he says. "That was a vicious, vicious murder. Reilly confessed. He was found guilty. Now what happened to this convicted killer? These people go up to the judge and they say they want to take him home with them. They want to look after him. When I read that, I thought they were stupid. How misguided can you get? But the more I thought about it, the more I realized what an extraordinary thing that was."

Conway thought that there might be something to Peter's claim of innocence if he was able to inspire such a degree of support. He admired the way the Canaan people were showing the courage of their convictions. An outspoken man with a colorful vocabulary and a strict moral code, he spoke well of anyone who had the "balls" to stand up and be counted on a public issue. He condemned "the eunuchs" who would not speak their minds or fight for their beliefs.

Conway followed the Reilly case in the newspapers through the summer of 1974. The most notable development was the intervention of Arthur Miller. The playwright and other celebrities had become involved in the raising of funds for Peter's appeal. Conway read that T. F. Gilroy Daly, an attorney in Fairfield, had succeeded Catherine Roraback as Peter's lawyer. Nothing was said, however, about engaging a private investigator to find out what had really happened in the Gibbons murder.

"I was down in Fairfield one day," Conway says, "and I decided to locate Daly and find out what the hell was going on with the Reilly case. I called him up and invited myself over. I told him I was a strong adherent of the idea that cases are won before you go into court. Get yourself someone who's going to come up with the answers. I'd like to know, I told him, and so would a lot of other people, whether or not this kid did this thing. I said: I'm not asking you to hire me, but get someone who can find out because this thing is dreadful."

Daly checked into Conway's history and was impressed. He asked him to take on the case, but warned him that little money was available. Money was being raised, however, by prominent people.

"I said to Roy," Conway relates, "that I'm not going to blackjack you. I wanted to take this on because I was curious. I wanted to know. I really did want to find out what the hell was going on."

Conway told Daly that he was going to start off by trying to prove that Peter Reilly was guilty. "I told him that as soon as I was sure of the kid's guilt I was off the case. I never defend anyone who's guilty. Lawyers say they have to, but I don't have to."

Conway looked into the Reilly case and the more he found out, the angrier he became. "The thing that really racked me up was the State Police saying they had a fingerprint that was identifiable but could not be identified. That's a contradiction in terms." He soon was confident of Peter's innocence and was willing to say it publicly. As the months went by, Conway, by talking to reporters about new disclosures in Peter's favor and condemning the evidence the State had presented in the trial, took a front-line position in the Reilly case that would ultimately cause him much grief.

Though his investigation turned the Reilly case around, so that Peter became the accuser, and the prosecutor the defendant, Conway received no fee for his services and only a portion of his expenses. And there was far less recognition of his work in the press than he deserved. At the end, he was almost the forgotten man.

The average case, Conway says, "takes about a month to knock off." The Reilly case consumed the better part of two years of his time, including seventeen months of intensive effort. Conway, who has a low boiling point, was often put off by Roy Daly's cooler style: "He believes in the Bobby Kennedy rule: Don't get mad, get even." He was miffed by what he took to be Peter's indifference and ingratitude. And he was angry with himself for investing so much of his time and energy in the case while turning aside other work that would have paid his bills. But he simply could not stifle the impulse to correct a miscarriage of justice.

"I'm a very independent S.O.B.," he says. "I operate on my own. I go my own way. I'm not a big shot. I'm not a wise guy or anything. I work hard and I think I know where it's at. I know what's happening. I'm not in this thing because of Peter Reilly. He's not important. But that this sort of thing could happen to any kid in the State of Connecticut! I don't buy that! I have five kids. I said to myself: They can't get away with this!"

Jim Conway's involvement in the Reilly case meant that Peter's future would be determined by the actions of three remarkable dissimilar individuals who came to his defense after he was convicted and sentenced.

Arthur Miller, T. F. Gilroy Daly and James G. Conway had never met one another. Except for the Reilly case, they might never have met, but Miller, once involved, discovered Daly, and Daly hired Conway. Each played a special role in seeking Peter Reilly's vindication: Conway found new evidence and fresh witnesses; Daly assembled the information and presented it in the courtroom; and Miller, the catalyst, used his influence to secure press coverage and public support.

They were three strong personalities who came to the rescue of a youth whose outstanding trait was his lack of personality.

Arthur Miller was particularly fascinated by Peter's chameleonlike character and his apparent lack of a strong sense of self-worth and self-identity. During one of many strategy meetings with Roy Daly and others who were helping with Peter's defense, Miller noticed someone else in the room. "My immediate reaction was, 'What the hell is this person doing here?' And then I realized it was Peter Reilly and that we were all here because of him."

When Jim Conway grumbled that Peter had failed to say thanks for things done for him, Miller pointed out that "Peter Reilly can't say 'I thank you' because there is no 'I' to say 'I thank you.'"

The celebrated trial lawyer Louis Nizer once said of Lord Louis Mountbatten that "He belonged to that small coterie of men whom nature had endowed with appearance suitable to their calling." That statement might as accurately have been said about the three men most responsible for establishing Peter Reilly's innocence.

Arthur Miller spent less time on the case than the others, but at strategic moments his presence was vital. The pipe-smoking playwright was the picture of the concerned intellectual who emerges from his country retreat to insist, as in *Death of a Salesman*, that "attention must be paid."

Roy Daly, a handsome, imposing man of 6 feet 6½ inches, who was used to action in the courtroom, was perfect for the role of crusading attorney. Though his detractors would later say that the politically ambitious lawyer was only seeking statewide prominence, Daly, a onetime prosecutor of organized crime, thought of himself in the Reilly case as "an advocate of the system that had gone off the track. I wanted to get it back on the track."

As for Jim Conway, he looks and talks like a hard-boiled streetwise ex-cop. After a lifetime of reading, however, he is erudite and philosophic, in the Eric Hoffer manner. A stocky man with an open Irish face and dark bushy eyebrows, he often wears a dirty white trench coat and rain hat as he appears unannounced on doorsteps to ask questions. "That way, people don't have time to rehearse their answers," he explains. His seemingly disorganized private-eye style and his exasperated way of speaking suggest a cross between television's Colombo and Archie Bunker. He pretends to be less sharp than he is. "Is that so?" Conway will say in an interview, making no notes but taking everything in. "Is that right? Gee, thanks a lot for the information."

The three men took charge of Peter Reilly's defense at a bleak time. He had been convicted by a jury; in all likelihood he would go to prison no matter what appeal arguments were made; and concern about his fate was pretty much limited to the Litchfield Hills. The Reilly trial had been well covered by a few Connecticut newspapers and had received periodic television coverage, but there was little statewide or national interest. The plight of another nineteen-year-old, Patricia Hearst, was receiving far more notice. She had been kidnapped on February 4, 1974, while Peter was still in the Litchfield jail. The FBI issued a warrant for her arrest a few days before Peter was sentenced. The struggle to free Peter Reilly would coincide with the efforts to find Patty Hearst.

In Canaan, Peter's supporters could only briefly enjoy their success in keeping him from spending even a single night in the penitentiary—at least for the moment. But they were at a loss about what to do next. They felt that the conviction should be appealed, but they wondered about Catherine Roraback's willingness to continue with the case. They questioned whether they should try to get another lawyer.

While there was universal appreciation of her willingness to take up Peter's cause in the first place, at no reward, members of the Reilly Committee were mystified by the loss in the courtroom and some were highly critical of Roraback's performance. She said little, but she clearly felt her critics had little understanding of the obstacles she had encountered and the problems of working with insufficient funds. On at least two occasions she indicated regret about not having given the jury a more tightly constructed account of the murder-night time sequence to show that Peter could not have done all the things that the prosecution said he had done. Mickey and Marion Madow remember Roraback saying, "I could kick myself," during a discussion at their home.

The attorney told the Committee that she was willing to continue working for Peter's vindication, but, since funds were so short, she suggested that the appeal be turned over to a public defender to whom she could give assistance. That way, the State would bear the cost of the trial transcript and pick up other expenses. Peter's supporters were wary about relying on a public defender and doubted that the case would get the skilled efforts that it deserved. They wanted a first-class criminal lawyer even though they had no money to pay him.

Arthur Miller made it his responsibility. Miller lived in Roxbury, a town at the southern end of Litchfield County, an hour's drive from Canaan. Joan Barthel had written to him and to a number of other celebrities who lived in Connecticut in hopes of provoking their interest in the Reilly case. When she went to see Miller he could tell that she was looking for more than financial help. "She had come into this as a sympathetic journalist," Miller says, "and now the group up there in Canaan seemed to be leaning on her to get things done. It was a difficult situation for her. I never fancied myself getting into a thing like that, but I did help get some people together at Styron's house."

William Styron, best known for *The Confessions of Nat Turner*, lived in Roxbury with his wife, Rose, who is also a writer. The gathering at their house included Mike Nichols, Lewis Allen, Renata Adler and others prominent in the film and literary worlds. The meeting resulted in immediate contributions and promises to contact friends. The Reilly Committee eventually received checks from a number of celebrities, including Jack Nicholson, Dustin Hoffman, Art Garfunkel and Candice Bergen. Elizabeth Taylor, in a personal note sent with her contribution, told Peter, "Hang in there, baby!"

Once engaged, Arthur Miller remained for the duration. A man who had some personal experience with false accusation during the McCarthy era, Miller was bound to be intrigued by a case that had, at its core, a confession that looked like the product of psychological coercion. He was disturbed by the apparent misuse of the polygraph during the police interrogation. "The purpose of a lie detector," he says, "is to tell whether someone is telling a lie and not to so manipulate the test that he's making a confession. A confession is supposed to be a remembered series of events, voluntarily given."

Miller went to Canaan to talk to residents and find out more about the situation. While sitting in on a Committee meeting in July he suggested that the group obtain tax-deductible status so that larger donations could be attracted. On that hot evening, the Reilly supporters were seated on folding chairs on the parish-house lawn. They paused when John Bianchi came strolling down Main Street, whistling to himself and seeming not to notice the gathering as he passed by on the way to his house.

The more Miller looked into the facts of the case, the more he became convinced that there had been no "explosion" by Peter Reilly, to use Bianchi's term. He would tell the *New York Times*:

> Do you realize what's involved in this? Peter, in the flow of blind rage, had to butcher his mother. He had to do it without getting blood on his hands. In a blind rage he

would have had to undress himself, kill her, get dressed, and then look up the numbers for the phone calls. . . .

I can't believe it was a premeditated act, either, because Peter's subsequent actions would have been different. When the cops, the ambulance and everyone else got there, Peter was shivering in shock. He was shaking.

Now that's an awfully quick transformation for someone who committed a premeditated murder. Did he go into a trance and commit the murder? No. He's shaking. He's just found his mother butchered.

The confession? There's Peter and authority—the absent father—and Peter saying, "I'm on your side," and the cops saying, "These are our terms. This is what you must say," and so Peter confesses.

Once Peter begins to relieve himself of his guilt and feels "free" of its oppressiveness, testifying to having cut Barbara with a razor, it is remarkable that no flow—even now—of hateful, resentful emotion takes place. In short, having now characterized himself as her murderer, it does not occur to him to justify the act or to explain it by the evocation of her persecution of him.

Instead, he maintains precisely the same attitude toward her as he had had before he confessed. No cathexis is reached, no discharge of a new order of feeling toward the hated mother he killed.

This is not believable. It is inconsistent with the confessional act, and it is simply the boy acceding to what powerful, respected and helpful (however threatening) policemen insist he say. They split him from himself and he joined them in blaming the mythical "Peter," not blaming the real Peter, the one they would not give some psychiatric care to. Instead, they dropped him, as he says, like a hot potato, charged him and locked him up.

Committed to Peter's cause, Miller looked for an experienced attorney who would take the case at a minimal fee. The task was more difficult than he had imagined. One lawyer who took a serious interest interviewed Peter and then asked for a fee of $100,000, with $25,000 down.

"I was getting nowhere," Miller relates, "so I called my

law firm in New York and told them that I was getting upset about this because it seemed to me that there had to be some kind of responsibility somewhere in this kind of thing. They went to work on it and finally told me that Roy Daly in Fairfield would be somebody who would respond to this. I contacted Daly. We had lunch. I explained the whole case to him and said there would be no money, but maybe, some way or other, it could be raised. But he didn't say much about a fee. He was interested in the case and finally agreed to take it on. He threw himself into it and spent an awful lot of time on it. Why did he do it? Whatever his reasons, I wouldn't for a moment underestimate his idealism."

T. F. (Thomas Francis) Gilroy Daly took charge in the late summer of 1974. He would be described two years later by the *New York Sunday News* as "The man who stopped the world spinning out of control for Reilly. . . . He restored order by dissecting the trial's many complexities; he attacked indiscretions of the State Police which led to the uncovering of indifferences by the prosecution which had ended with injustices in the courtroom."

Daly would say himself one day that "This was probably the most satisfying case of my career because Peter Reilly was going down the tubes. The State fought me every step of the way. They fought with every motion I presented, every piece of evidence I found. It was the greatest stonewalling operation I've ever seen."

The more Daly succeeded, the more the State Police were embarrassed and the more the State's Attorney system in Connecticut was revealed as ripe for reform. And yet, although he caused trouble for the State, the State was quite willing to make use of his talents. A few months after taking on Peter as a client, Daly was appointed Deputy State Treasurer by Connecticut's new governor, Ella Grasso. A year and a half later, while still representing Peter and still fighting the State in the courts, he was named Insurance Commissioner for Connecticut. In March 1977, Senator Abraham Ribicoff formally recommended to President Jimmy Carter that T. F. Gilroy Daly be appointed a federal judge.

Daly has a political heritage. His father was active in Connecticut politics and he is named after his great-grandfather, Thomas F. Gilroy, a Democratic mayor of New York in the 1890s who helped crush Tammany Hall. The family has a strong military accent too: his father was a hero of two world wars; his brother won the Congressional Medal of Honor; and Daly himself was decorated for his role in Korea as a reconnaissance officer with the Army Infantry Rangers.

During his last year at Yale Law School, Daly was recruited by Cyrus Vance for his New York law firm. During the Kennedy administration he served as an assistant United States attorney in New York, investigating and prosecuting organized crime and racketeering. He was commended by Attorney General Robert Kennedy for heading the prosecution in the conviction of eleven members of a $100-million international narcotics smuggling ring. He was a member of the Justice Department team that persuaded Joseph Valachi to testify against the Cosa Nostra. Later, he successfully blocked Valachi's attempt, in the U.S. Court of Appeals, to overturn a narcotics conspiracy conviction.

Leaving the Justice Department after President Kennedy's assassination, Daly returned to private practice. He served as deputy state attorney general and made an unsuccessful bid for a seat in Congress, on the Democratic ticket, in mostly Republican Fairfield County.

Roy Daly had taken no special interest in the Reilly case until he was approached by Arthur Miller. He had no opinion about Peter's guilt or innocence, but he did have an early sense that a miscarriage of justice might have occurred. At his first day-long interview with Peter, he says. "I was impressed with what appeared to be Peter's sincerity. I'm always chary of a defendant, though. I've been at the game too long."

He was willing to carry Peter's appeal through the courts, but soon concluded that the prospects were poor. "The judge didn't commit any grievous errors and the verdict wasn't outrageous considering the evidence. The jury, given what it heard, took a very likely course and not an unreasonable one." He did see as a possibility, at least in the federal courts, an appeal argument that rested on one of Catherine Roraback's major objections: the systematic exclusion of persons under twenty-one on both the grand jury and the trial jury. "That's a good point," Daly felt, "but you have to show more than that they were excluded under the rules. You've got to show that the exclusion worked to the detriment of the defendant, and that's pretty hard to find."

Daly considered another approach: a petition for a new trial on the basis of newly discovered evidence. That was an even dimmer prospect. Such new trials are rare in Connecticut because the restrictions are severe. For an attorney to produce evidence favorable to the defendant that had not been presented to the jury in the trial is not sufficient grounds. The evidence has to be so new that it could not have been found earlier by the defense by "due diligence." And it has to be so strong that the jury in a new trial would most likely reach a different verdict.

Daly had no way of knowing whether there was any evidence of this quality to be discovered. He would need a skilled private detective to find out. Jim Conway's visit to his office could not have been better timed.

Daly, the well-born master of the beagles at the Fairfield County Hunt Club, and Conway, the self-educated private eye, had little in common except their concern for the even-handed "administration of justice," a term Daly uses frequently. "I was born in Manhattan," Conway says, "about six blocks from Arthur Miller; Lexington Avenue and 106th Street, to be exact. My father was a bus driver for the Fifth Avenue Coach Company, driving the big double deckers, after working for years on the docks with his brother. My mother was a cook in the homes of wealthy people. She was an uneducated woman, but she had more character than most of these people trooping out of college with their sheepskins. She raised six kids the hard way and they all turned out very, very straight."

Within days of beginning work on the Reilly case, Conway was warned to keep out of it. The telephone rang while he was chatting with one of Connecticut's county detectives in the man's office. The detective answered and said to Conway, "It's for you." Surprised that anyone knew where he was,

Conway took the phone and heard the caller identify himself as Detective David Winslow of Troop C at Stafford Springs in the northeastern corner of the state, far from Litchfield County. Conway and Winslow were acquainted. Years later, Winslow would state under oath to a grand jury investigating the Reilly case that he had simply called Conway to inquire about his activities in Litchfield County and not to threaten him. At first he said he could not recall who had asked him to make inquiries but when called again to testify he said it was Trooper Calkins at the Canaan Barracks.

As Conway remembers the dialogue, however, Winslow asked, "Are you the Conway who's been over in the Canaan area, nosing around?"

"What do you mean," Conway said, "nosing around?"

"Well, look, I'm telling you, for your own good: stay out of there and mind your own business."

"Wait a minute! What are you talking about? Are you telling me I can't investigate a case in this state?"

"Look, I'm just telling you to mind your own business. Stay out of there."

"Wait a minute! Who's this coming from?"

"It's coming from where it should come from. Stay out. And wise up."

Immediately after the call, Conway discussed it with the detective and then with the local State's Attorney when he stepped into the office. "They can't do that to you," the State's Attorney told him. "You're a licensed investigator. You can talk to anybody. You can talk to State's witnesses."

Conway decided to call John Bianchi and report the incident. He had never met Bianchi, but he was accustomed to dealing on a cordial basis with prosecutors. "I was astonished by his response," Conway says. "When I told him about the warning, he asked me, 'Where's Troop C?' I said the location of Troop C wasn't the issue. I wanted to know where this order for me to butt out had come from. 'Where's Troop C?' he said. 'They're not involved in this case.' Well, he never did give me a straight answer to my question. He waltzed me up and down the aisle, playing his violin. I finally told him, 'I'm going to continue the investigation unless you want to put it in writing.' That was the beginning of all the things that were done to hinder us in this case."

Normally, Conway states, he is able to sit down with a prosecutor, look over the evidence and discuss a case professionally. "But this one was different. It was open warfare. We couldn't get the time of day. I never did talk to Bianchi face to face—not once in two years. When we finally got in the courtroom and he had to refer to me, he'd call me 'Conrad' or some other name. Arthur Miller told me that he didn't want to acknowledge my existence."

The biggest surprise for Conway as he dug into the case was the paucity of information at hand about the Gibbons murder. "The first thing I found out was that we had nothing. Absolutely nothing. Zero. All we had was what the police wanted the people to know." A number of witness statements and other police material had been passed on by Catherine Roraback but, as Roy Daly says, "we had a gut feeling that there was a lot more in Bianchi's files that should have been turned over to the defense." Their suspicions would eventually be justified. It was also true that they were further handicapped by Roraback's failure to turn over all of the Reilly case files that she possessed. They were not seen until 1976.

Conway did have a break, however, in the investigative work done after Peter's conviction by Roger Cohn and Joe O'Brien. Both reporters disclosed information that led Daly and Conway to believe that robbery had been associated with the Gibbons murder. O'Brien revealed that the wallet that had been stolen from Barbara Gibbons two weeks before her murder had been found by Elizabeth Mansfield within sight of the cottage six weeks after the killing. She had reported the finding to both Catherine Roraback and the State Police, and then expected that it would be brought out during the trial. When it was not, Mrs. Mansfield contacted O'Brien and he made the public disclosure.

An article by Cohn supported Peter's testimony that his mother had purchased a new wallet on the day of her death. That wallet had never been found. Cohn quoted Robert Drucker, the owner of Bob's Clothing Store, on the details of Gibbons' purchase. Drucker had given the police a signed statement before the trial, but it was never seen by the defense. No one had asked Drucker to testify.

Cohn's reporting was helpful in showing how the time sequence could be tightened up. He had contacted CBS and learned that the *Kelly's Heroes* scene, viewed by Marion Madow at the time of Peter's emergency call, was broadcast at 9:50. And he disclosed that Rev. Paul Halovatch had noticed 9:50 as the time on the clock in Johnny's Restaurant in Canaan some ten minutes after seeing Peter drive away from the church. Because his account, placing Peter at the church at about 9:40, challenged Barbara Fenn's story that Peter had reported his mother's condition to her at that time, Father Paul had expected to take the stand in the trial. But he was excused to attend his grandmother's funeral on the day he was scheduled to testify and then was not asked to come to the court another day.

Daly and Conway felt that the failure to attack Fenn's 9:40 testimony, in light of the police logging of her emergency call at 9:58, was one of three major defense lapses in the trial. The others were the absence of medical testimony to challenge Dr. Izumi's conclusions, and psychiatric testimony to question the validity of the confession. Conway went to Sharon Hospital and discovered that the emergency-room logs on ambulance activity contradicted Fenn's testimony.

"They tended to corroborate the police logs," Daly says, "as well as Joanne Mulhern's account of her call to the hospital after 9:50. So, we had one end of the time sequence pinned down. The police were called at 9:58; Trooper McCafferty arrived at the cottage at 10:02. Now we needed to determine when Peter made his first call instead of relying on when he said he did. It is elemental in preparation for a trial that you are always looking for evidence that is independent of what the defendant has to say.

"I called the assistant counsel at CBS and he came back with the answer that he had given Roger Cohn. We had 9:50 as the time Peter called the Madows for the ambulance. And we knew from the statements of both Jessica Bornemann and Barbara Fenn that Peter had said in his calls to them that he had already telephoned for the ambulance. Now the sequence began to make sense. We knew about when Peter had left the

church and where he had gone. We learned that the police
had timed that drive in his car at five and a half minutes from
the center of Canaan to the cottage, obviously going at high
speed. It was at that point when I had a session with Conway,
Miller, Peter and the Madows. I said that the appeal route in
my opinion was of no use to us. We would file it when we
had all the transcripts and we'd preserve it, but I was not very
sanguine about it. I proposed that we go the new trial route
even though it was extremely difficult. I thought it was worth
the gamble."

Much of Jim Conway's early work on the case was directed
toward firming up the time sequence. He discovered a number of persons who, though they had not testified, had information crucial to the time sequence. Elizabeth Swart, for
example, was the Sharon Hospital switchboard operator who
had taken Peter's call and passed it on to Barbara Fenn. She
was prepared to testify that the call had been received closer
to ten o'clock and that she had logged Fenn's report to the
police at about ten o'clock.

Jessica Bornemann, who had accepted the call that Peter
had made to her father-in-law, Dr. Carl Bornemann, remembered that she had been on the telephone with Peter for two
to three minutes because she sought to give him information
about other places he might call. That reduced the amount
of time Peter had to carry out the many activities claimed
by the State.

One valuable informant was John Sochocki's aunt, Mrs.
Judith MacNeil. Although he had testified in the trial, as a
sixteen-year-old friend of the defendant, she, a disinterested
adult, had not been contacted by Peter's attorney. She had a
vivid memory of her nephew arriving home in Peter's car
because he was unusually early. Normally he came back from
a Youth Center meeting at 11:00. She looked at the clock and
saw that it was only 9:45. She recalls that when she told this
to the police they seemed dissatisfied. She insisted on 9:45
as the time and said she was confident of her clock's accuracy because she checked it regularly with the firehouse noon
siren. (In fact, her clock almost surely was a few minutes

fast.) Even though Mrs. MacNeil was questioned on at least two occasions by the State Police, they did not take a statement from her, at a time when they were collecting dozens of signed statements from other persons.

The private detective's inquiries were greatly hampered by the fact that so many of those statements, containing information helpful to Peter, had not been turned over to the defense before the trial and were not being disclosed now. "Bianchi had given twelve statements to Roraback," Conway says, "but about people who had no role in this case. He wouldn't give us, to take one example, Dr. Lovallo's statement. Which was crucial because Barbara telephoned him between 9:20 and 9:40 the night she died. But we didn't know that! Can you believe it? They had this vital information from the last person Barbara talked to, almost surely, before the murderer turned up, but Bianchi never gave it to Roraback and he wouldn't give it to us. Lovallo didn't testify at the trial, so we didn't know what the story was. When I went to see him I cooled my heels in his office for a few hours and then he wouldn't talk to me. There were a lot of people who wouldn't talk to me. Fenn wouldn't talk. I ran into such an unbelievable wall.

"You can't imagine how frustrating it was and how much time I wasted because we couldn't get the stuff we were entitled to. For a long time we were trying to figure out how Gibbons got so wet: whether she had been running around the wet fields or whether somebody hit her with a car, smashed her legs and then brought her in the house to finish the job. But we were way out in left field. All this time Bianchi had Lovallo's statement which would put her in the house, on the telephone, before the murderer arrived."

Conway spent days tramping the roads, trails and fields in the area of the murder cottage, looking for clues and seeking to determine the route that the murderer had taken after fleeing out the side door, as he believed. While roaming about Falls Village, Conway became more and more interested in the character and behavior of a few young men, including Michael and Timothy Parmalee, and Wayne Collier, a youth who had been especially friendly with Barbara Gibbons. Each had been interviewed by the State Police and Tim had been given polygraph tests. The police seemed satisfied with their accounts of their murder-night whereabouts. Collier said he had been drinking beer with Tim Parmalee and Tim's relatives at their homes until 9:30, when his mother came in her car to take him home. ("I ate and went to bed and did not go out again.") Tim Parmalee said he had gone to sleep in his bedroom at about 9:30 and had not awakened until some time after one o'clock when Trooper Mulhern arrived at the house to ask questions. Mike Parmalee, Tim's older brother, also told the police that he went to bed at 9:30 but in a different place. He was living at the time in a trailer on a dairy farm on Undermountain Road, within walking distance of his family's house and the Gibbons cottage. He and a friend, Sandra Ashner, and her little boy were sharing the trailer with another couple. Ashner backed up Parmalee's story. She told the police that Mike had spent the night with her.

Conway took a special interest in the Parmalees because their names came up so often in neighborhood gossip. He learned, for one thing, that Tim Parmalee had been arrested shortly after the Gibbons murder for stealing a wallet from a neighbor, Howard Silvernale. The matter was dropped when Silvernale did not press charges.

As for Mike Parmalee, Conway found that Barbara Gibbons made a practice of taunting him and calling him a "fag" and a "queer" because he had attempted to involve Peter in a scheme to win a discharge from the Army as a homosexual. He had asked Peter to lie for him if army investigators ever checked his story.

It is noteworthy that the State Police were aware of the tension between Barbara Gibbons and Michael Parmalee within hours of the murder. It was mentioned to Trooper Mulhern by one of Peter's friends, Robert Belcher. And in a statement signed by Jean Beligni, she said, "I also knew from my own experience that a boy named Michael Parmalee had named Peter and my son Paul, and a boy from Massachusetts, as being homosexual. Parmalee used this to get out of military service. As a result of this, I know that Barbara was furious over this incident and that she used to really give the 'business' to Parmalee after this matter was investigated by the Army and found to be a lie."

320   DONALD S. CONNERY

Even though there was no evidence to show that Mike Parmalee had reacted to the epithets flung at him by Barbara Gibbons, the information was potentially useful to Daly if he sought to show, in the new-trial hearing, that persons other than Peter had a motive for doing her harm. Interest in Mike Parmalee deepened in April 1975 when Sandra Ashner, who had moved away from Falls Village and was no longer intimate with Parmalee, told a nurse that she had given false information to the police. She now said that he had not, in fact, spent the murder night with her. Jim Conway, on the heels of County Detective Sam Holden, talked to her and won her agreement to sign a statement—which she would not do for the police—and to testify at the new-trial proceedings.

Conway says that his Falls Village sleuthing "got a little hairy sometimes" because he investigated a number of local youths who were known for their drinking bouts and acts of violence. "I was caught out in a field one day by the guy who was my prime suspect at the time. He had a loaded .357 magnum. He fired a couple of shots at a can on a tree—trying to impress me, I guess. At one point he held the gun out to me and I figured if I ever reached for it, I'm dead. It might go off and he could claim it was an accident. I said I'd go up to the car and get my .38 and show you how to shoot. I didn't have any .38. Up to then, I never carried a gun. But it stopped him long enough to think about it. And I made tracks out of there. Later on, when I saw him in a garage, he said, 'Get out, you son of a bitch. I'll kill you.' There were a couple of other times when he threatened to get me. He's the reason, along with a mob situation I was investigating in Providence, that I finally bought myself a gun: a stub-nosed .38. I never had to use it."

While Conway, as he says, was "pounding around all that area on foot," Daly handled strategy, brought in expert assistance and prepared the motions and other legal papers. He held regular "think-tank" sessions on the Reilly case in his Fairfield office Saturday mornings and many evenings. Along with his young associate, Robert Hartwell, Daly had the invaluable (and free) counsel of two attorney friends, John Fiore and Alan Neigher. Conway would appear at the meetings with his latest findings and Arthur Miller sometimes attended. The detective frequently called on Miller at his Roxbury home to discuss the case.

"One of the things we could never figure out," Conway says, "was how Barbara's thighbones were broken. They're probably the two strongest bones in the human body. The idea that little Peter Reilly, wearing sneakers, broke them by jumping on his mother—well, it's unbelievable. We had various theories like the one about the car, but I don't think we'll ever resolve it unless we find out who did it."

The notion that Barbara Gibbons had been run over by an automobile before her throat was slashed had been seriously considered by the police. In the police scenario, however, it was Peter who rammed into his mother. His Corvette was meticulously examined. A detective, James E. McDonald, was prepared to testify that in his expert opinion Peter had run over his mother. He believed that rubber cleats on the Corvette's tires matched certain impressions he saw on the victim's body. He also concluded that an impression on the car's muffler matched her blue jeans.

Bianchi had not asked McDonald to testify, however, because his version of how Peter had assaulted his mother contradicted Dr. Izumi's testimony. Izumi, who had not observed any marks resembling tire treads on the body, had determined that the leg bones were broken after she had died of the throat wound. To make McDonald's conclusions fit with Izumi's, Bianchi would have had to claim that Peter slashed his mother's throat indoors, carried her bloody body outdoors, ran her over with the car, and then hauled her inside again to inflict the after-death wounds.

Daly asked for copies of the police photographs of the victim so that he could submit them to medical experts. He was refused. He was told that he would have to bring his experts to the Litchfield courthouse if they wanted to see the evidence.

According to Daly, "Two orthopedic surgeons and I, along with Conway and Hartwell, went up to Litchfield to look at the material in the jury waiting room. We went over all the slides, pictures, sketches and so on. They had already read the testimony. And they gave us different opinions about the killing." The doctors said that it was physically impossible for one person to break the thighbones by jumping on them if the victim was flat on the floor. And they thought it impossible for the assailant to have escaped being covered with blood when he slashed the throat and cut the trachea. Daly was sure now that he was going to have to find a forensic pathologist to give an opinion and testify.

Daly had already spoken to the State Medical Examiner, Dr. Elliot Gross, who had assigned Dr. Izumi to do the Gibbons autopsy. Gross recommended several experts including Dr. Milton Helpern. At age 72, Helpern was easily the most experienced and celebrated forensic pathologist in the world and the co-author of a 1,350-page book, *Legal Medicine, Pathology and Toxicology*, recognized as the definitive work on that subject. A self-styled "Sherlock Holmes with a microscope," he claimed to have personally conducted some 20,000 autopsies and supervised 60,000 more in his four decades in the Medical Examiner's Office of the City of New York.

"He knows more about violent and mysterious death than anyone else in the country," the *New York Times* had said. Helpern himself had once declared that "There are no perfect crimes. There are only untrained and blundering investigators [and] slipshod medical examiners." It occurred to Roy Daly that the eminent Dr. Helpern, who retired as New York's Chief Medical Examiner three months after the Gibbons murder, might respond to a plea from the eminent Arthur Miller to help out in the Reilly case.

Helpern did respond. And when he studied the evidence in February 1975, he came to the conclusion that, given the time available for the crime and the absence of blood on his person or clothing, Peter Reilly "would appear to be the least likely suspect." He also speculated that two persons might have participated in the murder. The spiral break of the right femur could have been caused by one person holding down the victim and another twisting the leg violently. In the police photographs, Barbara Gibbons' right foot appeared to have been wrenched out of place.

Enlisting Helpern as an expert witness for the defense was an important breakthrough. Daly was encouraged enough to submit to Litchfield's Superior Court, in the first week of

April, legal papers calling for a new trial. The papers had the effect of turning Peter into a plaintiff and John Bianchi into a defendant. Peter had just celebrated his twentieth birthday.

Nine more months were to pass, however, before a hearing was held in Superior Court to see whether a new trial was warranted, and it would be a full year before the answer was known, but this challenge by Peter's attorney had an important psychological impact on all of those who were caught up in the case. The State's Attorney and the State Police had thought they had put the Reilly case behind them. Now it was becoming a cause célèbre that received ever greater public and press attention. The headlines were indicative:

**SECOND REILLY TRIAL ASKED:
NEW EVIDENCE CLAIMED**

**REILLY LAWYERS SAY EVIDENCE
UNDERMINES CRUCIAL TESTIMONY**

**REILLY DEFENSE CLAIMS NEW
"SUSPECT" IN CASE**

**STATE ORDERED TO TURN OVER
EVIDENCE IN REILLY CASE**

**BIANCHI SAYS NO NEED SHOWN
FOR NEW TRIAL FOR REILLY**

The defense had taken the offense. The favorable publicity was encouraging to Peter's supporters and spurred their fund-raising efforts. The bake sales, benefit dances and other events arranged by the Reilly Committee, plus mailings that appealed for contributions, brought in badly needed dollars for the defense costs. By September 1975, two years after Barbara Gibbons' death, the Committee had raised $13,000, including donations from outside the community. (The amount would be doubled by the end of the case.) Unfortunately, most of the money had to go to pay the more than $400 interest each month on the $44,000 bank loan for Peter's bond. Four families then arranged among themselves to assume responsibility for the $60,000 bond by putting up their houses, to a limit of $15,000 each, as security for the bond. They were the Belchers, Belignis, Mickey Madow and Murray Madow. Their faith in Peter made it possible to return the $44,000 loan to Jacqueline Bernard and eliminate the monthly interest burden.

The fund-raising effort was impressive for a small-town group with scant experience in such matters and with only a dozen persons regularly active in the cause. On the other hand, the amount raised was sufficient—just barely—only because the two principals in Peter's defense, Daly and Conway, did not demand payment for their services. Both men, in fact, absorbed heavy out-of-pocket expenses.

During the nineteen months between his sentencing and the new-trial hearing, Peter led a surprisingly ordinary life. He had to meet with his attorney occasionally, and he could not leave the state without permission, but he moved about Canaan like any other youth. He was almost able to dismiss his manslaughter conviction as a bad dream.

To some of his supporters, in fact, Peter's desire for normalcy was disturbing because they felt that they were working harder than he was for his own vindication. Conway was angry when Peter did not help him out as much as he wanted in his search for the murder weapon and other evidence. Some Committee members thought Peter should attend their meetings more often. Reporters wished that he would sit still for longer interviews about the case.

"If I did everything people wanted me to do," Peter explains, "I wouldn't have any life of my own." Although he had been submissive to grown-ups most of his life, he was an adult now and he couldn't help being annoyed by the fact that so many people, including his most active defenders, were always telling him what to do and making decisions for him. He yearned for privacy and for relief from his role as either Convicted Killer or Victim of Injustice.

Partly because of the ongoing legal proceedings, Peter would say little about the case except that he preferred to "look on the bright side of things." On the other hand, when asked if he thought much about going to prison, he had this answer: "I know the possibility is there. I'm just trying to keep my head together and wait it out. What's going to happen is going to happen."

One major change in him was his attitude about his education. "I was really psyched about getting back to school after all I'd been through. My marks had always been below average, but I wanted to prove myself. I loved school when I went back." He did so well in his senior year that he earned honors for the first time.

In his Contemporary Problems course Peter studied the American Indian. He had hoped to be able to attend the Crime and Society unit of the course because the participants analyzed the criminal justice system. Police and prison officials appeared to lecture the students and John Bianchi was scheduled to preside over a mock trial. "After being hammered on the way I was—interrogated, going to trial and everything—I really wanted to get into it and hit the experts with a lot of questions they wouldn't expect from a high school senior. But I was talked out of taking it. I think they thought it would be too embarrassing."

Even so, Peter received permission to sit in on a few of the guest appearances. He restrained himself from questioning Bianchi after the mock trial, but when a rehabilitation expert from Somers penitentiary spoke to the class, Peter asked him, among other things, about certain details of a riot that had taken place at the prison a few years earlier. "He couldn't figure out where I got the inside information," Peter says. "Well, I got it in the Litchfield jail."

Only during those lectures, Peter says, did he feel separate from his fellow students. "To them it was all academic, but for me the criminal justice system was something I was living through." He had returned to the high school without experiencing a single instance of unpleasantness. Even though he was officially guilty of a bloodthirsty crime, Peter felt that everyone around him—students, teachers, administrators—assumed that he could not have done such a thing.

Peter was just one of 153 seniors who graduated from the high school in June 1975, but he was the only one to be featured in newspaper stories. A typical headline said that

"CONVICTED KILLER RECEIVES DIPLOMA." (Within the week, however, John Sochocki's name would be in the papers. He drowned in a nighttime swimming accident.) At the outdoor exercises, the class president urged his fellow students to "accept the challenges of a complex and confusing world." There were cheers when Peter's name was called and he was handed his diploma. "At-a-boy, Pete," someone shouted. After the ceremony, he said, "It took another year, but I did it anyway."

Peter went to work in the summer of 1975 as a custodian at the high school under a federally sponsored work program. He gave a portion of his pay to the Madows for his living expenses. He earned additional money playing his guitar in a rock band. Later in the year he attended night classes at Northwestern Community College, studying accounting. Jim Mulhern was a classmate.

Things were going more smoothly for Peter than for his new lawyer and the private detective. Roy Daly and Jim Conway had had a few lucky breaks (a Providence, Rhode Island, attorney, for example, had given them a lead on John McAloon's psychiatric history and his brother's willingness to identify McAloon as a habitual liar), but the struggle with the State's Attorney for exculpatory material, including the results of the police polygraph charts on Peter, was so intense and so often fruitless that Daly, in papers filed with the court, finally charged Bianchi with acting "in a manner verging on contempt."

"It was criminal what they were doing to us," Conway says. "I remember the day I met Hartwell after he picked up the stuff that Bianchi was supposed to give us. It was an absolute travesty. He didn't answer half our questions. He gave us a lot of junk. I'll give you an example. We had asked for a photograph they had of the Teen Center meeting that Peter went to. There was a clock on the wall that would pin down the time. So we wanted that picture. You know what they did? They took the photo and ran it through a Xerox machine so that we got a piece of paper with all kinds of dots and we couldn't read the time. I told Hartwell that this was ridiculous. You've got to realize that this was the middle of the summer. I had been on the case eight months already.

To me this was the straw that broke the back. I wanted to know how long are we going to let Bianchi get away with this stuff. I told Roy that this is a fight and we're still playing by their rules. I said that we have to go to the newspapers and tell people what's happening here. Roy said to me, 'I know you're very hot about this; relax.' But I said, 'Roy, I can't relax. I feel very strongly about this. People have got to know what's going on. They've got to know that this kid didn't kill his mother and the state cops and the State's Attorney can't get away with it.'"

For a time, Daly's cooler style prevailed. Conway continued his detective work and reports of the latest defense moves appeared in the press. "Then one day, out of the blue, Daly says, 'I heard from Arthur Miller and they're going to send a guy up from the *Times*.' We had been talking about it. Now we were getting somewhere."

According to Miller, "The press in Connecticut just wasn't doing the job. There were exceptions like the *Lakeville Journal*, but the story still wasn't getting out. It was time to break out of this cozy little Litchfield County courthouse and let the world at large hear about this. If this trial could have happened in the first place, and they convicted this boy without a case, then why couldn't they do it again? In fact, the second time might be easier if you had the same kind of silence.

"I knew some of the people at the *Times*. I told them the story of the case. I said to them that this happened to be an instance where there is a case of pure injustice. It had nothing to do with race prejudice or ethnic prejudice or anything else. It was just a case of the real failure of the court system to arrive at a just decision."

The *Times* gave Miller no encouragement. Roy Daly then suggested that Miller try again with the argument that "a poor white boy in Litchfield County has the same civil rights as a Hurricane Carter in New Jersey or a Joanne Little in North Carolina." The newspaper had given prominent coverage to the Carter and Little cases.

In mid-December 1975, the *Times* published a two-part, front-page exposé of the Reilly case. The articles were essentially a summation of Jim Conway's discoveries and information already reported in local newspapers, but they drew important new attention to Peter's story. Joan Barthel, who deserved credit for bringing Arthur Miller into the case (and thus Daly and Conway), went unmentioned while Miller, to his embarrassment, got most of the prominence. The headlines announced that the playwright had "turned detective."

Miller did accompany the *Times* reporter, John Corry, to the Sixth Homicide District in Harlem where they interviewed case-hardened detectives who investigated nearly three hundred murders a year. (The whole of Connecticut averages only a hundred homicides annually.) Skeptical of Peter's innocence until they looked over the interrogation transcript, the detectives took special notice of the sexual mutilation of Barbara Gibbons. "You're on the wrong track," they said. "A broad did it. It was a lesbian murder." That was a possibility that Conway had seriously considered. He had even concluded that a whiskey bottle was the most likely object in the cottage to have been used to cause the internal wounds.

Just as the *Times*'s reports appeared, the CBS television show *60 Minutes* sent Mike Wallace and a film crew to Canaan to prepare a feature on the Reilly case that was shown to a national audience in January. *Time* magazine was next in reporting the Reilly case. It was put in the context of "a long history of laymen trying to overturn what they see as injustice wrought by police, lawyers and judges."

Satisfying as it was to have so much attention paid to what the *Lakeville Journal* described as "the implausibility of the grounds on which [Reilly] was convicted of manslaughter," Roy Daly was painfully aware that all of the publicity and sympathy would do Peter no good if he could not present a package of new material that the court would find strong enough to warrant a new trial. At the close of 1975, with the hearing on the new-trial petition scheduled to start in mid-January, Daly knew that he did not yet have clinching evidence despite all their labors. "We knew that a grave injustice had been done but we were up against it: I didn't see how I could beat the legal standards in this state for a new trial."

Daly turned once again to a possibility that he had considered ever since his original interview with Peter. He wondered whether Peter knew something more about the murder than he was saying. "I didn't think he was consciously lying, but he might have pushed something he had seen far to the back of his mind. He had entered the cottage so soon after the attack on his mother that it was conceivable that something had registered that he would not or could not tell us about."

A polygraph expert from Hartford had been engaged in February 1975 to give Peter a lie detector test in the Madow house. The results enabled Conway to tell the press that Peter had no knowledge of how his mother was killed. Tim and Mike Parmalee agreed to be examined at the same time, and the expert said that they too had truthfully answered in the negative such questions as, "Did you have anything to do with the death of Barbara Gibbons?"

The following December, as he sought to understand more about Peter's psychological makeup, Daly arranged for Peter to be tested by a noted New York polygraph organization, Scientific Lie Detection, Inc. Two separate tests were administered by different experts. The result, according to Richard O. Arthur, president of the firm, was that "the polygraph recordings of Mr. Reilly were such that they could not be analyzed. Therefore, neither polygraphist is able to render any opinion as to Mr. Reilly's truthfulness. This does occur with approximately 3 percent of the persons we examine."

The jurors in the Reilly trial had been told to ignore the State Police polygraph test, but they had heard on the interrogation tapes the claim that Peter, the "textbook reactor," had lied to the examiner. Now it appeared that Peter is among the small percentage of individuals who cannot be accurately tested on the machine.

Still wondering whether some valuable piece of information might be lodged in Peter's subconscious, Daly decided that a psychiatrist using hypnotism might be helpful. After some search he was advised that the best man he could get was Dr. Herbert Spiegel of Manhattan, a professor of psychiatry at Columbia University and one of the nation's foremost authorities on hypnotism. "I called Arthur Miller," Daly relates, "and told him that Spiegel was the man we wanted.

I asked him to get him for me even if we didn't have any money for him. Arthur is a persuasive man. He arranged an appointment for us."

On the sixth of January, 1976, Murray Madow drove Peter, Daly and Miller to New York for Spiegel's examination. With another doctor assisting him and Daly and Miller observing, Spiegel examined Peter for three hours. His main objective was to determine whether Peter was suffering from amnesia as he recollected his observations in the cottage. Spiegel asked many questions and conducted a test of his own devising, the Hypnotic Induction Profile, that measures a person's ability to concentrate under given test conditions. Spiegel sought to hypnotize Peter and found that he was not hypnotizable. Nonetheless, he proceeded to examine Peter as if he were under hypnosis so that Peter could, if he chose to lie, make claims under the camouflage of a trance. Peter followed the psychiatrist's instructions to imagine himself looking at a movie screen and describe, in fifteen-second intervals, the things he had seen and done after arriving home from the Youth Center meeting.

Spiegel says that "I was able to tell Daly and Miller that one, Peter has none of the personality attributes, none of the measurements, that you would expect of a person who would develop amnesia; two, that he was able to give an accounting of every time segment; and three, when he was given the chance to lie, he didn't lie. So I came to the conclusion that he didn't have amnesia and that he was telling the truth."

From one point of view, the session with Dr. Spiegel was a disappointment and a waste of everyone's time. Nothing useful had been pulled out of Peter's subconscious. While he did have some impression of leaves rustling before he stepped into the cottage and of the drapes moving, he said himself that the wind was probably the cause, not another person. It was gratifying, nonetheless, to have Peter's truthfulness confirmed. "He was in an ideal situation," Daly says, "to give me the answers I wanted to hear, but he wouldn't do it because he had not, in fact, seen or heard anything. He knew at that point that we had strong suspicions about three persons who might have been involved in his mother's death. While he was supposed to be in a trance he could have elaborated on his story, but he didn't."

What no one realized at the time was that involving Dr. Spiegel in Peter's case was the wisest—and luckiest—step that Roy Daly could have taken. Within a matter of weeks the psychiatrist would be produced as a surprise witness in the Litchfield Court and decisively influence the outcome of the hearings.

"I had no intention then of calling Dr. Spiegel as a witness," says Daly. "I had gone to his office for the specific purpose of trying to probe Peter's recollection and I came away without any additional information from him. So I did not feel that the day was a success at all. The hearings were going to start one week later. Believe me, I was not optimistic. Our chances for a new trial were very, very small."

19 ▪ THE HEARING

PETER REILLY: And, I was wondering if some way—when you and I spoke man to man you said you'd help me because—is there any possible way I could possibly live with your family if you had the room? If you had the room. I wouldn't want to impose and I know my godmother would pay my way.

LIEUT. SHAY: Well, let's say this. It would be a rather unusual turn of events.

This time it was *Peter A. Reilly vs. the State of Connecticut*. Otherwise, the wintry scene at the Litchfield courthouse looked like a rerun of the 1974 trial. Peter's Canaan supporters came to town and huddled for warmth on the steps as they waited for the doors to open. The crowd on this opening day, January 15, 1976, was larger than before. More reporters were in attendance. Spectators in the courtroom saw familiar faces: Judge Speziale on the bench, John Bianchi representing the State and Peter Reilly sitting once again on the business side of the railing.

The list of witnesses heightened the feeling of *déjà-vu*. It appeared that there would be repeat performances from such figures as Fenn, Shay, Mulhern, Calkins, Pennington, Beligni and the Madows. Even Catherine Roraback and Peter Herbst were back in the courtroom again—this time as witnesses for Peter.

However, a fundamental shift in awareness had taken place in the twenty-one months since the manslaughter conviction. The Reilly trial, in a sense, had never really ended.

A judgment had been reached, but many questions were left unanswered. The public sense that something had gone wrong, and that the wrong man had been prosecuted for a horrible crime, was enhanced each time information not heard in the trial was revealed. Peter had become a sympathetic figure and a popular name in the news. He was on his way to becoming a symbolic victim of injustice. A classmate had published a poem about him. Someone else wrote a ballad. A book was being written.

All of this was infuriating and humiliating to John Bianchi. He was not used to being on the defensive. As far as he was concerned, he had simply done his job as State's Attorney. He had prosecuted a young man who, he was sure, was guilty. Now the bleeding hearts were in full cry, the press had made a hero out of Reilly, and T. F. Gilroy Daly had the audacity to subpoena him as the petitioner's witness even though he was the opposing attorney.

Although Bianchi would make a practice of referring to Roy Daly as "my brother" and even "my worthy brother," he saw Daly as a threat; he knew he was in for the fight of his life; and he knew that his reputation was at stake. The outcome of this hearing might well determine whether he would ever become a judge, as he hoped. Bianchi called in reinforcements: Assistant State's Attorney Robert E. Beach, Jr., from New Haven, and Joseph Gallicchio, a Torrington attorney who was made a Special Assistant State's Attorney. County Detective James Bausch joined them at the defense table. Roy Daly had his own back-up team: Robert Hartwell, John Fiore, Jim Conway and Elizabeth Morris, his secretary.

Judge Speziale, who was now the chief judge of the Superior Court, could have avoided the hearing. Connecticut's Superior Court judges work in a rotation system, taking turns in different counties, and Speziale was not due to be in Litchfield. But Judge Jay E. Rubinow, who was to conduct the hearing, urged Speziale to take his place because he knew more about the Reilly case than anyone else. Aware of the widespread concern that justice had not been done, Speziale decided that the Reilly case was something that he had to see through.

The beginning of the hearing for a new trial was delayed for more than an hour as extraordinary security measures were put in force. An Electro-Search metal detector was set up outside the courtroom doors and half a dozen state troopers in plainclothes were called in to help the sheriffs. The cause for concern was separate from the Reilly case. Someone had telephoned the judge's house and told his wife that "We're going to blow your husband's goddamn head off!"

The hearing lasted as long as the trial. It took seventeen days over a period of six weeks to hear fifty-four witnesses, some of whom took the stand two or three times. The legal arguments about whether particular witnesses should testify at all seemed to consume as much time as the testimony. There were so many objections made by the attorneys, Bianchi in particular, that the proceedings were often tedious. The hearing had several dramatic moments, however, including the kind of "bombshell" revelation that the press hopes for. Roy Daly would one day say of the Reilly case that "We felt if we kept on shaking the tree long enough, some things were going to fall out." He gave the tree a hard shake in the hearings; the fallout was considerable.

Judge Speziale, as he opened the proceedings, said that he wanted to "impress upon all counsel that we are not here to retry the criminal case . . . *State of Connecticut vs. Peter A. Reilly*. This is a hearing on a petition for a new trial. . . ." He continued:

> The petitioner, in the first and third counts of his complaint, relies on alleged newly-discovered evidence as a basis for a new trial. . . .
>   The petitioner has the burden of proving that the evidence was, in fact, newly discovered, that it would be material to the issue on a new trial, that it could not have been discovered and produced at the former trial by the exercise of due diligence, that it is not merely cumulative, and it must be sufficient to likely produce a different result in a new trial.

In his three-count petition Roy Daly claimed that 1) the time sequence proposed by the prosecution at the trial was

false and that Peter did not have sufficient time to commit
the crime without getting blood on himself or his clothes;
2) Bianchi had illegally withheld from the defense certain items
of exculpatory evidence; 3) newly discovered evidence elimi-
nates the "alibi defense" of a person "with one, and possibly
two, motives to do harm to Barbara Gibbons." That person
was Michael Parmalee, Peter's boyhood friend.

Testimony about the murder-night time sequence occupied the first days of the hearing. So many people talked
about specific or approximate times that an exasperated John
Bianchi eventually said, "All these clocks and watches, and
none of them seem to match." That was not quite true. The
times cited by the witnesses may not have matched exactly
but, using the *Kelly's Heroes* broadcast time as a basis, Daly
was able to show that Peter had arrived home from the church
meeting when he said he did—shortly before 9:50. Daly's
own conclusion, as he said in his petition, was that Barbara
Fenn had testified falsely about talking on the telephone to
Peter at about 9:40.

Daly put on the stand a number of witnesses who had not
testified at the trial. The Reverend Paul Halovatch, for example, spoke of seeing Peter drive away from the church and
then of going with the Reverend Peter Dakers on a brief journey (three or four minutes, he guessed) to Johnny's Restaurant. There he noticed that the time on the clock was 9:50.

Reverend Peter Dakers in his trial testimony had spoken
of their arrival at Johnny's as "I think, about 9:40, 9:45." Now
he said that "I definitely was" mistaken. He wished to stand
by his statement to the police of October 2, 1973. Speaking of when he had seen Peter's Corvette pull away from the
church, he had then said, "I can't pinpoint the exact time . . .
but it had to be 9:40–9:45, no earlier and no later."

The two clergymen were being too helpful. Convinced
that Peter had not driven at high speed from the church to
John Sochocki's house and then home, Roy Daly knew that
he would not have left the church later than 9:40 if he had
reached home at approximately 9:48 and taken a minute or
two to fix the headlight and lock the car. Peter's likeliest
departure time was about 9:35. "I knew that the testimony
was drawing the time sequence too tightly," Daly said after

the hearing, "but I had to go with the best recollections of my witnesses."

Michael Marden, the director of prime-time feature films for CBS, testified that the *Kelly's Heroes* scene that Marion Madow was looking at when Peter made his first emergency call was broadcast at exactly 9:50 and 10 seconds. Jessica Bornemann, who had taken Peter's second emergency call (after he had spoken to Directory Assistance), testified that she had said in her statement to the police after the murder that she had received the call sometime between 9:00 and 10:00. And yet, she said, "It was always my impression that it took place during the last part of that hour. When I gave my statement, I felt two constraints: the first one was my own constraint to err on the side of generality rather than too much specificity; and the second was the request or the instructions from the interviewer that I also do the same." She said it was her best recollection that she received Peter's call between 9:45 and 10:00.

Peter's third emergency call (after again calling Directory Assistance) was received at Sharon Hospital by the switchboard operator, Elizabeth Swart. On the witness stand for the first time, she testified that she had connected him to the supervisory nurse, Barbara Fenn. She stayed on the line while he talked to Fenn. Then, when she heard Fenn call for an ambulance, she noted in a log book that the call was made at about 10:00.

Her testimony set the scene for Barbara Fenn's return appearance. Since her few moments as the State's lead-off witness in the trial she had left Sharon Hospital to become the Assistant Director of Nursing in a Torrington hospital. Sworn in once again and facing Roy Daly, she identified Peter Reilly as the young man sitting before her wearing a purple shirt, sweater and light-colored slacks. She described the emergency call he had made to her and said that she had called out the Falls Village ambulance before notifying the police. Daly showed her the State Police log containing the entry establishing her call to the Canaan Barracks at 9:58 on the night of the murder. She agreed that that was probably when she made the call.

"Do you recall," asked Daly, "how long after receiving

the call from Peter Reilly . . . you notified the State Police?" She said she did not.

"Did you consider the situation at the Gibbons house an emergency situation at that time?"

"Yes."

"You are a registered nurse?"

"Yes."

"In an emergency situation, speed can be essential, is that correct?"

"Yes."

Fenn then said of Peter's call to her that "I remembered the time as approximately 9:40." She had stated at the trial that her 9:40 estimate was made "in connection with the fact that there was another ambulance arriving in the emergency room at the same time, and I checked with the ambulance log in time, which was approximately 9:40. . . ."

Daly handed her the ambulance log that she had referred to. "I ask you, does the time '9:40' appear anywhere on that document?"

Fenn's answer: "No."

Daly tried several ways to ask her whether she was accustomed to delaying action for eighteen minutes in an emergency situation, but Bianchi's objections were sustained. "Her recollection has been, in some areas, not total, Your Honor, to put it mildly," said Daly.

Fenn was a stubborn witness. When Daly asked whether she could have received Peter's call "later than 9:40," she said, "Could have received it before." She finally admitted that it could have been later. Daly's final question: "You are the wife of a state trooper, is that correct?" Answer: "Yes, sir, it is."

Not brought out at either the trial or the new-trial hearing was the fuller story of the emergency-room activity on the night of the murder. According to the entry on the log that Roy Daly showed Barbara Fenn, the Cornwall ambulance arrived at 9:45, but its exact accuracy is questionable (it seems to be up to ten minutes early) because the entry would normally not be made until after the patient had been brought into the emergency room and attended to.

The female patient with a broken hip was already in the room and receiving care, and the Cornwall ambulance attendants were present, when the telephone rang. The emergency-room nurse, Mrs. Jean Jones, would have picked up the phone, but Barbara Fenn, the supervising nurse, happened to be passing through the hall and took the call. Mrs. Jones as well as the ambulance personnel heard her part of the discussion with Peter Reilly. According to Mrs. Jones, Nurse Fenn called out the Falls Village ambulance almost immediately after the conversation. Fenn then told Jones she was going to call the State Police. Jones asked why. Fenn explained that the caller had said that Barbara Gibbons was bleeding a lot. Then she telephoned the police.

Nurse Jones is clear in her recollection that the two calls by Fenn were made without much delay after the conversation with Reilly. There was no quarter-hour interlude before the call to the police as Fenn's testimony has suggested. When Jones made out her own log after these events, she reported the Cornwall ambulance as having arrived at 10:00 P.M., and this was revealed in testimony given at the hearing by Dr. Paul Sternlof, the Sharon Hospital executive director.

In sum, there were no less than four log entries, all known to Peter Reilly's prosecutor, that contradicted Barbara Fenn's testimony: (1) Cornwall ambulance's 9:45, (2) Elizabeth Swart's 10:00, (3) Jean Jones' 10:00 and (4) the State Police's 9:58.

During his questioning of Barbara Fenn, Roy Daly established that neither Catherine Roraback nor her associate had spoken to Mrs. Fenn before the Reilly trial. In his turn, Bianchi brought out that Roraback had cross-examined Fenn at the trial. Since Fenn had simply repeated her trial testimony, Bianchi could not see how any of this could be considered newly discovered evidence. As with previous witnesses, he urged that her testimony be stricken. But Speziale said again, "The motion to strike is denied and may be renewed at a later time, should counsel so desire."

It was becoming more and more obvious that Judge Speziale was going to permit Roy Daly much leeway in his presentation of information. He seemed willing to hear anything that would shed light on the complex case. The *New York Times* reported that Peter Reilly's lawyers "won a small but potentially important victory" at the beginning of the new-trial hearing. "The victory came as Judge John A. Speziale of Superior Court repeatedly allowed the introduction into evidence of statements and documents that either had been part of the original trial record or had been available at the time of the trial."

Speziale could have refused to admit anything that was not genuinely newly discovered, but he gave way to Daly's repeatedly stated plea that the court hear "the totality of the situation . . . I cannot claim that every bit of evidence in this hearing was not, perhaps, discoverable with due diligence. I do claim that parts of it were, and when those parts are put into the whole, the whole picture is changed."

At one point, when Dr. Milton Helpern was introduced, Speziale asked, "Would it be your claim, ultimately, Mr. Daly, that if you are able to show that there is newly discovered evidence that you have proven to the Court, that, even though this witness's testimony may not ultimately be considered as newly discovered evidence, that it could go to the totality of the circumstances and show that an unjust result not only has been reached, but on a new trial it would likely produce a different result?"

"Precisely, Your Honor," said Daly.

It was clear, as the elderly Dr. Helpern took the stand, that the time sequence testimony was to serve as a platform for the pathologist to state whether he thought Peter Reilly had time enough to kill his mother and emerge without showing any sign of the event. Bianchi objected to his testimony being heard: "Dr. Helpern and many, many other men of his particular training and expertise were available at the time of the trial."

When Speziale allowed Helpern to testify, Daly put a hypothetical question to him. He was asked to assume that Peter had arrived home from the church meeting at roughly 9:50, saw the victim, took time to make several phone calls, and then was present without a trace of blood on his person or clothing when a state trooper arrived at 10:02. He was also to assume that Peter at that time was 5 feet 7 inches and weighed 121 pounds. Finally, Daly spelled out the condition of the corpse.

Daly asked Helpern if, given these assumptions and his review of the material, he had an opinion as to whether Peter Reilly killed Barbara Gibbons.

"In my opinion," Helpern replied, "the person, Peter Reilly, who is described to me as having undergone certain activities before he arrived home and then carried out certain procedures after he got home, would not have had time to have committed this homicide and appear in the way he did and undergo the kind of examination he went when the police took him into custody." He added that he would say the same about anyone: "I'd say that such a person could not have accomplished this homicidal act."

When Bianchi noted in his cross-examination that Dr. Izumi had testified that the assailant could have carried out the attack without getting bloodied, Helpern said that he disagreed with Izumi—"very much so."

Bianchi decided to try a hypothetical question of his own.

Q: Given the same set of facts that Mr. Daly gave you, but changing them to this degree: One, that Reilly arrived home ten minutes earlier than he did in Mr. Daly's hypothetical question and that there was evidence that Reilly disposed of the clothes that he was wearing, is your answer the same as it was to Mr. Daly's hypothetical?

A: Yes, my answer would be the same unless you ask me to assume that, in that rather short period of time, this boy would completely discard all his clothing so that when he was found by the time the police came, he was wearing an entirely different set of clothing.

Q: That's what I am asking you to assume.

A: I would say that, even if he threw all his clothing away, that he would still show some indication of blood on his person in that short period of time and in that situation.

Q: Let us add one more thing to my last question. Let us assume he washed off his body. Now, would you have the same conclusion?

A: My conclusion would be the same. . . .

Q: Now . . . we will add two other facts. One, assume that Reilly had thrown away his clothes and assume that he had confessed and admitted to the homicide, would your conclusion be the same, Dr. Helpern?

A: My conclusion would still be the same on that, yes.

Crucial as Dr. Helpern's testimony was to Daly's structure of proof, it was overshadowed by a courtroom disclosure on the third day of the hearing, January 20, that was worthy of Perry Mason.

"There has been a possibly substantial new development in this case, Your Honor," Roy Daly announced at the start of the morning proceedings, "with respect to the prints discovered by the State Police at the Gibbons home on or about September 28, 1973."

This was electrifying news for Peter's supporters. For two and a half years the police had failed to provide an answer to one of the most glaring mysteries about the murder: the identification of the fingerprint on the side screen door. "It is my judgment," Daly continued, "that it could, and probably will, lead to other things which may make a lot of the proof in the present petition necessary and I would move for adjournment, Your Honor."

Daly wanted a week's continuance in order to digest this development and reshape his case. Bianchi protested by belittling the fingerprint identification, saying it amounts to "a rather brief amendment to his pleadings." After a conference in chambers, Daly was satisfied with just a day's adjournment.

The owner of the fingerprint was described in the courtroom only as "a young man who is in military service." Nonetheless, the word quickly sped through the courthouse that the individual was Peter Reilly's boyhood friend, Timothy Parmalee. Because he had been subpoenaed as a witness by Daly well before the fingerprint disclosure, he was in the courthouse now, sitting in the State's Attorney's office. He was a slim, fair-haired youth, a high school dropout, who had joined the Army less than four months earlier, after his eighteenth birthday. He had been married for a year. His wife was still going to high school. He was the father of a little girl.

Although Roy Daly did not say so in the courtroom, the "identifiable" fingerprint had finally been identified, not because of persistence by the State Police, but because of his own initiative.

Largely because of Jim Conway's findings, Daly had become convinced that the fingerprint belonged either to Tim or Mike Parmalee. He called a friend at the Fairfield Police Department, Chief of Detectives Patrick Carroll, and told him that "I'm at a loss." He explained his frustration about the fingerprint. Carroll told him that Captain Paul Seaman at the State Police Bureau of Identification was a good man: "Call him and use my name." Daly contacted Seaman on the day before the hearing started and gave him the Parmalee names. Seaman instructed Sergeant Gerald Pennington, who had taken the fingerprint from the cottage in the first place, to go to the files and see if a match could be made. "The following Tuesday," Daly says, "I got a call from Seaman before going into the courtroom. He said the print was Tim's."

Daly says that he spoke to Tim Parmalee at that point "to tell him that I was not out to get him, but that I had to do what I could to help Peter." He suggested that he get a lawyer. "Tim told me that County Detective Bausch had already been to his house to tell him that the fingerprint had been identified as his, but to keep his mouth shut. I might have been more skeptical of this story if Joe O'Brien hadn't called me to find out what was going on in the Reilly case: he said that police cruisers had been seen at the Parmalee house. I realized that Tim Parmalee had the best lawyer he could have: the State's Attorney and the State Police."

Bausch denies telling Tim Parmalee or anyone else not to speak to members of the defense team, as was alleged. A grand jury investigation in 1977 found "no support for this charge." Even so, the inspector's call on Tim Parmalee, whether just before or just after the fingerprint identification was announced, gives an impression of exceptional solicitude for the Parmalees by John Bianchi's office. According to Michael Parmalee, Bausch merely told them not to worry because there was no way to tell how long the print had been on the Gibbons door and there was nothing that could be done to them.

Peter Reilly spent most of the morning of January 20 in the large waiting room of the Litchfield courthouse, playing blackjack with friends and reporters. He told the press that he thought it best not to comment on the fingerprint development. He never made a public accusation of the Parmalees. They, in turn, did not blame Peter for their sudden notoriety. They did accuse Roy Daly, however, of trying to throw the blame on them. According to Mike Parmalee, they asked John Bianchi what they should do about getting a lawyer. He told them not to worry about it because he did not intend to prosecute them.

Bianchi told reporters that he did not consider Tim Parmalee a suspect and said there were no plans to seek his arrest. "Arrest him for what?" he said. "There is no trial and there is no case before us at this time. This is just a hearing for a new trial, that's all. The suspect, Peter Reilly, was arrested, tried and convicted more than two years ago."

The press treated the fingerprint disclosure as the major news of the Reilly hearing and the name Parmalee was linked in the public mind with the Gibbons murder. The stories not only discussed Timothy, but his twenty-year-old brother, Michael, as well, because he had been named by Daly in court affidavits in connection with the third count of the petition. Both young men denied any involvement in Barbara Gibbons' death. Two years earlier, after Peter had been found guilty and Murray Madow had cried out on the courthouse steps, "Now all we have to do is find the killer," the mother of Mike and Tim Parmalee had gone to Murray and Dot Madow to assure them that her boys were innocent. And Tim's mother-in-law, Mary Sager of Cornwall, and her husband had organized a dance to help raise money for Peter's defense.

The public stance of the Parmalees and their in-laws was that they believed in Peter Reilly's innocence but they were *sure* that both Mike and Tim were guiltless. Now, with Tim's fingerprint having been disclosed, Mary Sager wrote an angry letter to the *Lakeville Journal,* saying that "Tim is innocent, but the radio, television and newspapers are trying to make him guilty." The *Journal* cautioned its readers against believing that either Tim or Mike was involved in the crime. "To rush to such a conclusion without either indictment or trial would be to do to others that sort of injustice that some of Reilly's defenders contend was done to him."

Concern about the rights of the Parmalees was shared by a number of Peter's staunchest supporters even as they recognized that Peter's chances for a new trial had been greatly improved. On the eighth day of the hearing, Judge Speziale ruled that the fingerprint identification qualified as new evidence. It was the first outright indication that the judge accepted at least part of Daly's new-trial argument.

Mike Parmalee said long afterward that "when I got the subpoena about three weeks before the hearing, I wasn't concerned about it—I figured I'd just be helping Pete. We were in school together from the second grade on and I knew he was innocent. I can't see Pete doing something like that. But they were the most depressing six weeks of my life. The whole experience ruined my name. They brought up a lot of skeletons there in court."

Tim Parmalee said that, "My mother's nerves are shot because of this." He pointed out that the police had tested him on the lie detector soon after the murder. "There were three different tests—the second time the machine broke down. They asked me if I knew Peter and his mother, whether I knew anything about the murder, whether I knew who did it. They told me, 'You have nothing to worry about; you're in the clear,' Later on, Mike took a test with me at the Madow house. We didn't have to take it but we did. A professional polygraph guy was there. He read the results and told both of us: no problem."

The Parmalees and their in-laws in Falls Village are so numerous that their immediate neighborhood is sometimes referred to as "Parmaleeville." Mike and Tim grew up with their two older brothers and four sisters in the ramshackle house on Route 63, a few minutes' walk from the Gibbons cottage. Their father, Jacob Parmalee, a laborer who used to work on the town's road crew, was eighty-one years old at the time of the hearing. He wore a pacemaker. Although sub-poenaed, his poor health prevented him from testifying. His wife, Margaret, who had gone to school with John Bianchi, is some twenty years younger than her husband. She had a nighttime job at the local Wash'n Dri factory.

Mike and Tim Parmalee are both a few inches taller than Peter. Mike is thinner and darker than his brother; Tim is more muscular. Both of them, like Peter and Wayne Collier, have tattoos on their arms. They have had occasional brushes with the police, both civilian and military. Mike, for example, received a five-day suspended sentence on a charge of assault and battery in 1972. He joined the Army after dropping out of high school, but soon found that he could not take the dis-cipline. He went AWOL three times and finally received an "undesirable" discharge. At the time of the Reilly hearing he was working as a kitchen helper at the Hotchkiss School in Lakeville. He lost six weeks' work because of the hearing, he says, and then the job.

Tim Parmalee was following in his brother's footsteps. He too tried the Army—"to get myself straightened out"—but it would not be long before he chafed under the restrictions and was given a discharge. On January 20, however, he was still in the service and, in answer to Daly's subpoena, had come home from his base in Maryland. He arrived at the courthouse in civilian clothes. When asked by reporters how he could account for his fingerprint being on the side screen door of the Gibbons' cottage, he said, "I don't want to talk, not now." Eventually his explanation would be that he used to open that door to adjust the television aerial when he was in the house watching TV with Peter.

During one of his three appearances on the stand during the hearing, Tim was asked by Bianchi, "Can you recall the last time that you were at the house . . . where Peter Reilly and the late Barbara Gibbons lived?"

Parmalee's answer: "Week and a half, two weeks and a half, not really sure." He said he had been to Peter's house "quite a few times" in the year before the slaying.

When Margaret Parmalee appeared as Bianchi's witness, she said that Mike and Tim had been "very good friends" of

Peter's during the months prior to the murder. In fact, she said that Peter visited her house at around ten o'clock on the morning of September 28, 1973, or the day before. And she said that her boys would stay overnight at Peter's house: "Often I would drop them off on my way to Canaan or some other place." Still speaking of the situation as it was in 1973, she said that "Timmy went up and stayed with him while his mother was in the hospital."

Tim Parmalee and his mother seemed to be saying that there were numerous opportunities in 1973 for his fingerprint to have been left innocently at the Gibbons cottage. Roy Daly's understanding was, however, that neither Tim nor Mike Parmalee had been allowed in the cottage by Barbara Gibbons for perhaps a year before her death—certainly not since an army investigator had arrived on the scene in the spring of 1973 to ask Peter, in his mother's presence, about Mike Parmalee's claim to be a homosexual. From that time, Daly told Judge Speziale, the relationship between Barbara Gibbons and the Parmalees "was one of extreme agitation, leading to taunts."

Daly produced school and hospital officials to challenge Mrs. Parmalee's testimony. Attendance records revealed that Peter was at the high school on the mornings of September 27-28. Hospital records showed that Barbara Gibbons had last been an in-patient in 1970, not 1973. When Peter testified, he said that Tim had not been at his house to watch television for more than a year before the murder. He stated that the TV antenna, which used to require adjusting, had been "permanently seated in the ground" for at least a year and a half: There no longer was a need to go through the side door to fix it.

As for Mike Parmalee, Peter testified that a year and a half before the murder, when Mike was visiting his house, he had accused him of stealing money from his mother. "He told me yes, he had. And he gave the money back to her."

Roy Daly questioned Peter about the occasion, three to four weeks before the slaying, when he caught Tim peering into his house.

"I was laying in bed," Peter said. "I was watching through the bedroom–living room door, watching the television."

"And when you first observed Timothy Parmalee, where was he?" Daly asked.

"Outside the house."

"Doing what?"

"Looking in the window."

"And what did you do then?"

"I got up, very quietly—well, I got up as if I hadn't seen him, and I walked through, out into the living room. And then I threw open the front door and said, 'What are you doing?' "

"Did Timothy Parmalee do anything at that point?"

"He was surprised. He—was just surprised."

This occurrence, while hardly important by itself, was one of a number of reasons why Peter had long ago concluded that Tim might be involved in his mother's death. When State Trooper Ronald Kamens transported him from the Litchfield jail to the Circuit Court for arraignment on October 1, 1973, Peter told him two things that Kamens thought important enough to set down in a report soon afterward. First, he said that he had signed a confession that he now realized could not be true; second, he spoke of his suspicions of Timothy Parmalee.

That report was never turned over to Peter's attorneys—not to Roraback, not to Daly—despite the discovery motions for all statements, admissions and confessions made by Peter Reilly. It also appears that Peter's comment did not inspire the prosecutor or the police to seek to link Tim Parmalee to the unidentified fingerprint. Peter was not alone in his suspicions about Tim Parmalee. The State Police gathered some ninety statements from persons in Falls Village and North Canaan while investigating the murder and a number of them mentioned the Parmalee brothers when discussing Barbara Gibbons' contacts or speculating about the event.

To Roy Daly and Jim Conway, the failure to identify the fingerprint for so long was a prime example of police work that was excessively directed toward establishing the guilt of one individual while neglecting other possible suspects. In Tim Parmalee's case, the police did have the excuse that his fingerprints were not available for comparison purposes in their central file until after the Reilly trial. His prints were taken in June 1974 because he and a friend were accused of stealing a pickup truck from Jacobs' Garage. His prints from an earlier theft had been kept in a separate file, under the juvenile offender statute.

"It's a very lame excuse," says Daly. "They're saying they couldn't put their right hand in their left-hand drawer. That might be true, strictly speaking, but if the police really wanted to match that fingerprint with Tim's they could have done it one way or another, even if they had to lift his print off something."

What were Timothy Parmalee's actions and whereabouts on September 28, 1973? When the police asked him soon after the murder to give an accounting he described an eventful day to them. He had tried to attend school that morning, but the assistant principal would not admit him "because I broke the conditions of my trial period." During the day he had helped one of his uncles, Howard Silvernale, "get a calf on his truck which had broken loose." He and Silvernale had gone on a shopping trip and had done some beer drinking. When they returned to Silvernale's house in the late afternoon, Tim told the police, "Howard stayed in the truck because he was drunk. When I got out I saw a brown wallet. It was old and worn. I just put it in my pocket and walked across the street to my house." Later that night, "I took the money, $55, out of the wallet and threw it into our garden."

Tim said that Wayne Collier came to his house at about 5:00 with a six-pack of beer. Later he went with Wayne and Ervin Machia, Tim's brother-in-law, to the local package store to buy two more six-packs of beer. He drank beer in his house and in his uncle's house. (In an interview after the hearing, Mike Parmalee commented on his brother's drinking: "That's normal down there. We like to get together on a Friday or Saturday night and enjoy ourselves. There's nothing wrong with that.") Tim said he made a long-distance call to his girlfriend in Massachusetts, using the telephone in his sister Marie's house. (The Parmalees have no telephone.)

His police statement concluded:

I talked to about 9:00. I went to [Uncle] Art's. I stayed until my sister [Marie] came home. I went over and I told her I owed her for the phone call. I stayed to about 9:25, went home and went to bed. At about 1:30 that morning I was awakened to talk to the police about Barbara Gibbons being murdered. Trooper Mulhern questioned everyone in the house. I got up at about 7:30 or 8:00 A.M. My sister [Judy Machia] asked me to wash some clothes. I did and washed my own. Friday night I wore a brown shirt, red pants and work shoes. I washed the shirt.

I stayed all day. At about 11:30 Howard told me of losing his wallet. Saturday night I went to a dance at the high school. At midnight I went to Chester, Mass., with my sister Lydia Saunderson and her husband. I stayed there to this Saturday, October 6, 1973. I slept at home Saturday night.

Sunday, October 7, Tom Killawee came down from Canaan. I gave him $25 which I had hid in my bedroom. We went to Sheffield. I spent the money at the Meadows, Johnnie's, Collins Diner. Sunday night we stayed in the woods behind the Drive-in Theater. I was afraid of the police I questioning me. Monday night I went home.

Tim Parmalee wore his army dress uniform when he took the stand for the first time. Judge Speziale asked him if he understood that he had a right to refuse to answer any questions that he thought might incriminate him. Tim said that he was willing to testify without the advice of counsel.

His responses to Daly's inquiries were along the lines of his 1973 police statement. Peter's lawyer was interested, of course, in the laundering Tim had done the morning after the murder. He had told the police that he had washed his shirt along with some clothing given to him by his sister. Now he specified a "few T-shirts and a pair of pants."

Tim's one-week trip to Massachusetts the day after the murder was explained. His purpose, he said, was to help his brother-in-law move furniture from one house to another. He conceded that only a single U-haul truckload had been moved all week.

Daly wanted to know why he had slept outdoors after returning to the area. Tim said he was "afraid of what was going on."

"Afraid the police were going to question you?" Daly asked.

"Yes," Tim said.

Bianchi's questions, however, gave Tim the opportunity to say that he feared police inquiries because he had, on the twenty-eighth, stolen Howard Silvernale's wallet and $55.

Bianchi produced several witnesses to confirm Tim Parmalee's story that he was at home and in his bedroom at the time of the murder. They were all members of his family.

One of Tim's sisters, Marie Ovitt, said that she had seen Tim just before 9:30 but not later. Another sister, Judith Machia, who lived in the Parmalee house with her parents, her brothers, her husband and her six children, told of seeing Tim at around nine o'clock and again after ten but not in between. She was sure, however, that he was sleeping in his bedroom during this important period of time.

Mrs. Machia said that she had been upstairs with her baby until about 9:35. Then she sat in the kitchen, alone, to do crossword puzzles. She noticed that Tim's bedroom door was closed. Soon after ten o'clock, her sister Marie, who lived across the road, came in to see if Tim would babysit for her. "I went in and tried to wake up Timmy in his bedroom. . . . He was sleeping. . . . I couldn't wake him up."

John Bianchi asked her, "Between twenty-five minutes of ten, and the time that you went in—shortly after ten o'clock—to wake Timmy up, did anybody come in or out of his bedroom door?"

"No," she said.

Could Tim Parmalee have entered or left his bedroom through one of the two windows? Not according to his mother. Margaret Parmalee, who returned home from work that night after 1 A.M., testified that the bedroom windows could not be opened because of the paneling that was in the way. State Trooper Dean Hammond also said that the windows could not be opened, but for a different reason: "I found that the sash around the windows had been painted sometime in the past, and that this paint was holding the window from being opened." Hammond claimed he had inspected Tim's bedroom on October 9, 1973. It was eleven days after the killing and Peter Reilly had already been arrested, but the police still considered Tim a suspect at the time, perhaps believing him to be Peter's accomplice. He had just been questioned and given a polygraph test; Hammond was told to check out his story.

Tim Parmalee's alibi received further buttressing from Trooper Jim Mulhern. He said that at about 1:40 A.M., while making inquiries in the Parmalee house, he saw Tim come out of his bedroom. "The only thing he had on was a pair of trousers. . . . He appeared as if he had been in bed, sleeping."

Michael Parmalee was not so fortunate in finding support for his story that he was asleep in a trailer bedroom at the time of the murder. His girlfriend at the time, Sandra Ashner, had originally confirmed his account, but she had since said that she had lied to the police.

Mike and Sandra, who was several years older, and her son, Robert, had moved into the trailer on Undermountain Road only a few days before the murder. The principal occupants were Sherwood Scanlon, who worked on the dairy farm owned by Albert Twing, and Jacqueline Watson, who liked to call herself Jacqueline Scanlon. There were three bedrooms. Sherwood and "Jackie" slept in one, Mike and Sandra in the other, and the child in the third.

When questioned by the police six days after the killing, Mike apparently had no trouble satisfying them about his activities on September 28. Nowhere in his signed statement does he account for his whereabouts. The document is devoted almost entirely to his comments about Peter's relationship with Barbara Gibbons. (He said that "Pete and his mother got along good" after her boyfriend Gregory stopped living with them.)

Michael Parmalee was questioned again by the police in April 1975 because Sandra Ashner had recanted and was saying that Mike had left the trailer on the night of the murder. Moreover, she said that earlier that day Mike had expressed a desire to see Barbara Gibbons dead. Parmalee now described to the police his comings and goings on September 28. He said that he had seen Peter's mother sitting outside of the cottage at about noon, but he denied making any statement about wishing to see her dead: "I have never made any threats or wished any harm to Barbara Gibbons." He said that everyone in the trailer, including himself, went to bed at about 9:30 P.M. "I never got up and left the trailer again." When he woke up at about 8:30 the next morning he was alone. "Sandra had gotten up a little before me."

When he took the stand in the hearing, however, Mike Parmalee changed his story somewhat. He had gone to sleep at about 9:00 P.M., he said, and awakened at 7:00 or 7:15 A.M.

Although Sandra Ashner in her original police statement had described the day as an uneventful one and said she went to bed with Mike at 9:30, she told quite another tale in the spring of 1975. In the statement she signed for Jim Conway she said that she was preparing to go to bed at about 8:30 when Mike came in and said, "Something's wrong at home, my mother and father are dead. I think I better go down to the house." She said he left for his parents' home (they were not, of course, dead) and that she went to bed at about 8:45. She had not mentioned his leaving the trailer to the police because she "had no desire to become involved in some police investigation." But later, "My conscience really troubled me" and she decided to speak out. Her statement concluded:

> I continued to live at the trailer with Sherwood, Jackie and Mike but I things became difficult. Every night Mike would wake up in the early hours of the morning about one, two or three o'clock shaking in fear. He would say, "Someone's coming, can't you hear it?" and because of his fear he would make me get up and sit on the living room couch with him. Usually we'd go back to bed but he would continue to imagine someone was coming in the doors or peeking in the windows. After two weeks of this I realized I couldn't continue living under these conditions. I returned to my folks [in Winsted]. Michael visited me there several times but I didn't want to have any more to do with him.

On the stand, obviously nervous, Sandra Ashner spoke so softly that Roy Daly had to urge her to keep her voice up so that the court reporter could take down her testimony. She described the events of September 28, then said that she awakened the following morning at 7:00 or 7:30. Mike returned to the trailer at 8:30 or 9:00.

When cross-examined by John Bianchi, Ashner insisted that Mike had left the trailer that night, but she admitted that she had not actually seen him depart. She simply "figured he had to leave" because "he was so concerned" and because he did not sleep with her.

"You just figured that," said Bianchi. "You just imagined this whole thing, isn't that true?"

"No," she said.

It was a good question, of course, whether Sandra Ashner, who said she had lied to the police originally when she and Mike were still lovers, was now telling the truth after the breakup of their affair. When Jacqueline Watson testified and Bianchi asked about their relationship, she would not agree that there was "bad blood" between Mike and Sandra, but she did say that Sandra had once hoped to marry Mike. She thought it fair to say, in Bianchi's phrase, that "There isn't any love lost" between them.

John Bianchi attempted to discredit Sandra Ashner's testimony by putting a woman named Gloria Bentley on the stand. She was identified only as a person who lived in the nearby town of Winsted and who had known Sandra Ashner socially for a four-year period. When asked by Bianchi what Ashner's reputation for veracity was in Winsted, she said, "She was not always a truthful person."

Daly sought to find out more about Gloria Bentley. It developed that she had come forward as a witness because she had been contacted by Marie Parmalee Ovitt. Daly did not discover until after the hearing, however, that Bianchi had put on the stand, as a character witness, a convicted felon who was, at that moment, awaiting sentence. Daly spelled out the details for Judge Speziale in an indignant footnote when he prepared his brief on March 12, 1976:

> Gloria Bentley was called as a witness by the State to impeach the credibility of Sandra Ashner. . . . The sentencing of Bentley in Common Pleas Court 14 in Hartford, following her conviction in October, 1975, for assault in the third degree, a Class A misdemeanor, and for interfering with a police officer, a Class D felony, was delayed to March 10, 1976; the result being that at the time of her

testimony in the present matter, she had not, as yet, been sentenced. This fact was unknown to the petitioner at the time of Bendey's [sic] testimony, and Bentley could not have been cross-examined on this point, despite the fact that the felony conviction of the witness was presumptively known to the State.

Jim Conway, who felt that it took some courage on Sandra Ashner's part to come forward and tell her story in court, was inclined to give it credence because of something he had learned from Jacqueline Watson. He found in his investigation that the State Police had never interviewed Watson and yet she had something to say about Mike Parmalee's behavior that had troubled her for some time. In a statement she gave Conway she said that she did not know whether or not Mike had spent the murder night in the trailer because she and Woody Scanlon had gone to bed early, at about 8:00. Scanlon, she said, awakened at 4:00 A.M. to do his farm chores. When he returned to the trailer at about 7:15, he "woke up myself, Sandra and Mike." (This conflicts with Ashner's story about Mike returning to the trailer at 8:30 or 9:00.) She continued: "As I was preparing breakfast shortly after, Mike suddenly said, 'I've got to go, someone down the road got killed.' He left the house at approximately 7:35 A.M."

Watson told Conway that she first learned of the Gibbons murder when Mike returned to the trailer that noon. His earlier comment "someone down the road got killed," had bothered her because there was no radio or television set in the trailer "and I wondered how Mike knew of the murder if he had been in the trailer all night."

During her appearance in court, Jacqueline Watson repeated a number of these details, though not the hearsay about Mike's comment. Then Sherwood Scanlon confirmed that he had awakened Mike Parmalee as well as the others soon after 7:00 A.M.

Observers at the hearing were bewildered by all of the conflicting accounts. Ambiguities and unanswered questions seemed to litter the Reilly case and the clutter was getting worse with each witness. The confusion of it all was expressed in the testimony of a Rhode Island man named

Thomas McAloon, the brother of the convict who had testified against Peter in the trial. Saying that his brother John had received psychiatric treatment "on and off" since he was fifteen years old, he added that John was considered "no more than a liar and a thief" in his hometown.

Asked Bianchi, "You voluntarily came down here to call your brother a liar, is that right?"

"I am not calling him a liar. I was asked to tell the truth. If the truth is he is a liar, then that's the truth."

What was the truth about the Parmalees and Barbara Gibbons? In all of the thousands of words of testimony about them there was nothing that was not in dispute—except perhaps for the reason behind Barbara Gibbons' taunting of Mike Parmalee. Both Peter Reilly and Paul Beligni told of Mike's effort to involve them in his homosexual hoax of the Army and he admitted that it was true. Thereafter, Peter testified, his mother made a practice of opening the door and yelling at Mike whenever she saw him walking by. In her "bad-mouthing" of Mike, Paul Beligni testified, she would say things like, "Hey, queer, how are things in fairyville?" Mike's reaction, he said, was "not too good a one."

Parmalee did not deny the taunting while on the stand because he was not asked about it He said after the hearing, however, that "Nobody ever got along with the old bat. Me and Timmy weren't the only ones she picked on. She picked on everybody."

Despite the inconclusive quality of so much of the hearing testimony, it was sufficient for Roy Daly's purposes to demonstrate that there were enough questions about the Gibbons murder—on matters that had not been presented to the trial jury—to warrant a new trial for his convicted client. Some of the items he laid before the judge would have to be ruled as newly discovered, like the fingerprint, but the "totality" was important too.

A number of witnesses, for example, testified about Barbara Gibbons' several wallets and the Sincerbeaux check that she cashed on the day of her murder. A third Parmalee brother, Jacob, told of selling cigarettes to Barbara Gibbons when he waited on her at the Falls Village Market late that afternoon. His boss said he had noticed that she had "a lot of money" in her wallet when he saw her in the store earlier. There was nothing in any of this to prove that the victim's attacker or attackers had set out to steal her money or had taken her wallet as an afterthought, but it could be supposed that at least one juror in another trial might have a reasonable doubt about Peter's guilt if such information were presented.

Confusing as the testimony may have been, there was no doubt that Roy Daly had gained the upper hand on John Bianchi. He had, as one attorney put it, introduced "Daly's rules of evidence" on Bianchi's home ground. The effect on the State's Attorney was visible. "You could see him deflating," the attorney said, "right in front of your eyes."

It was not all smooth sailing for Daly. One morning, early in the hearing, an angry Judge Speziale chastised Jim Conway for making "extra-judicial statements" on the CBS *60 Minutes* broadcast. He warned Daly, as Conway's employer in the Reilly case, that "any future infractions will be regarded very seriously by this Court." But it became more and more obvious, as the days went by, that the hearing was a devastating experience for the State's Attorney. Roy Daly's second count was aimed directly at his competence and his integrity. Daly proposed to put John Bianchi on the witness stand and ask him why exculpatory information had been withheld from Peter Reilly's defense. But first he had to show that such withholding had indeed happened. In his new-trial petition, Daly claimed that seven statements and seventeen pieces of evidence that the defense was entitled to had not been turned over to Catherine Roraback and Peter Herbst.

For a defense attorney to question his client's previous attorneys on the stand was unusual, and Daly's intention to question the prosecutor even more so. A number of lawyers came to the courtroom to hear the testimony. Perhaps more than other spectators, they were able to appreciate the undercurrents in the courtroom. The ill feeling between Daly and Bianchi, beneath the gentlemanly surface, was obvious enough, but there was antagonism too between Daly and Roraback. They had clashed soon after he had taken over Peter's case. He felt that she was being less than cooperative as he sought information; she resented his tactics and complained about his manners. Obliged by Daly's subpoena to produce those records on the Reilly case that she had not given him in 1974, Roraback arrived at the courthouse bearing two large and bulging expansion files. Most of the documents were not essential material, or else had been obtained elsewhere by Daly, but many of the items—including the reports of the psychiatrist and psychologist who had studied Peter Reilly—would have been helpful to Daly and Conway in their work since the 1974 trial.

Daly's questions to Catherine Roraback and her former associate about their dealings with John Bianchi painted a picture of official intransigence. She did not disguise her annoyance about being on the witness stand. Daly would later describe it as "the most difficult direct examination of my own witness in my career at the bar."

Peter Herbst in his testimony spoke of the two motions for disclosure and inspection that the defense had made late in 1973 and of the many oral requests made to Bianchi. He said that all specific requests for statements had been granted, but that numerous statements and pieces of evidence that Daly believed to be exculpatory were not given to Roraback or himself. He told of a conversation with Bianchi that he had put in a memorandum: "He said that he was not going to give any further statements at this point because . . . it was such a hassle to go through the process of Xeroxing them. He said he would view them himself, and if he felt they were exculpatory, he would provide us with copies of the statements."

That, of course, was the problem. It was the State's Attorney's privilege to decide which of the material at hand was favorable to the accused, and thus helpful to the defense, and should be turned over. He was supposed to show some of the cards in his hand but not all of them—and he alone could decide which ones. One card, for example, was Joanne Mulhern's statement. Despite having earlier assured Roraback that all exculpatory statements had been delivered, Bianchi did not give her this document until February 24, 1974, just days before trial testimony began. The statement not only included Mrs. Mulhern's observation that Peter was wearing the same clothing before and after the murder, but told of her call to

Sharon Hospital at close to 10 P.M. when she learned that there was an emergency situation underway. "That statement," Daly told the judge, "is the first indication that I am aware of that anybody should have been alerted to the fact that that switchboard was tied up between 9:50 and 10:00 P.M. on September 28 and not at 9:40 as Mrs. Fenn has continued to insist."

Daly's contention was that much of the withheld material, including the hospital logs, gave information about the murder-night time sequence that, if used by the defense, would have shown the jury how little time Peter Reilly had to carry out the killing and cleanse himself of bloodstains.

Before the testimony of Peter Herbst and Catherine Roraback, Peter was asked by the judge whether he was willing to waive the usual attorney-client privilege and permit "any and all matters" that transpired between himself and his attorneys to be disclosed. Peter said he was. Bianchi quickly took advantage of this new situation. After Herbst's first appearance on the stand he asked him to step into his courthouse office. Several of Bianchi's associates were present.

"Peter," said Bianchi, "your privilege is gone. At any time, before, during or after the trial, did Peter Reilly admit his guilt to you?"

"No," Herbst said.

On February 6, several days after the two former defense attorneys testified, Daly announced, "Your Honor, I call John Bianchi." But Bianchi did not come to the stand. Instead, his associate, Robert Beach, said that "We have a motion in opposition to Mr. Bianchi testifying as a witness."

Lengthy arguments were made by both sides. Essentially, Daly was saying that only by putting Bianchi on the stand to testify under oath could he find the truth about the State's resistance to providing exculpatory material to the defense. Beach, however, disputed that there had been resistance and pointed out that Roraback had not complained to the Court about it. In any event, he said that "an attorney for one litigant should not call the attorney for the other litigant, regardless of whether it is the State's Attorney or not, except in the most extreme circumstances."

Judge Speziale, in his ruling four days later, agreed that the circumstances were not extreme: "This Court finds that there is no reasonable necessity, here, and without just cause, this Court will not allow the State's Attorney to be called as a witness in his capacity as a State's Attorney." Furthermore, said Speziale, because Daly had been seeking a number of documents from Bianchi, "This Court will not permit his confidential files to be subjected to a fishing expedition."

While the ruling was a defeat for Daly, he succeeded in turning the occasion to his advantage. Just before Speziale announced his ruling, Daly spread on the record a series of questions that spelled out some of his suspicions about the conduct of the prosecutor and the police in the Reilly case. Among them were these:

—Whether Bianchi knew of John McAloon's history of mental illness before putting him on the stand in the trial.

—Whether he made a deal with McAloon, promising a suspended sentence for his testimony.

—Whether Barbara Sincerbeaux "was questioned for six to eight hours by the State Police in Canaan Barracks before the trial and . . . was threatened with criminal prosecution."

—Whether James Conway was told "as early as November of 1974 to stay out of this case and to mind his own business . . . by a state trooper."

—Whether Bianchi "was aware of or knew or had any role in the efforts to obtain a bench warrant for Mr. Conway's arrest in an unrelated case."

—Whether, after the identification of Tim Parmalee's fingerprint, he sent an officer "to go out to see Timothy Parmalee and to advise him to keep his mouth shut and . . . not to talk to Mr. Conway."

—Whether or not that same officer advised Timothy Parmalee "that there would be no new investigation as a result of the identification of that print."

—Whether, after learning of the print identification, and before Daly was informed of it, Bianchi made an effort "to have Mr. Parmalee rushed to the Army at the Aberdeen Proving Ground in Maryland outside the jurisdiction of this court."

Some of these items were outright accusations of misconduct

on Bianchi's part. Daly, at this point, was playing a rough game. Perhaps putting such matters so starkly was unfair. But the questions were laid out before the judge's ruling and Bianchi, who was present, could have agreed to take the stand and answer them and the accusation that he had withheld exculpatory evidence. "The fact that he did not choose to respond," says Daly, "is a fact that speaks volumes."

The defense rested at 2:28 P.M., Friday, February 13. John Bianchi's last-minute action was to move that the transcript of the Reilly trial "be made a part and parcel of this petition for a new trial."

Said Judge Speziale: "You are asking the Court to take judicial notice of the entire criminal file—that would include all of the pleadings, the exhibits and the entire transcript?"

"Yes, I am, Your Honor."

"The entire public record of the prior trial, Docket 5285, is that correct?"

"Yes, sir."

"Any objection?" Speziale asked Daly.

"None whatsoever, Your Honor," Daly replied, barely concealing his delight.

"And the Court," said the judge, "does take judicial notice of all that."

The State's Attorney did not realize until later what he had done. He had just opened the door for Roy Daly to bring Dr. Spiegel into the courtroom to testify about the validity of Peter's confession.

Daly recalls that earlier that week, while dining in a restaurant, "I suddenly had the feeling in my gut that Bianchi was going to give me an opening. He was going to make the confessions an issue by moving in the whole trial transcript. I was going to have a chance to rebut Peter's admissions in the interrogation and I was going to do it with Spiegel. I didn't want to put the confessions in myself because then I couldn't attack them; I could only attack them if Bianchi put them in."

Daly telephoned Spiegel to say that he thought Bianchi was likely to give him the opportunity he wanted. He asked him if he would be willing to testify. "Even though Spiegel was fascinated by Peter and saw him as a classic case of the impressionable personality," Daly says, "he works such an incredible schedule that he really didn't want to testify. I didn't blame him, but I reminded him that the confession isn't worth the paper it's written on and said that his testimony could make all the difference in the outcome. He agreed to come up if his testimony could be used. I told him that he had better read the transcripts first. I sent them down to Manhattan by special messenger Lincoln's Birthday morning. That was Thursday. Friday night I told him that we had the opening and that we needed him next Tuesday."

Herbert Spiegel is a striking man. His bald head, black moustache, searing eyes and strong facial features are those of a man who could pass for a Cossack. He is, in fact, a skilled horseman. He began his career in psychiatry not in an office but in nine months of World War II combat in North Africa as a battalion surgeon with the First Infantry Division. A German shell fragment put him out of action. He says that "I learned more about psychiatry, people and my ability to deal with crisis than in any other single year in my life."

John Bianchi was stunned when Daly announced that Dr. Spiegel would be his next witness. Psychiatric testimony was unheard of in a new-trial hearing. In any event, he protested to the judge, this was not proper rebuttal.

Daly countered that Bianchi's move to bring in "the entire criminal proceeding known as *State of Connecticut vs. Peter Reilly*" had changed the situation. "Part of that is the confession; and this is, therefore, proper rebuttal."

Spiegel was allowed to testify. He outlined his professional training and his academic associations and noted that he had conducted an examination of Peter Reilly in early January. Daly explained that what "I am driving at is the personality that was Peter Reilly . . . as best it can be reconstructed on September 28, 1973." Spiegel was asked to give his opinion.

The outstanding features that became apparent during the examination and the history were these: That he was, in essence, a somewhat immature young man who has a serious deficit in his ability to identify who he is as a person.

This is known, clinically, as an identity diffusion. As a result of this, he has difficulty in integrating his concept of self, and, at the same time, has confusion and difficulty and a poor ability to integrate his conceptions of others.

This combination of being so terribly uncertain about who he is as a person and who he is relating to, especially people in authority, leads to a great deal of confusion and, certainly, a great deal of difficulty in trying to withstand any efforts at interrogation and to make critical judgments about the difference between a statement and an assertion or a question.

For that reason, I had the impression that, because he had such a low self-esteem, and justifiably so from the nature of his whole family background, he went along. Under conditions of interrogation, he needs support, protection and understanding of a question and formulating an answer to that question. Without that support and guidance, he can easily be confused. He, most certainly, can easily accept as a fact something that he knows nothing about. This is especially true because of his long-standing respect for authority, especially police authority. As a matter of fact, he, at that time, told me he aspired to become a policeman. These become important issues in trying to understand the quality of the interrogation and the nature of his response to the questions.

Daly asked how Spiegel's opinion would relate to Peter's personality as it was when he was subjected to police questioning. Spiegel said, "I have every reason to believe that the quality of his integration was as high as it possibly could have been at the time of my examination of him in January of '76" and that Peter's ability to identify himself and so forth "was as defective, if not more defective, a few years before."

When asked about "brainwashing," Spiegel described one kind "which is done subtly with implied threat or deception and with misleading cues that takes advantage of the deficit in the critical judgment of the person being interrogated. In a sense, he is tricked into believing premises that may or may not be true but are consistent with what the interrogator wants to impose upon the subject." He went further:

There is related to that, the other phenomenon that is often called [mistakenly] "amnesia." This is where the deception takes place—that an event may not occur in the presence of an individual, and, if it does not occur, he has no way of recalling that the event took place.

Now, if, in the context of a coercive brainwashing interrogation, or where, even if not coercion, deception was used, if a person with a low self-esteem and having a problem with his ego identity, and his sense of self is shaky, if he is told what happened—that events happened that he does not remember because he has "amnesia"—his shaky confidence in himself, combined with his respect for authority, may lead him to believe that, perhaps, the event did take place.

Because he is so weak and anemic in the mind he has to take their word for this. In deference to this authority, he may well agree to accept this as having happened, even though he has no recall of it, at all, and will accept the idea that it did happen. It comes under the category of "amnesia."

Speaking specifically of Peter Reilly and the interrogation, Spiegel said that Peter came to rely on the polygraph "as a means of trying to clear up his memory and to understand what happened because he felt that he had nothing, at all, to do with the killing."

In the course of this procedure, he developed the notion that, possibly, because he doesn't remember how the killing took place, that, possibly, he did have something to do with this because of the nature and the atmosphere of the interrogation.

This is where his condition of being what we call a "borderline" condition, a man with a shaky identity diffusion, by having nobody else to refer to, he interpreted this lack of memory and lack of knowledge of what took place to account for the killing as possibly a defect in his own memory. Under the atmosphere of the interrogation, he then accepted the inferences of the questions that he may have done this, but he knew not how he did it.

He accepted the "scientific" atmosphere of using the polygraph as a means of touching something within himself, as a means of accepting the proposition that, perhaps, he should confess because the police authority believed he did it. He had no proof that he did not do it, and he accepted the notion that he must have had an amnesia for an event that took place.

It's in that sense that he mistook the fact that something that never took place, in his own awareness, he couldn't possibly remember. He accepted in his unstable condition the notion that, not knowing it took place would be accounted for by "amnesia." In deference to the police authority, he then accepted their authority and accepted the responsibility for the killing on the basis of their assertions.

"Do you have an opinion, Doctor," Daly asked, "whether or not, at the time in question in 1973, Peter Reilly was a victim of amnesia?" Spiegel said he found no evidence of it.

"Do you have an opinion as to whether or not Peter Reilly is the type of person to cry in public?"

In his answer, Spiegel spoke of "a kind of alienated way in which this kind of person responds to terribly charged situations; and the least likely thing for a person in this category to do is to openly display any emotion of sadness or tears."

Daly then put a question that was in the minds of at least a few spectators: "Do you have a professional opinion, Doctor, as to whether or not Peter Reilly . . . is the type of personality who would fly into a rage?"

After Bianchi's objection was overruled, Spiegel said: "Because of his extreme modesty and appropriate modesty and because, again, of his uncertainty about himself, not only doesn't he have the likelihood of taking on the right of an emotional outburst or rage against somebody, but I suspect strongly that it doesn't occur to him that he has that right in the first place."

After the hearing, some spectators said Dr. Spiegel had "psyched" John Bianchi. They noticed that the psychiatrist, while answering Daly's questions, had a way of looking directly at Bianchi, as if to say that the answer was meant for him in particular. Bianchi was trying to take notes as Spiegel testified, but he would often stop doing so as he watched the doctor watching him. More to the point, Bianchi seemed uncertain about what to do with a surprise witness who spoke so authoritatively as he attacked the validity of Peter Reilly's confession.

Bianchi had no psychiatrist of his own to counter Spiegel's observations and his own attempts to find fault with Spiegel's qualifications and his conclusions repeatedly backfired. He asked, for example, who was paying him for appearing as a witness. Spiegel said he was not asking for a fee. (His customary charge for a forty-five-minute session with a private patient is $100. "It's a kind of fee that allows me to live the way I want to and do the research that I like to do.") When Bianchi, for reasons unclear, asked him to repeat the names of the medical schools where, in addition to his regular work at Columbia, he had lectured, Spiegel named Harvard, Yale, Chicago, Cornell, Pennsylvania, Stanford, N.Y.U., Emory, Rome, "and several others that I cannot recall."

Bianchi asked Spiegel whether he had, in the January examination, given Peter a Rorschach test, an I.Q. test and other elementary tests. This gave Daly the opportunity to show that the Rorschach, for example, is normally given by a clinical psychologist, not a psychiatrist, and that Spiegel's tests were on a more sophisticated level.

The State's Attorney's biggest mistake, however, was to continue his cross-examination of Spiegel into another day instead of cutting his losses and letting the hearing conclude in the late afternoon of February 17. Understandably, he wanted to see if he could counter Spiegel's testimony in any way, but by bringing him back to the stand the next day he cleared the way for two revelations: Spiegel's qualification as an expert on police interrogations and, more importantly, the fact that the key test he had given Peter could be considered newly discovered evidence.

Arthur Miller invited Dr. Spiegel and his son, Dr. David Spiegel, also a psychiatrist, to spend the night at his Roxbury home. "We were sitting around talking about the hearing,"

Spiegel relates, "and Miller was telling us about the importance of coming up with new data in the hearing if there was going to be another trial. Well, I had been living with my Induction Profile Test for eight or ten years—it's part of a long research project—but it's only recently been recognized in the literature. David came up with the idea about how we could use this. He remembered that my profile test had been described as something new in the field in an article published only a year ago, well after Peter's trial. Miller really got excited about this because it looked like it might qualify as newly discovered evidence. We telephoned Daly. He loved it."

Back in the courtroom for the final day, Bianchi's continued cross-examination was futile. Because Bianchi had asked Spiegel to list his academic associations, Daly was able, on redirect, to draw out the fact that Spiegel taught as a guest lecturer at the New York University Law School. He participated in a course conducted by Professor Henry Foster which "deals with the quality of confessions and the psychological factors that have to be taken into account in the atmosphere of a confession and how safeguards are necessary to maintain the integrity and the truthfulness of a confession." He said that he was referring specifically to police interrogation.

"Would you tell the Court," Daly then asked, "when, if at all, the tests you administered became acceptable and accepted by the medical, scientific community?"

Bianchi, clearly rattled, protested that "The doctor didn't testify that he had given him any test. . . ."

Said the judge: "Mr. Bianchi, in response to you, the doctor several times referred to tests that he administered to the plaintiff."

Spiegel testified that the profile test he gave Peter—"that measures the ability to concentrate under given test conditions"—had been in development over a period of eight years, but its first acceptance or recognition in medical literature was in February 1975: an article in the *Annual Review of Psychology,* Vol. 26. Spiegel described himself as the principal investigator in the development of the Hypnotic Induction Profile Test.

Daly said he had no further questions. "May I have a few minutes, Your Honor?" Bianchi asked. He took a few minutes and then said, "I have no further questions of this witness."

Bianchi's words were the climax of the hearing. The judge signaled Daly and Bianchi to come to the bench with Dr. Spiegel. Speziale wished to tell the psychiatrist that "While I am not going to prejudge what weight I'm going to give to your testimony I wish to say that you are the most credible expert witness that I have ever heard in my years on the bench and as a private attorney."

Peter and his friends had good reason to be hopeful about the prospects for a new trial, but they would have to wait five long weeks for the judge's decision.

20 ▪ "WHERE THERE'S A WILL . . ."

SGT. KELLY: Oh, Pete, come on. You know it was you.
PETER REILLY: What would you do if something came up where it turned out that it absolutely wasn't me? If it happened?
SGT. KELLY: I'd apologize to you. But this isn't going to happen, Peter.

Peter was in the kitchen drinking iced tea. He wanted to be near the telephone. He had planned to go to work at his high school janitor's job this morning, March 25, but he took the day off after learning that Judge Speziale's decision was about to be announced. "Roy told me not to get my hopes for a new trial up too high," Peter said, "but I had to because I wanted it so much."

A swarm of reporters at the Litchfield courthouse scrambled at nine o'clock to get the first copies of the judge's thirty-four-page, 7,500-word ruling. Judith Liner, one of the most active members of the Reilly Committee, was also present. After glancing quickly over the decision, she raced to a telephone and dialed the Madow house in East Canaan. Peter picked up the phone.

"You've got it, kid," Mrs. Liner said.

"I've got it!" Peter yelled. "I've got it!"

He was crying. So was Hannah Lavigne, "my grandmother." They hugged each other. "I've been crying for a long time," she said to Joe O'Brien. "For almost three years, since this all started." O'Brien had been waiting with them for the call.

Peter telephoned the news to his "mom," Marion Madow. She too wept with happiness. Later, she told a reporter that "All morning I've been trying to describe my feelings. I've been using dumb words—terrific, marvelous, wonderful. But do you know what it's really like? It's like having had a child with an incurable disease and then finding out that there really is a cure."

Peter telephoned his relatives and a number of the people who had helped him, including Arthur Miller and Catherine Roraback. "I'm surprised," Roraback said later when asked about Speziale's decision, "but I'm pleased for Peter."

As the *New York Times* reported in its front-page story, Peter said, "This was my birthday and Christmas present rolled into one." He had reached his twenty-first birthday only three weeks earlier. He was described as "impassive as ever." Reporters asked if he was really as calm as he looked. "Not in here," he said, tapping his chest. He made the front page of the *Daily News* in New York: "WINS NEW TRIAL IN MOM'S DEATH."

Peter was not sure whether he had won just the battle or the war, but he was delighted with the forcefulness of Judge Speziale's decision. The judge had not simply approved the petition for a new trial; he had ruled that "a grave injustice" had been done in his own courtroom when Peter Reilly was convicted of manslaughter. He said that a different result would "more than likely" be reached in another trial.

John Bianchi did not react immediately. He was on vacation in the West Indies. Arthur Miller, applauding the judge's ruling, said, "Do you know what this shows? It shows that if people don't simply accept what's handed down from above, and if they don't surrender to despair, then they change things. They can get justice." Added Miller: "I think Jim Conway was decisive. He spent long months trudging country roads, roaming all over the state, doing quiet, precise, endless work. Without him there might have been a different result in this case. He literally did the work of the State Police."

Roy Daly called it "a long, hard ordeal. A long, long road. I'm happy for Peter Reilly. I'm happy for justice." He called it "a very gutsy decision" on Speziale's part. He said the judge could have refused a new trial by adhering to the established interpretation of new evidence but, instead, "he has written new law."

It is noteworthy that Speziale was not deterred by the prevailing public belief, understandable enough in a nation plagued by crime, that the accused have too many rights and that the courts are too lenient with criminals. The judge knew that those rights exist precisely to protect the Peter Reillys. In a different society, one that is more concerned with punishment than justice, Peter, the certain killer in the minds of the police and prosecutor, would long since have been executed. "Judge Speziale's ruling," said Daly, "is one of the strongest decisions in criminal law in favor of the defendant, including one of the strongest in favor of a convicted defendant, that I have seen in twenty years of practicing law."

Long after the ruling was announced, when she had time to think about the Reilly case in its entirety, Marion Madow said something that many of Peter's supporters believed: "The greatest man in all this was Judge Speziale. To sit there and reverse what happened in his own court!"

Speziale had sequestered himself in his home for two weeks while he struggled with the decision. He knew what he wanted to do, what he felt he had to do, but justifying the unprecedented ruling was something else. He was bound to be criticized for loosening the limitations on new trials even as he was applauded for giving Peter Reilly another chance. He slept little during the fortnight and lost 14 pounds. When he went to Florida soon afterward to rest for a week, he explained to friends who commented on his appearance that he had been on a "Reilly diet."

Roy Daly's brief, written for Speziale after the hearing, must have been convincing: It is reflected in many passages of the judge's decision for a new trial. Daly listed four items of newly discovered evidence: 1) the fingerprint identification; 2) the fixing of the exact time of the phone call to Marion Madow and the resultant shifting of the time of events immediately following; 3) the methods used by Dr. Spiegel in his testing of Peter Reilly; 4) the introduction of a new suspect because of Sandra Ashner's recanting of her statement to the police about Michael Parmalee ("The Ashner statement," Daly wrote, "opened an avenue of investigation which was closed to the defense at the original trial."). He stressed the importance of Dr. Spiegel's testimony because "without the 'confessions' and purported 'admission,' the petitioner is tied to the crime by the barest of threads."

Daly made no argument in his brief about his charge that the State's Attorney had withheld exculpatory evidence. He had been unable to develop sufficient proof. He did say in footnotes, however, that he thought Bianchi had made a deal with the convict John McAloon for his testimony against Peter, and that Bianchi had introduced Gloria Bentley as a witness about Sandra Ashner's truthfulness while knowing that she was a convicted felon awaiting sentence.

John Bianchi, at the start of his own brief, repeated a charge he had made in his closing argument in the hearing. He said then that "Never in Connecticut's history has there been such great media coverage of such a hearing. . . . This is seen by the defense in this case as a calculated effort to influence the judicial determination of this matter. They have attempted to throw a pall over our entire judicial system here and in the country." Bianchi said that "The representatives of the People, however, have confined the presentation of their case to the four walls of the courtroom."

By venting his anger about the pro-Reilly publicity, he risked offending the judge. Speziale surely would maintain that no amount of newspaper, television or public pressure would influence the decision he alone would make.

After the judge's decision was announced, however, an embittered senior police officer said that Speziale was obviously "oversensitive" to public opinion. "The decision is horse-shit," he said. "It's Monday morning quarterbacking." He saw the judge as "grasping at straws" so that he could overturn the conviction. Speaking of Peter Reilly, he maintained that "We had an awfully good case against the little bastard."

Bianchi argued in his brief that the evidence claimed by Daly to be either newly discovered or worthy of consideration within the "totality" of the situation was not. He made no mention, however, of the CBS information establishing 9:50:10 [seconds] P.M. as the time Peter telephoned the Madows for an ambulance.

Bianchi said that the fingerprint identification was new, but that it did not change anything. He said that it only shows that Tim Parmalee "had visited the Gibbons' home sometime probably within a year. This fact contradicts nothing presented at the previous trial. Crucially, this fact does not remove the Petitioner from the scene . . . it does not remove a history of violent quarreling; nor does it eliminate a plethora of admissions." (No history of "violent quarreling," of course, had been established at either the trial or the hearing.)

As for Dr. Spiegel, Bianchi questioned his motives and said that the way he came into the case, at Arthur Miller's request and without asking for a fee, "indicates to the State that he appeared as a friend rather than a purely objective psychiatrist." In any event, Bianchi maintained, Peter's original attorney could have found someone like Spiegel to testify in the trial if she chose; she herself had argued in her summation that the interrogation of her client was "the ultimate in brainwashing."

Peter Reilly, Bianchi concluded, "was convicted on a great deal of evidence. . . . Even if this court should take the extraordinary step of assuming that the jury had before it all of the evidence elicited at the Hearing on the Petition, the result would still be the same. The bottom line, unchallenged and uncontradicted, is that Peter Reilly was present when his mother was alive, and that postmortem wounds were inflicted with the same weapon which caused a premortem wound."

Bianchi urged the judge not to do anything drastic: "The traditional approach, which the State suggests is the only proper one, is, first, to consider whether each individual piece of evidence is, in fact, newly discovered and not previously discoverable; if not, that piece is to be discarded and withdrawn from consideration." He urged the judge to reject the theory, "for which the State knows of no authority," which "would allow one iota of newly discovered evidence to trigger the consideration of any and all evidence a Petitioner may choose to raise, regardless of its relationship to that which is newly discovered."

* * *

In his explanation of his ruling, Judge Speziale said that he was "mindful of the unusual, bizarre and complicated nature of the facts and circumstances of this case. The proceedings before this Court, both at the original trial and at this hearing, have been long, arduous and complex. This Court has virtually lived with all of the many and varied aspects of this case for over two years, and is very much aware of its grave responsibility to exercise cautiously the awesome power of the Court to grant or deny this petition for a new trial. It is well established that sound public policy requires that all litigation come to an end at some point."

However, referring to a principle laid down in two previous cases, Speziale said that a new trial should be granted when it is "apparent that a grave injustice has been done and that the result at a new trial would probably be different" even if all the traditional criteria for granting a new trial on the basis of newly discovered evidence are not satisfied. In a key passage certain to intrigue professionals in the law, the judge said, "It is obvious that newly discovered evidence can logically and reasonably lead to other evidence, not necessarily new, which would then take on new dimensions and importance."

"Concerning the defense case at the original trial," he wrote, "it is important to note the complete lack of any medical testimony to rebut Ernest Izumi's very damaging evidence, i.e., that the plaintiff could have inflicted all of the injuries on the victim without being contaminated by her blood, and also the total absence of any psychiatric testimony to explain the reasons for the plaintiff's confessions to the state police." He called this "a lack of due diligence. Those two serious omissions created gaps in the defense and it is likely that the plaintiff was unable to perceive those gaps because of his immaturity and inexperience."

While criticizing Catherine Roraback, Speziale praised John Bianchi, but he carefully limited himself to the State's Attorney's work before and through the 1974 trial. Bianchi's post-trial conduct was a different story. Speziale said that "The plaintiff has not proved that the State withheld exculpatory material from the defense at his original trial. . . . It is clear to the Court that prior to and during the trial the State's Attorney carried out his duties in accordance with the highest traditions of his office, and that, within the limits of his responsibilities, he made every effort to be fair to the plaintiff."

Speziale generously did not fault Peter's trial defense for not finding out the time of the CBS broadcast. "At the original trial," he said, "Marion Madow testified that the plaintiff called between 9:40 and 9:50 P.M. Since her testimony was consistent with Barbara Fenn's testimony that she spoke with the plaintiff at approximately 9:40 P.M., there would have been no reason for defense counsel, in the diligent preparation of the plaintiff's case, to investigate that issue further."

He said the CBS broadcast time of 9:50:10 "opened an avenue of investigation which was not apparent at the original trial. A new time sequence is not only material but crucial to the issue of whether the plaintiff committed the crime. An injustice was done the plaintiff since he was convicted without an opportunity to frame a defense based on the new time sequence evidence."

The judge was impressed by Dr. Helpern's testimony and "highly impressed" by Dr. Spiegel's. He accepted Daly's argument that Spiegel's testimony counts as newly discovered evidence "since the method of analysis was not available at the time of the plaintiff's trial [and] no amount of due diligence could have discovered it."

Realistically, Dr. Spiegel probably could have testified about Peter Reilly's personality much as he did without his Induction Profile Test. Or another competent psychiatrist could have spoken about Peter's desire to please. Speziale thought highly of Spiegel's analysis; he wanted to fit it into his decision for a new trial; and Daly gave him a good excuse to do so.

The judge did not, however, blame the police for any impropriety in the interrogation.

The State Police were engaged in investigating a brutal and violent slaying. They were justified in considering the plaintiff as a suspect and questioning him at length because of many factors, including his uncertainty, his vacillation, his claim that his mother was breathing when he arrived home, and other behavior, such as his request for a polygraph test.

Nevertheless, this court believes that an injustice was done the plaintiff at his original trial because of the absence of any expert testimony to raise the issue of the reliability of the plaintiff's confessions and admissions. The confessions and admissions went totally unexplained except in the testimony of the plaintiff himself.

Judge Speziale concluded his decision by saying "it is readily apparent that a grave injustice has been done and that upon a new trial it is more than likely that a different result will be reached."

Even though the basic wording echoed an earlier precedent-setting new-trial decision (*Taborsky vs. the State of Connecticut*, 1955), some lawyers considered the judge's phrasing and the overall tone of the ruling to be exceptionally strong and unprecedented. It was characterized as a "hundred-gun salute" because it was such a clear signal to State's Attorney Bianchi to drop the prosecution of Peter Reilly unless he had significant new evidence against him. Speziale had even considered stating it directly in a closing paragraph but decided that it would be improper. He had restrained himself from expressing his criticism of the State's Attorney's actions and utterances in the two years since the 1974 trial in order to allow him to make a graceful exit from the wreckage of the Reilly case. Speziale was not alone in his astonishment when Bianchi either did not get the message written between the lines of the decision or could not bring himself to abandon the position he had staked out so stubbornly.

Peter and his supporters were torn between a desire to see the whole business concluded, without the enormous expense of another trial, and their wish to have his innocence irrefutably established. Peter himself told reporters that "I'm ready to go to trial any time they're ready to take me. The way I feel, I would rather be found not guilty by a jury than have the case thrown out."

When Bianchi was finally reached by reporters on the telephone, he said he still believed Peter to be guilty and would take him to court again later in the year. He expected to base his case on the same information he presented in 1973: "Our investigation is concluded unless something comes up in the interim." He said he would not conduct any inquiry into the whereabouts of the Parmalee brothers at the time of the murder even though the judge had said that the new evidence raises "the possibility of a new, legitimate suspect or suspects in the death of Barbara Gibbons." Said Bianchi: "I consider both Parmalee boys completely innocent. They had nothing whatsoever to do with the crime." He said, "I've seen nothing that changes my mind about this case."

Although at least four newspapers, after separate telephone interviews, published Bianchi's comments that he still considered Peter "guilty," he denied saying so soon afterward when he was confronted by Roy Daly's motion to dismiss the charges against Peter. Daly called Bianchi's comments to the press "highly improper" in that they caused "considerable pretrial publicity." The State's Attorney, he said, while intending to try Peter Reilly on a murder charge, was already proclaiming the guilt of the accused in the press. Bianchi told Superior Court Judge John Bracken that he must have been misunderstood; "The [telephone] connections between Connecticut and St. Maarten's in the Netherlands Antilles leave something to be desired." Daly's motion was denied.

On the very day of his return from vacation, Bianchi engineered the arrest of Jim Conway. Now there were new headlines: "REILLY DETECTIVE SEIZED ON A WEAPONS CHARGE" and "PRIVATE EYE CLAIMS COPS HARASS HIM."

Reported the *New York Times:*

James G. Conway, a 58-year-old former New York City policeman, surrendered at the State Police Barracks [in Litchfield] this afternoon and was released pending a hearing on charges of unlawful possession of a revolver while attending a court hearing on the case. . . .

If convicted, Mr. Conway could be sentenced to serve up to five years in prison. Even if given a suspended sentence, he would lose his private investigator's license and be unable to help with Mr. Reilly's defense in the new trial this fall.

"One does not have to be a genius to figure out what's going on," Mr. Daly, who is also Mr. Reilly's attorney, said after Mr. Conway was released in his own recognizance.

The experience was a novel and humiliating one for Jim Conway. He was accustomed to making arrests, not being arrested. He was booked, photographed and fingerprinted by the State Police. "They read me my rights," he said. In court, he pleaded "Not guilty." Some time later he told Joan Barthel that "When I came into this case, I used to feel like the Man of La Mancha, always falling off the rear end of a horse. Now I feel more like a character in *One Flew Over the Cuckoo's Nest*."

To Conway, Daly and others who were involved in Peter Reilly's defense, the arrest of the private detective was obvious harassment—a continuation of a campaign to discredit Conway and prevent him from helping Peter. To John Bianchi's defenders, Conway's arrest was just another example of the prosecutor doing his duty. Bianchi denied that it had anything to do with the Reilly case. He did have grounds for going after Peter's detective: Conway had a gun permit, but he mistakenly believed that it was good throughout the state whereas it was valid only for the township where he lived.

"Since he seems so diligent in following up this violation," the *Lakeville Journal* commented, "it would be interesting to know how many other persons Mr. Bianchi has prosecuted as State's Attorney for carrying pistols with improper permits."

Bianchi had delayed asking for Conway's arrest until Judge Speziale made his decision, more than two months after he learned that Conway lacked a proper gun permit. On February 2, midway through the hearing, Bianchi told Speziale that Conway had tried to get into the courtroom with a loaded gun. The judge, greatly concerned, asked Daly about it. Daly, himself concerned, checked and reported that nothing of the sort had happened.

The facts were that that day Conway was carrying a gun—a Colt .38 revolver—for the first time in Litchfield County because "I thought I might run into my prime suspect.

He had told me and half a dozen other people he was going to kill me if he got the chance." Just inside the courthouse entrance, Conway told a bailiff that he had a gun and turned it over to him for safekeeping. Later in the day he tried to reclaim the revolver and was asked to show his permit. Conway produced the permit that he had obtained in the town of Vernon. To his great embarrassment, he was told that it was only good for that town and not, as he had supposed, for the state. "It was dumb," Conway says, "I know that. When I got the permit in the first place I just put it in my wallet without looking at it because I was talking to a guy who was there. I hadn't looked at it since."

That there may have been a mission to "get" Peter's detective is evident from the fact that the police made an immediate effort, after Conway checked in the weapon at the courthouse, to determine whether it was a stolen gun. They quickly learned that Conway had rightful title. He had purchased the reconditioned second-hand revolver (which, incidentally, had earlier figured in a criminal case as a stolen weapon) from Colt Firearms in Hartford.

After Conway's arrest, Bianchi told reporters that Conway had taken the gun with him to the second floor of the courthouse and tried to go into the courtroom with it while the hearing was in progress. He said a policewoman at the metal detector had taken the gun away from him. This version appeared in the press. Conway calls it a total falsehood. He is supported by the receipt for the gun he received from a clerk in the downstairs office and by an affidavit signed by Policewoman Irene Welsh which says nothing about Conway attempting to take the gun upstairs or into the courtroom. "Anyway," Conway says, "I never used that staircase or went through the metal detector. I always went through the back way to get to the courtroom since I was part of the defense team."

Roy Daly argued in Superior Court that the new Conway case and the Reilly case were inextricably linked. If there were to be a Conway trial first, he said, it might discredit information that the detective had uncovered on Peter Reilly's behalf. Conway remained under arrest but at liberty while action on his case was deferred indefinitely.

*   *   *

In early July, in chambers with Judge Luke Martin, Daly argued that the reprosecution of Peter Reilly for murder after he was prosecuted for murder and convicted of manslaughter "constitutes a transgression of the double jeopardy clause." He said it would also be a violation of the standards of fundamental fairness of both the United States and Connecticut constitutions and a "conscious overcharging of the defendant by the State in violation of the American Bar Association's standards of criminal justice."

Bianchi, who had told reporters after the Reilly trial that he had believed all along that Reilly had committed manslaughter, not murder, did not object to dismissal of the original murder charge. He declared, however, that he fully intended to prosecute Peter for manslaughter.

In an off-the-record interview in early August, Bianchi said that there would not be any surprises or dramatic new prosecution evidence at the next trial, but the approach and emphasis might be different. He wasn't worried about the outcome: "I don't look at cases in terms of winning or losing. My job is to present a set of facts to a judge and jury. It's up to them to decide a case."

He portrayed himself as a craftsman: a true technician of the courtroom unaffected by petty personal motives. He said he had nothing personal against Peter Reilly. He recalled that he had once helped him out, at his mother's request, so that he could get his driver's license at sixteen. He arranged for an affidavit to be drawn up stating that the person listed on his birth certificate as Peter Gibbons was Peter Reilly.

Two years after that favor, Bianchi was sure, Peter killed his mother. But he offered an important qualification inasmuch as "I can't be sure how the killing took place." His theory was one that a senior detective and other police officers had been advancing in private to reporters ever since Roy Daly had tightened up the time sequence. Bianchi said he thought it possible that another individual was involved in the killing, but he admitted that there was no evidence to support the idea. It was a convenient fallback position for the prosecutor and the police because it provided a way of

explaining how Peter could have appeared unbloodied after
the slaying.

At the time of his arrest, Jim Conway said of the Reilly case
that "This is like an afternoon soap opera. There's one thing
after another. Tune in tomorrow. It just goes on and on. You
never know what's going to happen next."

What happened next was the sudden death of John Bianchi. On a hot Sunday afternoon in late August, while playing golf on the fourth fairway of the Canaan Country Club,
he suffered a massive heart attack and died on the spot. He
was fifty-four years old. He was survived by his wife, his
young daughter and his father.

Inevitably, people said that anxiety about the Reilly case
killed the prosecutor. Close friends called such speculation
nonsense. They spoke of his serenity and self-confidence.
Although some of his Canaan neighbors no longer excused
his actions, Bianchi had maintained, during the two years
and eleven months of his work on the Reilly case, cordial
relations with a number of his friends who were most vocal
in proclaiming that he was prosecuting the wrong man. "I'm
not mad at John," said one of Peter's supporters shortly before
Bianchi's death. "It's just that I can't understand why he has
done the things he has done to Peter. He always waves and
says hello when we see each other on the street and I always
say, 'Hi, John.' " Peter said to reporters, after learning of the
death, "It was a shock. I haven't even thought about how it
affects anything. I'm just very, very sorry about Mr. Bianchi
and for his family."

Bianchi's closest friends and associates found it galling
to see that every news account of his passing described him
first of all as "the prosecutor of Peter A. Reilly" or simply
as "Reilly prosecutor," as if his three decades as an attorney and his many years of community service counted for
nothing. One old friend, Irving Marsh, said, while pointing
out that Bianchi had been especially helpful to young people,
"He was probably the most cordially liked and respected
citizen in our town." The *Lakeville Journal* described him
as "a genial man and an able lawyer doing what he thought

was right in the Peter Reilly case." But the Reilly case had gravely damaged his reputation and at least one friend was certain who was to blame. Patricia Keilty said in a letter to the *Journal* that "It chanced to fall that this man became the object of mingled opinion, simply for doing a job assigned to him. Those who were opposed to him crusaded vigorously, their campaign of hatred masked thinly as a campaign for justice."

Bianchi's funeral in St Joseph's Church was described by the newspaper as "the largest in the remembrance of the community."

> State officials such as Senator Lewis Rome and former Governor Thomas Meskill stood shoulder to shoulder with Superior Court judges and personnel, educators, former Pittsburgh Pirate pitcher Steve Blass, friends and neighbors.
>
> Quiet tears were shed by many in the crowd as five priests sang John Bianchi's soul to its repose. At the close of the Requiem Mass the congregation joined in singing the patriotic anthem "God Bless America."
>
> The casket bearing Bianchi's body was carried from the church by some of his closest friends, passing through an honor guard of about 35 state troopers.

Peter Reilly was in limbo. Technically, he was still under arrest and still out on bail, but Roy Daly had persuaded the court to reduce the bond from $60,000 to $25,000—and a month after Bianchi's death it was cut again to $15,000. In the eyes of the State, he was still a killer, but it sometimes seemed to Peter that if he just waited long enough the State would stop playing games with him and admit that a mistake had been made. John Bianchi, five months after announcing that he would take Peter to trial again, had not even gotten around to filing the "substitute information" charging him with manslaughter.

Peter seldom spoke of how he felt about having to live midway between freedom and prison. "It's hard to get Peter to talk about his feelings," said Geoff Madow. "We mostly talk about cars and when we don't talk about cars we don't talk much." But Geoff also said that "He's been cheated out of two and a half years of his life. Before this happened we were normal American kids. We went around in our cars, never broke any laws. We were friends with all the cops—really friends. Then this happened. We've had to be cautious ever since—no cars, no fooling around, nothing."

Saying that "I'll be happy when it's all over and people won't recognize me again and I can just earn a living," Peter worked hard at living as normal a life as possible. He was anxious to find a more satisfying, better paying job. Largely because the Madows were so involved in volunteer ambulance work, and because his "brothers," Art and Geoff, had jobs with a Hartford ambulance company, Peter decided to take an eighty-one-hour course to qualify as an emergency medical technician. The owner of the ambulance firm promised him a job as an ambulance attendant if he passed. He could double his income.

For several weeks, Peter drove to the Enfield Police Training School to take the course. Three quarters of his fellow students were policemen. "They knew who I was," he says, "but we got along fine." After successfully passing the course in early May, he went to the Canaan Barracks to fill in a standard form so that he could receive a license to work on an ambulance. He soon learned that he would not be treated like any other youth who had passed his emergency medical technician exam.

One question on the form asked, "Have you ever been arrested?" Peter answered, "Yes."

Next question: "Have you ever been convicted of a crime?" Peter thought it over, realized that Judge Speziale had thrown out his manslaughter conviction, and decided to give a negative answer. The attending officer said that he should write down that his case was still in the courts. Peter, no longer so susceptible to suggestion, decided to stick to his guns. He wrote, "No."

Lieutenant James Shay had been transferred from Canaan to a desk job at the State Police Detective Division soon after the Reilly trial. (It was a loss-of-command move, just a year after assuming the Canaan post, that encouraged speculation that his superiors were less than pleased with his performance.) His successor as Troop B commander, Lieutenant Charles Rust, felt that Peter Reilly should not do ambulance work right away. He wrote on the application, "At the present time the applicant has a criminal charge of murder pending against him. I feel that the application should be held in abeyance until the case is disposed in court."

Peter was disheartened by the turn of events. "It isn't fair," he said. "I feel when I have not been convicted, I'm just as innocent as anyone else." But Peter was no longer anyone else, and this now worked in his favor. His effort to get a license and do ambulance work made the newspapers. The stories suggested that the police were determined to make life difficult for Reilly. This was not true, insisted Lieutenant Rust. "It is strictly up to the Department of Health to reject or accept. What I put on I put on as factual." As the pressure mounted, a Department of Health official granted the license.

After that, Peter was frequently photographed on the job. When he and his partner administered cardiopulmonary resuscitation and successfully revived a fifty-nine-year-old woman who appeared to be clinically dead, the Associated Press story about it was published across the country. The press was fascinated by the paradox of a youth saving lives while being accused of taking a life most brutally. His boss praised him as one of his best employees and said he was good for business. Some of the emergency calls to the company asked specifically for Peter Reilly's ambulance.

The Reilly case was stalled until John Bianchi's successor was named and found the time to study the record and decide what to do next. But one formality was disposed of in late September: the acting State's Attorney, Robert Beach, filed the substitute information charging Peter with first-degree manslaughter. Once again, Peter stood in the center of the Litchfield courtroom and pleaded not guilty.

A month later, on Judge Speziale's recommendation, a thirty-one-year-old Torrington attorney, Dennis A. Santore, was appointed to the $31,000-a-year post of State's Attorney by a committee of Superior Court judges. At his swearing in, Santore heard Speziale speak of the "awesome decisions" he would have to make in the future.

The new prosecutor knew that he had inherited the most

controversial criminal case in the state's history. "It was a real baptism by fire," he said later in the year. "This case is one of the most amazing things I've ever come across." As he immersed himself in the history of the Reilly prosecution, he was astonished by the sheer volume of the material. "If anything, it was a larger investigation than the case really warranted."

The more he read, the more he felt that the evidence against Peter Reilly was insufficient to warrant a new trial. On Friday, November 12, he mentioned at the conclusion of a telephone talk with Connecticut's Chief State's Attorney, Joseph T. Gormley, Jr., that he was thinking of filing a nolle prosequi in the Reilly case—in short, to drop the case against Peter. Gormley was the former prosecutor for Fairfield County who had assumed the newly created post of Chief State's Attorney less than three months before the Gibbons murder. He advised Santore to speak to the State Police first.

Joseph Gormley at that stage had no familiarity with the Reilly case and, he insists, no opinions about it. "But if you throw a case out," he says, "you tell the police why. Is it fair to let the cops just sit there and wonder what the hell happened?"

The advice was reasonable. Santore, in fact, had already scheduled a meeting with Lieutenant Shay for the following Monday. He would, in time, be accused of acting impulsively in disposing of the Reilly case but if he had, at this point, simply dropped the charges against Peter without consulting anyone further, none of the revelations, accusations, investigations and general commotion of the following months would have happened. And Peter Reilly, though no longer under threat of imprisonment, would have remained under a cloud: still guilty in the eyes of the State Police and others who would not accept his innocence.

The police did not share Santore's opinion about the futility of the Reilly prosecution. Individual officers were furious at the idea that the charges be dropped. When Santore sat down on Monday, November 15, with James Shay and Captain Thomas J. McDonnell, commander of the Detective Division, he listened to Shay argue vehemently in favor of another trial. Shay was utterly convinced of Peter's guilt. He pulled from the files a pair of documents that he said made it obvious.

Santore had read the trial and hearing transcripts and many other documents but the file was so voluminous that he had missed these items. They were statements by an auxiliary state trooper and his wife, given to the State Police soon after the killing, that told of seeing Peter in his Corvette in the middle of Canaan village and on his way home at about 9:40 P.M. Shay said the statements by Frank and Wanda Finney were important because they indicated that Peter could have arrived at his house at approximately 9:45 and had time enough to assault his mother before making his telephone calls.

Santore was confused. If the statements were that important, why hadn't they been used by the prosecution in the original trial or in the hearing for a new trial? Shay said that he personally had wanted them to be employed against Reilly but Bianchi had decided otherwise.

The first statement, dated September 29, 1973, read:

I, Frank E. Finney, age 24, of North Elm Street, North Canaan . . . make the following voluntary statement.

On Friday night, September 28, 1973, at about 9:40 P.M., I left the Canaan Drive-In movie with my wife, Wanda. We drove south on Railroad Street toward the center of Canaan, and I saw a blue Corvette with a gray scoop on the hood and wide tires enter Railroad Street from Bragg Street. This car followed me to the center of town, but I didn't notice where it turned off.

I have seen this car parked at Barbara Gibbons' house in Falls Village. The driver had long, blond hair and he appeared to be short. I got home at 9:45 P.M. It took me about five minutes to drive home from the movie.

On Saturday, September 28, 1973, I came to Troop B to work as an auxiliary trooper and saw this same Corvette in the troop garage.

The second statement, dated October 4, 1973, was more detailed:

I, Wanda S. Finney, age 31, of North Elm Street, North Canaan . . . make the following voluntary statement.

On Friday night, September 28, 1973, I went to the

Canaan Drive-In Theater with my husband Frank. The movies that were playing were called *Slaughter Hotel* and *Don't Look in the Basement.* We left during the second feature about 9:40 P.M. My husband drove down Railroad Street toward the center of town; and as we passed Bragg Street, a blue Corvette, with a white top with a scoop on the hood stopped on Bragg Street.

As we passed, I looked at the driver who was alone in the car, and I recognized him by sight as the boy who was always driving this car. I am positive of his identity because he used to come in to Mencuccini's Market where I worked as a cashier. I identified this boy as Peter Reilly from a picture that Trooper Moran showed me, today.

This car followed us to the center of town. Then, I didn't notice where it turned off. We drove home. I got out off *[sic]* the car, went into the house, and used the bathroom, then went into the bedroom and noticed that it was 9:45 P.M.

On Monday night, October 1, 1973, my husband and I retraced our steps of Friday night, accompanied by Trooper Moran. We viewed the movies at the Drive-In and left during the same scene and arrived at Bragg Street at exactly 9:39 P.M. We then drove home and duplicated our movements of Friday night and noted it was 9:45 P.M.

Both statements had been witnessed by Trooper Donald Moran and turned over to Lieutenant Shay. Other officers had taken part in a reenactment of the Finney movements on the night of the murder and in the clocking of the drive from the center of Canaan to the Gibbons cottage. A statement was taken from the projectionist at the drive-in theater. He had started the showing of the horror film *don't Look in the Basement* at 7:20 on September 28, 1973, and then had duplicated his actions for the police on October 4.

After the Finneys, in the reenactment, reached the corner of Railroad and Bragg Streets at 9:39, the police clocked the five-mile journey from that point to the Gibbons cottage at five minutes and twenty-nine seconds. Faster and slower speeds gave three other times for the trip: 4:40, 6:30 and 6:40.

The Finney statements had obviously played a major role in the police investigation in its earliest days. That the statements had not been revealed earlier could not be because they had been forgotten. The possibility that Peter Reilly had seen the movies gave the police reason to believe that he had been inspired to butcher his mother by watching the horror-film action. But no one had seen Peter at the outdoor theater and he says himself that "the thing is so crazy. That kind of stuff is the last thing I want to watch when I go to the movies." The drive-in theater manager, Dennis Togninalli, has revealed that he gave special screenings of the murder films for the State Police and that on two or three occasions at an indoor theater he showed them for the police with doctors and psychiatrists present. They were particularly interested in "a part where a woman was all cut up. The woman was slashed in the throat and she was cut up around the breasts and kicked and beaten."

State's Attorney Santore, so new to the case, did not at that point fully realize the explosive character of the Finney statements. They were virtually time bombs that had been ticking away in John Bianchi's files for three years. While he did not agree with Shay that they leaned more toward Peter Reilly's guilt than his innocence, he was persuaded that so much of the detail of the case was in dispute that it would be better to have a trial to straighten the whole thing out. A trial would be fairer for Peter, and the State, than a decision of his own to drop the prosecution.

The day after learning of the existence of the Finney statements, Santore called on Judge Speziale. "I was advising him as a simple courtesy that I intended to retry the case." As he was taking his leave he mentioned, almost in passing, that he had some evidence that had not been used in the first trial: the Finney statements.

"The judge," Santore relates, "expressed great surprise. He indicated to me that, in his opinion, the statements were, in fact, exculpatory and advised me to bring them to the attention of the presiding judge, the Chief State's Attorney and defense counsel."

Speziale was as much horrified as he was surprised. He knew immediately that the Finney statements stood in direct contradiction to Barbara Fenn's testimony about Peter's supposed 9:40 telephone call. John Bianchi had been willing to give credence to her testimony, in the opening minutes of the Reilly trial, even though he knew his files contained evidence placing Peter five miles from the murder scene at 9:40.

Speziale—who had sponsored Bianchi for the State's Attorney's job and had praised Bianchi for having "made every effort to be fair to the plaintiff" in the trial—could only wonder about Bianchi's motives and feel aggrieved by the seeming concealment. He knew that Catherine Roraback, in a motion for discovery and inspection on December 21, 1973, had asked Bianchi for any exculpatory information and specifically for the name of "any person who saw the defendant driving his car on the night of September 28, 1973, after 9:30 P.M."

Bianchi should have handed the Finney statements to the defense at that time, if not earlier. He had kept them locked in his files even as he, and later his associate, Robert Beach, assured the court that all exculpatory material had been turned over to the defense. By his own account, Beach, who had assisted Bianchi outside the courtroom in the 1974 trial as well as in the courtroom in the 1976 hearing, had never seen the Finney statements until just before or just after Bianchi's death.

Beach, who had begun his law career only months before the Gibbons killing, was still on the staff of Chief State's Attorney Joseph Gormley. And he was, as Dennis Santore soon discovered, passionately devoted to the idea of Peter Reilly's guilt.

On Wednesday, November 17, Santore went to Gormley's office in Woodbridge in southern Connecticut to seek his advice. Gormley was glad to help; that's what he was there for. The Chief State's Attorney does not direct or control the independent and autonomous prosecutors in the several counties but he coordinates their work and provides support and guidance when asked. Gormley was a veteran prosecutor who would one day say that "I have a reputation for being one of the fairer people in this business. This doesn't mean I'm easy or a pushover. I'm obviously disturbed that that reputation of fifteen years has taken such a shellacking."

The shellacking would begin not long after this first conference about the Reilly case between the two men. The good feeling at the start would disintegrate into charges several weeks later that one had acted impetuously in his desire to avoid prosecuting Peter Reilly while the other had exceeded the powers of his office as he tried to save the Reilly prosecution in order to spare the police embarrassment. Long afterward, when the dust had settled, Santore would simply say, "Joe Gormley and I no longer talk about the Reilly case."

Santore told Gormley about the Finney statements. Since Gormley had never studied the Reilly case, Robert Beach was called in. He argued vigorously that the statements were *inculpatory* and need not be revealed to the defense. Santore countered that the documents might well be *exculpatory* but he was at a disadvantage in pressing the point. Judge Speziale, perhaps feeling that it would be improper to discuss the situation in detail, had not told Santore about the obvious contradiction with Barbara Fenn's testimony. Santore would have to find that out for himself. Gormley was in the middle of the dispute but he was bound to be concerned about the repercussions of dropping a prosecution that had become so famous, or infamous, in the state. He recalls Santore saying, before taking his leave, "I agree that the Finney statements and the other information provide enough time for Reilly to have committed the murder. How he did everything else after that and made all the phone calls is a problem, but I am going to try him."

Santore maintains that he was not that set on going to trial. "I was still not certain about the significance of the statements. I hadn't put the thing together."

On Thursday, Santore went to John Bianchi's old office in Canaan and rooted through the Reilly files. He read Judge Speziale's new-trial decision and looked over the transcripts. "That's when I put things together and saw the exculpatoriness of the statements—how the defense had been blocked from going beyond 9:40. Then it really hit me. I called [County Detective] Jim Bausch in. I said, 'This is it. This is why the judge feels they must be disclosed.' And he understood it. Then I had Shay come in that evening and I explained it to him, and he understood it. He agreed that the statements had to be revealed."

But Shay did not agree that the charges against Peter

Reilly should be dropped. He "expressed great resentment," according to a judge who later investigated the incident. "Mr. Santore was reminded that he was young and new to the job and it was suggested that if he expected to have the cooperation of the State Police in future prosecutions, he should try the case and allow the jury to render the final decision."

Captain McDonnell telephoned Santore at his home to argue for continuing the Reilly prosecution. He would later berate Santore for not giving the police enough support.

Dennis Santore might easily have followed the example of his predecessor. The late State's Attorney had decided to hang tough, in Watergate parlance, in the cause of Peter Reilly's guilt, and he had been popular with the cops. John Bianchi had been a close friend. Santore and his wife had been on holiday with him on St. Maarten's Island when the bad news about Judge Speziale's granting of a new trial was received. Like Bianchi in Canaan, Santore in Torrington with its even larger Italian population was a local boy who had made good. He had something of Bianchi's appearance, charm and fondness for golf and other sports. He was a husky young man, built for combat. And right now he had the feeling that he was in the battle of his life.

Santore telephoned Joseph Gormley Thursday night, November 18, to say that he now considered the Finney statements exculpatory, without question. Gormley, who was about to go out to dinner with friends, urged Santore to do nothing further until the next morning when they could talk on the phone and arrange another conference.

"When I woke up Friday morning," Santore relates, "that's when I said to myself, 'Whoa! That's enough!' My teaching as an attorney was that on questions of this kind you go to the court," It had just dawned on him that "there might have been some kind of covering up of these statements and I refused to get into any part of it."

Santore took the Finney statements to Judge Simon Cohen in the Litchfield court. And *then* he arranged to meet Gormley and Beach for further discussion. (This sequence of events is misstated in a grand jury report that was eventually made on the Reilly case.) "It was a fait accompli when Santore got here," says Gormley. When Santore pointed out the contradiction of the Finney observations of Peter Reilly in Canaan with Barbara Fenn's testimony, Beach remained adamant that the statements were inculpatory, but Gormley allowed that "if any seven Superior Court judges were to rule on the issue, all would conclude that the statements are exculpatory." (He would express the completely opposite view in a public report several weeks later.)

The problem now was to decide how to deal with the motion to dismiss the charges against Reilly that T. F. Gilroy Daly would be sure to introduce as soon as he learned about the Finneys. Gormley was anxious for Santore to challenge such a motion or at least make the argument in court that the statements were double-edged: useful to the defense but nonetheless incriminating. Santore would later say that "I didn't feel that I should make that argument because I didn't think it was right. I am convinced to this day that they were concretely exculpatory."

Roy Daly, much less Peter Reilly, knew nothing of the crossfire going on among the police, the prosecutors and the judges. Then he received a telephone call from Court Clerk Paul Brown advising him that an additional disclosure had been filed by the State's Attorney and that he should appear in the Litchfield courtroom with Peter for a hearing the following week. He could give no further details.

Daly realized that this could be good news for Peter. On the other hand, it could be bad enough to put him back in prison.

He asked Brown, "Does Peter need to bring a toothbrush?"

"No, no," said Brown, "he doesn't have to do that."

Daly knew then that the news was favorable. He called Peter to tell him about the court appearance, but avoided saying anything that might raise his hopes.

The hearing was scheduled for Wednesday morning, November 24. By that time, Santore had arranged for the Finney statements to be read to Daly on the telephone. Despite the efforts at secrecy, the news leaked. The *Waterbury Republican* announced on its front page that "NEW DATA MAY CLEAR REILLY." Arthur Miller, the Madows and a number of Reilly

Committee members had already learned that something dramatic and perhaps climactic might occur in Litchfield. Once again, the press and spectator seats in the courtroom were filled for the Reilly case.

Roy Daly, with Alan Neigher assisting him, conferred in private with Santore. It was their first meeting. They agreed on procedure. "As I walked out," Daly relates, "I met Judge Speziale's secretary. She said that the judge had called the court that morning to hope that I understood that this development was really coming out of the blue as far as he was concerned. I knew that, of course."

When Daly entered the courtroom he saw Peter, grinned, and gave him a thumbs-up sign. "I knew then," Peter said later, "that it would be okay."

The hearing lasted just sixteen minutes. Daly and Santore stood before Judge Cohen. "First matter on the docket, this morning," said Santore, "is number 5285, *State vs. Peter A. Reilly.*" He explained that while reviewing the case file in depth, "I have discovered two statements in the file which are consistent with the time sequence set forth by defense counsel on the hearing for a petition for new trial." He said that "I cannot advise the Court as to any reason for their nondisclosure" to the defense. After describing the action he took in disclosing the statements, he gave a cue to Daly by saying, "It is my understanding that defense has a motion to present to the Court, at this time."

"If Your Honor please," said Daly, "I do." He mentioned that Peter Reilly was present in the courtroom. Judge Cohen asked Peter to come forward.

Daly said that he viewed the statements "in the same light as the State's Attorney has said Judge Speziale views them"— that is, exculpatory—and so he moved that the manslaughter charge be dropped and that "The defendant be discharged on the grounds that there is not sufficient evidence or cause to justify continuing the information in effect or placing Peter Reilly on trial."

The young State's Attorney said softly to the judge, "Your Honor, for the record, the State would have no objection to the Court entertaining this motion."

The State had dropped its case against Peter Reilly!

Judge Cohen asked Daly to spell out the grounds for his motion to dismiss.

Daly said that the State, despite having in its file these statements placing Peter Reilly "in Canaan and some distance from the scene of the crime at 9:40," put on the stand in the criminal trial "one Barbara Fenn whom I charged on the hearing for a new trial had not told the truth. She testified under oath that she received a call from Peter Reilly at that precise same time and that the call was coming in from the scene of the crime." He noted that the journey from the place where the Finneys had seen Peter in Canaan to the cottage took five minutes and twenty-nine seconds, according to the test run done by Trooper Mulhern. (Mulhern drove faster than Peter says he did on the murder night.)

Therefore, Daly said, the statements are exculpatory and "should have been turned over before the original criminal trial, as they should have been turned over pursuant to my requests during the hearing, and they are inconsistent with the statements made by the then State's Attorney as to whether or not there were exculpatory statements in the file." He added that they were "clearly encompassed in my offer of proof when I wanted to put the State's Attorney on the stand."

The future of Peter Reilly was now in Judge Cohen's hands. A gray-haired man of sixty-seven with a thick moustache, Cohen had long experience as a lawyer, United States District Attorney and Superior Court judge. In somber tones, he read aloud the Finney statements for the record and then said that he wished to make a short statement in regard to the motion to dismiss.

The responsibility of those in the administration of justice, of course, is not to win cases but to see that justice is done. When justice is done, everybody wins. The duty and obligation imposed on the State's Attorney as an officer of the Court is a heavy one. He must be antiseptically free to carry out his responsibilities without fear or favor, and the Court has that same duty.

The rights of the defendant, as expressed in the motion filed by his counsel, require the Court to consider, not only this motion, but the previous trial and the exhaustive decision of Judge Speziale on the motion for a new trial.

This defendant was arraigned before me in this court on a charge of manslaughter, and he pleaded not guilty in the early part of this term, some time, and you appeared with him, Mr. Daly.

This new information which has been brought to the attention of counsel for the defendant and to the Court by the State's Attorney raises issues which make probably effective prosecution of this charge extremely doubtful.

The time sequence involved in the elements of proof in this case augur for less than even—not only positive proof, but circumstantial proof of guilt.

What has gone on before in this case has been an honest and dedicated effort by all involved to bring these issues to a conclusion. This is the final chapter.

I can quote from Daniel Webster in his statement that he made, many years ago; and he said this, "Justice, sir, is the great interest of man on earth. It is the ligament which holds civilized beings and civilized nations together."

I believe, in the best interests of justice, that this case should be dismissed.

Purely as a formality, knowing that the Reilly case was over, Santore requested the opportunity to appeal the decision.

"Under the rules," said Judge Cohen, "I presume you have that opportunity, but I believe that, in order to write F-I-N-I-S to this case, at least at this stage of the proceedings, the motion that you filed, Mr. Daly, is granted, and the accused is discharged. . . . He may be released from custody."

It was over. The audience in the courtroom, having virtually held its breath for a quarter hour, erupted with cries of relief and congratulation. The end had come so suddenly and unexpectedly that it was still too much to grasp. Again, there were tears to go with the cheers. Peter could only repeat over and over again that he was just "so happy" as friends and strangers rushed up to hug him and shake his hand.

"Thank God," Roy Daly said, "for an honest prosecutor."

"This wasn't just a miscarriage of justice," Arthur Miller insisted. "This case was the prosecution of a man whom they knew from the outset was innocent. A few hundred thousand words later and a few million dollars later and we're still back where we started: Who killed Barbara Gibbons?"

"We've gone further than that," Daly interjected. "American justice and the system have finally been served."

Tomorrow was Thanksgiving Day, someone said. Peter agreed that he had plenty to be thankful about. He said that he wanted to give a party for all his friends as soon as he could make arrangements. Right now, the morning was still young in Litchfield and at least two dozen people clustered about as they tried to realize that it was all over—no more money to be raised, no more trips to the courthouse, no more fear that it would all end with Peter in prison. They moved down the road en masse to a local inn and persuaded the manager to open the bar. They celebrated for a while, but Peter looked uncomfortable. "I've got a bad cold," he explained, "and I've just been working a forty-eight-hour shift on the ambulance. I pulled my back out lifting a very large lady. Right now I feel very confused. I just want to go home."

That evening, as the telephones rang constantly, reporters arrived to do interviews and visitors came to offer congratulations. Peter lay in the den, wrapped in a blanket, blearily watching television. He mumbled that he wished everyone would just go away.

Peter was himself again a few days later when he went to work in Hartford and found that his colleagues had strung a printed banner across the ambulance company office: "CONGRATULATIONS, PETER. WE ALL KNEW THE TRUTH. EVERYONE ELSE WAS JUST A LITTLE SLOW." And then the following week he was the happy host when 75 of his supporters gathered at Alexander's Inn in Falls Village for a victory party. Snow was falling as the guests arrived. CBS filmed the event for its national television news. This was the first time in the three years of the Reilly case that the most important figures in Peter Reilly's defense, except for Catherine Roraback, had gathered in one place. It was a mingling of those Canaan citizens who had spontaneously risen to his support and those outsiders—Daly, Conway, Miller, Spiegel, Barthel, Styron, Jacqueline Bernard, and others—who provided reinforcement.

Peter was dressed more conservatively than anyone could

remember in a dark-blue, double-breasted suit, white shirt and a tie bearing the legend "Where there's a will . . ." As he cut the cake for dessert, he said, "It's really been a long, long three years and I guess everybody here has looked forward to this party as I have." He thanked everyone for helping him.

"It's too bad," said one guest to his partner, "that Barbara Gibbons can't be here to see this. I think she would really enjoy being in on the end of the story and seeing how Peter has turned out."

Barbara Gibbons lay in her still-unmarked grave half a mile away. She had been largely forgotten since her death because of the attention focused on her son. But now she was remembered as the Reilly case once again became the Gibbons case. In an editorial, "Shadow Over Connecticut," the *New York Times* commented, "Though the charges that Peter Reilly murdered his mother, Barbara Gibbons, have finally been dropped, questions about this case and the distortions in Connecticut's criminal justice system still abound. Not the least of the questions is: Who actually did kill Barbara Gibbons?"

The *Times* asked:

> Why did Mr. Bianchi prosecute a youngster when he had in his own hands convincing proof that refuted the state's case? Why did no state trooper come forward during the previous proceedings and make known the existence of the exculpatory material? Was there a conspiracy among law enforcement personnel to convict Peter Reilly of a crime he obviously didn't commit?
>
> Something is rotten when a lot of people would go to such extraordinary lengths to cover up the truth in this case. Most of them were law enforcement people or persons close to them. It is an extraordinary scandal which will require of Governor Grasso extraordinary measures designed to re-establish the integrity and credibility of the State Police and the prosecutor's office.

There was a storm of editorial comment, of course, in Connecticut newspapers. The *Vernon Journal Inquirer* said that "If the people of Connecticut care about justice, they should demand an investigation not only of the victimization of Peter Reilly but also of police and prosecution practices generally. Someone must be held accountable."

The *Lakeville Journal* noted that "The job of the State's Attorney is not only to prosecute; in a larger sense, it is to help in the attainment of justice. This, for whatever reason, Mr. Bianchi plainly did not do. . . . The late Judge Learned Hand quoted a warning that seems highly appropriate in this situation, and it applies to police, prosecutors, judges, newspapers and all the rest of us alike. It was Cromwell's plea to his generals before the Battle of Dunbar: "I beseech ye in the bowels of Christ, <u>think that ye may be mistaken</u>."

After Judge Speziale's ruling for a new trial eight months earlier, there were editorial calls for a reopening of the murder investigation and efforts were made by private citizens to persuade Governor Ella Grasso, State Police Commissioner Edward Leonard, and Chief State's Attorney Joseph Gormley to take notice of the apparent scandal. The Governor said it was up to the Commissioner. The Commissioner made some inquiries, talked to the Chief State's Attorney, and announced that he would do nothing further. The Chief State's Attorney said that it was John Bianchi's case and not his responsibility: "I have no control over his decision. I could not command an action one way or another."

The revelation of the Finney statements and the dismissal of the charges against Peter made it impossible to ignore the scandal any longer. Governor Grasso ordered the State Police to reopen the investigation of Barbara Gibbons' murder. "Fantastic," said Peter. "Really fantastic. It's about time," The Governor also directed Joseph Gormley to investigate "the questions raised concerning the use of evidence" in the Reilly case.

The assignment received immediate and widespread criticism because Gormley's own assistant, Robert Beach, had joined John Bianchi in giving assurances to Judge Speziale and Roy Daly that all exculpatory material had been turned over to the Reilly defense. And Gormley had already announced that "I really don't believe John Bianchi would consciously withhold evidence that he thought would be advantageous to the defense. I believe if he did withhold it, he did it for some proper motive in his own mind."

Less than a month later, the Chief State's Attorney issued a twenty-five-page report which insisted that the Finney statements were not exculpatory. He had spent two weeks reviewing the Reilly case and had consulted with "four other State's Attorneys from our largest offices." Despite the Governor's very broad directive about looking into the "use of evidence," Gormley chose to limit his inquiry to the Finney statements.

Gormley argued that "No single definition of exculpatory material has been adopted" and that all of John Bianchi's actions made it plain that he considered the Finney statements favorable to the prosecution, not the defense. Gormley said the statements "could clearly be construed as inculpatory and incriminating" because they were "inconsistent with the defense position that he had no time to commit the offense." (In fact, the defense had not argued that there was "no time" for Peter to kill but no time for him to do that and such other things as removing all traces of blood and disposing of the murder weapon.)

Gormley said the Finney statements contradict those defense witnesses who thought Reilly was still in the village at 9:45. He dismissed the obvious contradiction with Barbara Fenn's 9:40 testimony by saying that "No one," presumably including John Bianchi, "seriously considered her estimation of time as accurate because of its relation to the time her call was logged in at the State Police barracks at 9:58 P.M."

Gormley said he did not know why Bianchi had not used the Finneys in the trial but he noted that Lieutenant Shay and Sergeant Norman Soucie had understood Bianchi to say that he intended to call them in rebuttal. (This would have been difficult to do since it would mean impeaching his own first witness, Barbara Fenn, and raising questions as to why he had not turned over the Finney statements to the defense.) Gormley's own view was that Bianchi, relying mainly on "Peter Reilly's admissions and the medical evidence supporting several postmortem wounds," simply considered the Finney statements to be of little importance. "Mr. Bianchi placed no emphasis on the time sequence, which is borne out by the fact that there is not one single reference to a time in his final argument."

Exactly the opposite, of course, could be argued: that Bianchi, realizing full well the importance of the statements and the hospital logs and knowing that they all contradicted Barbara Fenn's testimony, made a conscious decision to put Fenn's "9:40" into the minds of the jurors and thereafter to steer clear of references to time. For example, Bianchi drew from the witness who had followed Fenn to the stand, Trooper John Calkins, the fact that he had received Fenn's telephone call on the night of the murder but he did not ask when that call had been received.

Denying that Bianchi intentionally concealed the statements, Gormley said that names of Frank and Wanda Finney, as well as the drive-in theater projectionist, were on the original list of witnesses. The defense had been free to contact them. (According to Frank Finney, Catherine Roraback did telephone him but he declined to speak to her. Roraback has said she cannot remember the call.)

Gormley noted that Roraback had stated in court, just prior to jury selection, that "Mr. Bianchi had been most thorough" in responding to her discovery motions. He said of Peter's defense: "They never filed any additional motions for disclosure, never brought the Finneys' unwillingness to speak to them to the attention of the court, and never placed the Finneys under subpoena. The foregoing facts repudiate the accusation of a blatant cover-up in this case."

Concluded Gormley: "I do not believe there is a need for a special prosecutor to further investigate the prosecution of this case."

At a press conference, Gormley described John Bianchi's successor as "a young man who has not had experience." He said Dennis Santore acted hastily in concluding that the Finney statements were exculpatory. Gormley criticized Judge Cohen for freeing Peter Reilly. He believed that the judge had not spent enough time studying the case. Judge Cohen was incensed when he heard this. He told reporters that Gormley "should keep his mouth shut."

Gormley's report amounted to a whitewash of the issues. Roy Daly described it as "irrelevant." Leaders of both parties in the State Assembly were unimpressed. They began calling for the appointment of a special prosecutor to investigate any misconduct by officials in the Reilly case. Instead of dealing directly with the Reilly question, Governor Grasso proposed creating an Office of Special Prosecutor to look into all manner of citizen complaints about the administration of justice in the state.

When it appeared that nothing would be done soon, if ever, Roy Daly complained to reporters about "the continuing conspiracy of silence. They'll continue to investigate themselves and find themselves innocent."

Daly wrote to the Chief Justice of the Connecticut Supreme Court urging him to name a special prosecutor. His appeal to the jurist and his reasons for calling for an independent inquiry were prominently reported in the press. Chief Justice Charles S. House, whose former law clerk was Robert Beach and who had appointed Joseph Gormley to his position, wrote Daly a scathing and sarcastic letter saying that he had no intention of appointing a special prosecutor.

The danger of a cover-up of police and prosecution misdeeds in the Reilly case was real. There were heavy pressures on both Dennis Santore and John Speziale to let things be, but it was obvious to both men that the integrity of Connecticut jurisprudence was at stake. The atmosphere at the time was described by Superior Court Judge Maurice J. Sponzo as one of "concern, criticism, mistrust and lack of confidence in the administration of justice in the state of Connecticut." Santore had spent a number of sleepless nights after the issuance of the Gormley report agonizing about the "constipation of the system" and the constitutional issues raised by the handling of the Reilly case.

Two days before Christmas, 1976, State's Attorney Santore faced Judge Speziale in the nearly empty Litchfield courtroom and filed a "petition for order of inquiry" in the Reilly case. It was a direct challenge to Joseph Gormley's conclusions that no wrongs had been done by the authorities and no further investigation of official behavior was necessary. Santore said in his petition that he has charge of the investigation and prosecution of criminal violations in Litchfield County and "is under a duty not solely to obtain convictions but, more importantly, to determine that there is reasonable ground to proceed with a criminal charge."

He appeared to have John Bianchi and the long-withheld Finney statements in mind when he said that a prosecutor's role is to "see that impartial justice is done the guilty as well as the innocent and to insure that all evidence tending to aid in the ascertaining of the truth be laid before the court, whether it be consistent or not with the contention of the prosecution that the accused is guilty."

Santore asked the judge to take "appropriate action" because of the Gormley report and "other matters" which he spelled out in a sealed affidavit. Those matters had to do with what he saw as an assault on the independence and authority of his office. Recent actions by the police and the Chief State's Attorney had given him the distinct impression that he was being elbowed to the sidelines in the reinvestigation of the Barbara Gibbons murder. This was *his* county, *his* murder, and he was supposed to be in charge, not Joseph Gormley.

Judge Speziale may one day tell the story of the appeals that were made to him to resist any effort to open the Pandora's Box of the Reilly case. All that the public record now shows is that he, like the prosecutor facing him in the courtroom, stood his ground. He accepted and acted on Santore's petition. And then the two men left the courtroom together, visibly affected by what they had done. Connecticut's newspapers made the brief legal exchange and Speziale's "appropriate action" the top story in their Christmas Eve editions.

"JUDGE ORDERS SPECIAL PROBE OF REILLY ARREST, PROSECUTION," said one headline. Speziale had created a one-man grand jury in the person of Superior Court Judge Maurice Sponzo "to determine whether or not there is probable cause to believe that a crime or crimes have been committed within this county" in connection with the Reilly case. Judge Sponzo was directed to name a special prosecutor to help him in his work.

A veteran jurist at sixty-two, Sponzo is a heavy-set, white-haired man of cheerful countenance who soon selected one of the state's foremost trial lawyers, Paul J. McQuillan, as his prosecutor. John A. Danaher, Jr., a private investigator who had served twenty-eight years as an FBI agent, was engaged as a special detective for the grand jury investigation. Sponzo, McQuillan and Danaher dug into the mountain of evidence and paid visits to Canaan and the murder scene. Once again, in the late winter and early spring of 1977, a succession of Reilly case witnesses passed through the Litchfield courthouse, this time to a judge's office in the rear of the building. Virtually everyone who had been caught up in the Reilly case was sworn in and questioned at great length.

Short of a sudden solution of his mother's murder, Peter Reilly considered the announcement of the grand jury probe "the best Christmas present anyone could give me," but he could not help feeling that he was living a roller-coaster life. "It's bad news one day and good news the next," he said. "We keep going up and down and it never comes to an end." Even in the midst of his jubilation about being freed of all charges, he was warned by Roy Daly, as they walked out of the courthouse, not to be surprised if the State Police found some excuse to arrest him again.

The possibility of Peter's rearrest was greater than either Peter or Daly realized. On November 25, the day after the charges were dropped, the State Police received an anonymous telephone call at the Westport Barracks advising them to search the church near the murder cottage for bloody clothes that Peter Reilly might have stashed away after the killing. The abrupt appearance of detectives and troopers at the old wooden church and their collection of bags of dirt and other items made sensational headlines. It was rumored that clothing had been found but State's Attorney Santore would only admit to "something of a material fabric." The articles were sent to the FBI in Washington for examination but it appears that the whole exercise was a false alarm.

Unknown to the press and public, however, was the fact that the anonymous caller contacted the police a second time and identified himself as Robert Joyce, a truck driver and resident of Stratford, Connecticut. He explained that he and his family were friends of Robert Erhardt, the convict who had befriended Peter Reilly in the Litchfield jail and testified on Peter's behalf in the murder trial. Joyce said he had telephoned about the possibility of clothing hidden under the church because of something Erhardt had told him four months earlier. And he said he had reason to believe that the prisoner might have something to reveal about Reilly's guilt if he were transferred away from Somers penitentiary.

Understandably enough, the State Police were intrigued by this information and the possibility that Robert Erhardt would provide proof that the police had been right about Reilly all along.

Chief State's Attorney Joseph Gormley was notified of this development and proceeded to take charge of the Barbara Gibbons murder investigation, at least temporarily, even though the case was the direct responsibility of Litchfield State's Attorney Dennis Santore. Gormley would later insist that he had kept Santore fully informed.

Robert Erhardt was immediately moved from Somers to a cell in Bridgeport prison along with his large scrapbook of newspaper clippings about the Reilly case and his correspondence with Reilly supporters (all of which ended up in Joseph Gormley's office). Soon afterward, Gormley and the police obtained a wholly new account from Erhardt of what Peter Reilly had told him in the Litchfield jail. Peter had murdered his mother, the convict said.

And yet everything in the evidence of the Reilly case indicates that Erhardt's original story of his Litchfield jail conversations with Peter was and is true. Erhardt told the author of this book in a prison discussion in June 1977 that his new version was a total invention because "they" had finally worn him down. He claimed that he had not meant to change his testimony about Peter and had done so only after cracking under "unbelievable pressure." He said it had reached a point "where I would say anything they wanted me to say and sign anything they put in front of me." Explaining himself further in a letter, Erhardt said that "Peter's nightmare started in 1973 and mine was to begin in 1976," on December 2, "and it still haunts me." He had assumed that Peter, Jim Conway and others who had taken him into their confidence would forgive anything he might say under pressure and be aware of how a man can be dehumanized in prison and reduced to "a piece of crap."

Robert Erhardt's tale of psychological torture (he did not charge physical abuse) is not confirmed by anyone else or by the tape recording of at least part of his encounter with the authorities in Bridgeport prison. "People who want to write fiction," says Joseph Gormley, "can say that I and the State Police beat him over the head to change his story and that we ran to the prison to drag him out and promise him all kinds of things. But I've been in this business fifteen years. I was very careful in dealing with Mr. Erhardt because I've dealt with people like him in the past. He is obviously very suspect."

With some justification, however, Erhardt may truly believe that he has been living through a nightmare, and not only since the end of 1976, and that all kinds of pressures led to his apparent rejection of Peter Reilly. His role in the Reilly case is a story within Peter's story, and one that seeks understanding. It is likely that the most decent and admirable thing that Robert Erhardt did in his long history of wrong turnings was to listen to Peter Reilly sympathetically when they first met in the jail, to advise him to get a lawyer, to warn him about other prisoners and to testify for Peter in his trial.

Robert Joyce, whose family had tried over the years to help Erhardt "go straight" and make use of his artistic talents, was not the only person to tell him that he had been a complete fool for going out on a limb for an accused murderer who might well be guilty. Erhardt did not agree, and in fact was proud to be "a stand-up guy" for a youngster he knew to be innocent. He did come to believe, however, rightly or wrongly, that he had jeopardized and perhaps destroyed his chances for furloughs, assignment to a prison farm and other privileges. Certain guards at Somers were "leaning on him," he claimed, and he would one day write that "someone very high up" had said to him, "If it was not for you, you son of a bitch, telling Peter about his rights, phone call, etc., etc., there would not have been all this investigating." And always in his mind, of course, was the memory of his fellow inmate in Litchfield, John McAloon, spinning his garbled story about Peter Reilly's guilt and then, at John Bianchi's recommendation, walking away to freedom with a suspended sentence.

Erhardt also seems to have expected a greater show of gratitude from "the Reilly people." He felt used and forgotten because, once he had given his trial testimony, there were few signs of interest apart from an occasional note from Peter and infrequent visits to Somers by the author and Jim Conway, whose son was a guard at the prison for a time.

Erhardt saw confirmation of his belief that "the system" was determined to make his life miserable in the fact that his application for parole was denied in September 1976. Given his long record of armed robbery and other crimes, and his current five-to-ten-year sentence, it was wholly unrealistic to expect to be granted a parole so soon. Nonetheless, the first questions put to him at the parole board meeting were about his involvement in the Reilly case.

It is not surprising, then, given his bitterness and his desire to be free of prison walls, that Erhardt should have indicated to Robert Joyce that he might change his testimony about Peter Reilly under the right circumstances. On a hot Sunday in August 1976, one month before his parole hearing, Erhardt asked Joyce to contact John Bianchi. Joyce says that he was not told what Erhardt planned to tell the State's Attorney but "he requested me to mention something about Peter Reilly, and about clothes being hidden in an air vent [at the church], and I was to tell Mr. Bianchi that he would not talk to him as long as he was inside Somers." The bit about the clothes, says Joyce, was "to make Mr. Bianchi's ears perk up."

That evening, as telephone records confirm, Joyce did try to reach Bianchi, first at his office, then his home. A state trooper answered the telephone and informed him that John Bianchi had died that day of a heart attack.

Uncertain what to do next, Joyce telephoned Jim Conway to ask him to explain why he thought Peter Reilly was innocent. Joyce felt that he should do something further about Erhardt's message if there was a good chance that Peter was guilty. Conway was convincing; Joyce did nothing more. And he put the subject to the back of his mind after receiving a note from Erhardt telling him to forget the little matter they had discussed on the Sunday of Bianchi's death.

Even so, Joyce relates, "I was sitting on something. I don't know what I was sitting on. The truth? I don't know." He suspected that Erhardt would say anything to get out of prison; some time earlier the convict had made overtures to the authorities about helping the police look for the body of

Jimmy Hoffa, his onetime cellmate in a federal prison. "Bob has lied to me in the past but I can usually tell when he is lying. I like the guy. I'd move heaven and earth to help him get out and go straight and narrow."

Joyce made his move after learning on November 24 that all the charges against Peter Reilly had been dismissed. In Joyce's mind, Peter was now free to walk the streets—and maybe kill again, if he had killed before. And so he called the police anonymously.

Joseph Gormley states that he drove to the Bridgeport prison on the night of December 2 because it appeared that Erhardt wanted to talk to him personally as the Chief State's Attorney. It was a cold night and Gormley says he "damn near froze to death" as he waited in his car outside the prison while State Police officers talked to Erhardt: he was going to drive home if he received a signal that the prisoner did not wish to make a statement about the Reilly case. Also sitting and waiting in his own car was Captain McDonnell. After half an hour, soon after eight o'clock, the two men were told by an officer that Erhardt appeared ready to talk. Robert Joyce, his wife and their grown-up daughter had been brought to the scene to plead with him to cooperate with the police. Erhardt asked to speak to Gormley out of the hearing of the police. "I sat there," Gormley remembers, "with Mr. and Mrs. Joyce and their daughter. We smoked a lot of cigarets. And I could see that Erhardt was thinking: what are you going to do for me? I said, 'Mr. Erhardt, I'm going to do *nothing* for you.' I said, 'If that's what you're looking for we can ring the buzzer now and I'm going home.'"

Gormley stayed, the police came back and Erhardt talked. As a tape recorder was switched on, he proceeded to deliver "a rambling dissertation of about two hours," according to Gormley. He denied his original account of Peter Reilly's first days in the Litchfield jail. He had lied about it before, he explained, because of his hatred for John Bianchi, the man who had prosecuted him for robbing a movie house. (Supposedly, Bianchi had failed to honor an agreement with his attorney to recommend a lighter sentence.) He said that Peter had told him privately that he had killed his mother. They had then set up a personal signalling system so that Erhardt could warn him when he was revealing too much to other prisoners. He stated that Peter had used a bayonet for the throat slashing and other wounds and then had rammed a whiskey bottle into his mother's vagina. Peter had then hidden his weapons and bloody clothes under the church.

(It is noteworthy that Jim Conway, in private discussions about the case, would often speak of his theory that the murderer had used a whiskey bottle for the sexual injuries. Conway would also grumble about the time he asked Peter, because he was so much thinner, to crawl under the church to look for bloody clothes or a weapon, and how Peter was too squeamish to help him. Erhardt had a number of discussions with Conway and such details might have been remembered.)

The convict said he was sorry to have fooled all of Peter's gullible defenders with his original story and to have done an injustice to John Bianchi. But now he was telling the truth, he said.

Soon afterward, Erhardt was transported to a minimum security prison. He says he was so shaken by the whole experience and by the fact that he had changed his testimony that "I lay on the bed for eight days, unable to move." Nonetheless, when Joseph Gormley called on him in late December with a statement giving the highlights of his taped "dissertation," Erhardt signed it. It was not long before he was able to enjoy a day's furlough with the Joyces.

What was the consequence of the convict's recanting of his original testimony, both to the police and to a grand jury inquiry some time later? Noting that "this is the most unbelievable case in all aspects that I have ever been involved in," Chief State's Attorney Gormley says of Erhardt's story that "if we believed what he told us one hundred percent and felt it totally credible, we would have rearrested Peter Reilly, right?"

Peter was not arrested but Erhardt's new version of what had happened in the Litchfield jail triggered an elaborate State Police exercise in the questioning of convicts and ex-convicts who had known and spoken to Peter after his mother's murder. At least a few prisoners were indignant enough to telephone Roy Daly and alert him to the latest efforts of the police investigators.

It is conceivable that, in different circumstances, the combination of Erhardt's new statements and gleanings from other prisoners would have inspired the police to arrest Peter again. But the police knew that the uproar would have been deafening. Once so alone in the world, Peter was now protected against arbitrary moves of the authorities by the sheer weight of public opinion and press attention. Yet this was small comfort at a time when the State Police were actively and expensively engaged in the pursuit of any information that might confirm their belief in his guilt. It was reported that the police had found his old and battered Corvette somewhere in New York State and purchased it. A *Hartford Courant* headline announced that "EX-POLICE OFFICIAL CLAIMS EVIDENCE IMPLICATES REILLY." But the supposed evidence was more than three years old and the story was no more than the belief of James E. McDonald, the former head of the State Police crime laboratory, that "In my opinion, [Barbara Gibbons] was run over by Reilly's car, no question about it."

The reinvestigation of the murder, as ordered by Governor Grasso, took a strange form. The man in charge, Captain Thomas McDonnell, did not have the uncommitted fresh mind that the situation required. He had joined Lieutenant Shay in urging that the prosecution continue. In private conversations he talked about Peter Reilly as the likeliest killer.

The police would not divulge the extent of their operations but it was known that two large investigating units had been formed: one to find evidence against Peter, the other to look into other possibilities. McDonnell assured Roy Daly that the investigation was being handled fairly because the two squads were equal in size and funding.

"Equal?" Daly protested. "You've got one unit going against Peter Reilly and the other against the rest of the world."

At least the unit going against the rest of the world seemed genuinely interested in other suspects. And it had become known that a number of troopers shared the view of an officer who had worked on the Reilly case and had always said that Peter "didn't do it." The new inquiries by the police in Falls Village were welcomed by some residents who believed that one or two murderers were in their midst, but some of the police methods brought reminders of things done in 1973 to firm up the case against Peter. Mrs. Florence Collier, for example, charged in mid-April 1977 that she and her 25-year-old son Wayne had been harassed by the police. She said that Wayne had provided his fingerprints and a handprint and a sample of his hair, and that they had both taken lie detector tests. "They told me they weren't going to leave us alone until we did these things." Later Mrs. Collier appealed to the Reilly Defense Fund for help in paying a lawyer who would advise Wayne as he went before the grand jury. Little was left in the fund but a contribution was made to the Colliers.

The overall activities of the State Police, however, made it obvious that they were still transfixed by the idea of Peter's guilt. Captain McDonnell flew to California to talk to Fran Kaplan about her knowledge of what had happened when she accompanied the ambulance crew to the murder scene in response to Peter's call. Hair samples were taken from persons who attended the Youth Center meeting with Peter. The Reverend Paul Halovatch, who had moved to Washington D.C., refused to provide a sample of his hair, calling the request "outrageous."

Peter Reilly had no expectation that the police would find enough evidence to arrest anyone for his mother's murder. Too much time had passed; the trail had grown cold; and their enthusiasm was suspect. He had greater faith that the grand jury probe would produce fresh information. He was one of 92 witnesses who appeared before Judge Sponzo during the 48 days of hearings over a span of five months. Several witnesses who appeared to be suspects made as many as four visits to the grand jury room. One former resident of Falls Village, known for his violent temper, kicked the doors and yelled his way out of the courthouse after being ejected as too intoxicated to testify that day.

Important events in the Reilly case had often occurred on or close to the big holidays of the year. Now, on June 1, 1977, just after Memorial Day and the dedication of a plaque at Canaan's Little League field in memory of John Bianchi, Judge Sponzo was ready to reveal the findings of his grand jury investigation.

Peter stayed home ("I've seen enough of courtrooms"), but dozens of his supporters went to Litchfield's Superior Court, perhaps for the last time, to watch Judge Sponzo, the grand juror, submit his report to himself as the presiding judge. In his few remarks from the bench he quickly dispelled any notions that he would reveal the true murderer. He seemed to have some idea, however, of whom that person or persons might be. He said he was ordering an addendum to the report kept secret because it contained the list of individuals "who I feel possess the motivation, the opportunity and the capability of committing the homicide of September 28, 1973. This does not mean that there is a basis for prosecuting individuals at this time." The State Police and the State's Attorney would have to make the next move.

Those who purchased (for $30.50 each) the first copies of the 61-page grand jury report learned that Judge Sponzo, while not proclaiming Peter Reilly innocent, had satisfied himself that he had been the victim of police and prosecutorial mistakes and misjudgments; that it was foolish to have arrested him in the first place even though he was a logical suspect; that an injustice had been done to him; and that, "on the basis of evidence uncovered to date, there is no likelihood that a conviction of Peter A. Reilly could result."

Peter's initial reaction to the Sponzo report was one of disappointment. Perhaps unrealistically, he had hoped for a more ringing denunciation of the authorities who had pursued him with excessive zeal. The *Lakeville Journal*'s editorial, while generally praising the report, echoed Peter when it spoke of "the lack of indignation about what happened to Peter Reilly. . . . Perhaps Judge Sonzo was merely being judicious; it is possible to argue that his report is the more effective because of his restraint. Nonetheless, an enormity, a huge wrong was committed because of the system—because of authorities who were blinkered, who were unwilling to admit error. Someone ought to shout about it."

Peter felt that those responsible should not be allowed to go about their business. As he scanned the report in the Madow living room, he found this conclusion:

> As a result of this probe the undersigned concludes that no crime or crimes have been committed by anyone in the Reilly matter. There were errors in judgment. There has been a misapplication of the law. Many persons have failed to appreciate the scope and limits of their powers and duties. Rights of individuals have been violated but the undersigned concludes that this was brought about unintentionally because of overzealousness and overreaction caused by the pressure of massive publicity.

Judge Sponzo, of course, had asked Peter and dozens of other witnesses whether they knew of specific crimes committed by any officials. Amateurs in the law were unable to say whether concealment of exculpatory evidence or harassment of the defense team's private investigator, among other things, amounted to lawbreaking, but witnesses told Judge Sponzo that the whole Reilly case was a crime even if no individual crimes could be identified.

Peter threw down the report in disgust. "After three and a half years and maybe a million dollars," he said, thinking of the whole chain of events, "all they've managed to do is remove one suspect from the list." Marion Madow and others told him, however, that the Sponzo report was more powerful than it appeared at first glance. The judge's details were damning and his criticism of everyone from Lieutenant Shay to the Chief State's Attorney was blistering. As the *Hartford Courant* said in its editorial, Judge Sponzo's findings give "the distinct impression that Connecticut's criminal justice system—especially the State Police and the State's Attorneys—is stuck back in an earlier era, one glimpsed on TV's 'Kojak' or the comic's 'Dick Tracy.'"

* * *

In his summary of the essential facts of the Reilly case, the judge raises questions about the determinations of the authorities to bring out the full truth about the actual circumstances of the murder night. He notes that the distance from the intersection of Railroad and Bragg Streets in Canaan, where Peter was seen by the Finneys, is 5.23 miles from the Gibbons home. "The distance was never revealed at the two trials [1974 trial and 1976 hearing] although the state has possession of a scaled map which had been prepared by a professional engineer." Sponzo says that Peter followed the Finney car for some distance to Route 7. "Frank Finney testified that Peter Reilly operated his vehicle at a normal rate of speed. While driving northerly on Route 7 at this approximate time, Trooper Bruce McCafferty noticed a blue Corvette travelling in a southerly direction at a normal rate of speed."

This is a revelation. It had never before been disclosed that the officer who was the first State Policeman to arrive at the murder scene had seen Peter's car heading home at a moderate speed only a few minutes earlier.

The judge describes the police efforts to reduce the amount of time that it took Peter to drive home that night. Apparently dissatisfied with the first police driving tests of October 5, 1973, Lieutenant Shay one month later drove Peter's Corvette at speeds of up to 70 miles per hour, thus clocking the distance from Railroad and Bragg in 5:29 minutes. Trooper Mulhern, the next day, raced to the cottage in 4:40 minutes at speeds of up to 90 MPH. "There appears to be no basis," the judge comments, "for the driving tests conducted by Lieutenant Shay and Trooper Mulhern at high speeds in view of the observations made by Frank Finney and Trooper McCafferty. In their re-investigation of this case, the State Police have conducted new driving tests at speeds ranging from zero to 50 and 55 miles per hour and these tests place Peter Reilly at his home between 9:47 and 9:48."

The report gives another intriguing time detail. Dr. Frank Lovallo said in his original police statement that he had received a telephone call from Barbara Gibbons about her medical tests at some point between 9:20 and 9:40. But Sponzo writes that the physician "distinctly and unequivocally remembers speaking to her on that evening at 9:35–9:40 P.M."

It would seem, then, that one or more persons carried out their assault on Barbara Gibbons in the ten minutes or so before Peter wheeled his loud Corvette up to the front door. The coincidence of their attack and Peter's arrival is so startling that Joseph Gormley, as an experienced State's Attorney, will argue that the times cited by Judge Sponzo lean more toward Peter's guilt than his innocence. At least, if he had been the prosecutor in the case he would have used the Lovallo and Finney times to show how unlikely it would have been for anyone else but Reilly to have done the killing, and to show that Reilly did have a few minutes to murder. It would be up to the defense to make the case that there was no time for the defendant to rid himself of all traces of blood and dispose of the murder weapon. Judge Sponzo, however, in stating that "there is no factual basis for the police conclusion that Reilly arrived home between 9:43 and 9:45 P.M.," states:

> The Finney statements would have tended to exculpate Peter A. Reilly and if they were not furnished to him it would be constitutional and prejudicial error. When the totality of the circumstances is considered, particularly that Reilly was inspected and examined within an hour after the murder and no blood was found on either his person or his clothing, the failure to furnish the statements becomes of greater significance. It is highly unlikely that a person of Reilly's size could have committed such a bloody murder without getting blood on him if he caused and inflicted the massive injuries, including an oblique fracture of the right femur and a spiral fracture of the left femur, within a period of two or three minutes. Some members of the State Police now theorize that Reilly drove his vehicle over his mother's legs. Under the established time sequence this would mean that Reilly would have had to drag his mother from under the car, carry her into the house, place her on the floor of the bedroom, and inflict the multiple and massive injuries all within a period of two or three minutes.

In exploring whether John Bianchi believed the Finney statements to be exculpatory, Sponzo notes that "It is argued

that neither Mr. Bianchi nor Catherine Roraback appreciated the significance of time in this case." The prosecutor
did not divulge the Finney statements when the defense
attorney made a specific request for the names of persons
who had seen Peter driving home on the murder night. On
the other hand, he did not hide the existence of the Finneys.
Their names were not only on a list of possible prosecution
witnesses for the trial but on a police report of November 7,
1973, describing test drives between the center of Canaan
(including the drive-in theater) and the Gibbons house.

> Although Miss Roraback does not deny the fact that she
> received this report, apparently she did not appreciate its
> value, probably because no reference was made in it that
> Reilly was seen by the Finneys at Railroad and Bragg
> Streets, as described in the Finney statements. The failure
> to provide the Finney statements to the defense defies a
> logical explanation.
>
> The undersigned concludes that State's Attorney Bianchi
> committed serious and prejudicial error in failing to fur-
> nish the Finney statements to the defense inasmuch as
> these statements were definitely exculpatory. Based on
> the theory on which the case was tried by Mr. Bianchi,
> if the Finney statements had been revealed and if their
> contents were presented to the jury, it is more than likely
> that Peter A. Reilly would not have been found guilty of
> manslaughter in the death of his mother, Barbara Gib-
> bons, on September 28, 1973.

The judge concludes that "The conduct of defense counsel during the murder trial was not in the best interest of the
accused. . . . It is evident that if the Finneys had been contacted
and if the time sequence had been probed fully, the conviction
of Peter A. Reilly would have been difficult to attain."

A major portion of the Sponzo report is devoted to the police
handling, or mishandling, of the Reilly case. Lieutenant
James Shay, "described as a versatile, dedicated, hardwork-
ing officer with a strong and domineering personality," was

the man in charge. Some of his work was praiseworthy. The judge relates that Shay, upon learning that Trooper James Mulhern was acquainted with Reilly, called him to duty immediately. He was "purposely used by Shay in the initial stage of the investigation," but "there is nothing to indicate that Mulhern took advantage of his acquaintance with Reilly to obtain any admissions which Reilly may have made."

Sponzo finds little to criticize about the detention of Peter in the Canaan Barracks and the subsequent interrogation except for observing that "on at least two occasions Reilly indicated he was getting tired and would like to discontinue the interrogation, but the requests were not honored." He faults the police, however, for focussing their inquiries so quickly and thoroughly on one suspect: "Although the active part of the police probe continued until the early part of November 1973, one gets the impression that after Reilly was charged with murder the remainder of the investigation was concerned primarily with the elimination of any other suspect." There were many developments that "should have caused the police to review their investigation."

The judge denounces the police for relying too much on lie detector tests, especially since "it is clear the tests were used principally to eliminate suspects and to prepare a stronger case against Reilly."

The great reliance on the polygraph tests seemed to impede the investigation. The use of polygraph tests in this probe confirms the wisdom of our rules of evidence in prohibiting the admissibility of the polygraph results as evidence. In one instance Michael Parmalee and Sandra Ashner made contradictory statements about the whereabouts of Parmalee on the evening of September 28, 1973. Both persons consented to take the polygraph test administered by the State Police and both were found to be truthful. As a result of these tests and tests given to other suspects the police curtailed their investigations of those persons in the early stages of the investigation. The failure to investigate other reasonable suspects with the same intensity and vigor as applied to Peter A. Reilly is hard to understand.

"Very little was done" to identify the identifiable finger-print and palm print found on the cottage doors. "Much of the questioning of suspects was cursory and superficial," Sponzo continues. "This is attributed to lack of morale and efficiency. Troopers testified that while they complied with the orders of their superior, they would do nothing further because they were not permitted to voice suggestions or opinions." Coordination of the investigators and the police laboratory specialists was so bad that, for example, "the contents of the bathtub trap were never analyzed and this was not discovered until recently."

Judge Sponzo severely criticizes the State Police in their reinvestigation of the Gibbons murder for pursuing the dis-credited theory that Peter Reilly ran over his mother with his car. "The only conclusion drawn by undersigned is that some State Police are determined to vindicate their position that there was no error made in the arrest and conviction of Peter A. Reilly."

Disclosing that Robert Erhardt had changed his testimony about Peter's innocence, Judge Sponzo comments:

> During the re-investigation the police have taken numer-ous statements from persons who were inmates at the time of Reilly's incarceration and some indicate that Reilly made damaging statements and others indicate otherwise. The undersigned rejects the testimony of these inmates because their motives are suspect. Many inmates make statements with the hope of ingratiating themselves to the authorities in the expectation of receiving a lenient sentence, such as the suspended sentence received by McAloon, or in the hope of having their request for parole favorably considered as in the case of Erhardt.

In contrast to his denunciation of the police investigation, Sponzo has high praise for the private detective who "devoted countless hours" to Peter Reilly's cause: "The conduct of the private investigator, James G. Conway, is to be commended. He embarked on an investigation more than a year after the homicide had occurred and after Reilly had been convicted. He met resistance from the police and certain witnesses, whose activities were suspect. He persisted in his investigation which led to evidence that brought about the granting of the new trial."

There was more than just resistance to Conway's efforts. After confirming the harassment charges made by Roy Daly and Conway in and out of court, Sponzo says that "This conduct on the part of an organized police organization has to be terminated if the constitutional right to a fair trial is to have any meaning. A thorough investigation on behalf of the accused is a necessity in providing a proper defense."

(Jim Conway, of course, was still under arrest and facing trial on charges of carrying a dangerous weapon. Two weeks after Judge Sponzo's report was issued, Dennis Santore announced that he did not choose to prosecute, and a judge dismissed the charges. Now as free as Peter Reilly, Conway called it the "final vindication.")

The grand juror is equally strong in condemning the police pressures on State's Attorney Dennis Santore prior to the dismissal of the charges against Peter. "While it is understandable that, in a case saturated with publicity, a *nolle* or dismissal of a charge might be construed as inefficiency or incompetency on the part of the police or might result in adverse comments or publicity, this cannot be of concern to a prosecutor. His duty is to see that justice is done. If justice demands a trial, a trial must be held, and if justice dictates a *nolle* or dismissal, then that course must be pursued."

Saying that the State Police "in no way were involved in the suppression of the Finney statements," Judge Sponzo observes that Lieutenant Shay's "strong and exaggerated" expression of feelings to Santore "was more out of frustration than a threat to the State's Attorney's office." Chief State's Attorney Joseph Gormley, however, is less generously described. In the judge's opinion, he exceeded his jurisdiction in taking charge of the reinvestigation of the Gibbons murder "to the complete exclusion of the State's Attorney of Litchfield County." (Gormley denies that he took charge of the case or tried to undercut Santore.) As for Gormley's own investigation into the alleged concealment of the Finney statements, the Chief State's Attorney is said to have depended too much for his information on the very persons he was probing. "It appears that the primary objective of his investigation and subsequent report to the Governor was to justify and protect the actions of the State Police, Mr. Bianchi and Mr. Beach with respect to their insistence that the Finney statements were inculpatory. . . . This conclusion is bolstered by Mr. Beach's opinion that the guilt or innocence of Reilly should be determined by a jury and not by the court or a prosecutor. Mr. Beach has failed to understand and appreciate the primary duty of a prosecutor . . . which duty is not merely to convict but to see that justice is done."

(In late June 1977, despite Judge Sponzo's findings and the protests of Justice Speziale and another justice, Chief Supreme Court Justice Charles S. House reappointed Gormley to a second four-year term as Connecticut's Chief State's Attorney. If Gormley was in error in the Reilly case, the jurist told the press, "it was an error in judgment and, after all, we're all human and make mistakes in judgment from time to time.")

The one-man grand jury, in finding so many people to blame for the scandal of the Reilly case, did not spare Reilly himself. It appears that he was at fault for being himself and for reacting as he did, in keeping with his personality at the time, to the most shocking and devastating experience of his young life. In Judge Sponzo's view, "Peter A. Reilly himself caused many problems which contributed to his arrest and conviction. During the initial stage of investigation, his abnormal behavior was a significant factor leading to the judgment of the police that he was a suspect. His failure to exhibit natural emotions, such as crying, hysteria, remorse or concern, impressed the investigators that he might be involved." And then, of course, he had made "strange and unusual remarks" and ultimately signed a confession.

The judge might have considered what would have been Peter's fate if he had acted "normally" and had hysterically entered the bedroom to try to revive his butchered parent. He would have been found by the police covered with blood.

Every so often, in an interview or an encounter with a stranger, Peter Reilly would be asked to explain how it was possible for an innocent person to be judged guilty—and why, in the wake of his mother's death, he had believed for a while that he was guilty. He would say of the interrogation that "It really got down to a point where I was almost two people, one looking at the other. One of me looking at the other of me. It's kind of hard to understand."

By the time the grand jury report was issued, Peter was twenty-two years old, and when he looked back to the eighteen-year-old Peter of 1973, he could scarcely recognize him. He found it difficult to believe that he had once been so naive and gullible. "I'd always believed the justice system worked," he would say, "and then for a while I saw it wasn't working. I lost my faith in that. And now I can see how people can make it work." He had learned that "I have to push for what I believe is right. I learned to depend upon myself, to stand up for myself." And he would tell his friends, "You know, in a funny kind of way, this whole experience has done some good things for me. It made me grow up—very fast."

He had grown up. Indeed he was two inches taller. He had become a mature young man who had survived his ordeal with uncommon grace. His sense of humor was intact. He could see the irony in the way the tables had turned, but he rarely spoke meanly of those authorities, now so discomfited or dead, who had accused him.

Peter often wearied of all the attention he received as well as the tension he lived under, and he would say that "I'd still like to think of myself as an unknown kid from northwest Connecticut." But he was shrewd enough to realize that the Peter Reilly case had been the making of Peter Reilly. He had self-confidence now. He was a member of a family. He had a legion of friends, including persons of fame and influence. He thought now that he would seriously take up the study of the guitar while attending courses in business administration and business law; perhaps someday he could combine his love of music with a management career, working within the music industry.

"I wasn't able to make plans before," he said in early 1977. "Now anything is possible." He was not the same person he would have been if a murderer had not torn his life apart.

Peter would often say of his mother that "I can't describe how much I miss her. When I think of her now, I think of her sense of humor. She would do anything for a laugh." In his remembrance of things past, he chose the good parts and put aside the bad.

Perhaps this was an escape of sorts. Dr. Spiegel believed that Peter was still putting his emotions "on hold." He had yet to react fully to the tragedy he had walked into one September night. But this was Peter's way to be happy and he was without bitterness. And he could still say, as he did so soon after the murder, "This is an interesting case."

EPILOGUE

My home in the Litchfield Hills is half an hour's drive south of Falls Village. Until September 1973 I had never heard of Barbara Gibbons or Peter Reilly. After his arrest and conviction I became aware of Peter only as a name in our weekly newspaper and as the central figure in a criminal case that had captured the imagination of my wife and my younger daughters.

Julie and Carol often talked about Peter because he had been a high school classmate of theirs. I thought it was loyal of them to speak with such certainty of his innocence but I remembered other cases involving angelic youths who, in the eyes of their friends and neighbors, could not conceivably be guilty, but were.

I was working on a book about India, and I made a deliberate effort not to become too interested in the Reilly case. My journalistic experience is as a foreign correspondent, not a crime reporter, and I had problems enough trying to understand the difficulties of 600 million Indians. However, Carol became a friend of Peter's friends in Canaan; they, and he, began calling at our old farmhouse in Kent. They were a lively, light-hearted group and we enjoyed seeing them. Peter stayed for dinner one Sunday, and my mother-in-law remarked afterward that "he was such a nice boy I could hardly believe that I was dining with a convicted killer."

I became increasingly aware of the incongruity of Peter's situation. After all, he had been charged by the State and condemned by a jury for a slaying of frightful savagery. Yet here he was, dating the local girls, finding doors open to him everywhere, and living the life of Reilly. Seemingly, everyone—or just about everyone—in our corner of Connecticut took for granted that the authorities had made a terrible mistake. To know Peter Reilly was to know that he was innocent. It was as simple as that.

So simple, in fact, was this supposition that I could not accept it. I was confident that the State would not have prosecuted Peter without good cause. Only later did I see that the case was, as Arthur Miller has said, an instance of pure injustice. Like others who had taken an interest in Peter, I felt an obligation to act once I recognized that a miscarriage of justice almost surely had occurred and that his imprisonment was being sought by officials too irresponsible or too cowardly to admit the error that had been made.

I proposed to Peter and his attorney that I write a book about the case under an exclusive arrangement that would provide him with half of all my earnings from this work and from the motion picture that is to follow. If all went well, he might be able to settle the huge debt of the three-year defense effort mounted on his behalf and have something for his future.

The terms of my collaboration contract with Peter have left me completely free to follow the truth wherever it led—even to his guilt, if that be the case. Neither he nor Roy Daly ever asked for the right to approve, or disapprove, the content of this book. Peter's automatic acceptance of my conditions, like his refusal of the prosecutor's plea-bargaining offer, can be seen as the natural act of a young man who knows that the truth is his best defense. I think it noteworthy that Peter's demeanor throughout his long ordeal, including the hours of interrogation when he was accused of playing "head games," has been straightforward and free of guile. Indeed, his openness was his undoing. If he had not cooperated so willingly with the officers he trusted, if he had exercised his constitutional right to remain silent, there would have been no case against him.

My early skepticism about the claims for Peter's innocence was not the result of naiveté about the shortcomings of our judicial system. I was familiar with celebrated cases of defendants victimized by corrupt policemen, overly ambitious prosecutors or prejudiced judges. In the season of Watergate I was not surprised by instances of misbehavior by those sworn to uphold the law.

In Peter's case, however, not even his most fervent defenders in Canaan were claiming that the authorities had deliberately set out to railroad him. To the contrary, they spoke of the prosecutor, John Bianchi, as a genial fellow townsman and of the Canaan barracks officers as familiar and friendly figures who had lost their way in the Reilly case. Only in the later stages of the case did they see what was apparent to Peter's more experienced supporters and ultimately to myself: that some of the authorities were not truly concerned about seeing that justice was done. So long as the police and their defenders within the State's Attorney system could insist on Peter as the undoubted murderer, so long would the magnitude of their mistake be disguised.

Unlike a youth in a violent city ghetto, where the police and many juveniles are virtual combatants, a youngster in a small town like Canaan benefits by the protective instincts of the community. A boy like Peter who has a good personal reputation and who is notably respectful of his elders can feel assured that the impulse of the authorities is to help rather than hurt him in a time of trouble.

Although no one in a small town is anonymous, Peter was particularly known to the man whose actions would determine his future. John Bianchi had generously given legal advice to Peter's mother from time to time. If he had concluded, surely with reluctance, that Peter was guilty of her slaying, I reasoned, and if twelve jurors had heard the evidence and reached the same conclusion, then in all probability he was guilty.

Nothing then so astonished me in my research for this book

as the discovery that there was no case against Peter Reilly—
at least no case that could stand the scrutiny of an independent
observer. Expecting to find at least a fragment of physical evidence or the testimony of a reliable eyewitness to link him to
the murder, I found that all the evidence was circumstantial
and much of it implausible. As in the fable about the emperor's
new clothes, the State's case seemed to have substantial gar-
ments of evidence when, in fact, there was nothing there.

The case against Peter was nothing more than an artful construction of his own confused utterances in the aftermath of
the most traumatic experience of his life: his stated belief that
his mother was still breathing when he found her; his speculation about how he might have killed her after succumbing to
police assertions that he had done so; and his repetition of his
"confession" to two state troopers after the interrogation.

These words, plus his bad luck in arriving home so soon
after the attack on his mother, were all that John Bianchi
had against him. The prosecutor added certain embellish-
ments while making sure that the defense did not see all of
the material to which it was entitled.

Most useful to the prosecution's case was the testimony
of four persons: a state trooper who claimed that Peter had
actually said "I killed her"; the wife of another state trooper
whose version of events put Peter on the murder scene
at 9:40; a convict whose tale of Peter's disposal of bloody
clothes helped save the convict from paying the penalty for
his various crimes; and a pathologist all too willing to state
that a particular kitchen knife was the precise instrument that
caused the postmortem mutilation of Barbara Gibbons.

The case against Peter Reilly was a travesty. Why did it happen? And why did the State persist in its folly despite innumerable signals that a mistake had been made?

G. K. Chesterton once said that "The horrible thing about
all legal officials, even the best, about all judges, magistrates,
detectives and policemen, is not that they are wicked (some
of them are good), not that they are stupid (some of them are
quite intelligent), it is simply that they have got used to it."

In the matter of Peter Reilly, the concerned legal officials were so accustomed to processing criminal cases (even though a homicide as gory as the Gibbons killing is a relative rarity in Litchfield County) that they failed to see that they were dealing with an exceptional personality in exceptional circumstances.

Routinely, a confession was extracted from the handiest suspect, Peter Reilly. From then on, the few incriminating sentences of the signed document were all that mattered in the minds of the police and the State's Attorney. The interrogation tapes were put on the shelf. "The nature of the confession is irrelevant," one officer told me. "The fact that he confessed is what counts."

John Bianchi did not listen to the tapes before taking Peter to trial, as if unaware of the possibility of a false confession. (Yet he must have known that the famous Miranda ruling of the Supreme Court centered on the quality of statements drawn from suspects under the coercive conditions of police custody. The majority opinion stated that "The aura of confidence in his guilt undermines [the suspect's] will to resist. He merely confirms the preconceived story the police seek to have him describe.") Although the police in the Reilly case should have suspected that they had arrested the wrong man when the physical evidence of the crime failed to confirm the confession details, they blundered on with their investigation. While the true killer or killers escaped detection, the police concentrated their efforts on establishing Peter's guilt.

Bianchi accepted the results of the investigation uncritically. Then the highly vocal public concern about Peter, expressed within hours of his arrest, appears to have solidified the police and the prosecutor in their commitment to Peter's guilt. Very likely they were sincere in their belief that he was the murderer. Even if they had doubts later, there was no turning back.

When I began my research into the case I listened with great skepticism to the claims of some of Peter's supporters that the State Police would go far to prove that they had not arrested the wrong man, In fact, I was greatly impressed when Police Commissioner Edward Leonard, who was then not well informed about the Reilly case, spent four hours in April 1976 listening to my reasons for believing that the police had bungled. "I know it would be embarrassing for the department to reopen the investigation," I said. He assured me that "I'm not concerned about embarrassment. We'll do what's right." I was later informed that the commissioner had studied the case and could find no reason to reopen the investigation.

At that same time I called on Cleveland Fuessenich, the retired police commissioner, to ask him to read the Reilly interrogation transcripts and other case materials and to advise me whether I was wrong in my belief that something was obviously and terribly wrong about what had happened to Peter Reilly. I offered the opinion that the State's Attorney for Litchfield County seemed dedicated to putting an innocent person behind bars. Fuessenich was disturbed enough by the documentation to suggest that I take my story to Chief State's Attorney Joseph Gormley. In fact, he offered to telephone Gormley and recommend that he see me. Gormley, however, said in effect that he knew nothing about the Reilly case and wanted to know nothing. It was John Bianchi's responsibility and it was not his place to interfere.

What about John Bianchi? The police behavior in this case might be suspect, but it was his responsibility, not theirs, to take the case into the courtroom. Although sworn to see that justice is done, prosecutors have been known to place the winning of a conviction ahead of other considerations. Was this true of Bianchi, a proud and ambitious man under fire?

A psychiatrist who has studied the Reilly prosecution characterizes the late State's Attorney as "an evil man." I disagree. I think it fairer to say that John Bianchi was more careless than calculating at the start of the Reilly case and then fearful and desperate at the end. Though he brought his troubles on himself, I consider him to be the most tragic figure of this long, sad story and I think it likely that the tension he lived under did indeed contribute to his early death.

He was caught in a trap of his own making. He had proclaimed his intention to stage a second Peter Reilly trial but the only fresh evidence that he could introduce, unless more convicts would agree to testify against Peter, could only be revealed at great risk. If he tried to show that Peter ran over his mother with his car before killing her, using the three-year-old beliefs of former State Police Lieutenant James McDonald, then he undermined Dr. Izumi's conclusions about the before-death and after-death injuries and wounds. If he tried to employ the statements of Frank and Wanda Finney, he would expose himself as a prosecutor who had concealed obviously exculpatory evidence from the defense and the Court.

Judges and attorneys who knew Bianchi well and considered him a good man and a valued friend say that he became a different person as Peter Reilly's new defense team pressed on and triumphed in the new-trial hearing early in 1976. Even one of his own associates in the hearing knew that the prosecutor had been less than scrupulous in honoring defense motions for exculpatory material. Joseph Gallicchio, the widely respected Torrington attorney who had been assigned to assist Bianchi, found himself in frequent disagreement with the State's Attorney. "John gave Roy Daly a helluva time with regard to producing evidence," Gallicchio recalls. "He would say he'd turn something over, then he wouldn't do it. He would require Daly to go through the whole legal process: if you want this from me, file a motion. That type of thing. Whereas my attitude was, what the hell's the difference? If he's entitled to it, give it to him. What are we trying to do here?" On one occasion, seeing Bianchi stalling about giving Daly the army report on Mike Parmalee's homosexual hoax, Gallicchio announced that he was going to give Daly the document, and did.

The attorney believes that Bianchi became bitter about Peter Reilly's defender. "Roy Daly is a very, very effective cross-examiner and very good at chipping away at everything. As a trial goes on you can get emotionally involved and that's what happened here. I think John lost his cool now and then."

John Bianchi's state of mind was revealed midway through the hearing when he muttered "You bastard!" at Roy Daly loudly enough to be heard by Mrs. Daly, Joe O'Brien and others in the courtroom but not by Daly, Judge Speziale or even the court reporter. It was an uncharacteristic comment because Bianchi, the almost priest, rarely used profane language. The highly unprofessional outburst could have disrupted or even scuttled the hearing, but Daly and Speziale, after learning of it, agreed to let it pass. Word was sent to the press that the judge would take a stern view of any reporting of the "You bastard!" incident, and it was not made public.

A friend and defender of Bianchi's said after the decision for a new trial that "John has to feel very defensive these days. You can see physically how much this case has hurt him when questions are raised about his integrity and his character. He won't let on, however, because he is so used to being in the public eye and being admired. He's a man who really does enjoy life. He liked to relax, let his hair down, hang around with the cops." Other friends noticed that he had begun to drink more heavily than usual.

Relaxing and being one of the boys was part of Bianchi's undoing. His colleagues in the law would admit that he could be surprisingly casual about important legal matters—sometimes "lazy" and "sloppy." Even in the midst of the Reilly trial he would go off to the Caribbean for weekends at a St. Maarten's resort hotel. One lawyer called him "a good, earnest attorney but he was not what you would call meticulous."

I believe that John Bianchi simply did not realize—or take the trouble to realize—the kind of case he had in his hands when he embarked on the prosecution of Peter Reilly. He virtually dismissed as unimportant the nature of the interrogation that produced the confession. He did not mean to railroad Peter, at least not at the start, because he was sure of Reilly's guilt and doubtless felt no qualms about twisting the circumstantial evidence or even concealing evidence to win a conviction. He certainly could argue to himself that he was only doing what is all too common under our adversary system of justice: going all out to win. In his inspirational speeches to Little Leaguers and at sports banquets he was accustomed to saying that winning is the most important thing.

Joseph Gallicchio, musing about the ways of prosecutors, says that "they rely so much on police evidence, and they associate so much with the cops, that if the police are convinced, they're convinced. If you're as prosecution-minded as John Bianchi was after so much experience representing the State, it goes against their whole law upbringing to deliver stuff out of their files. These rules for disclosure and production are still new. Eight or ten years ago prosecutors wouldn't give you the time of day. They're all fine gentlemen, of course, but they feel their duty is to convict."

A few months before his death, John Bianchi, as charming

and easygoing as ever, spoke to me for over an hour about his
confidence that no mistake had been made in the prosecution
of Peter Reilly. Not only was Peter guilty, he said, but he
failed to see what the fuss was about and why people thought
the case was exceptional. It had all been quite routine. He had
on his hands two other homicides that were "more interesting
than the Reilly case."

I asked him how he reacted to the support that Peter was
receiving in the town and elsewhere. "Do you feel that it is
you versus the community at this point?"

"Oh, gosh no," he said.

"Well, you are trying to put into prison, it would seem, a
kid who has a lot of friends in the area. What does this do
to you?"

"Not a thing," he replied.

"You're a very popular man in Canaan," I said. "Or you
were until September 1973."

Bianchi laughed and said, "Well, you've heard of that old
term, the Silent Majority. You ought to hear my phone ringing on and on with people saying just the opposite of what
you hear in the press. Now, the people who are helping Peter
are good friends of mine. I don't think they hold any animos-
ity towards me. They realize I have a duty to do, that I represent the people of our county. And I think I do my job as best
I can and, of course, *I* don't make the decision to send him
to jail, sir. That is done by the jury and the Court. I simply
present to them the evidence that is available to me in the
best manner that I can."

"But why," I persisted, "are you personally so convinced
of Peter's guilt?"

"Somewhere along the line, Mr. Connery," he answered,
"ask yourself this question: How would I have reacted if I had
spent eighteen years living with Barbara Gibbons?"

And so, at the end, it all comes back to Barbara Gibbons—
and Peter's guilt by association. Nothing is more apparent to
me in the Reilly case than the complete misreading by the
authorities of the relationship between Peter and his mother.
That relationship was something they could not or would not

understand, just as they misread Peter's personality. They were led astray by their failure to perceive that between mother and son there was more tenderness than hostility and more comradeship than conflict.

Once settled on their theory of the case, they either lacked the imagination to realize that they had erred or the courage to admit it. To what extent did they realize that Peter was innocent but pursued him nonetheless to save face?

I think it likely, in a case that is striking for its psychological overtones, that the authorities brainwashed themselves into believing that they had caught the true killer. Willfully ignorant or woefully unprofessional, they closed their minds to every development that should have inspired them to reexamine their conclusions.

When I asked legal officials at all levels, from the police commissioner and the prosecutor down to the troopers who followed orders, how they could believe something that seemed unbelievable to so many citizens, their answers betrayed their mentality. "The press is always criticizing us for one thing or another." "The public doesn't understand these things." "We don't have enough manpower." "They expect us to play Sherlock Holmes." "These people are just looking for the publicity." "We know many cases where guilty people go free. This one is no different." And in the words of one trooper, "How do I know how Reilly killed his mother without getting blood on him? Maybe he took off all his clothes before he did it. All I know is that he did it."

In the normal course, Peter Reilly would have disappeared into prison, just one more penal-system statistic. He resembled the young man described by Piri Thomas in *Down These Mean Streets:* "A baby-faced, small-framed, good-looking kid who looked about fourteen years old, he was perfect prey for the jailhouse wolves."

Peter was saved from the wolves by the intervention of friends and strangers who were not content to accept the official doctrine over their own perceptions. His case was the stuff of melodrama, but it was real life too, and all who were drawn to his cause were bound to ask, How many more Peter Reillys are there?

AFTERWORD

A conceit of old-school journalism is that "Good reporters have no friends, only sources." Keep your distance. Just tell the story. Don't become part of it.

But what do you do if you see a law enforcement juggernaut crushing the life out of a boy who did nothing wrong?

At the beginning of the Reilly case, my acquaintance with cops, courts and prisons was confined to the mockery of justice carried on in the dictatorships I had known during the Cold War. Sharing the popular belief that America has the best of all justice systems, even if imperfect, I was as uninformed as everyone else about wrongful convictions.

Mistaken prosecutions and imprisonments were still viewed as rare. This was before the present age of DNA exonerations and innocence projects. Now we are flooded with new knowledge about the magnitude of false eyewitness identifications, false confessions, junk science, police ineptitude and perjury, mindless or overzealous prosecutors, lazy or dimwitted judges, and clueless or corrupt defense attorneys.

Back in the 1970s, when correcting an unjust conviction

was close to impossible, the best known victims of the legal system were fictional characters.

Henry Fonda was *The Wrong Man* in the Hitchcock film. Jimmy Stewart played the Chicago reporter who saved an imprisoned innocent man in *Call Northside 777*. Alabama justice was on trial in the book and film, *To Kill a Mockingbird*. Television's long-running drama, *The Fugitive,* told of a falsely accused man roaming the country to find his wife's actual killer.

But Peter Reilly was real. He was a sympathetic figure. His plight captured hearts all across the land as few cases ever had. And his ordeal spoke volumes about why the law flies off the tracks so often. Like Tommy Lee Jones in the 1993 movie version of *The Fugitive,* Peter at any time might have cried out to his pursuers: "But I'm innocent!" He would have received the same cold reply: "I don't care!"

For me, being so close to the scene of the Barbara Gibbons slaying and the claims of Peter's innocence, I felt driven to know the truth. Fidelity to journalistic objectivity led me at first to almost ridiculous efforts to prove his guilt just to be sure I was not gullible.

Even much later in the case, I had to check out the State Police claim that they now knew how Peter had *really* killed his mother. Despite contradicting the medical evidence, the "car theory" accused Peter of letting his Corvette roll backward onto Barbara's legs as she was supposedly trying to remove the vehicle's license plate during a fit of anger. I had my wife lie down behind our own car on the driveway to see if this scenario was plausible. It was not.

My role became intense as I worked intimately, for four years, with playwright Arthur Miller, private investigator Jim Conway, defense attorney Roy Daly, prosecutor Paul McQuillan, State's Attorney Dennis Santore and even Judge John Speziale (who would soon become Connecticut's chief justice) to expose the terrible wrong.

At one turning point, Governor Ella Grasso told McQuillan, as her legal counsel, to discreetly recruit me as a well-informed person independent of the system to dissect Captain McDonnell's error-strewn, self-justifying, 58-page report of the Gibbons murder reinvestigation she had ordered.

McDonnell had selected September 28, 1977, the exact fourth anniversary of the killing, to announce the results of his hugely expensive nine-month probe. He had reached "the inescapable conclusion" that Peter Reilly "is, in fact, the sole perpetrator in the Barbara Gibbons homicide."

The document was supposed to be secret but the cops leaked its allegations to the media even as they delivered the first copy to the governor. There was a powerful whiff of déjà vu as news broadcasts and headlines ("NEW POLICE REPORT CALLS REILLY SLAYER") portrayed Peter as guilty once again.

In a dark corner of a restaurant, McQuillan let me read the still confidential report but not take notes or make a photocopy. My point-by-point analysis became a media event days later. Denouncing the document as a hoax and the investigation the worst in police history, I called for the immediate firing of Captain McDonnell and State Police commissioner Edward Leonard.

At the same time, and more importantly, State's Attorney Santore rejected the State Police insistence on Peter's guilt as "contrived," "unworthy" and "blatantly contradictory." The car theory was "completely untenable."

All of which gave Governor Grasso the cover to call in Leonard and demand that he denounce the document. The commissioner obediently told the world that he had been "misled" by his chief detective. He now "wholeheartedly" supported Santore's decision not to prosecute Peter Reilly a second time. Leonard resigned a few months later, but only after touring the state to tell assemblies of troopers that the department was not at fault. He received a standing ovation from 150 cops and civilian personnel at one key location.

These were exciting times. Not since the Cuban Missile Crisis in 1962 had I been so close to the sweat and strain of the powerful. But when it came time to write the book I knew this was Peter's story, not mine. I would use the first-person pronoun only at the end of the tale.

Even then, I was restrained by my fetish about being fair-minded. Speaking of the chief perpetrators of the injustice as self-deluded, I held back from charging that they *knew*

Peter was innocent, almost from the start, yet plunged ahead anyway.

To be honest, I could not find the words to express my outrage. I saw evil personified but lacked the skill to set it into the framework of the long, sordid history of man's inhumanity to man. Fortunately, Arthur Miller came along in his 1987 autobiography, *Timebends,* to explain why, for a full decade, he had found it impossible to write about the case despite having been a principal player:

> It is still difficult to describe with any precision, but I think I was oppressed by a certain brute repetitiveness in the spectacle of the Reilly prosecution. It was simple enough to understand that the police, once locked onto Peter, could not relent lest they endanger their professional reputations. Quickly the question changed from who murdered Barbara Gibbons and might still be walking around loose to who was impugning the State Police. But as simple as the explanation was, it offered a vision of man so appallingly unredeemable as to dry up the pen. . . .
>
> It all seemed to bespeak an evil transcending any commensurate gain or motive, as one understands gain and motive, and I could not escape the feeling that I was watching a shadow play of mindless man dumbly miming roles of very ancient authorship, rather than a spontaneously new and real event.

The dire picture painted by the great playwright was offset at every stage of the drama by the performance of the central character. Peter was always and entirely the good-hearted person his friends, neighbors and advocates claimed. He never failed them.

After his exoneration, Peter was done with celebrity. Always forthcoming with serious interviewers yet never seeking publicity, he wanted a normal life, not the role of victim of the law. He remained more country than city in his ways even after the Madow family moved to suburban digs in central Connecticut.

Mickey and Marion never officially adopted him, but there was no need. He was simply one of their three sons.

After Mickey's death, followed by Marion's failing health, he became her principal caregiver.

Only once did he live elsewhere, and that did not go well. The fabled dream life in sunny Southern California ended after a rocky two-year marriage. "It didn't work out," he told me, citing "irreconcilable differences."

To see him now in his middle age is to see a youthful-looking average man. You wouldn't know, and he won't say unless you ask, that anything extraordinary has ever happened in his life.

His laid back personality still intact, Peter has not lost his easygoing charm or his devotion to the things he most enjoys: playing guitar in a rock band (known for a time as "Voodoo Justice"), tinkering with his primer red 1940 Ford Deluxe coupe and just being with his family and friends.

His working life began after graduating the regional high school in Falls Village. While serving as a school janitor, he took an evening Accounting course at a community college. (He studiously ignored a fellow student, state trooper Jim Mulhern.) Nearly six years as an emergency medical technician for ambulance services followed—earning him the gratitude of a patient whose life he saved.

Still, determined to make a living by following his passions, he mostly worked in the music business, as a member of setup crews for traveling rock bands; and in the automobile business, as a salesman for a national distributor of hot rod parts.

The two of us have had an enduring friendship even though I am twenty-nine years his senior. It is always "Don" and "Peter" or "Pete." We have clung together on the roller coaster of the never-ending murder case ever since his exoneration. No cat has had more lives than the unsolved Gibbons slaying.

In June 1977, as Judge Sponzo made public the report of his grand jury findings on the botched investigation, he gave the State Police a secret addendum naming five persons he considered prime suspects. One of them soon killed himself—but for reasons other than involvement in the death of Barbara Gibbons. The State Police had already given a free pass to the four others.

In 1978, there was an explosion of media interest, led by the *New York Times,* when Tim Parmalee's recent live-in girlfriend, Vanessa Olysheytz, surfaced with the claim that he had boasted to her of being responsible for the Gibbons murder. A second blast came with a similar claim by Wallace Wilcox, who had worked on a farm with Tim.

Parmalee denied everything. A furious search for corroborating information—by leading Reilly supporters and the new chief state's attorney—raised great dust but no data. The state assigned Paul McQuillan to conduct the *third* investigation into Barbara Gibbons' murder. His eight months of digging produced only brief prison sentences for Tim Parmalee and one other person (for lying to the grand juror).

Meantime, the State Police did a little dance. They took one step forward by creating major crime squads of better-trained detectives to handle murder and rape, and a big step backward, by making it an unofficial policy to *not* record interrogations.

When reporters called about the status of the Gibbons case, a statement was always ready: "To our satisfaction that investigation was concluded and made available for prosecution with the person we believe to be responsible for the murder."

Peter bristled at such backhanded assertions of his guilt. As the years went by, his frustration grew. His mother would never get the justice she deserved. Yes, he had been exonerated, but the only lawman ever to apologize to him was Cleveland Fuessenich, the head of the State Police at the time of the crime. Fuessenich publicly took the blame for failing to more closely supervise Lieutenant Shay's flawed investigation. Shay went on to become East Hartford's police chief.

In 2001, producers for the A&E network show, *American Justice,* asked Shay for an opinion about Peter for its hour-long documentary on the old case. "I don't think that he should have gotten away with—," Shay said before interrupting himself. "I don't think anybody should get away with murder." Retired Captain McDonnell was far less restrained: "Peter knows he did it. I know he did it. And that's that."

These statements, coupled with a failed attempt by Peter and me to match any known suspect to the DNA of certain hair strands found at the crime scene, triggered our effort to discover any overlooked or concealed evidence that might lie buried in the giant State Police case file.

We were told that the file did not exist. We appealed to Connecticut's Freedom of Information Commission. There the attorney for the cops explained that the file had not been burned or shredded but simply "erased" under a state law denying public or media access. The purpose was to protect the privacy of a person whose crime conviction had been vacated. The file cabinets were gathering dust at headquarters.

We asked that Peter be allowed to invade his *own* privacy. The police resisted. We went to a superior court judge to untangle this knot. He ruled that Peter could see his files, and so could I as his assigned power-of-attorney researcher.

So, one fine day, with CNN cameras rolling, we marched into the police headquarters in Middletown. The officers were polite but not pleased. In a secure room with a trooper keeping watch, I spent the next few weeks in a daily search for a needle of new evidence in the great haystack of crime-scene photographs, suspect interviews and the not-surprising data revealing that the so-called "tire marks" on the victim's shattered legs, the basis of the "car theory," were almost surely made by the boots of a killer.

There were clues aplenty about the lack of police zeal to go after suspects other than Peter in the original investigation, but no smoking gun was found. Except for the names of two possible suspects with dangerous reputations who had vanished long ago, we came up empty.

As Peter once told a reporter, the case was a learning experience. Both of us now knew volumes about the workings of the justice system. While I began a career investigating miscarriages of justice across the country, Peter became a frequent spokesman for the falsely accused—and the not-yet accused. At high school and college gatherings, he told students to protect themselves by knowing their constitutional rights. "You need a lawyer even if you're innocent," he would say. "*Especially* if you're innocent!"

In 1995, he, Arthur Miller and top experts on interrogation-room tactics were speakers at an all-day public forum in Hartford centered on the case of a mentally and physically impaired Connecticut man named Richard Lapointe who, in

1989, had gone to prison for the rape and murder of his wife's 88-year-old grandmother.

Lapointe's actual innocence was obvious. No good evidence connected him to the crime. But a nine-hour Manchester police interrogation had produced such statements as, "I killed her, but I don't remember being there." The forum was a landmark event, the first-ever major conference on confessions, but it was no help to Lapointe. At this writing, he remains incarcerated even though, as he says, "Everyone here, even the guards, knows I didn't do it."

No "wrong man" case captivated Peter more than that of Martin Tankleff of Long Island. The similarities to his own ordeal were eerie despite the great difference that he, a poor small-town boy, had been rescued before long imprisonment, while Marty, a rich kid raised in a posh New York suburb, would lose two decades of freedom.

Marty Tankleff, then seventeen years old and about to start his senior year in high school, woke up in his home one morning in 1988 to find his mother murdered and his father near death after an attack by intruders. Led by detective James McCready, the Suffolk County cops had Tankleff's confession within hours.

When told, falsely, that his dying father had come out of his coma just long enough to say that his son had attacked him, Marty Tankleff, like Peter, believed he might have "blacked out" his memory of the terrible crime he had not committed. At trial, testimony by Dr. Herbert Spiegel about the teenager's susceptibility to intimidation did not keep the jury from delivering a guilty verdict.

All the while, the avalanche of knowledge about who actually had committed the crime was ignored by authorities. Suffolk County prosecutors had a long history of using coerced confessions, true or false, to win cases. As Tankleff sat in prison writing thousands of letters seeking attention to his plight, an epic struggle through the courts by teams of top defense attorneys finally led to his freedom and full exoneration.

Peter and I were more than just witnesses to this drama. Seeing Marty Tankleff in prison and in court proceedings, we re-lived much of the trauma of the events of the 1970s. Back then, a victory party in Falls Village, attended by almost all of Peter's defenders, sealed the many friendships that had been made.

On a September night in 2008, in the great space of a renovated, hollowed-out old synagogue in lower Manhattan, Marty was feted at his own victory celebration. Family members and major supporters were there under the banner, "MARTY GRAS" and the slogan, "Freedom Is Never Too Late."

Peter and Marty embraced. Their smiles lit up the room. It was a priceless moment for me, knowing that these two men, no longer naive adolescents, would surely go into the future as eloquent voices calling for reforms of the broken justice system that had turned their lives upside down.